IMAGINING VIETNAM AND AMERICA

THE NEW

COLD WAR HISTORY

John Lewis Gaddis, editor

IMAGINING VIETNAM AND AMERICA

The Making of Postcolonial Vietnam, 1919–1950

MARK PHILIP BRADLEY

Foreword by John Lewis Gaddis

The University of North Carolina Press

Chapel Hill and London

© 2000 The University of North Carolina Press
All rights reserved
Manufactured in the United States of America
Set in Electra and Champion types by Tseng Information Systems
The paper in this book meets the guidelines for permanence and durability
of the Committee on Production Guidelines for Book Longevity of the Council
on Library Resources.

Library of Congress Cataloging-in-Publication Data
Bradley, Mark.
Imagining Vietnam and America : the making of postcolonial Vietnam,
1919–1950 / by Mark Philip Bradley ; foreword by John Lewis Gaddis.
    p.   cm. — (The new Cold War history)
Includes bibliographical references and index.
ISBN 0-8078-2549-2 (cloth : alk. paper) — ISBN 0-8078-4861-1 (pbk. : alk. paper)
1. Vietnam—Politics and government—20th century.   2. Vietnam—Foreign
relations—United States.   3. United States—Foreign relations—Vietnam.
4. United States—Foreign relations—20th century.   I. Title.   II. Series.
DS556.8 .B73   2000
959.7′03—dc21   99-088185

Portions of this work have been previously published, in somewhat different form, as "Imagining
America: The United States in Radical Vietnamese Anticolonial Discourse," *Journal of American–
East Asian Relations* 4, no. 4 (Winter 1995); "Making Revolutionary Nationalism: Vietnam,
America and the August Revolution of 1945," *Itinerario* 23, no. 1 (1999); and "Slouching Toward
Bethlehem: Culture, Diplomacy and the Origins of the Cold War in Vietnam," in *Cold War
Constructions: The Political Culture of United States Imperialism, 1945–1966*, ed. Christian G. Appy
(Amherst: University of Massachusetts Press, 2000), © 2000 by the University of Massachusetts
Press, and are reprinted here with permission, respectively, of Imprint Publications, Inc., the
editors of *Itinerario* and the University of Massachusetts Press.

04   03   02   01   00   5   4   3   2   1

For my parents,

Paul and Anna Bradley

CONTENTS

FOREWORD

It is rare to find a historian who actually demonstrates the relationship between culture and diplomacy. Historians talk frequently enough about the need to make this connection, but when they begin to write, their sensitivity to cultural differences tends to fade. Knowing how easily the documents they find in the archives crossed borders, they often forget that the ideas these documents contain were not equally transportable. Words like "democracy" and "liberation" can carry very different meanings across time and space. Culture has a way of particularizing the significance, even of what appear to be universal concepts.

Mark Bradley's *Imagining Vietnam and America* is a welcome departure from this pattern of writing history. It shows how a culturally rooted particularization of universals brought about, in Southeast Asia, a costly and protracted Cold War conflict. Anyone who read only the *words* of American and Vietnamese leaders at the end of World War II would have thought such an outcome unlikely. Franklin D. Roosevelt's bitter denunciations of French colonialism seemed to clear the way for Ho Chi Minh's declaration of independence, with its quotations from Thomas Jefferson. But appearances deceived, for as Bradley makes clear, these converging pronouncements arose from remarkably divergent expectations.

The Viet Minh regarded the Americans along with the Russians as revolutionaries whose history of turning words into deeds provided a model for overcoming imperialism—and perhaps also a basis for actual support. The Americans, however much they despised French colonialism, still saw the Vietnamese as naive, passive, and ineffectual people whose independence in an emerging Cold War could only create opportunities for international communism. The very infrequency of contacts prior to World War II had led Ho and the Americans to assume compatibility, but as they got to know one another better, they trusted each other less. The resulting antagonism, therefore, was not just the product of missed opportunities or of an expanding Soviet-American rivalry; it reflected deep cultural differences.

Based upon an impressive array of Vietnamese, French, and American sources, *Imagining Vietnam and America* is at once a multiarchival and multicultural history of the early Vietnamese-American relationship. It reminds us that the expectations people hold shape what they make of the experiences they have. It shows how artificial distinctions between domestic and foreign policy can sometimes be. And it reveals how many fresh insights can emerge, even on a familiar topic, when a young, accomplished, and imaginative scholar accords culture an equal status with diplomacy in researching and writing international history.

John Lewis Gaddis

ACKNOWLEDGMENTS

This project, which has involved sustained research in Vietnam, France, Great Britain, and the United States, has incurred more than the usual share of intellectual debts. My research in Vietnam was made possible by the National Center for the Social Sciences in Vietnam and the Institute of History. I particularly wish to thank Tran Huy Dinh, Vu Huy Phuc, and Nguyen Van Ku for their untiring efforts to help me secure access to Vietnamese archives and libraries and to make arrangements for my interviews. I am also grateful to the historians and researchers who assisted me in my work, including Bui Dinh Thanh, Van Tao, Phan Huy Le, Pham Xanh, Luu Doan Huynh, Do Quang Hung, Hoang Phuong, and Duong Kinh Quoc. In France I am indebted to Professors Pierre Brocheux and Daniel Hémery of Université Paris-VII for their help in conducting my research. I am also grateful to the archivists and staff at the Archives du Ministère des Affaires Étrangères Diplomatiques and Bibliothèque National in Paris, Dépôt des Archives d'Outre Mer in Aix-en-Provence, and the Service Historique de l'Armée de Terre in Vincennes. In Great Britain I was fortunate enough to receive the assistance of Professor Ralph Smith of the School of Oriental and African Studies as well as his kind efforts to introduce me to the Vietnamese studies community in London. I am also grateful to the archivists and staff of the India Office Library and Records, London; Public Records Office, Kew; Liddell Hart Centre for Military Archives, King's College, University of London; Christ Church College, Oxford University; and the Harley Library, University of Southampton. In the United States I am indebted to the archivists in the military and diplomatic records branches of the National Archives and National Records Center; the archivists at the Roosevelt, Truman, and Eisenhower presidential libraries; and the curators of the Wason-Echols collection at Cornell University.

I could not have undertaken this project without the assistance of my thesis advisers, Professors Ernest R. May and Hue-Tam Ho Tai, who shepherded it through its first incarnation as a dissertation. They provided me with the intellectual capital in American diplomatic and Vietnamese history that allowed me to conceive of this project and have interjected needed guidance and financial resources at a series of critical moments. I also benefited from the suggestions of Akira Iriye, whose work on American-Japanese relations provided a model for this study. My colleagues in the history department at the University of Wisconsin, Milwaukee, were particularly patient and unfailingly helpful in seeing an earlier version of this work through to its completion. I am particularly grateful to David Buck, Reginald Horsman, David Healy, and Margo Anderson for their insightful readings and comments.

This work has also been shaped by my association with the Cold War International History Project at the Woodrow Wilson Center in Washington, D.C., which helped to support financially my first research trip to Hanoi. As I have come to know the quite wonderful group of international scholars who are a part of the project, their warmth, encouragement, and models of scholarly rigor have sustained my work. Among them are Warren Cohen, Jim Herschberg, Odd Arne Wested, Chen Jian, Vlad Zubok, Mari Olsen, Bob Brigham, Vojtech Mastny, and Kathryn Weathersby. I particularly appreciated the opportunities to present my work at workshops and conferences organized by the project in Washington and Hong Kong and the many useful comments that emerged in them.

Over the last two years, as a faculty member in the history department at the University of Chicago, I have been fortunate to be a part of a rigorous, probing, and supportive intellectual community. My colleagues have challenged me to conceive of Vietnamese-American relations in a larger and, I hope, ultimately more persuasive way. The department and the university have been immensely supportive of my work, providing much-appreciated leave time and financial support for my research and writing. I am indebted to Bruce Cumings, George Chauncey, Kathy Conzen, Michael Geyer, Tom Holt, Leora Auslander, Tets Najita, and Ralph Austen for their comments on various portions of this manuscript, as well as to my undergraduate and graduate students, whose interest and engagement in the theory and practice of international history has enriched what I brought to this project.

Portions of this manuscript have been presented at a variety of conferences, lectures, and workshops at Oxford University; the School of Oriental and African Studies; the National Center for the Social Sciences and Institute of History in

Hanoi; Ohio University; the University of Hong Kong; the Nobel Institute; the Center for Southeast Asian Studies at the University of Wisconsin, Madison; Indiana University; the University of Leiden; Princeton University; the University of Chicago Workshop on Colonialism; and panels at the annual meetings of the Association for Asian Studies, the Organization of American Historians, the American Historical Association, and the Society for Historians of American Foreign Relations. I am grateful for the comments and ideas these presentations elicited. I also wish to thank a host of scholars who have generously provided helpful comments on various portions this manuscript: Warren Cohen, George Herring, Chris Appy, Frank Ninkovich, Walter LaFeber, Marilyn Young, Keith Taylor, Nancy Tucker, Ben Anderson, David Marr, Stein Tønnesson, Chris Goscha, Michael Adas, Arif Dirlik, Yuen Foong Khong, Robert McMahon, Mel Leffler, Lloyd Gardner, Ellen Fitzpatrick, Judy Stowe, Gary Hess, Anne Foster, Shawn McHale, Bradford Perkins, and Victor Lieberman. It also has been a great pleasure to work with the University of North Carolina Press. I am particularly grateful for John Lewis Gaddis's keen interest in publishing this work in his new series there and for his enormously helpful advice and comments as I have revised the manuscript. I feel very fortunate to have had as my editor Lew Bateman, who has been unfailingly patient and supportive.

The research and writing of this project was made financially possible through the Fulbright-Hays Doctoral Dissertation Research Abroad Fellowship; the National Endowment for the Humanities Dissertation Fellowship; a Bernadotte E. Schmidt Grant for Research in the History of Europe, Africa, and Asia from the American Historical Association; a Sidney J. Weinberg Research Fellowship from the Franklin and Eleanor Roosevelt Institute; an Abilene Travel Fellowship from the Eisenhower World Affairs Institute; research grants from the Woodrow Wilson International Center for Scholars, the Harry S. Truman Library Institute, and the John Anson Kittridge Educational Fund Trust; and a Foreign Language and Area Studies Fellowship for Vietnamese language study at the Southeast Asian Studies Summer Institute. At Harvard University my work was also supported with grants and fellowships from the Charles Warren Center, the Center for International Affairs, the John King Fairbank Center for East Asian Studies, and the Graduate School of Arts and Sciences. Generous faculty research funds from the University of Wisconsin, Milwaukee, and the University of Chicago were essential for its completion.

The contribution of my wife, Anne Hansen, to this project has been enormous. It could not have been completed without her encouragement, intellectual companionship, and love. The birth of our children, Ilsa Lillian and Peter Johan, at different stages of this project have not exactly quickened the pace of my work, but I hope with its completion that they will be happy to spend more time with their father. Finally, it is to my parents, Paul and Anna Bradley, that I owe the greatest thanks. By the time I was eighteen months old, they had whisked me off for the first of many sojourns in Southeast Asia, an event cataloged in family albums by a photograph of a somewhat imperious looking toddler posed next to the ruins at Angkor Wat. Although they might be rightly skeptical that this study of Vietnamese-American relations had its origins some thirty-five years ago at Angkor, I hope they know that their love not only made this project possible but sustains all that I do.

Chicago, July 1999

ABBREVIATIONS

The following abbreviations are used in the text.
For source abbreviations used in the notes see pages 193–94.

CAC   Country and Area Committee on the Far East
CCP   Chinese Communist Party
DRV   Democratic Republic of Vietnam
ICP   Indochinese Communist Party
OSS   Office of Strategic Services
MO   Morale Operations
PRC   People's Republic of China
SEAC   South East Asia Command
USIS   United States Information Service

IMAGINING VIETNAM AND AMERICA

Pac Bo
Cao Bong
Yen Bai
Lang San
Dien Bien Phu
Red River
Hanoi
Haiphong
Thanh Hoa
Vinh
VIETNAM
Hue
Danang
Dalat
Nha Trang
Tay Ninh
Saigon
Vinh Long
Mekong River Delta
Con Son
(Poulo Condore)

Chunking
CHINA
Kunming
YUNNAN PROVINCE
Red River
KWANGSI PROVINCE
Canton
Hong Kong
Hanoi
LAOS
Mekong River
area of enlargement
THAILAND
Bangkok
CAMBODIA
VIETNAM
Phnom Penh
Saigon
Con Son
(Poulo Condore)

INTRODUCTION
Liberty and the Making
of Postcolonial Order

On 15 March 1887, the first French colonial exhibition in Hanoi was opened to Vietnamese and French residents of the city. At the center of the exhibition, the organizers erected a replica of sculptor Frédéric-Auguste Bartholdi's *Liberty Enlightening the World*. Bartholdi's monumental original had been unveiled in New York Harbor five months before the Hanoi exhibition opened, a gift to the United States from France to honor the centenary of the American revolution. For the French officials organizing the colonial exhibition, who saw no contradiction between the ideals of liberty and their imperial vision, Hanoi's *Statue of Liberty*, an exact if smaller copy of the one France sent to the United States, was intended to dramatize the political, economic, and cultural promises of French rule and tutelage to its new colonial subjects.[1]

After the exhibition closed, *Liberty* was moved to a more permanent installation at the nearby Place Neyret, where it anchored a figurative spatial geography of French power and authority in Vietnam. *Liberty* rested on the southernmost tip of the expansive Avenue Puginier, named to honor the well-known Catholic missionary who had played a central role in the French conquest of northern Vietnam. From *Liberty*'s visage the avenue traversed the Citadel, which housed the colonial military forces; passed the beaux arts mansions that provided offices for the civil colonial administration; and finally, at its northernmost point, flowed into the imposing Place Puginier, dominated by the grand residence of the *gouverneur-général* for French Indochina.[2]

Some fifty years later on 2 September 1945, a day that marked the symbolic passing of the French colonial order in Vietnam, *Liberty* remained in place at one end of the Avenue Puginier. At the other end, a crowd of almost 400,000 people filled the Place Puginier, now renamed Ba Dinh Square by the new Vietnamese provisional government to honor a failed but tenacious Vietnamese battle against French colonial forces in the 1880s. From a raised wooden podium in front of the *gouverneur-général*'s palace, Ho Chi Minh proclaimed Vietnam independent of French colonial rule. In his speech, which opened with quotations from the American Declaration of Independence and the French Declaration of the Rights of Man and the Citizen, Ho contrasted the revolutionary ideals of liberty with what he termed eighty years of French colonial oppression in Vietnam.

Joining the crowd of Vietnamese revolutionaries gathered in the square were a small group of American officers from the wartime OSS, one of whom had helped Ho Chi Minh ensure the words he borrowed from Thomas Jefferson about the meaning of liberty were accurately rendered. Ho closed his speech with a plea to the United States and Allied powers to recognize the right of the Vietnamese people to self-determination in the spirit of the wartime Tehran and San Francisco conferences where the principals animating the newly formed United Nations had emerged. "Vietnam," he concluded, "has the right to enjoy freedom and independence, and in fact has become a free and independent country."[3]

As Ho's words reverberated through the crowds in Ba Dinh Square, echoed down the Avenue Puginier, and met *Liberty*'s gaze, the imposing symbolic edifice of French colonial power that lined the avenue lay in ruins. The beaux arts offices were emptied of their French civil servants. French military forces were under house arrest in the Citadel. Hanoi's *Liberty* now seemed to embody an alternative set of meanings: an ironic reminder of the yawning chasm between French rhetoric and colonial realities, an astute recognition of the power of the United States to shape international order at the close of World War II, and a reverent, if somewhat inchoate, vision of the promises of postcolonial independence.[4]

The transnational circularity of *Liberty*'s image and the multiple meanings it came to represent in Vietnam illustrate the central concerns animating this study of the encounter between Vietnamese revolutionaries and the United States from 1919 to 1950. For much of these transformative three decades, the relationship between Vietnamese and American political elites was often more symbolic than real. If perhaps the only Vietnamese in Hanoi in September 1945 who had actually seen the original *Liberty* was Ho Chi Minh himself, who passed it in the French steamer that brought him to New York City in 1912, an imagined America occupied a central place in anticolonial political discourse as a symbol of the qualities that Vietnamese revolutionaries believed were critical for reshaping Vietnamese society. The *Statue of Liberty* could easily have joined an existing dialogue that gave sustained attention to figures such as George Washington, Abraham Lincoln,

Thomas Edison, and Henry Ford in indigenous accounts of American revolutionary virtue, commercial strength, and technological achievement. The heroic voluntarism many Vietnamese revolutionaries favorably equated with the United States during the colonial period, along with their embrace and indigenization of Marxism-Leninism and the ideals of socialist internationalism, formed a diverse and enduring repertoire of symbolic language and perceptual experience. As Vietnamese anticolonial elites worked to overthrow the French colonial order and establish an independent Vietnamese state, much of their effort rested on a postcolonial vision informed by this fluid discourse of revolutionary nationalism.

Although American policy makers would come somewhat slower to their apprehensions of Vietnam, the assessments of Vietnamese society and French colonialism that made up America's imagined Vietnam are also refracted in revealing ways by the predominant meanings white Americans ascribed to the *Statue of Liberty* after its installation in New York Harbor. The gift of the statue to the United States in the 1880s was intended by the French to serve as an icon of their national greatness as the original home of liberty and as a reflection of their contemporary technological and cultural prowess. But many Americans were quick to claim the symbolism of liberty for themselves. As the *New York Times* argued in an editorial the day after the statue's dedication,

> It will stand as a perpetual reminder of the realization in America of political ideals of which the origin may fairly be claimed for France, but of which the realization in France itself seems more precarious and less complete. On our shores, and under the tendency of a race less theoretic, less excitable, and less impatient than the French people, the germinal idea has been realized in what all Americans believe to be, with all its imperfections, the most successful and the most hopeful of all the social systems that have grown up in the history of mankind.[5]

These assertions of American exceptionalism and innate French weaknesses, along with *Liberty*'s increasing association with remaking immigrants as Americans, presaged key aspects of American apprehensions of colonial Vietnam. The first sustained American assessment of Vietnam emerged during the period between the two world wars in the writings of journalists, scholars, missionaries, and diplomats. In part these observers offered a withering critique of the failures of French colonialism in Vietnam that implicitly reflected the contemporary celebratory discourse surrounding America's state-building efforts at home and its colonial project in the Philippines. At the same time American observers found little to praise in what they saw as a backward and primitive indigenous

Vietnamese society, views that echoed the fundamental beliefs in racialized cultural hierarchies that underlay the broader American encounter with nonwhite peoples at home and abroad. The coming of war in the Pacific in the late 1930s brought Vietnam to the consciousness of the highest level of American policy makers in Washington. Sharing the deprecating interwar perceptions of colonial Vietnam and an unwavering belief in the ability of superior American political, economic, and social models to cross cultures, many American policy makers, including Franklin Roosevelt, were increasingly convinced that Vietnam should be reformed and remade in America's image.

Strikingly, Vietnamese and American perceptions of each other and their imaginings of Vietnam's postcolonial future drew on a shared vocabulary, but one mediated though external sources and then reproduced and transformed in a variety of Vietnamese and American idioms. The perceptions of the United States and articulations of postcolonial Vietnam by Vietnamese revolutionaries were shaped by modernist currents of thought that entered Vietnam through the works of reformers and radicals in China and through the lived experience of French colonial rule. The ensemble of assumptions through which Americans apprehended the Vietnamese, often posed in Social Darwinian, neo-Lamarckian, or Orientalist terms, were a part of the culturally hierarchical discourse that infused the theory and practice of Western imperialism. To borrow the categories Lydia Liu proposes in her study of modernity in China,[6] one might think of Vietnamese and American perceptual discourses as "host" languages and the broader transnational circulation of modernist and colonial ideas as "guest" languages. In the mutually constitutive processes that shaped the making of both Vietnamese and American visions of postcolonial Vietnam, the guest languages of modernism and colonialism were sometimes usurped, at other times transformed, and in the American case, sometimes complicit in them.[7]

From the perspective of Vietnamese and American political elites in the fall of 1945, the subsequent course of Vietnamese-American relations was surely an unimagined contingency. Neither side could have anticipated they would face each other as enemies in 1950 when the colonial war between the French and the Vietnamese was transformed into an arena of the Cold War. Nor could they envision that they would send troops into battle against one another by 1965 as Vietnam became the central Cold War battleground. But as the Cold War came to Vietnam, the overlapping and intertwined meanings accorded to the historical rupture of decolonization in 1945, and the relationship between the colonial past and the postcolonial future, remained central to the subsequent course of Vietnamese-American relations. For both Vietnamese and American policy makers, the largely imagined Vietnam and America that were constructed during the interwar and World War II periods fundamentally shaped the contours of the postcolonial Vietnamese state and its place in the articulation of post-1945 international order.

My analysis marks a sharp departure from the Cold War narrative that has informed most accounts of the early history of Vietnamese-American relations. In this existing literature, the coming of the Cold War in the late 1940s forms an almost axiomatic starting point from which Vietnam is quickly subsumed within the escalating global rivalry between the Soviet Union and the United States. Although the explanatory variables offered in these works are diverse—ranging from fears of revolutionary political instability in France and the rest of Western Europe to the need for a liberal capitalist trading order in the Pacific, the vulnerability of Southeast Asia with the rise of a communist state in China, or the domestic political threat of McCarthyism at home—they share a common focus on the geostrategic dimensions of American decision making.[8]

Embedded in this narrative is a broader assumption of American exceptionalism that has structured much of the writing on American diplomacy in the postwar period. The United States is not just portrayed as different from other state actors but remains fundamentally apart from the historical relationships and processes that surround it and shape the nature of states and peoples with which it interacts.[9] Operating within this prevailing exceptionalist prism, existing accounts of Vietnamese-American relations see the period after World War II as a virtual tabula rasa in which the colonial past and emerging postcolonial order is of marginal utility for understanding the exercise of postwar American power.

The Vietnamese themselves are also virtually absent in all of these accounts. The central historical agents of the Cold War narrative are always American policy makers and sometimes their French and British counterparts. In more recent works, drawing on the opening of primary source materials in the former Soviet Union and the PRC, Soviet and Chinese actors play more prominent roles. But the perceptions and policies of Vietnamese revolutionary elites remain almost completely ignored.[10] By muting the voices of Vietnamese actors and artificially separating American policy toward Vietnam from the Euro-American colonial project in its broadest terms, the Cold War narrative renders opaque the processes through which Vietnamese revolutionaries and American policy makers sought to construct the postcolonial Vietnamese state and the transnational circulation of ideas that gave their efforts shape and form.

This work does not claim that the Cold War is epiphenomenal to the Vietnamese-American encounter. Nor does it aim simply to trace an alternative history of the neglected colonial and postcolonial dimensions of that encounter. Rather, it seeks to locate and analyze the relationship between Vietnam and the United States within the larger sweep of the international history of the twentieth century in which the global discourse and practices of colonialism, race, modernism, and postcolonial state making at once preceded, were profoundly implicated in, and ultimately transcended the dynamics of the Cold War.

In these aims my approach to Vietnamese-American relations is part of a broader effort since the end of the Cold War to reconsider its meaning. With the opening of archives in Russia and Eastern Europe after the collapse of the Soviet Union and the loosening of Chinese restrictions on the availability of primary documents, what has been termed "the new Cold War history" of the last decade has internationalized the largely American and European focus of previous scholarship and begun to reveal the dynamics of decision making among the leadership of the Soviet Union, the PRC, and Eastern Europe. In a similar fashion, my work provides the first analysis of Vietnamese perceptions and policies toward the United States during the early Cold War period based on Vietnamese-language sources.[11]

In its more expansive temporal frame and analytical concerns, however, this study also seeks to engage ongoing efforts to reconceptualize the international history of the twentieth century in ways that more fully transcend the traditional Cold War narrative and the premises of American exceptionalism that have guided much of past scholarship. Among the most important of these works is Robert Latham's *The Liberal Moment*.[12] As Latham revealingly asks about the central premises of Melvyn Leffler's magisterial study of American Cold War foreign policy,[13] What are the "core values" that Leffler believes American policy sought to defend? And how were they conceived? In his answers Latham provides a supple and transformative account of structure, contingency, and agency in the making of a postwar world order. A cluster of what he terms liberal modernist values—free trade, domestic market economies, liberal (though not necessarily democratic) governance, individual and collective rights, and self-determination—animated the views of both American policy makers and their European allies at the end of World War II. The rise of the Cold War, Latham argues, was an unanticipated contingency but one that Americans and Europeans mediated through the processes of liberal modernist order building.

This probing, and ultimately more satisfying, interpretation of international history in the twentieth century, however, is virtually silent on the challenges presented to world order by decolonization. Its rapidity was another unforeseen contingency of the postwar era. But apprehensions of the colonial world and the meanings of its collapse in the United States, Europe, and the newly decolonizing world were shaped by the same transnational circulation of ideas and beliefs that informed the larger liberal modernist order-building process. This study of Vietnamese-American relations is an attempt to address that inexplicable but critical omission.

1

EUROPEAN WIND, AMERICAN RAIN
The United States in Vietnamese Anticolonial Discourse

In the winter and spring of 1919, as the Paris Peace Conference deliberated over the postwar peace settlement for Europe, members of the Vietnamese expatriate association known as the Groupe des Patriotes Annamites often gathered in a small Parisian apartment in the thirteenth arrondissement. Inspired by the Wilsonian rhetoric of self-determination, the focus of their meetings was to draft a proposal for the gradual emancipation of Vietnam from French colonial rule to present to the leaders of the Great Powers in Paris. The final document, titled "Revendications du Peuple Annamite," set forth an eight-point program that included calls for a general amnesty for political prisoners, equality of legal rights between French and Vietnamese, freedom of the press, the right to form political associations, and permanent Vietnamese representation in the French parliament.

Although the drafting of the proposal had been a collective effort that included the participation of Phan Chu Trinh, among the most famous and influential of Vietnamese anticolonial leaders, the "Revendications" bore the signature of a relative unknown, Nguyen Ai Quoc, or Nguyen the Patriot. Shortly before the deliberations in Paris came to a close, the Groupe des Patriotes Annamites submitted its "Revendications" to the heads of various national delegations, including President Woodrow Wilson, asking that their proposals be added to the conference agenda. Their request was ignored.[1]

Some twenty-five years later, Nguyen Ai Quoc, who reemerged on the Vietnamese political stage as Ho Chi Minh, would again pursue American support, this time as the leader of the communist-led Viet Minh movement that sought independence from the French during World War II. The passage of a quarter-century, however, fundamentally transformed the nature and aims of Vietnamese anticolonialism. The refusal of the Paris conference to consider the relatively modest demands of the Groupe des Patriotes Annamites marked the eclipse of a generation of scholar-gentry patriots, such as Phan Chu Trinh, who had embraced Social Darwinism and new currents of neo-Confucian thought to apprehend the humiliation of French conquest and chart a path of indigenous societal reform and anticolonial resistance. In their place arose a younger generation of anticolonial activists in the 1920s who conceived a more radical critique of Vietnamese society and French colonialism. By the 1930s, Marxist-Leninist internationalism had become the driving force in Vietnamese anticolonialism.

Just as the spirit of Wilsonianism hovered over the drafting of the "Revendications" by the Groupe des Patriotes Annamites in 1919, the United States occupied a persistent though often elliptical role in the transformation and radicalization of Vietnamese anticolonial thought and politics. Although Ho Chi Minh visited New York City in 1912, rarely, if ever, did most Vietnamese political elites encounter America or Americans directly.[2] Reflecting the importance of East Asia and Europe as the primary source of foreign influence on Vietnam under French colonial rule, Vietnamese perceptions of the United States were refracted through Chinese, Japanese, French, and Russian commentaries on American history and society. Viewed at such a distance, an imagined America came to represent the shifting currents and tensions in Vietnamese anticolonial thought. As Ho Chi Minh and the leaders of the Viet Minh embarked on their path to power and Vietnamese independence in the 1940s, the legacies of the anticolonial political discourse under French colonial rule, and the place of America in it, would frame their vision of national liberation and the nature of their diplomacy with the United States.

Between Neo-Confucianism and Social Darwinism

Vietnamese images of the United States first emerged through the Reform Movement, which dominated anticolonialism in Vietnam during the early decades of the twentieth century. Members of the generation of elites that led the Reform Movement were born in the 1860s and early 1870s into scholar-gentry families often from north and north-central Vietnam. Like their fathers and grandfathers before them, they had studied Chinese classical texts in preparation for the imperial examinations that would enable them to enter government service and symbolically mark their right to rule as virtuous Confucian "superior men" (*quan-tu*). The examination system, reflecting centuries of cultural borrowing from the

Chinese, inculcated Confucian values into the political culture of Vietnamese elites and served as the foundation of the administrative structure through which the Nguyen emperors had ruled Vietnam since 1802.[3] Prizing stability over change and viewing the wider non-Confucian world beyond East Asia with suspicion and derision, it was a profoundly conservative political and social order that proved unable to withstand the French colonial challenge in the late nineteenth century.

Members of the reform generation, who came of age in the 1880s at the time of the French conquest of northern Vietnam, watched as the slow French enervation of Vietnamese political, economic, and social life undermined the neo-Confucian premises that had shaped their view of the world. For these young men, the failure of scholar-gentry resistance to French conquest, like the Aid the King (Can Vuong) Movement in which many of their fathers had played a leading role, demonstrated that Confucian principles alone provided an inadequate response to French rule and heightened the urgency of reversing what they termed "the loss of country" or "national extinction" (*mat nuoc; vong quoc*). As the author of one reform poem asked of the situation Vietnam faced under the onslaught of French colonialism,

> Why is the roof over the Western universe the broad lands and skies,
> While we cower and confine ourselves to a cranny in our house?
> Why can they run straight, leap far,
> While we shrink back and cling to each other?
> Why do they rule the world,
> While we bow our heads as slaves?[4]

To explain Vietnam's predicament and formulate a new vision for the reconstruction and transformation of Vietnamese society, the reform generation increasingly looked outside their own tradition. For the first time, the European and American historical experience became a major part of Vietnamese political discourse. Reformers were captivated by the philosophical writings of Jean-Jacques Rousseau and Montesquieu; the nation-building efforts of Peter the Great, Giuseppe Garibaldi, and Otto von Bismarck; and the inventiveness of James Watt. Americans, including figures such as George Washington, Patrick Henry, and Thomas Edison, were also widely celebrated as deserving emulation by the Vietnamese. Among the most compelling Western thinkers for the Reform Movement was Herbert Spencer. To Vietnamese reformers, Social Darwinism offered a powerful explanation for the weaknesses in traditional society that had led to Vietnam's domination by the French. It also pointed to the strengths of the West that offered a potential path for Vietnam's future.[5]

Significantly, Social Darwinism, or what reformers more broadly termed the

"European wind and American rain" (*gio Au mua My*), entered Vietnam indirectly. Unable to read European or American texts themselves, Vietnamese reformers encountered Western thought and experiences in the writings of Liang Ch'i-ch'ao and K'ang Yu-wei, the leading intellectual advocates of self-strengthening reforms in China, and through what they came to know about the reform of Japanese society under the Meiji restoration.[6] Discussions of the West in works by Chinese self-strengtheners in particular were a revelation to Vietnamese reformers whose training in the Chinese classics was bounded by the conservative curriculum of the Nguyen imperial examinations that favored the study of Sung neo-Confucianism and ignored contemporary intellectual innovations in the Sinic tradition.[7]

But viewed within the interpretative veil of Chinese and Japanese informants, the revolutionary new currents of Western thought that animated the discourse of reform in early twentieth-century Vietnam were refracted through the persisting neo-Confucian sensibilities of the East Asian classical world. While the reformers in Vietnam were remarkably open to European and American ideas, they continued to see themselves as Confucian superior men and mediated Western thought through Confucian norms and values. As one reform text argued, "Among these European winds and American rains, who knows but what there may be men who on behalf of their country will sweep away the fog, lift up the clouds, and create a radiant and expansive horizon for us all."[8] By emulating the achievements of the West, the leaders of the Reform Movement believed they could transcend French colonialism and regain their rightful place as the leaders of a newly strengthened Vietnam. Poised between neo-Confucianism and Social Darwinism, the articulation of this reformist vision would produce the earliest enduring Vietnamese images of America.

The Reform Movement was launched in 1904 with the publication of an anonymous tract titled *The Civilization of New Learning* [*Van Minh Tan Hoc Sach*]. Infused with the Social Darwinian themes that had characterized the writings of Chinese reformers, the manifesto offered a wide-ranging critique of Vietnamese society and a prescription for the future. It argued that Vietnamese civilization was "static" (*tinh*) and Western civilization was "dynamic" (*dong*). Using Spencerian rhetoric, the manifesto suggested that ceaseless change produced a strong civil society: "The more ideas, the more competition; the more competition, the more ideas." Appreciation for the importance of Darwinian intellectual competition in Europe and America, it continued, produced innovations in political thought, education, commerce, and industry. In Vietnam, by contrast, the rigid adherence to classical Chinese learning and suspicion of foreign ideas had foreclosed dynamic change.

Despite this grim Spencerian critique of traditional society, Vietnamese reformers were not without hope for the future. Because Chinese interpretations of Spencer's thought downplayed its relentless determinism in favor of a more optimistic voluntarism, Social Darwinism as it was received by the Vietnamese also presented a path to national revival. Much of *The Civilization of New Learning* was devoted to outlining a program of Vietnamese self-strengthening patterned on Western models that included plans for educational reform and the development of indigenous industry and commerce. Sharing the neo-Confucian perspective of Chinese interpreters of Social Darwinism, the manifesto insisted these projects were to be led by and directed to Vietnamese elites, arguing one could not "open up" the intellects of the masses until elite attitudes had been changed.[9]

The critique of Vietnamese society and reform proposals contained in *The Civilization of New Learning*, aimed at bringing the dynamism of the West to Vietnam, would underlie much of the Reform Movement's activities.[10] An Eastern Study (Dong Du) movement brought Vietnamese students to Japan, where they not only came in closer contact with the works of Chinese reformers such as Liang Ch'i-ch'ao, who was living in Yokohama, but also with the ideas of Japanese thinkers who had guided the country's rapid economic modernization and bid for Great Power status under the Meiji restoration. In Vietnam itself, reformers organized the Dong Kinh Free School (Dong Kinh Nghia Thuc) and the publication of a newspaper, *Old Lantern Miscellany* [*Dang Co Tung Bao*], which served as critical forums for the introduction of new currents of thought. They also worked to establish indigenous commercial enterprises and agricultural societies to reverse the traditional scholar-gentry disdain for commerce and to emulate what reformers perceived as the sources of Western wealth and power. Reinforcing their optimism that these projects could successfully bring about the transformation of Vietnamese society was the Japanese victory in the Russo-Japanese war of 1905. As the *Asia* ballad [*A-te-a*] that was popularized by the Dong Kinh Free School suggested, the Japanese experience confirmed that Asian peoples could match and even exceed the achievements of the West.[11]

Within the broader consensus of the need to reform Vietnamese society along Western lines, substantial differences existed on the ultimate aims of the Reform Movement, illustrated by the careers of the two leading reformers, Phan Boi Chau and Phan Chu Trinh. Like others in the movement's leadership, both men were classically educated sons of scholar-gentry families who embraced reform after the failure of the Aid the King Movement. Phan Boi Chau, born in 1867 in Nghe An province in north central Vietnam, passed the regional imperial examination with the highest honors in 1900. Phan Chu Trinh, born in 1872 in Quang Nam province, passed both the regional and metropolitan imperial exams by 1900. Coming to reformist ideas through the medium of Chinese writers and short sojourns in Japan after 1900, both men played critical roles in establishing the Vietnamese movement for reform. Phan Boi Chau organized the Eastern Study Movement in Japan, and his writings were among the most important and influential reform works, forming the basis for much of the curriculum at the Dong Kinh Free School.[12] Phan Chu Trinh, second only to Phan Boi Chau in the Reform Movement, became a widely read essayist, a particularly influential figure in the Dong Kinh Free School, and a strong advocate of scholar-gentry involvement in commerce and industry. But while Phan Boi Chau saw reform as part of a larger effort to organize effective anticolonial opposition against the French, Phan Chu Trinh believed political change should come to Vietnam only after a long process of social and cultural transformation.

Phan Boi Chau's calls for reform in Vietnam were accompanied by sustained efforts at political organization, including the development of the Reformation Society (Duy Tan Hoi) and the League for the Restoration of Vietnam (Viet-Nam Quang Phuc Hoi). The Reformation Society, active in the first decade of the twentieth century, aimed at Vietnamese independence under a constitutional monarch. The league, inspired by the Chinese revolution of 1911, sought to put into place a democratic republic. Little came of these ambitious goals, but both organizations reflected Phan Boi Chau's willingness to use political violence to bring about anticolonial ends. Members of the Reformation Society were instrumental in the wave of anticolonial demonstrations that erupted in 1908, including tax protests in central Vietnam and a plot to poison the food of the French colonial garrison in Hanoi. The league, too, was involved in a series of terrorist incidents that eventually brought Phan Boi Chau's imprisonment in 1914.

For Phan Chu Trinh, a lifelong opponent of violence whose father had been assassinated when Phan Chu Trinh was in his late teens, the educational and cultural projects of the Reform Movement were ends in themselves. Phan Chu Trinh uncompromisingly opposed the old order in Vietnam. In his best-known work, a letter to French governor general Paul Beau in 1906 seeking French support for institutional reform in Vietnam,[13] Phan Chu Trinh was intensely critical of French colonial rule. But he reserved his harshest scorn for the traditional mandarinate whose obscurantism and petty jealousies, he believed, had prevented the emergence of reforms necessary for the transformation of Vietnam into a dynamic society. Because the indigenous barriers to reform were so great and the gap between Vietnam and the West was so vast, Phan Chu Trinh argued, independence could only follow an extended period of internal reform. Despite Phan's gradualist tone and repeated denouncements of anticolonial violence, French colonial officials found his vision of reform radical enough that he was sentenced to life imprisonment on the penal island of Con Son in the wake of the anticolonial protests of 1908, a sentence later commuted to fourteen years of exile in Paris. In the prison poetry he composed on Con Son and in essays written from Paris,[14] he continued to criticize the traditional elite and call for the social and cultural transformation of Vietnamese society.

Although important differences divided them, both Phan Boi Chau and Phan Chu Trinh shared and advanced the Social Darwinist critique that informed the Reform Movement. In their writings and those of other Vietnamese reformers, the European wind and American rain, filtered through the East Asian cultural prism, was essential to the discourse of reform. For Vietnamese reformers, as for the Chinese and Japanese reform movements, Europe was without question the dominant influence in shaping their broader agenda. American models were often undifferentiated from those of the other Western powers that, with the United States, provided reformers with an essential rhetorical trope for Vietnam's failure to keep pace with the world struggle for national survival and served as an idealized representation of the salutary benefits of Darwinian competition that awaited Vietnam under the reformist vision. Reflecting the Vietnamese reform generation's embrace of the meanings Chinese and Japanese reformers ascribed to Social Darwinism, a poem written for the Dong Kinh Free School sharply delineated the Vietnamese and Western experiences and warned of the need to shift Vietnamese sensibilities:

Our country from a very old time
Always diligently and uninterruptedly followed Chinese learning.
Aping old-fashioned and narrow-minded skills,
We are paralyzed in a state of near-exhaustion.
What do we know from the outside? From America? From Europe?[15]

Similarly, American and European models infused prescriptions for the future offered by the reform generation in Vietnam. Chastising the traditional elite for "following the old ways" and blocking the development of modern industry in Vietnam, *The Civilization of New Learning* asked, "Has anyone shown the skill or the talent . . . of a Watt or an Edison?" The "talents of men like these," it argued, "truly merit awe." In using the word "talent" to describe Edison and Watt, the manifesto not only reflected the popular Vietnamese belief that talent (*tai*) could allow individuals to exert control over their destiny (*mang*) but revealed the Reform Movement's insistence that Western thought and experience was a more reliable and powerful weapon than the traditional repertoire of talents Vietnamese had used to shape their future. America and Europe were also an inspiration for the publication of the *Old Lantern Miscellany* in Hanoi. Pointing in wonder to the fact that "the United States had more than 14,150 newspapers" and noting the vitality of the European press, *The Civilization of New Learning* advocated the immediate establishment of a Vietnamese newspaper to provide information about foreign innovations and local news so that the competition of ideas that had stimulated the rise of American and European power could be replicated in Vietnam.[16]

The place of the United States in the exhortative essays and poetry of Vietnamese reformers, however, did depart from contemporary discursive practices elsewhere in East Asia. Significantly, the unwavering praise lavished on the United States in the writings of the Vietnamese reform generation far exceeded that of Chinese and Japanese reformers. While respectful of American power and political culture, leading reformers in China such as Liang Ch'i-ch'ao came to be wary of the United States, unsure of how its imperialist aspirations in the Pacific might affect China, and critical of the deleterious role big business played in American life. In Japan, too, appreciation for American models was tempered by the threat the United States posed to its own imperialist ambitions.[17] For Vietnamese reformers, the European wind carried some of these ambivalent connotations as French colonial power threatened Vietnam's survival while European models offered a path to national reform. But Vietnamese depictions of the American rain raised none of the qualms that troubled many Chinese and Japanese reformers.

If the Social Darwinian sensibilities of reformers in China and Japan shaped the purposes to which Vietnamese writers put their images of the United States, the images themselves more closely resembled the admiring portrait of America and its political leaders that emerged in the first sustained Chinese writings on the United States in the mid-nineteenth century. Constructed in the wake of the Opium War, images of a powerful but benign America underlay Chinese hopes at mid-century that the United States might serve as a counterweight to the continuing European demands for expanded diplomatic and commercial intercourse. The terms the Vietnamese reform generation employed to refer to the United States and the meanings they conveyed were borrowed from Chinese usage that became common in this period. Vietnamese reform authors used "Beautiful" (*My*; Chinese *Mei-kuo*) to mean "America" or "Americans" and "Flowery Flag" (*Hoa Ky*; Chinese *Hua-ch'i-kuo*) for "the United States" to reflect their admiration of American models.[18]

These earlier Chinese images of the United States also presaged the celebration of America's benign wealth and power by the Vietnamese reform generation. In a poem titled "Telling the Stories of the Five Continents" ["Ke Chuyen Nam Chau"], written by Phan Boi Chau in 1905 to introduce Vietnamese youth to developments in Europe, America, and Japan, Phan Boi Chau began his flattering description of the United States by drawing attention to American wealth, one of the critical factors mid-nineteenth-century Chinese had ascribed to American dynamism and power:

Now we come to America [My] or the United States [Hoa Ky],
Where business is carried on in every profession
And there is great wealth on one hundred sides.[19]

The Asia ballad popularized by the Dong Kinh Free School after the Russo-Japanese war of 1905 lauded American efforts to broker the peace between Japan and Russia as evidence of U.S. beneficent power:

Luckily the United States was willing to negotiate
And skillfully brought peace to raise the Japanese siege.
If not, the court at St. Petersburg might not exist today![20]

The most sustained representations of American experiences by the Vietnamese reformers, utopian narratives of the life of George Washington and the American revolution, borrowed from admiring mid-nineteenth-century Chinese images as well. But the didactic purposes they were meant to serve also reflected both the strong influence of the more recent Chinese embrace of Social Darwinism and indigenous forces such as the enduring elitism of the Vietnamese reform generation and the differences of approach that divided its leaders. In his 1905 poem "Telling the Stories of the Five Continents," Phan Boi Chau offered a paean to the exemplary life of George Washington:

To develop the mind who do Americans rely upon?
They all rely upon [George] Washington;
Everyone relies upon the genius of Washington.
They tell the story of the time when as a young man he enlisted [in the
    British army],
At a time when the country felt humiliated by the British presence.
He intended to quell this unpleasant situation
By uniting all the soldiers.
For eight years he acted as he pleased;
Then he was able to fight and defeat the British.
Venerate Washington who served as commander-in-chief;
Follow the example of Washington who served as commander-in-chief.[21]

Phan Boi Chau's evident admiration for Washington closely follows the portrait of Washington in Hsü Chi-yü's 1848 treatise on world geography, the first widely disseminated Chinese text to devote substantial attention to the United States and Washington. Hsü's treatise was known among classically educated Vietnamese elites. Phan Boi Chau may have encountered its depiction of George Washington directly or through the writings of reformers such as Liang Ch'i-ch'ao and K'ang Yu-wei, whose own representations of Washington were based on it. As members of the Vietnamese reform generation relied almost exclusively on these Chinese writings for their knowledge of figures such as Washington, the central place of Hsü's account in shaping both contemporary Chinese and Vietnamese views of the United States is particularly important. Presaging the language of Phan Boi Chau's poetic narrative, Hsü's sustained account of the pivotal role he believed Washington played in overthrowing British colonial rule and establishing the American state concluded by asking, "Can he not be called a hero? Of all the famous Westerners of ancient and modern times, can Washington be placed in any position but the first?"[22]

Ironically, Americans themselves may have also indirectly contributed to Phan Boi Chau's approving rendition of Washington's life. In preparing his account of Washington's accomplishments, Hsü relied on works in Chinese written by American missionaries that were intended to introduce the United States in an idiom the authors believed readily comprehensible to their intended Chinese readership. As the leading scholar of Hsü's work argues, much of Hsü's account of Washington, including the Confucian biographical mode in which he placed Washington's accomplishments and the praise he showered upon him, are directly lifted from these American-authored texts.[23]

But for Phan Boi Chau, who was organizing anticolonial resistance through the Reformation Society at the time, the experiences of Washington's career and the shared colonial heritage of the United States and Vietnam also offered very specific weapons for anticolonial political agitation in Vietnam. Phan Boi Chau's narrative concentrates on Washington's decision to become a soldier in the British army to acquire the skills necessary to undertake a successful military campaign against British colonialists. The intended lesson Phan Boi Chau offered to his readers was that Vietnamese revolutionaries should emulate Washington's efforts by infiltrating the French colonial militia and winning over to the anticolonial cause the Vietnamese serving the French. Another poem written at the same time for the Dong Kinh Free School, titled "Advice for Fellow Sisters," urged Vietnamese women "to be worthy of marriage" to young Vietnamese who emulated heroes like George Washington.[24]

The United States also played a hortatory role in the tracts that marked Phan Boi Chau's establishment of the League for the Restoration of Vietnam in 1912. In a manifesto that was distributed throughout Vietnam, the now familiar reformist image of America was put to use to support the league's aim of independence:

> While we have servilely imitated the Chinese,
> The people of America and the people of Europe have been their own
>   masters.
> Knowing the power of these nations
> Lets us know that the strength of the people can transform our country.

Another proclamation took the image of the European wind and American rain to underlie its call for the establishment of an army to fight against the French.[25]

Perhaps the most sustained and revealing reformist depiction of America emerged in Phan Chu Trinh's *Rare Encounters with Beautiful Personages* [*Giai Nhan Ky Ngo*], a poetic adaptation of a Japanese novel from the 1880s completed during Phan's exile in Paris, intended to introduce Vietnamese readers to the revolutionary histories of Europe, the United States, and Japan. How Phan Chu Trinh came to adapt this work reveals the processes through which Japanese and Chinese reformist thought influenced the form and content of the Vietnamese discourse on reform. Phan's verse rendition of this work is itself based on a translation of the original Japanese novel by Liang Ch'i-ch'ao that appeared in 1898. In deciding to recast the novel as poetry rather than the prose of the Japanese original and the Chinese translation, Phan Chu Trinh followed a tradition by which Vietnamese authors had translated Chinese literature into a Vietnamese cultural milieu using the six-eight couplet form that was the most common and popular style of indigenous poetry. While the work was first published, though quickly banned by the French, in Hanoi in 1926, Phan Chu Trinh and other members of the reform generation first encountered and began to discuss Liang's Chinese translation as early as 1904.[26]

Phan Chu Trinh's epic poem opens with the visit of a "young and virtuous" Japanese scholar to Philadelphia. Because his country has met with "unfortunate hardships," the scholar's teacher sent him to America to study the "noble and distinguished" origins of the American revolution. As the young scholar gazes up at the Liberty Bell and reads the text of the Declaration of Independence, he encounters two women "activists," one Spanish and the other Irish, who explain the American struggle for independence in heroic terms:

> In the old days, when Americans gathered together,
> They initiated liberty here, in group discussions;
> Heroes left their imprint on the rivers and mountains of their homeland.
> It was truly the year 1774;

The Americans anxiously cast their eyes north and south.

There was the De-Thuy [Delaware] River and over there the Tao-Khe
[Erie?] Lake.

The state House drafted proclamations in those rooms.

From that point freedom was increasingly emblazoned on the hearts of the
people;

Far and near the clouds clustered and bees drifted down from the skies,

Righteous assistance, aiding the ancestors, women and men with one heart.

Old Mothers forgot their hardships;

Shedding tears, they counseled their sons to win victory on the battlefield.

Think of the love of the soldier's wife,

Attached to her husband who might die in the path of battle.

But if defeated his spirit will not be vanquished nor discouraged.

Freedom is won by renowned heroes;

Hundreds of brave youth met tens of thousands of British soldiers.

Seven bloody years passed but the struggle for freedom was never put aside.

Boston was destroyed into cinders;

New York, filled with smoke, was routed; Philadelphia became a cloud of
ashes.

Washington endured a period of bitterness.

Remnants of his army deployed themselves at Erie;

The weather was brutally cold,

Snow fell for many miles, the route was freezing.

As the remnants of Washington's army moved forward there were no food
supplies;

Gathering enough vegetables and grasses along the way was difficult.

Meanwhile the leaders discussed

A bold pledge to begin a truly courageous battle;

At midnight, the order to move out was transmitted.

Rolling up his flags, holding his [mandarin's] badge of office in his teeth,
Washington crossed the Delaware,

Destroying the English in a terrible battle.

From that point on his military prestige echoed like thunder on all four sides;

The more you think about hundreds of officers enduring hardship and
poverty,

The more you sympathize with them.

With decaying shoes and torn sandals they wandered about,

Soaked by frost, treading upon snow, drops of blood falling on the road.

Alas! How exhausting and deplorable life could be!

Feeling many passions: love of life, hatred of death and sorrow,
Why did they renounce their bodies?
Concerned with repaying the debt of their nation, they thought little of
    themselves!
When you think about it your heart is inflamed and aroused.
How commendable are the Americans, who truly are a civilized race;
That was why they opposed the oppressive English,
Improved their schools, developed industry and commerce,
And built a rich and powerful country.
Everywhere on the four horizons the words peace and security were
    radiant.[27]

Phan Chu Trinh's rendering of the American revolution in part reflects his differences with Phan Boi Chau over the ultimate aims of the Reform Movement. Unlike Phan Boi Chau's use of American models as a call to immediate anticolonial action against the French, Phan Chu Trinh's more deliberate depiction of the sacrifices and hard-won victory of American revolutionaries aimed to evoke the rewards that awaited unwavering disciples of the arduous and protracted process of reform. In Phan Chu Trinh's account, military victory over the British was inseparable from the Americans' development of educational and commercial skills that allowed them to "build a rich and powerful country." By Social Darwinian criteria, the Americans were a "civilized race" and a "commendable" model for the Vietnamese reformers.

But the imagery and narrative structure of Phan Chu Trinh's poem also captured the place of America in the persisting neo-Confucian boundaries that framed the Social Darwinist vision for Vietnamese reform. Confucian imagery familiar to the classically educated elite Vietnamese audience for whom Phan Chu Trinh intended the poem abounds in his depiction of the American revolution. To some extent, the similes and metaphors derived from traditional Chinese verse that Phan scattered throughout the work—"clouds clustered," "bees drifted," and "military prestige echoed like thunder on all four sides"—functioned as rhetorical signposts to guide readers through the potentially unfamiliar American historical terrain. Similarly, reference to the plight of the wives of U.S. soldiers would have heightened sympathy for the American cause and suggested historical parallels with American experiences for Vietnamese readers as it recalled the themes of the well-known eighteenth-century Vietnamese poem *The Song of the Soldier's Wife* [*Chinh Phu Ngam*].[28]

Most substantively, Phan Chu Trinh's use of Confucian imagery betrayed the enduring elitism that infused reform thought. Like George Washington, in whose teeth he places a mandarin's badge of office for the commander's fateful trip across the Delaware, the leaders of the American revolution in Phan's poem displayed all of the virtues that Vietnamese elites commonly ascribed to Confucian superior men: righteousness, self-sacrifice, courage, and devotion to their country. His emphasis on the role of properly cultivated heroes in the American struggle reflected the broader reformist sentiment that politics and social change remained an elite domain. Given his disdain for the contemporary practices of much of the Vietnamese elite, Phan Chu Trinh's idealized portrait of American patriots as virtuous Confucian heroes offered a model for what a reformed and revitalized elite could accomplish in Vietnam.

Perhaps most important, the voluntarism and progressive character of the narrative structure through which Phan Chu Trinh ordered the American experience illustrate the influence of Chinese reformers on the Vietnamese reform generation in tempering the implicit determinism of the reform generation's Social Darwinist critique within a neo-Confucian framework readily understandable by the classically educated Vietnamese elite. There was a substantial voluntarist thrust to Phan Chu Trinh's rendering of the almost overwhelming odds Americans overcame to prevail against the British. Employing a measure of poetic license, Phan pitted "tens of thousands" of British soldiers against only "hundreds" of American patriots who faced every obstacle to success: cold, hunger, poverty, and destruction of their homes and families. Yet through force of will, he suggested, their "spirit" remained unvanquished, and the Americans attained their goals. This optimistic portrayal of American revolutionary perseverance was undoubtedly intended to urge his Vietnamese audience to adopt Western voluntarist models to surmount the barriers that traditional society and French colonialism posed to the process of reform in Vietnam.

Phan Chu Trinh's faith in the boundless capacity of human will was rooted in his reading of the subtle but transformative shifts in neo-Confucian thought that emerged in the works of the Chinese reformers. In the neo-Confucian tradition, perseverance, or will, usually referred to sustained efforts to improve moral character for the purpose of realizing Confucian moral ideals. But for the Chinese reformers who encountered European and American thought in the late nineteenth century, willpower took on a Western-inspired emphasis of an enterprising and adventurist spirit relentlessly working to master the world. This recasting of the transcendent power of human will allowed Chinese reformers and, later, their Vietnamese counterparts to look past the deterministic and impersonal sociohistorical forces fundamental to Western conceptions of Social Darwinism and formulate a voluntarist Darwinian prescription for social evolution.[29]

The carefully constructed narrative progression that Phan Boi Chau adopted to present his account of America also reflects the importance of Chinese reform authors in shaping the neo-Confucian dimension of the reform generation's Social Darwinist vision and the place of the United States in it. In Phan Chu Trinh's narrative, the American struggle for independence begins not with impersonal Darwinian forces of power, economics, or culture but through the appearance of properly cultivated individual heroes such as George Washington. Nor did Phan Chu Trinh end his story with the Spencerian competitive quest for wealth and power but, rather, in a peaceful Confucian utopian universe. At one level, Phan Chu Trinh's narrative order self-consciously mirrored the path to self-cultivation and social harmony outlined in *The Great Learning* [*Dai Hoc*; Chinese *Ta-hsüch*], one of the four books that made up the neo-Confucian canon and formed the basis of the Vietnamese imperial examinations. By juxtaposing a central passage from *The Great Learning* with the narrative progression of Phan Chu Trinh's poem, it is possible to see the neo-Confucian sensibilities that shaped his conception of the American experience:

> Things being investigated, knowledge became complete [Americans gathered together and initiated the idea of liberty]. Their knowledge being complete, their thoughts were sincere [Through discussions, freedom was emblazoned on the hearts of the people]. Their thoughts being sincere, their hearts were then rectified [The pledge to seek freedom recalled virtues of righteousness and filial piety]. Their hearts being rectified, their persons were cultivated [American patriots renounced and overcame their individual passions and suffering]. Their persons being cultivated, their families were regulated [Mothers and wives supported their sons and husbands who worked to defeat the British in order to honor their ancestors]. Their families being regulated, their states were rightly governed [The Americans defeated the British and built a civilized and powerful state]. Their states being rightly governed, the whole kingdom was made tranquil and happy [The aftermath of the American struggle led to peace and security radiant on the four horizons].[30]

Phan Chu Trinh's step-by-step rendering of the American revolution, however, must also be viewed within the context of the challenges to the neo-Confucian canon posed by Chinese reformers. In the writings of the Chinese reform scholar K'ang Yu-wei, which were a particular source of inspiration for Phan Chu Trinh, the meaning of a utopian peace, the penultimate step in *The Great Learning*, took on radically new connotations. K'ang argued that human history inexorably moved through three stages, from the age of disorder through the age of approaching peace to the final age of universal peace. While the neo-Confucian tradition emphasized the links between individual and societal moral cultivation in these stages as well as their cyclical and repetitive character, K'ang focused on their linear development and the accompanying emergence of new political forms, placing absolute monarchy in the age of disorder, constitutional monarchy in the age of approaching peace, and republican government in the age of universal peace.[31]

Phan Chu Trinh's admiration for the Chinese reformer along with his virulent antimonarchism lead one to believe that the image of utopian peace—"Everywhere on the four horizons the words peace and security were radiant"—with which Phan closed his depiction of the American experience more fully reflected the republican vision of K'ang Yu-wei rather than neo-Confucian ideas. A speech Phan Chu Trinh delivered several months before his death in 1926 reinforces this interpretation. In it, he refers to the United States in support of his call for the eventual establishment of a republican government in Vietnam after the long process of internal cultural reform had been completed.[32]

The reform generation's admiration for America cannot be understood without reference to these larger forces that shaped its critiques of Vietnamese society and prescriptions for reform. This imagined America, with its Confucian heroes who knew the path of social evolution led to a glorious future and used their conscious will to guide society toward it, was a central theme in works by Phan Chu Trinh, Phan Boi Chau, and other Vietnamese reformers. It reflected their own idealized self-image and articulated their aspirations for the movement they led. The reform generation passed from the Vietnamese political stage in the 1920s, as did the centrality of Social Darwinism for Vietnamese anticolonial thought. But the images of America that emerged in the radicalized political discourse of the next generation of Vietnamese anticolonialists betrayed the echoes and lingering potency of the neo-Confucian and Social Darwinian voluntarism that animated the reform generation's vision for Vietnam.

America and Vietnamese Radicalism

The political and intellectual upheavals of the 1920s in Vietnam set the stage for a reconsideration of the place of America in indigenous political discourse. Student demonstrations in Hanoi to protest the French decision in 1925 to sentence Phan Boi Chau to life imprisonment for his anticolonial activities and the public funerals organized by students throughout Vietnam to observe and commemorate the death of Phan Chu Trinh in 1926 marked the symbolic passage of leadership in Vietnamese anticolonial politics. These events ushered in a new generation of young nationalists whose embrace of more radical paths to Vietnam's social transformation and political independence would dominate indigenous political life in the interwar period. Among them were many of the future leaders of Vietnamese communism, including individuals who would guide Vietnam to independence in the 1940s and shape Vietnam's postcolonial diplomacy toward the United States.

Despite the homage this younger generation paid to the two leaders of the reform generation, students—along with clerks, interpreters, primary teachers, and journalists recently graduated from school or expelled for their anticolonial activities—who made up the radicalized "new intelligentsia" (*gioi tri thuc*) that emerged in the 1920s were dissatisfied and impatient with the scope and pace of the reform generation's prescriptions for Vietnamese society. But the student-led mass demonstrations and strikes of 1925–26 were not only an expression of a revitalized and radicalized patriotic anticolonialism. Viewed within the continuing social dislocations of French colonial rule, they also provided a vehicle for students to challenge the traditional authority of their parents and older teachers. The United States would play a critical symbolic role in the struggle of young radicals to redefine the relationship between the individual and society and articulate a new revolutionary anticolonial vision.[33]

The sons, and sometimes the daughters, of mandarin families who formed the new intelligentsia of the 1920s were products of the French-controlled educational system that superseded the traditional academies that had taught the Chinese classics and Confucian morality. For their secondary education, many of these students attended French lycées and Franco-Annamite schools concentrated in urban centers. Some also undertook advanced study at the University of Hanoi, founded by the French to offer training in medicine, law, and teaching. A few, usually the children of wealthy southerners, were sent to France for university training, a practice that accelerated in the wake of the expulsions that followed the student protests of 1925–26.[34]

The French and French-trained indigenous teachers at the secondary and university levels provided students with a Western-oriented curriculum that differed sharply from the Confucian examination system that had shaped the worldview of their fathers and grandfathers. The experience of French education, particularly its veneration of Western ideas and values, had a corrosive effect on the relationship between student radicals and their families as it accelerated the fraying of Confucian familial and social bonds under French colonialism. As one young radical of the period wrote, "Vietnamese youth is caught as if in whirling waters, not knowing where to swim for. Faced with a moral choice, it does not know on which morality to base its actions and its judgments."[35]

Reflecting these profound differences in generational sensibilities, student activists aimed to address the dilemmas of youthful alienation with calls for the recreation rather than reform of the moral and social order in Vietnam. Indeed, the political discourse of the new intelligentsia, and its increasingly radical critique of Vietnamese society, was initially driven by individual and familial concerns as many students came to perceive disturbing links between what they saw as the confining boundaries of traditional family life and the burdens of colonialism. Young radicals sought to break with the Confucian past and the colonial present by investigating and internalizing new, often Western, ideas and values.

They took full advantage of a modest French loosening on restrictions governing freedom of expression in 1925 to participate in the indigenous publishing boom of the late 1920s. In an outpouring of books, pamphlets, and periodicals, the new intelligentsia reexamined and debated the Western thought and experiences that had captured the imagination of the reform generation. Radicals also introduced into Vietnamese discourse the ideas of a more far-reaching and sometimes potentially subversive range of Western thinkers: philosophers such as Immanuel Kant, Georg Wilhelm Friedrich Hegel, Baruch Spinoza, and Friedrich Nietzsche; political theorists such as Karl Marx, Pierre-Joseph Proudhon, and Lenin; and scientists such as Albert Einstein and Marie Curie.[36] As in the reform generation, their investigations of Western ideas and values focused on Europe, with the United States playing a secondary but important role. But as the shared experience of French education removed the necessity of relying on Chinese and Japanese informants for their perceptions of Europe and America, the new radicals apprehended Western morality, ethics, history, politics, and science in ways that substantially departed from the neo-Confucian imaginings of the Reform Movement.

The place of America in the shifting perspectives on Western ideas and values that inspired the investigative studies of the new intelligentsia is best revealed in a 1928 pamphlet titled *European and American Civilization* [*Van Minh Au My*].[37] Published in Hue by a small group of influential young radicals led by Dao Duy Anh, the likely author, the pamphlet was one of a series of works that formed one part of an ongoing indigenous debate in the 1920s over Vietnamese national essence (*quoc tuy*). On one side neotraditionalists such as Pham Quynh argued that Confucian norms should continue to shape the inner spirit of the Vietnamese, while new Western ideas were more properly thought of as outer or secondary and utilitarian components of modern Vietnamese society. Against this neotraditional division between substance and application (*the-dung*), young radicals such as the author of *European and American Civilization* asserted that Western thought offered fundamentally transformative paths to Vietnam's future.[38]

The pamphlet opened with a review of the achievements of European societies, including a discussion not only of the ideas of individual liberty that had given rise to the French revolution, the constitutional structure of the European nation-states that emerged in the nineteenth century, and the rise of imperialism but also a summary of the critiques offered by Marx, Lenin, and others for the inequalities within European societies and the coming of the Bolshevik revolution in Russia. These powerful intellectual and political developments, it argued, rested on the European commitment to the advancement of knowledge. Along with praise for Europe's universities, book-publishing industry and periodical press, and expansive infrastructure for the rapid communication of ideas, the pamphlet's analysis of European intellectual curiosity and vitality drew particular attention to the development of the physical, natural, and social sciences and their shared emphasis on the principles of experimentation, classification, and inductive and deductive reasoning.

Turning to the United States, *European and American Civilization* suggested that the "essential elements" of American civilization were similar to those of Europe, as they shared "the same father and mother," an image that drew upon the familial language that characterized radical discourse during the period. But unlike the relatively undifferentiated portrait of European and American societies in the writings of the reform generation, it argued that the essentialist underpinnings of both civilizations produced quite different results in the United States because of the divergent historical experiences of Europe and America. When the European settlers first came to America, the pamphlet observed, they encountered "a largely uninhabited land of dense forests." Their initial efforts were directed at the formidable task of developing the land to support agriculture and commerce, activities in which "workers were more esteemed than intellectuals." For this reason, it argued, American civilization was more "materialist" than its European counterparts, "a nation of . . . buying and selling."[39]

The distinction between the idealism of Europe and the materialism of America shaped the pamphlet's explication of the "special characteristics" of the United States. In comparison with the European class system, *European and American Civilization* suggested, "people who live in America work for a living. They are all common people. Therefore American civilization is the civilization of the common people, without adornment but successful. Because of this, American society is more altruistic and equal, its civilization more materialist. . . . The United States is a nation of commerce and industry." Similarly, it viewed Americans as less philosophically inclined than the Europeans: "The American people think more highly of the practical than philosophic ideas; they think more highly of character or feelings than intelligence." Such sentiments, the pamphlet implied, also promoted greater social equality: "The bosses in big factories, the majority of whom were once employees, worked their way upward because they had the characteristics of endurance and mechanical cleverness." [40]

In its analysis of the United States, *European and American Civilization* revealed the exposure of the new intelligentsia to Western ideas through the prism of the French educational system. Many of the characteristics it identified as peculiarly American—materialism; commercial, industrial, and technological prowess; Yankee ingenuity and probity; and the deprecation of intellectual inquiry —mirrored contemporary French perceptions of the United States. [41] The author and other Vietnamese radicals might well have encountered these views in school or through more indirect means. For instance, works by the leading interwar French interpreters of America, such as Georges Duhamel and André Siegfried, were available in Vietnam in the 1920s, as were French translations of novels by American authors, such as Sinclair Lewis, Theodore Dreiser, and John Dos Passos, that enjoyed particular popularity in France because of their critical views of American culture. [42]

But while many contemporary French observers saw American society in derogatory, if not hostile, terms, the distinctions between the United States and Europe that emerge in *European and American Civilization* are largely descriptive rather than judgmental. Even though the intellectual dimension attributed to European society by the pamphlet's author resonated more fully with the sensibilities of the new intelligentsia, America was nonetheless approvingly rendered as a conventional, though extremely powerful, Western nation. Commenting on recent American history, the pamphlet noted that the United States "retained the doctrine of 'no intervention in the affairs of the world' until the beginning of the twentieth century, preferring to concentrate on the development of commerce and industry." But more recently America had imitated European imperialism, "searching for colonies, territories, and concessions." As a result, "The United States at present stands at the top of the list of the world's strongest nations." Although U.S. materialism offered an "ideal" (*ly-tuong*) to order society that was different from European models, the pamphlet concluded, the critical lesson of both the American and the European experience for Vietnam was the need to embrace an ideal with the capacity of releasing powerful forces for revolutionary change in society. [43]

Like the author of *European and American Civilization*, young radicals assumed their quest for self-knowledge and self-realization would in time bring both individual and national liberation. But the processes by which this transformation should take place were never fully articulated by the new intelligentsia of the 1920s. Far more diffuse than the Reform Movement in its overarching vision, radical thought left vague the precise relationship between new sources of Western knowledge, the shifting behavior of individuals, and the coming of revolutionary social, cultural, and political change. In part, continuing French censorship prevented the application of these analyses of the West to Vietnamese conditions. Aware of the potentially subversive uses to which the Vietnamese could put Western thought, the French often banned or censored portions of books and articles that presented Western ideas, a practice that eventually prompted a measure of indigenous self-censorship.[44]

The vagaries of the new intelligentsia's vision were also related to the nature of radical political discourse itself and the French educational experiences that shaped it. Self-consciously experimental and iconoclastic, radical thought was never as firmly anchored around a body of shared principles as those that guided the Reform Movement. Unlike the unifying experience of the traditional academies with their emphasis on common Confucian values, the impersonal structure and diverse curriculum of the French educational system left the new intelligentsia much more fragmented than the reform generation that preceded it. Though eager to debate a wide range of issues, radicals never formed a consensus on a single set of guiding ideals to bring individual and societal change to Vietnam. Nor did the diffuse inclinations and leadership of the movement leave its members well placed to organize for unified anticolonial political action.

In the absence of an integrative vision for Vietnam's future, the new intelligentsia's disparate search for individual and societal transformation rested on an almost romantic belief in revolutionary heroism that both recalled and reshaped the voluntarism of the Reform Movement. It was expressed most forcefully in the numerous biographies authored by student radicals that were the dominant mode of indigenous publishing on historical issues in the late 1920s. Most prevalent were biographical accounts of indigenous cultural heroes such as the Trung Sisters or Le Loi, who had led the Vietnamese to victory in the repeated Chinese invasions of the precolonial period. But contemporary Asian nationalists such as Sun Yatsen and Mohandas Gandhi received substantial biographic attention, too, as did a variety of European individuals ranging from Christopher Columbus, Napoleon Bonaparte, and Louis Kossuth to Catherine the Great and Florence Nightingale. A number of American figures also received biographical treatment, including George Washington, Abraham Lincoln, Benjamin Franklin, and Thomas Edison.[45]

The new intelligentsia's celebration of individual voluntarism in biographies of these Asian, European, and American figures served as a central vehicle to realize their romantic yearnings for fundamental change in Vietnam. In part, the structure and aims of these biographical accounts bore more similarities to the neo-Confucian past than the new intelligentsia might have cared to admit. Echoing the works of Phan Boi Chau and Phan Chu Trinh, radicals used biographic forms to glorify the triumph of individual will over historical destiny and often ascribed Confucian virtues to their subjects. But the biographies authored by the new intelligentsia were also framed by a fuller appreciation than that of the reform generation for the role of political, economic, and social forces in shaping individual experiences. Often highly emotional in tone, radical biographies urged readers to emulate the personality traits of the indomitable indigenous and foreign heroes they described in the belief that these figures offered exemplary models for collective action to overcome the impersonal political and social forces of French colonialism that had brought about the subjugation of the Vietnamese.

A 1929 biography of Abraham Lincoln illustrates both the rhetorical conventions of the genre and the meanings ascribed to the American experience in this form of radical political discourse.[46] Lincoln's life is presented through a didactic series of vignettes interspersed with "commentary" (*phe-binh*) designed to explicate the appropriate lessons for Vietnamese readers. The biography opens with Lincoln's humble origins in Kentucky. But although his family was poor, the reader is told, Lincoln's parents brought their son up to be "righteous," "courageous," "hard-working," and "honest." On his deathbed, Lincoln's father told him "to make every effort to work to be a good person like I taught you everyday: respect and venerate God and your family." Shortly after his father's death, the biography continues, Lincoln studied the story of another American hero, George Washington, which inspired him to serve his country as well as honor his family. Washington's model inculcated in Lincoln a commitment to the democratic ideals of the American republic. As a young man, Lincoln sought to cultivate a virtuous life for himself and his country as a lawyer and congressmen, a path approvingly recommended to readers "if we want to be great men in these times."

Rewarded for his virtue, the authors of the biography suggest, Lincoln became president only to face the crisis posed by slavery, a condition they equated with French colonialism in Vietnam. Aware that slavery violated the American commitment to individual freedom and threatened to destroy the state, they argued, Lincoln drew upon his inner resources to mobilize the nation for victory over the slaveholders of the south in the American civil war. Tragically, they noted in the highly emotive language typical of these works, Lincoln's assassination prevented him from seeing the benefits his sacrifices had won for the nation. The biography concludes with a "general lesson" (*tong-binh*), calling upon young Vietnamese to learn the story of Lincoln to acquire the behavior and morals necessary to transform themselves and society: "From the story of Lincoln, we know that fate does not control individuals if they know how to establish and show their resolve. From the story of Lincoln we know that any misery can be reduced if the politics of one's own country are democratic. From the story of Lincoln we know that his accomplishments were in all cases due to his inner virtue. If we aspire to the accomplishments of Lincoln we must first develop his virtues." [47]

Within this radical intellectual milieu, with its calls for individual and social transformation and embrace of revolutionary heroism, Ho Chi Minh founded the Vietnamese Revolutionary Youth League (Viet Nam Thanh Nien Kach Menh Hoi) in the spring of 1925. The Youth League, one of several radical Vietnamese anticolonial associations that emerged in the late 1920s, proved no more effective than the others at drawing on the voluntarist ethos expressed in biographies like that of Lincoln to restructure Vietnamese society and bring an end to French colonial rule. But while the lasting significance of most radical anticolonial groups proved ephemeral, the Youth League served as the forerunner of the Vietnamese communist movement, providing much of the latter's leadership and ideological orientation.[48]

The Youth League's membership of young radicals included Pham Van Dong and Truong Chinh, whose importance for Vietnamese communism and its diplomacy in the 1940s was second only to Ho Chi Minh's. Pham Van Dong, born in 1906 to a mandarin family in Quang Ngai and active in the student protests at the prestigious Lycée Albert Sarraut in Hanoi, joined the league in 1925. Truong Chinh (a pseudonym he adopted in the 1930s meaning "Long March") was born Dang Xuan Khu to an impoverished scholar-gentry family in Nam Dinh province in 1907. A leader in student efforts to commemorate Phan Chu Trinh's death at the Franco-Annamite School of Nam Dinh, Truong Chinh became a Youth League member in 1927. Only Vo Nguyen Giap, who formed the third member of the leadership troika under Ho Chi Minh in the 1940s, was not a member of the league. He was, however, an active participant in the radicalizing events that shaped his generation. The youngest of his future compatriots, he was born in 1911 to a scholar-gentry family in Quang Binh province. As a student at the Imperial Academy in Hue, he was active in the student protest movement there. He also became a member of the New Vietnam Revolutionary Party (Tan Viet Cach Mang Dang), which had close links with the Youth League and eventually became a part of the Vietnamese Communist Party.[49]

Central to the establishment of the Youth League and its revolutionary ideology was Ho Chi Minh. Several decades older than the students who made up the membership of the league, Ho Chi Minh was born sometime between 1890 and 1894 in Nghe An province to a poor scholar-gentry family. Through his father, a minor scholar official closely involved in anticolonial activities, he came to know many of the leaders of the reform generation, including Phan Boi Chau and Phan Chu Trinh. As a student at the National Academy in Hue, he joined in the anticolonial agitation organized under the auspices of the Reform Movement in 1908 and later taught briefly in one of the movement's schools. He left Vietnam for Europe in the summer of 1911, embarking on an intellectual and political odyssey that prefigured the experiences of many of the new intelligentsia in the 1920s. After traveling to southern France, northern Africa, New York City, and London, Ho Chi Minh eventually settled in Paris, where he worked with Phan Chu Trinh to draft the petition he presented to the peace conference at Paris in 1919. In the wake of the conference's unwillingness to consider these demands for greater Vietnamese political rights and responsibilities under French colonial rule, he turned from the more gradualist anticolonial ideas and strategies of the reform generation to Marxism. He became a founding member of the French Communist Party in 1920, a student at the University of the Toilers of the East in Moscow in 1923, and a leading spokesmen for the anticolonial cause at the Fifth Congress of the Communist International in 1924. Sent to China as a Comintern agent in 1925, he began the organizational work that resulted in the establishment of the Youth League.[50]

The ideology of the Youth League was most fully expressed in *The Road to Revolution* [*Duong Cach Menh*],[51] prepared by Ho Chi Minh in 1927 as a training manual for the organization's members. Marxism, particularly its Leninist formulations, occupied a dominant place in the analysis Ho presented in *Road to Revolution*. It provided an overarching framework to universalize the Vietnamese colonial experience and an organizational path to realize anticolonial aspirations and the transformation of Vietnamese society. But Ho emphasized the immediate imperative of the "national question" rather than "social revolution" or class issues and employed conceptual language that borrowed as much from indigenous political discourse as it did from Marx and Lenin. While the determinism of Marxism-Leninism injected a compelling note of historical inevitability into his consideration of Vietnamese national liberation, Ho devoted particular attention to the voluntarist dimension of revolutionary struggle. In discussions shaped by both Leninist themes and the voluntarist modes more familiar to his radical student readers, Ho drew not only from the Russian revolution and Marxism-Leninism as guides for the Vietnamese struggle for national liberation but also from the French and American revolutionary experiences and the ideas of Jefferson, Gandhi, and Sun Yat-sen. He also freely mixed neo-Confucian maxims with Leninist rhetoric from *What Is to Be Done?* to explicate the virtues necessary for young revolutionaries to bring about Vietnamese independence.[52]

These diverse Marxist and indigenous intellectual legacies informed Ho's sustained discussion of the American revolution that, with analyses of the French and Russian revolutions, formed a substantial component of *Road to Revolution*.

He opened his consideration of the American experience with a brief review of the European settlement of North America that foreshadowed both the materialist thrust of his analysis and its more traditional emphasis on the threats colonial rule posed to colonized peoples.[53] Next, Ho turned to a consideration of the causes of the American revolution. At one level, the materialist emphasis of Ho's analysis of the reasons for the revolution substantially departed from the neo-Confucian renderings of the reform generation that attributed the success of American patriots to the emergence of virtuous elites:

America is very rich in agricultural land, iron, coal, cotton, rice, cattle, and other resources as well. The English secretly wanted it all for themselves, so they promulgated the following three rules of behavior: 1) the Americans must always grant their resources to the English; they were not allowed to sell them to other nations; 2) the Americans were not permitted to set up factories or trading associations; 3) other countries were not allowed to trade with America; only the English could trade. These three laws, which also added heavy taxes and duties, made the American economy extremely poverty stricken.

But his analysis of revolution itself also reflected the persisting radical appreciation for the wealth and power of American society and its admiration for the voluntarist capacities of the Americans to exert their will to overcome historical circumstances:

Angered, the Americans decided to "boycott" the English in 1770. The boycott against the English royal government lasted for five years. The English brought soldiers to suppress it and imposed their own officials. Every time they imposed one of their own officials, all the people felt more angry. In 1775, when the English army imposed a number of their own officials as well, the people pulled together to fight, and the English army killed nine people. This event, like adding fire to gunpowder, prompted the angry Americans to explode. In this life and death matter, they resolved to expel the new English government. After a year, on 4 July 1776, the revolution took place, and America declared itself independent and became a republic. Now, the United States has 48 states and 110 million people.[54]

Finally, Ho combined aspects of Marxist-Leninist analysis with more traditional neo-Confucian formulations to present three lessons his Vietnamese readers should learn from the American revolution. The first lesson suggested in part that the shared experiences of imperialism and colonial rule made the United States a valuable model for Vietnamese to study. But Ho's efforts to differentiate aspects of the Vietnamese and American experiences drew less on Marxist-Leninist categories than on the familial images of reformist and radical rhetoric, reflecting the persistence of indigenous fears that colonialism threatened the very spirit and existence of the Vietnamese people:

> French policy toward Vietnam today is more shameful than English policy was toward America because the French put their grip on everything belonging to our people, hindering our people's labor and other affairs. They also forced us to smoke opium and drink liquor. The English were only fond of American money; the French want money but they also want to do away with our race, leaving Vietnam bereft of its children. Nonetheless, the Vietnamese people should still continue to study the American revolution![55]

A second lesson focused on the gap between American rhetoric and contemporary reality. It also expressed an admiration for American ideals one might not expect to find in a Marxist-Leninist analysis. But its emphasis on the collective rather than the individual nature of the rights ascribed to Americans fit both Confucian and Marxist conceptions of the subservient relationship of the individual to the state:

> In America's declaration of independence, there are these lines: "Under heaven all people have the right to liberty, the right to defend their lives, and the right to earn their living happily. If any government injures its people, they must bring down that government and build up another one. . . ." But now the American government does not want anyone to speak about revolution or attack the government![56]

Significantly, Ho's concern with collective rights and responsibilities prefigured the movement away from the individualistic concerns of many student radicals in the 1920s toward a focus on mass politics in subsequent decades.

In a final lesson that expressed an even more emphatic assertion of the importance of collective rights and responsibilities, Ho warned of the limitations of the American experience:

> Although the American revolution was successful more than 150 years ago, American workers and peasants are still extremely poor and carefully organize for the second revolution. The American revolution then is a capitalist revolution, but a capitalist revolution is not a complete or world revolution. We lay down our lives for revolution, but to make a complete or world revolution we must work in such a way to deliver rights for all the masses rather than for a few people. Only by struggling many times over can all the people have happiness.[57]

But if America proved an imperfect guide to realizing Vietnam's revolutionary aspirations, Ho's larger vision of a complete or world revolution was not rendered in conventional Marxist terms as a dictatorship of the proletariat in *Road to Revolution*. While Ho offered the "courage," "spirit of sacrifice," and "unity" of workers and peasants in the Russian revolution as models that came much closer to a world revolution than the American or French experiences did, he used a Confucian rather than a Bolshevik idiom to articulate the ultimate aims of the Vietnamese revolution. Ho suggested "the great unity under heaven—that is, world revolution" (*thien ha dai dong—ay la the gioi cach menh*), a characterization that both recalled the reform generation's use of the Confucian utopian peace to denote Vietnam's idealized postcolonial future and revealed radical efforts to recast and transform traditional categories of analysis for revolutionary purposes.[58]

Ho Chi Minh's account of the American revolution and other radical commentaries on America from the 1920s reflected the experimental, iconoclastic, and fluid nature of the new intelligentsia's search for a new political and social order in Vietnam. As it had for the reform generation, America remained an important source of inspiration for the celebration of voluntarism, which continued to infuse radical political thought. The radical embrace of American figures such as Washington and Lincoln shared aspects of the reformist concern with the cultivation of individual neo-Confucian virtue and its respect for the wealth and power of the United States. The new intelligentsia's training in French schools, its superior command of a wider range of Western ideas, and its probing curiosity about the material sources of the ideals that animated the European and American collective wills, however, served to recast indigenous understandings of how revolutionary voluntarism could be exercised in Vietnam. For Ho Chi Minh and the radical students such as Pham Van Dong, Truong Chinh, and Vo Nguyen Giap who were attracted to the ideas of the Youth League and the universalism of Marxism-Leninism, the American experience was no longer rendered as the ultimate objective of anticolonial politics but, rather, as one stage in Vietnamese revolutionary development. But even in this case, indigenous categories of analysis drawn from neo-Confucian, reformist, and radical discourse shaped the articulation of Marxist-Leninist thought in Vietnam and the place of America in it.

At the close of the decade, much of the radical agenda remained unrealized. With the rise of the mass politics of the 1930s and its focus on collective rather than individual interests, the radical effort to redefine the role of the individual in Vietnamese society was forestalled. The symbolic space occupied by the United States in the political discourse of the 1920s, like the broader eclectic contours of radical thought itself, would continue to frame the Vietnamese intelligentsia's ongoing search for social transformation and political independence and shape the

Vietnamese encounter with the United States during and after World War II. But both the domestic and the international agendas of Vietnamese revolutionaries, however, would also bear the legacies of the mass politics of the 1930s.

The Legacies of Internationalism

The United States was often barely perceptible in the internationalist political discourse of the radical mass politics that dominated Vietnamese anticolonialism in the 1930s. Ho Chi Minh's efforts to transform the membership and ideological emphasis of the Youth League into the Vietnamese Communist Party between 1928 and 1930 foundered with the decisions of the Sixth World Congress of the Comintern. At its Sixth Congress in 1928, the Comintern shifted to an ultra-leftist revolutionary line with a heavy emphasis on class struggle, proletarianization, and social revolution. In Vietnam this new internationalist revolutionary agenda challenged the Youth League's focus on the primacy of the national liberation struggle and its eclectic blend of Marxism-Leninism and indigenous political thought. The collectivist orientation of the Comintern strategy also brought a retreat from the individualistic yearnings that had initially stimulated the youthful radicalism in the preceding decade.

Some middle-class advocates of radicalism were wary of Vietnamese efforts to promote the Comintern agenda in the 1930s, preferring what one scholar has termed an "oratorical progressivism" that opposed mass violence and class conflict.[59] In their continuing endeavors to perpetuate the radical reform agenda of the 1920s, they devoted some attention to the United States. *Ladies' News* [*Phu Nu Tan Van*], the leading journal of progressive thought in the south, often featured stories about American figures. A few items were comical, such as a photograph of Herbert Hoover placed next to one of a bulldog that bore a remarkable resemblance to the American president. Most, however, were serious, if cursory, explorations of aspects of American life, including the ideas of John Dewey and other educational reformers, nineteenth-century literature, recent technological advances, and the achievements of outstanding American women such as Eleanor Roosevelt. In tone the journal closely followed the materialist analysis of American society that informed much of the radical discourse in the 1920s.[60]

But the United States received scant attention from the increasingly factionalized radical advocates of mass politics that were the leading force of anticolonialism during the 1930s. The incarceration of Youth League members such as Pham Van Dong and Truong Chinh by the French and the arrest of Ho Chi Minh in Hong Kong followed the widespread incidents of anticolonial agitation that swept Vietnam between 1929 and 1931. In the absence of these leaders, a group of Moscow-trained proletarian internationalists were left to run what was now termed the Indochinese Communist Party under the ultra-leftist Comintern line. In southern Vietnam, ICP cadres were joined by students returning from France who had been active partisans in French debates between Stalinists and Trotsky-ists. Adherents of Trotskyism and Stalinism established a tenuous rapprochement with the ICP upon their return to Vietnam, but ideological divisions persisted, as did endemic fighting with the ICP. The differences that separated them, often far removed from indigenous concerns, were expressed in debates that mirrored the contemporary European leftist polemics of the period on the Spanish civil war and on the ideological purity of the revolutionary lines of Joseph Stalin and Leon Trotsky.[61]

If America had little symbolic resonance in a dialogue increasingly bounded by issues of class and social revolution, the rise of mass politics in the 1930s did have subtle implications for the perceptions of the United States formed by the individuals who would lead Vietnamese communism after 1940 and conduct its postcolonial diplomacy. For the much of the period from 1930 to 1935 when the ultra-leftist line was ascendant, Ho Chi Minh, Pham Van Dong, Truong Chinh, and Vo Nguyen Giap watched from the sidelines as the Moscow-trained prole-tarian internationalists oversaw a period that would prove to be the nadir of the party's fortunes. Ho Chi Minh was arrested in Hong Kong in 1931 but was either released or allowed to escape through the efforts of a sympathetic British lawyer several years later. He returned to Moscow in 1934, where he remained until 1938. Pham Van Dong and Truong Chinh were arrested by the French in 1929 and 1930, respectively, but were not released from prison until 1936. Vo Nguyen Giap was also arrested in 1930 but was released in late 1932. Despite their lack of any direct control over party activities, the experiences of these men in this period would have lasting significance for how they apprehended Marxism-Leninism and per-ceived the relationship between Vietnam and the wider world.

Ho Chi Minh's long and desultory exile in Moscow undoubtedly reinforced his inclination to meld internationalist ideology to Vietnamese realities and may have prompted an enduring suspicion of Stalin and Soviet ideological direction. Ho's activities after he reached Moscow remain somewhat obscure, but recently released Comintern documents suggest that he was critical of the new Comintern line. In a 1931 letter to the Comintern's Far Eastern Bureau in Moscow, Ho com-plained about the illiteracy of workers and peasants who were new party recruits, arguing that "in spite of their courage and self-sacrifice they work badly, their ideo-logical and political level being too low." Comintern materials also reveal that Ho underwent severe criticism for his alleged nationalist proclivities and his sympathy for the bourgeoisie. His Comintern minder in Moscow reported, "We feel that in the coming two years he must apply himself seriously to his studies and will not be able to handle anything else," a decision that prevented Ho from assuming any meaningful role within the Vietnamese Communist Party during this period. Reports that Ho was put on trial in 1934 or 1935 remain unconfirmed without access to KGB archives, but as one observer who has worked most closely with Comintern material on Vietnam argues, some sort of tribunal would not have been impossible in a time of widespread Stalinist paranoia and terror. A June 1938 letter from Ho to the Comintern on the seventh anniversary of his arrest in Hong Kong and absence from party affairs suggests the depth of Ho's eclipse: "One this occasion, I write to ask you to change this situation. . . . Do with me what you think is useful. What I ask is that you do not leave me to live too long without activity and apart from and outside the party." Although available documentation is elusive, Ho left Moscow for China at the end of 1938 more likely to work as a clandestine operative in building the anti-Japanese coalition between the Chinese communists and the Kuomintang rather than to oversee the struggle for independence in Vietnam. When Ho did reemerge as a leader in Vietnamese anticolonial politics, his articulation of Marxism-Leninism, shaped by his experiences in China and the national liberation strategies of the Youth League, bore only cursory nods to Stalinist discourse and direction.[62]

For Pham Van Dong, Truong Chinh, and Vo Nguyen Giap, the legacies of the early 1930s were somewhat more ambiguous. From their vantage point in French prisons, they, too, learned of the failures of the Stalinist ultra-leftist line in Vietnam. But their experiences in prison were also deeply shaped by Marxist-Leninist ideology. French colonial prisons, which held more than 10,000 political prisoners between 1930 and 1936, became centers of Marxist education, or what some Vietnamese have termed "universities of revolution." On Con Son, a large French penal colony off the southern Vietnamese coast, where Pham Van Dong was incarcerated, prison halls were adorned with portraits of Marx, Lenin, and Stalin and with hand-drawn maps of Europe, Indochina, China, and the Soviet Union, which allowed prisoners to follow the progress of the Spanish civil war as well as political developments in the rest of Europe and Asia. Pham Van Dong led ICP efforts to organize prisoners at Con Son, offering long-term courses in Marxist theory and briefer study sessions on Marxist-Leninist texts. Truong Chinh, who was incarcerated at Son La prison in northern Vietnam, undertook similar efforts there. Both men were also regular contributors to the clandestine journals published at Con Son and Son La, *Shared Opinion* [*Y kien chung*] and *Red Star* [*Sao do*], respectively.[63]

Several aspects of the prison experience had critical implications for the leaders of Vietnamese communism after 1940. Prison writings from this period suggest that the psychological support derived from being part of an international movement helped prisoners endure the often brutal experience of French imprisonment. In turn, this spirit of connectedness emphasized in prison strongly reinforced the internationalist component of Vietnamese communism. Leninist tactics of collective organization and unified action received particular emphasis in the curriculum of prison study sessions, giving rise to a more pragmatic voluntarism than the romantic revolutionary heroism of the 1920s. The common bond of incarceration may also have contributed to the remarkable unanimity of purpose that appears to have guided key party leaders in the early postcolonial period.

But despite the universalizing comfort of Marxism-Leninism, prison life was also an isolating experience that limited revolutionary breadth of vision about the world. During their more than five years of imprisonment, Pham Van Dong and Truong Chinh gleaned their knowledge of contemporary events either from a limited range of books and journals that made their way into Vietnamese prisons or from what they learned from other prisoners and the prison staff. Incarceration served to perpetuate their narrow range of experience with the world beyond Vietnam and southern China, perhaps contributing to the postcolonial sense of Vietnam and Vietnamese communism as encircled and isolated that informed later policies and initiatives. By contrast, although Vo Nguyen Giap's experience of the world also remained bounded by Vietnam and southern China, his earlier release from prison in 1932 and subsequent experiences as a law student, high school teacher, journalist, and editor in the mid-1930s may account for his comparatively more cosmopolitan outlook.

Events in the Soviet Union and France in the mid-1930s brought Pham Van Dong, Truong Chinh, Vo Nguyen Giap, and other Youth League members back to prominence in northern Vietnamese radical politics at the end of the decade. In 1935 the Comintern reversed its emphasis on class consciousness and social revolution, adopting a Popular Front policy that called for an antifascist alliance regardless of class background. The rise of the Popular Front government in France prompted the release of most Vietnamese political prisoners in 1936, including Pham Van Dong and Truong Chinh, and loosened restrictions on indigenous political expression. Although the Popular Front policies relegitimated aspects of the Youth League's ideological orientation, the ICP's leadership remained fragmented and its ideology diffuse. In 1938 the ICP Central Committee established the Indochinese Democratic Front (Mat Tran Dan Chu Dong Duong) in an effort to build a broad coalition to advocate indigenous political rights. But little came of these ICP efforts. Noncommunist groups remained wary of ICP intentions; Moscow-trained proletarian internationalists remained suspicious of the new revolutionary line; and the deepening factionalization of southern radical politics mitigated against renewed coalition building.[64]

Of more enduring significance was the renewed vigor of the indigenous press during the Popular Front period in which Pham Van Dong, Truong Chinh, Vo Nguyen Giap, and eventually, Ho Chi Minh played an important role. Throughout the late 1930s the United States remained a muted presence in the outpouring of radical books, pamphlets, journals, and newspapers. Some attention was devoted to Franklin Roosevelt's promise of Philippine independence, but the strength and dedication of the Huk communist insurgency in the Philippines received considerably more emphasis than admiration for the comparative benevolence of U.S. colonial policies.[65] More commonly, the Popular Front press was characterized by the internationalist polemics that had animated political discourse earlier in the decade, with vociferous ideological debates between Trotskyists and advocates of the new Comintern revolutionary line.

After the outbreak of the Sino-Japanese war in 1937, however, the northern Vietnamese press devoted increasing attention to events in China, a development that held future repercussions for the leaders of Vietnamese communism after 1940 that were as important as their experiences in prison. Here, too, the ICP supporters of the anti-Japanese coalition in China sparred with Trotskyist opponents of United Front tactics. But more importantly, expanded knowledge of the Chinese experience and Maoist formulations of internationalism provided Ho Chi Minh and former Youth League members with an alternative to Soviet models for the national liberation struggle that better fit indigenous realities and prompted an ideological affinity with China that would persist and deepen after 1940.

The interest of the ICP in Chinese developments in the late 1930s built upon a series of earlier encounters and affinities between Chinese and Vietnamese revolutionaries. Ho Chi Minh's links with Chinese communism began in the 1920s when he was an active member of the French Communist Party. After the founding of the European Branch of the Chinese Communist Youth Corps in 1922, Ho served as the official liaison between the group and the French communists. Chou En-lai, one of the leaders of the European Branch, became acquainted with Ho in this way, as did a number of other young Chinese radicals who would later occupy important positions within the CCP. Here the subsequent patterns of ideational influence were reversed, with the older Ho Chi Minh, who tutored them in Leninist thought and tactics, considered an "elder brother" by Chou and others.[66]

With Ho's establishment of the headquarters of the Youth League in Canton in 1925, much of the focus of radical Vietnamese politics shifted to southern China. Ho regularly invited important CCP figures such as Chou En-lai, Liu Shao-ch'i, and P'eng P'ai to lecture in the political training program for the league's young

Vietnamese recruits. The most promising students were sent to study at the nearby Whampoa Military Academy, where Chou was the director of the political department. Both Pham Van Dong and Truong Chinh studied under these Chinese teachers in Canton as members of the Youth League.[67]

Against this background it is perhaps less surprising that the ICP press followed events in China after 1937 in considerable detail. *News [Tin Tuc]*, a weekly paper that included Truong Chinh as one of the members of its editorial board, followed the progress of the Chinese communist Eighth-Route army in the spring and summer of 1938 and praised the union of communists and noncommunists in the anti-Japanese struggle. Another ICP paper, *People [Dan Chung]*, ran a series of articles on the Sino-Japanese war in the fall of 1938 that included an extended interview with Mao Tse-Tung and discussions of Chinese communist military strategy. Several pamphlets published under the auspices of the ICP in 1938 provided the first comprehensive introduction to Maoist thought and the workings of the Popular Front in China. Among the most important were Nguyen Duc Thuy's *The Method of the Anti-Japanese Resistance of the Chinese Red Army [Phuong Phap Khang Nhat cua Hong Quan Tau]*, containing twenty-one translations from tracts by Mao and other Chinese strategists on political questions and guerrilla warfare, and Nguyen Van Tay's *What Can the Chinese Do to Defeat the Japanese? [Lam Sao cho Tau Thang Nhat?]*, which provided summaries of Chinese communist strategic thought.[68]

The introduction of these Chinese texts into radical political discourse was vital to the efforts of Vietnamese communists after 1940 to advance the Youth League vision of a national liberation revolution within a framework that preserved their larger commitment to Marxist-Leninist internationalism. As one key passage from Mao included in Thuy's *Method of Anti-Japanese Resistance* argued, "We temporarily stop the class struggle between workers and peasants and the bourgeois classes within the country because in a semi-colonial country like China the contradictions between China and external imperialism are greater than the internal contradiction between classes." Tay's *What Can the Chinese Do?* provided a detailed outline for "implementing the armed protracted resistance" and organizing a general economic and military mobilization across class lines "to save the country."[69] These Chinese formulations, through which Mao and other Chinese communist leaders sought the "sinification of Marxism,"[70] found immediate resonance in the Vietnamese political context, illustrating the willingness of many Vietnamese communists to look beyond Stalin and the Soviets for internationalist models.

Appreciation for developments in China informed Vo Nguyen Giap's *The Proper Path: The Question of National Liberation in Indochina [Con Duong*

Chinh: Van De Dan Toc Giai Phong o Dong Duong], published by an ICP publishing house in 1939. As the title suggests, Giap gave primary place to the struggle
for national liberation in Vietnam under the ICP. With events in China as an immediate backdrop, he warned of Japanese intentions in Indochina and the possibility that the French might collaborate in fulfilling them. The "road to liberation," Giap asserted, must be what he termed a "Leninist solution" that combined
the antifascist with the anticolonial struggle.[71] But underlying the Leninist rhetoric he used to support his argument was the Maoist model of the Popular Front
as a conceptual framework for mass mobilization in Vietnam. Vo Nguyen Giap's
intense interest in Chinese models emerged in a work he authored that was published by the ICP earlier in 1939, *Understanding Clearly the Military Situation in
China* [*Muon Hieu Ro Tinh Hinh Quan Su o Tau*]. In this detailed examination
of Chinese communist military and political strategy, Giap explicated concepts
such as national salvation associations, mass mobilization, and guerrilla war that
would become central to Vietnamese Communist Party strategy after 1940.[72]

Throughout the spring and summer of 1939, the radical press continued to
focus on developments in China. *Notre Voix*, a weekly paper also dominated by
the ICP, took up the Chinese cause with particular fervor, running regular stories
about the anti-Japanese resistance as well as calls to organize Vietnamese support
for the Chinese war effort. Among the articles on China that appeared in *Notre
Voix* was an eight-part series titled "Lettre de Chine," authored by P. C. Line, a
pseudonym for Ho Chi Minh, who had left Moscow for China the previous year.[73]
Ho's letter of 14 July 1939, a review of the political and military successes of the
first two years of the United Front against "Japanese fascist aggression" in China,
concluded in this way:

> Against a very strong and dangerous enemy, but one which is rapidly weaken-
> ing, we have all manner of favorable conditions: the atmosphere fortifies us for
> our struggle; this immense country with indisputable riches and a great popula-
> tion provides a reservoir for our army; France, Great Britain, the United States,
> and all democratic peoples aid us; the Soviet Union is our most faithful and
> interested friend. We have "clement weather, favorable terrain, and concord
> among the people," the three elements necessary for victory. But in order not to
> appear to be bragging, I will borrow the words of a foreigner who knows China
> well—the American ambassador. "The attitude of the Chinese people is very
> self-possessed," said the ambassador. "The spirit of the soldiers is very high. All
> of the leaders have absolute confidence in their final victory. They are deter-
> mined to fight to the finish." Although this quotation is a bit old—the ambas-
> sador made this speech on 4 February in New York—it remains true today. To

conclude, I invite my friends to recite the final couplet of a song written to celebrate the second anniversary of our war for independence and liberty: "All who have money contribute it. All who can be soldiers are soldiers. Each of us is a valiant combatant. Advance! The enemy will be vanquished. We give all! We give all! For victory is before us!"[74]

Some six weeks after this letter appeared in *Notre Voix*, the announcement of the nonaggression pact between Stalin and Nazi Germany on 23 August 1939 made the Soviet Union seem a less "faithful and interested friend" and rendered even more compelling the Maoist model for national salvation. In its broad outlines, Ho Chi Minh's sketch of the favorable revolutionary conditions facing China and his celebration of the United Front prefigured the broad-based appeals for national liberation in Vietnam that he and other leaders of Vietnamese communism offered in the 1940s. But Ho's special emphasis here on America was an unusual departure from the internationalist register that continued to frame radical discourse in the late 1930s and, significantly, foreshadowed the willingness on the part of Vietnamese radicals to chart an independent path as they sought international allies, including the United States, to sustain their struggle.

In many ways, Vietnamese communists were no closer to transforming indigenous society and achieving independence at the end of the 1930s than the leaders of the Reform Movement had been in the early decades of the century. With the fall of the Popular Front government in France in 1939 and the onset of renewed and more vigorous anticolonial repression in Vietnam, the prospects for their success grew even dimmer. But as the revolutionary situation became more favorable in the 1940s, the shifting contours of indigenous political thought under French rule that characterized the efforts of Vietnamese anticolonialists to understand and overcome the threatening forces that surrounded them had an enduring impact on Vietnamese communism and the future course of its diplomacy.

The movement from the neo-Confucianism and Social Darwinism of scholar-gentry reformers to the radicalism and internationalism of the new intelligentsia was less an evolutionary line than a continuing dialogue across generations that lacked a fixed or final synthesis. From this dialogue emerged a diverse repertoire of symbolic language and perceptual experiences that reflected not only an appreciation for Maoist internationalism and Leninist voluntarism but also an embrace of revolutionary heroism and Confucian moral virtue. As Ho Chi Minh, Pham Van Dong, Truong Chinh, and Vo Nguyen Giap organized the struggle for national liberation during World War II and turned to a largely imagined America for support, they relied on these powerful, if sometimes contradictory, legacies.

REPRESENTING VIETNAM
The Interwar American Construction of French Indochina

"Backwaters of Empire in French Indo-China" was an apt title for American journalist Gertrude Emerson's 1923 account of her first experiences in Vietnam.[1] Like much of Southeast Asia beyond the Philippines, Vietnam remained on the periphery of American foreign relations for much of the period between the two world wars. For diplomats and businesspeople, American political and economic interests in Vietnam were marginal. Of the fewer than one hundred Americans who lived in Vietnam, most were Protestant missionaries associated with the Christian and Missionary Alliance operating small missions in Hanoi, Saigon, and several provincial capitals. Until 1940 a single consul in Saigon represented American interests in the French colony. Consular duties in Saigon were not considered particularly taxing, with one consul asking to be excused from preparing monthly departmental reports because "there were almost no political developments to report."[2]

Nor did Vietnam hold much promise for American business interests. As another American consul remarked in the 1920s, the country was "almost cut off, commercially, from the United States." Despite an increase in exports of Vietnamese rubber to the United States in the late 1930s, American imports to and exports from Vietnam were a fraction of its interwar trade in Southeast Asia, far behind its more substantial commercial relations and investments in the Philippines, British Malaya, and the Dutch East Indies.[3] On a few occasions Vietnam did permeate the consciousness of official Washington. Along with Ho Chi Minh's attempt to put Vietnamese independence on the negotiating table at the Paris Peace Conference in 1919, several members of the French parliament sought to sell Vietnam and the rest of French Indochina to the United States in 1920 to pay

French war debts. But like Ho's efforts, those of the French parliament went unanswered by American policy makers.[4]

If Vietnam held only marginal significance for American diplomats and businesspeople, it did occupy the attention of journalists such as Gertrude Emerson as well as a number of scholars and travel writers writing in the interwar period. Vietnam was the focus of regular attention by journalists who contributed to periodicals such as *Asia, Current History, Living Age, National Geographic,* and the *New Republic.* Virginia Thompson and Thomas Ennis, both noted American specialists on Asia, prepared detailed studies of Vietnam in the 1930s. Missionaries, hunters, and travelers also produced a number of accounts of their experiences in Vietnam. Taken together, the works of these authors, along with the reports of consular officials from Saigon, provide the first sustained body of American commentary on Vietnamese society, French colonialism in Indochina, and Vietnamese nationalism.[5]

The primary impetus for American writing on Vietnam may have been the emergence of an enormous body of reportage literature in the United States that chronicled the everyday impact of the Great Depression. Most of the interwar American commentary on Vietnam was produced in the 1930s when works such as Theodore Dreiser's *Tragic America,* Edmund Wilson's *American Jitters,* Sherwood Anderson's *Puzzled America,* and the photo documentaries of depression-era life by Walker Evans and Dorothea Lange for the New Deal's Farm Security Administration enjoyed a wide domestic audience.[6] Primarily exposés of rural poverty and the human costs of joblessness in industrial cities, they provided a familiar conceptual vocabulary for Americans to report on the unfavorable conditions they found in Vietnam. The popularity of these works also offered some reassurance to editors and publishers that the relatively obscure Vietnam might attract an attentive American readership.[7]

Despite the common experience of worldwide depression, however, conditions in Vietnam seemed far worse than those in the United States to most American observers. "Primitive," "lazy," "cowardly," "vain," "dishonest," "unclean," and "somnolent" were the adjectives most frequently used to describe the Vietnamese. French colonial rule was judged to be an administrative, economic, and moral failure. And expressions of Vietnamese nationalism were dismissed as the work of external, often Soviet, agents. Embedded in these harsh judgments of colonial Vietnam was a broader interwar discourse on the relationship between what was seen as the backward character of nonwhite peoples and the more progressive West. American images of Vietnamese society and nationalism reflected a fundamental belief in racialized cultural hierarchies that had underlain the American encounter with nonwhite peoples at home and abroad since the mid-nineteenth century. Much of the vociferous critique of French colonialism rested on the wide-spread notion of the unique success of the American colonial project in the Philippines and the superior claims of American political and social models to reshape backward peoples.

But if the assumptions guiding American commentary on Vietnam were rooted in a domestic context, they also displayed revealing commonalities with the patterns of perception and behavior of European colonialists. Notwithstanding their anti-French rhetoric, Americans relied almost exclusively on the writings of French scholars, colonial officials, and journalists in forming their judgments of the largely unfamiliar Vietnamese. These deprecating French assessments of Vietnamese society were part of a wider Orientalist discourse on the non-Western "other" through which European colonial powers used a culturally constructed conception of the negative essence of colonized peoples to denote Western superiority and reinforce colonial military and economic dominance. Although Americans often celebrated what they saw as their own exceptionalism as a colonial power, their apprehensions of Vietnam point toward the shared rather than antithetical nature of interwar colonial discourse and practice in Europe and the United States.[8]

Had it not been for the outbreak of the Pacific war in 1941, interwar American perceptions of Vietnamese society, French colonialism, and Vietnamese nationalism might best be viewed as little more than a historical curiosity. But when the war with Japan heightened the geopolitical significance of French Indochina for the United States, the perceptual legacies of the interwar period, and the intertwined domestic and Euro-American currents of thought that shaped them, provided an essential starting point for American policy makers during and after World War II as they sought to articulate their own vision of postcolonial Vietnam.

Orientalizing the Vietnamese

Most interwar American accounts of Vietnam began with an examination of what one scholar termed "Annamite psychology."[9] With very few exceptions, the Vietnamese were found wanting. "Natural laziness," wrote Virginia Thompson in the most comprehensive American study of Indochina before World War II, "keeps the Annamite in a state of chronic poverty and often vagrancy." For Thompson, the "Annamite's total lack of initiative" characterized all important aspects of Vietnamese life, a view reflected by most observers, including U.S. consul Leland L. Smith, who reported to Washington in 1924 that the "Annamites as a race are very lazy and not prone to be ambitious." In discussing rice cultivation, which employed the bulk of Vietnam's largely rural population, writers commented that the "native farmer works within the strict orbit of his needs, which may be summed up in his philosophy that it is easier to do without something than to work for it. If his daily needs are satisfied, the Annamite takes no thought of the morrow." Traditional forms of education were thought to be important for urban and upper-class Vietnamese largely as "emancipation from manual labor." [10]

An image of Vietnamese society and culture as primitive also emerges in these accounts. The veteran Asia correspondent Mona Gardner, in a 1939 book chronicling her travels throughout Southeast Asia, summarized a common view of living conditions in Vietnamese villages: "Houses . . . were layers of desiccated mud, and might have been fashioned just slightly after the Stone Age. . . . Inside everything was sliding down as though the earth were drawing these people and their few possessions back unto it." Similarly, Gertrude Emerson, an associate editor of *Asia* magazine, was struck by the "groups of flimsy thatched hovels often standing in stagnant waters" that she observed in Vietnamese villages during her 1924 journey through northern Vietnam. "Annamites at best are never clean," Thompson claimed, "but sickness shows up this trait in its most revolting form. To have his pulse taken, the patient clothed in be-vermined rags extends a grimy fist covered with layers of dust." Indigenous cultural practices drew contempt from American observers. Thompson's view that "native eating" illustrated "general negligence" and "indelicacy" was echoed in accounts of diplomats such as Leland Smith, who, in upcountry trips, described the preparation of an "exceedingly Annamite meal" that he "could not eat (having seen it prepared)." Vietnamese modes of expression were also seen as inadequate. The "Annamite language," Thompson, like many observers, argued, "is adapted to the mentality of a primitive people. The vocabulary is limited and lacking in words to express the major emotions and complex ideas." [11]

With perceptions of the Vietnamese as lazy and primitive, many American observers argued that the Vietnamese were, by nature, liars. "Lying does not trouble the Annamite conscience," Thompson reported in her discussion of indigenous government. "Facts makes little impression on . . . a chaotic state of mind." The Vietnamese "flair for imaginative lying," according to many observers, pervaded indigenous society. Popular legends, one writer noted, glorified "graft, ruse and lies." Mandarins and other native administrators were "venal" and "dishonest." Villagers had "a natural tendency" to say what was "agreeable to their superiors." American travelers and hunters frequently referred to incidents of Vietnamese duplicity. For example, Harvard University zoologist Harold J. Coolidge Jr., in his narrative of the Chicago Field Museum's expedition to Vietnam in 1928–29, tells the story of his Vietnamese guide, Vinh, who overcharged the expedition for needed supplies. At first Coolidge was skeptical, as the accusation came from the expedition's Vietnamese cook, who allegedly "hated" Vinh and whom Coolidge assumed might be lying himself. After verifying the accusations with local merchants, however, Coolidge "summoned" Vinh and "told him he was not to lie to me or he would be punished." But, Coolidge recounted, "he persisted in his story, his Annamite face not changing a bit." [12]

Observers also pointed to cruelty and hate as dominant traits of the social order in traditional Vietnam, while at the same time arguing that the Vietnamese often appeared effeminate and weak. "Two pin-points of distilled hate in his eyes were curious to watch," Mona Gardner remarked in an effort to characterize several Vietnamese she met in Hanoi and Haiphong. "It wasn't hate of any one person . . . but of mankind and life. One generation or two of French rule hadn't put it there . . . for it was too fundamental." Gardner's metaphor informs the analysis of other authors, who pointed to the use of corporal punishment for minor crimes and the death penalty for robbery and the misuse of funds in traditional society as evidence to support the contention that the "indifference of the Annamites to their compatriots' sufferings is unbelievable." [13] Along with these common perceptions of the oppressive character of Vietnamese society, many authors criticized Vietnamese men for their lack of virility and military prowess. Gardner considered them "weak husks of men" whose "faces are long and thin, and so delicately featured that it is difficult to tell a man from a woman," as "the women put their thin flat bodies in the same identical clothes . . . as their men wear." Others commented on the "puerile vanity" of Vietnamese men, discussing the reticence of most Vietnamese to join local militias, and what Thompson called "the conspicuous absence of epic virility" in Vietnamese literature.[14]

The perceptions of Vietnamese inferiority formed by interwar American observers might at first appear unexceptional, given the more familiar deprecatory images articulated by most white Americans of the non-Anglo-Saxon peoples they encountered at home and abroad in the nineteenth and early twentieth centuries. In fact, the explanations Americans offered to account for the deficiencies they identified in the Vietnamese character were sometimes almost casually dismissive. As one observer remarked, "[Centuries] have resolved the Annamite into a type character. If one succeeds in understanding a single *nhaqué*, or peasant, one understands them all." [15] In the more fully developed explications that inform many of these works, the renderings of Vietnamese incapacities resonate closely with the qualities often ascribed to African Americans and Native Americans; to southern European, Chinese, and Mexican immigrants; and as the United States became an imperial power, to the peoples of the Caribbean, Latin America, East Asia, and the Philippines. These pervasive images, as many scholars of fin de siècle

America have demonstrated, were rooted in a shared discourse of racialized cultural hierarchies that placed American Anglo-Saxons at the apex of civilization.

An emerging view of the interwar era, however, suggests the period saw the beginning of a transformative shift in U.S. attitudes toward and assumptions about race and culture. Much of this recent scholarship has focused on the rejection of racism within the scientific community that had played a key role in legitimating racial discourse and the embrace of cultural relativism in the works of influential social scientists such as anthropologists Franz Boas, Margaret Mead, and Ruth Benedict.[16] But in a stronger version favored by some cultural historians, the attitudinal shift is seen as reaching farther, with Americans in the 1930s making an "epochal transformation" in popular beliefs as they embraced "relativizing, nonracial explanations of cultural difference."[17]

American images of Vietnam belie these far-reaching claims for the interwar period, demonstrating the persistence of fin de siècle assumptions about nonwhite peoples and the superiority of Western civilization. The writings of interwar Americans on Vietnam drew on a neo-Lamarckian environmental discourse that, along with heredity, shaped the ubiquitous faith in racialized cultural hierarchies. American observers frequently pointed to the critical role of the environment in shaping the inferior qualities they attributed to Vietnamese society. Vietnam, Virginia Thompson claimed, was a "land of extremes:"

> wild and desolate mountain scenery alternate[s] with the monotonous and drab rice-fields or the rampant tropical forest. Its restless and destructive vitality created a . . . malaise. Man no longer seemed to count, he was too much at the mercy of uncontrollable forces. . . . The violence of the Tonkinese rivers is in keeping with the excesses of the climate. Typhoons and inundations from the monsoons alternate with droughts . . . which make human efforts seem futile and unavailing. . . . The struggle with implacably hostile forces [has] left an imprint . . . on native character.[18]

Interwar accounts by missionaries and hunters of their experiences in Vietnam also pointed to the inhospitable character of the Vietnamese physical environment. Vietnam's landscape called forth images of "heathen darkness" for many of the missionaries with the Christian and Missionary Alliance in Indochina. While the "mystery" and "magic" of the Vietnamese jungle held an exotic appeal for many big-game hunters, most found the country hostile and forbidding. In a 1920 account of his tiger hunt in Indochina, H. C. Flower Jr. frequently complained of the "oppressive and torrid atmosphere" in Vietnam. The American consul Leland Smith, whose duties did not preclude frequent trips to hunt for tiger and elephant, told of being "plunged into the dark country away from the white man's land . . .

in a tangle of tropic growth . . . [that] is strangely silent." In a narrative of the expedition he led to southern Vietnam for Chicago's Field Museum in the late 1920s, Theodore Roosevelt Jr. called Vietnam "a strange land where sickness lurked behind every tree."[19]

For many American observers, Vietnam's tropical climate explained a variety of Vietnamese weaknesses that they believed were not present in more temperate, or Western, climates. "Apathy, insensitivity and placidity," qualities commonly imputed to the Vietnamese by American authors, appeared to be "forced upon them" by climate. The Vietnamese were believed to "age more quickly than men who lived in temperate zones" because "the climate exhausts the nerves and stimulates the circulation of blood." A "less highly developed nervous system," Americans believed, prompted Vietnamese "indifference to suffering." Even more striking were efforts like those of Virginia Thompson to demonstrate the inferiority of Vietnamese mental development by reference to tropical climate: "A more subtle effect of climate upon Annamite psychology is their inability to receive sharp, clear-cut impressions. Perhaps it is the brilliant sunshine that has weakened their sensory reactions along with their will power. The Annamite dreams a perpetual melancholy reverie uncontrolled by any critical faculty. His thinking is confused and indecisive . . . incapable of separating the essential from the trivial."[20]

Though seldom acknowledged, American observers' use of environmental explanations for the failings they identified in Vietnamese society suggests the persisting influence of environmental theories of racial inequalities formulated in both Europe and the United States long before the interwar period to account for perceived deficiencies of nonwhite peoples. As early as the mid-eighteenth century, Montesquieu's *Esprit des lois* popularized the idea that climate played a degenerative role in determining human development. French and British commentary on the New World reflected this belief, arguing that the New World's humid climate rendered Native Americans physically, morally, and intellectually inferior to Europeans. Most white settlers in America, who viewed Native Americans and African Americans in British North America as distinct and inferior peoples, followed these European formulations.[21]

In the nineteenth century, race joined, and eventually superseded, the environment as the predominant factor Americans used to explain these differences. The belief in innate distinctions between the races no matter what environment they inhabited became widespread among Americans by the 1840s. As a number of scholars have argued, these attitudes shaped antebellum approaches to slavery, Native Americans, and manifest destiny. They were codified in the late nineteenth century with the passage of Jim Crow laws to govern the behavior of African Americans and the consignment of Native Americans to reservations.[22]

As the United States pushed beyond its continental boundaries to become an imperial power at the end of the nineteenth century, the attitudes of white Americans toward the peoples they encountered in the Caribbean, the Philippines, and elsewhere in what later would become known as the Third World often reflected the explanations they had used to denote the inferiorities of Native Americans and African Americans. Racial and environmental assumptions were essential components of the prevailing belief among fin de siècle Americans in a cultural hierarchy of races. In this hierarchy—which placed whites on top, blacks at the bottom, and Hispanic and Asian peoples, if somewhere in the middle, distinctly inferior to whites—the historical development of humanity was seen as a unilinear process moving from the more primitive stages of savagery and barbarism to the florescence of advanced and superior Euro-American civilization.[23]

Social Darwinism provided much of the intellectual underpinnings of the faith in cultural hierarchies. Unlike the more optimistic vision of Social Darwinism favored by Vietnamese reformers in this period, U.S. conceptions stressed the competitive struggle for the survival of the fittest among individuals, nations, and races and the relentless determinism of the forces of heredity impervious to the influences of the cultural or physical environment. But at the same time, many Americans also embraced a neo-Lamarckian doctrine that depicted human behavior as shaped by direct environmental influences or by hereditary traits influenced by the environment and passed from parent to children. Herbert Spencer, whose views framed American thinking on these issues and who is often portrayed as the archetypal Social Darwinist, borrowed from Lamarckian notions of environmental inheritance to explain the social and cultural origins of racial difference. Despite more rarefied scientific debates between Darwinian and Lamarckian views, the blurring of these two conceptualizations in the articulation of racialized cultural hierarchies was more common at the level of popular discourse.[24]

Among the most influential popular works that sought to explicate the links between environment and racial inferiority were Alleyne Ireland's *Far Eastern Tropics* (1905) and Benjamin Kidd's *Control of the Tropics* (1898).[25] They reiterated the degenerative effects of tropical climates, or what was sometimes termed "the heat belt," within a framework that recognized and affirmed theories of innate racial differences. Ireland, an English journalist who frequently traveled to the Caribbean, settled in the United States in 1898 at the height of the Spanish-American War and quickly established a reputation as a leading expert on colonial issues. His study of European and American colonization in Asia exemplifies the approach to what contemporaries termed "the general laws that govern civilization in the tropics."

Ireland used the heat belt to divide the world into two categories. Within the belt were the "primitive" societies of Latin America, Africa, the Middle East, and South and Southeast Asia. Outside the belt were Europe, North America, and according to Ireland, the more "civilized" Japan and China. The "comparative barbarism" of tropical societies, Ireland argued, was manifested in their lack of achievement compared with more temperate societies:

Apart from the work done by Europeans and Americans in the tropics, the civilization of the heat belt has remained stationary for a thousand years, and the advancement of humanity during that period has been carried on entirely by the inhabitants of those countries which lie outside the heat belt. . . . The people of the heat belt have added nothing whatever to what we understand by human advancement. Those natives of the tropics and subtropics who have not been under direct European influence have not during that time made a single contribution of the first importance to art, literature, science, manufactures, or inventions; they have not produced an engineer, or a chemist, or a biologist, or a historian, or a painter, or a musician of the first rank; and even if we include half-castes and such natives as have enjoyed European education, the list of eminent men in the domain of art, science, literature, and invention, produced by the heat belt can be counted on the fingers of one hand.

The cause of these "great differences," Ireland argued, was the "permanence of race characteristics" shaped by the interaction of "weaker" tropical peoples with their physical environment. For Ireland, the "climatic discipline of the West" permitted the accumulation of capital "necessary to the development of peoples" and "man's emancipation from the tyranny of his surroundings." In tropical countries, however, the "extreme" climate mitigated against capital accumulation as labor was "sure to be irregular." The result, he argued, was "a general condition of apathy and helplessness" that over long centuries acquired "the rigidity of a race characteristic." Tropical peoples, Ireland concluded in a view shared by many early twentieth-century American commentators, suffered from an environmentally induced racial inferiority that left them without "strength of character" or "vigor of mind." [26]

American writing on the Philippines best reveals the pervasiveness of Ireland's framework and the broader contemporary belief in cultural hierarchies. The Filipinos were usually characterized in terms that both recalled the categories and explanations white Americans had used to denote Native and African Americans and presaged the tenor of U.S. interwar commentary on the Vietnamese. In the debates over Philippine annexation and in the reports of colonial officials during the first two decades of U.S. rule in the Philippines, Filipinos were commonly rendered as "ignorant and superstitious," "nothing but grown up children," "one of the less advanced races," and "living in a tropical slough of ignorance and sloth."[27]

In the majority of cases, American authors writing on Vietnam did not draw explicit attention to these links between environment, race, cultural hierarchies, and perceptions of the Vietnamese. But rather than indicating that interwar attitudes toward tropical peoples had undergone any fundamental transformation, their silence suggests these linkages were so widely understood and accepted that they did not require substantial elaboration. Studies chronicling the resurgence of a virulent nativism in the 1920s and unchanging interwar perceptions of African Americans indicate a highly charged domestic racial climate.[28] Highly suggestive of the broader commonalities between fin de siècle and interwar attitudes toward nonwhite peoples abroad is a 1924 Yale University survey that asked eminent American diplomats, missionaries, and scholars to rank the civilizations of the world based on climatic and racial characteristics. Vietnam's ranking, low in relationship to both the West and other Asian societies, was not singled out for particular discussion, but the results of the survey suggest that many American elites continued to view non-Western peoples, the Vietnamese included, as their inferiors.[29]

Interwar American writings on the indigenous peoples in other parts of Asia echoed the findings of the Yale study and closely mirrored perceptions of the Vietnamese. American works on Southeast Asia are filled with descriptive markers denoting the "backward" Indonesians, the "feudal" Malays, and the "inevitable indolence" of the Thais.[30] More popular interwar works on India and China also point to the ubiquity of these images and the assumptions of cultural hierarchies that shaped them. Katherine Mayo's influential and widely read *Mother India* (1927) was a scathing attack on Hindu customs and practices. Its gendered title, as one scholar has recently noted, built on a long-standing tradition of feminized representations of a backward, passive, and servile India.[31] The case of Pearl Buck's bestselling novel *The Good Earth* (1931) is somewhat more complicated. *The Good Earth* has recently been characterized as a primary agent in the transformation of U.S. attitudes toward Asian peoples, "exchanging stereotypes of earlier American representations of Asia for a more firmly grounded portrait."[32] But if Buck succeeded in shifting American images, her portrait of the Chinese remained tied to the larger framework of cultural hierarchies. The stolid Chinese farmer and his family at the center of the novel are an idealized version of a hardworking and thrifty American farm family. In *The Good Earth* the Chinese only become more comprehensible and sympathetic by seeming more like Americans, a narrative device that substitutes a racialized paternalism for the racialized contempt that had characterized much of the previous writing on China.[33]

Buck's use of an American idiom through which to portray the Chinese finds important, if more subtle, parallels in American writing on Vietnam. Concerns about immigration and morality at home appear particularly salient in conditioning U.S. critiques of Vietnamese society. In the Americanization campaigns of the late 1910s and 1920s, which emerged in a period of heightened anxiety about the deleterious impact of immigrants on American society and the necessity for their moral regeneration, many reformers sought to impose white, middle-class notions of domesticity on the dietary, clothing, housekeeping, and child-rearing habits of immigrant households. As George Sánchez argues in his study of Mexican Americans in Los Angeles, such campaigns were a "tool in a system of social control intended to construct a well-behaved, productive citizenry."[34] In addition, cultural studies of the United States in the 1930s suggest the dislocations of the depression era prompted the widespread embrace and valorization by middle-class Americans of a deeply conservative vision of family and social structure.[35] The perceived links between the reform of immigrant household practices and Americanization as well as the conservative moral climate of the 1930s provide a framework for the seeming obsession of interwar Americans with the "lack of comfort" in homes, "drab" clothing, "indelicate" eating, "primitive" medical practices, and "general negligence" they found in Vietnam as well as the use of tropes such as laziness and lying to denote their observations of the deleterious effects of poverty and vagrancy on Vietnamese society.

While interwar images of Vietnam were rooted in a familiar domestic context, they were also reflections and reworkings of the broader Orientalist discourse central to European writings on the non-West. Given their own lack of familiarity with the Vietnamese, Americans often consulted French Orientalist scholarship to account for many of the deficiencies they found in Vietnamese society. American renderings of the absence of virility among Vietnamese men, for instance, drew upon a substantial body of French writing on Indochina that characterized Vietnamese men as effeminate "boys" who were indistinguishable from women and that dismissively termed indigenous troops "*soldats mamzelles.*"[36] More broadly, their discussions of Vietnam's "immutability" and "stagnation" relied on what they viewed as authoritative works by former French administrators in Vietnam, such as Eliacin Luro's study of political and social institutions in Vietnam,[37] which highlighted the deleterious effects of Vietnam's historical experience with China. Reflecting the sinological emphasis of most French Orientalist scholarship on Vietnam, Luro argued that the thousand-year Chinese occupation of Vietnam between 111 B.C. and A.D. 939 exposed Vietnam to a "superior" civilization and prompted the Vietnamese to adopt Sinic laws and mores in a process he termed "the vulgarization of Chinese civilization." Despite Vietnamese successes at maintaining their political independence from the Chinese after the tenth century, Luro asserted in a passage typical of prevailing French views, "Annamite civilization in its present state has preserved the archaic forms long discarded in China."[38]

Drawing upon the conclusions of French scholars such as Luro, American commentators viewed Vietnam as a fossilized "little China." Vietnam's major traditional institutions—monarchy, administration, legal codes, and family structure—were seen as "servile" copies of their counterparts in China. Vietnam's ready acceptance of Sinic influences, argued Virginia Thompson and other American observers, rendered it an imitative and static society: "Annamites forgot their past and adopted Chinese civilization. . . . In their life as a nation and individuals, the Annamites to this day bear the indelible print of Chinese culture left by the first conquest. . . . The lack of a vital national culture resulted in a complete spiritual stagnation, which was the heavy price paid by Annam for China's moral domination."[39] These perceptions were reinforced by the accounts of French journalists that appeared in the U.S. popular press during the interwar period and emphasized the persistence of traditional Chinese practices in Vietnam. "Annam has inherited the traditions of China," many of these authors claimed, and "religiously preserved them." Others suggested that Vietnamese society held largely antiquarian interest, particularly as Vietnam's imperial capital of Hue, modeled on the Forbidden City in Beijing, provided the sole extant example of Confucian-inspired state ritual after the fall of the Ch'ing dynasty in 1911 and the rise of republicanism in China.[40]

The deference American writers showed to the French as authoritative sources of knowledge about the Vietnamese was often quite remarkable. For instance, Virginia Thompson's claims that climate was "a major influence on native character" were a natural outgrowth of contemporary American thinking on race. Yet Thompson supported her assertions with the writings of Paul Giran, a French colonial administrator who served in Vietnam in the late nineteenth century. Giran's 1904 text, *Psychologie du peuple Annamite*, presented a hodgepodge of racial interpretations for Vietnamese inferiority, including an illustrated cranial analysis that purported to explain the less-developed Vietnamese brain by reference to the effects of tropical climate.[41]

By embracing these French interpretations of Vietnam, Americans signaled a willingness to locate their representations of the Vietnamese within a larger Orientalist framework common to many contemporary Western interpretations of Asia. As Edward Said and other post-Orientalist scholars have argued in their analyses of European discourse on non-Western societies, European colonial powers formulated essentialist differences between the immutable Orient and the dynamic West as a tool to reinforce European political and cultural mastery.[42] As

Said suggests, Orientalism provided a stable, durable, and authoritative vocabulary through which European scholars, writers, and colonial officials both rendered Oriental backwardness, degeneracy, and inequality and described the Orient as a locale requiring Western attention and reconstruction.

The language of Orientalism, filtered through a French prism, provided U.S. observers with a critical means of explaining the character of Vietnamese society. In his 1936 study of French Indochina, Thomas Ennis used the terms "Indochina," "China," and the "Orient" interchangeably to illustrate the ways in which traditional Vietnamese legal practices departed from Western or Occidental models. He argued,

> In order to comprehend Indochina fully, the different emotional structures of . . . this oriental land must be analyzed. . . . The legal procedure of old Indochina . . . did not differ materially from that of China. . . . In the Orient, codes are generalized, allowing magistrates wide interpretation. In the Occident, judges are restrained by the precision of jurisprudence. In the Occident, the interest of the great number (i.e., public order and security) is the core of legal theory and practice. In the Orient, the whole is sacrificed for the part (i.e., the family).[43]

The distinction between Oriental and Occidental societies was rarely employed by interwar American observers of Vietnam for simple descriptive purposes. Their use of Orientalist constructions, like those of European observers, more often revealed perceived sources of Vietnamese inadequacies. By implicit contrast to the more dynamic and progressive West, Vietnam came to embody the inertia these American authors ascribed to all Oriental civilizations. Virginia Thompson made frequent reference to such rhetorical figures to account for a number of the weaknesses she and others identified in Vietnamese society. The Vietnamese were "indifferent" farmers, she argued, because of an "age-old Oriental prejudice" against manual labor and "a life so impregnated with ritual and static . . . philosophy that it makes antique methods meritorious simply because they are old." The lack of "public spirit" among the Vietnamese, Thompson claimed, arose because "the Oriental had no concept of person dignity. He is insolent in good fortune and obsequious in misfortune. . . . [This] has been a primary cause of their immaturity as a people." The impotent Vietnamese response to French conquest, she argued, was characterized by "interminable delays and contradictory interviews in the best Oriental manner." As Thompson dismissively concluded, "The country slumbers on in its traditional Oriental rut." The deprecatory image of Oriental somnolence also emerged in the observations of other Americans, such as Mona Gardner, who suggested that the Vietnamese "seem too finely bred, as though the long civilization behind them has made them tired, too tired to change, and that in the process strong emotions and passion have been drained from them."[44]

If the appropriation of Orientalist discourse allowed interwar authors to universalize their disparaging critiques of Vietnamese society, it also prompted U.S. observers to localize the deficiencies they perceived in Vietnamese society within Vietnam's tradition as a cultural borrower. Viewed as cultural imitators rather than innovators, the Vietnamese attracted considerable American opprobrium, suggesting the presence of subtle, hierarchical distinctions within the largely negative view of Oriental civilizations. For many Americans, Vietnam was not only a smaller China but a lesser civilization as well. American observers often followed French interpreters to argue that China was "infinitely more disciplined and cultured" than Vietnam. Vietnamese political, social, and cultural norms were considered to be "a saddened and simplified version" of their Chinese precursors. In a discussion of the overseas Chinese community in Vietnam, Virginia Thompson claimed that both the Chinese and the Vietnamese recognized these differences: "The Chinese do not disguise their feelings of contempt for their former vassals. The Annamites, on their side, resent the Chinese . . . yet they admire them for their success. It is, however, the deadly hatred of the inferior for the superior . . . a weak vanity wounded by unending and forced admissions of inferiority. . . . The Chinese have more endurance, intelligence, and industry than any of their Asiatic rivals."[45] The widespread perception of Vietnam as a second-rate Oriental nation helped U.S. observers to explain what they believed to be the particularly conservative and immutable character of Vietnamese society. By viewing the Vietnamese as dedicated preservers of appropriated Chinese cultural forms with no indigenous civilization of their own, many American authors echoed Thompson's comment that "the Annamite is the enemy of all change, as sacrilege. . . . He is the tranquil observer and defender of law and custom."[46]

The vocabulary of Orientalism was not the only commonality that joined American and European perceptions of the Vietnamese and other non-Western peoples. Fundamental aspects of the more domestically rooted American critique of Vietnamese society closely followed European thought and practice. Just as concerns about immigration and the moral quality of society at home made their way into American analyses of Vietnam, several scholars of European colonialism have noted what they term the "embourgeoisement" of European images of colonized peoples. They argue that descriptions of the colonial "other" often corresponded to existing patterns in the metropole, particularly anxieties about the moral standards of the rapidly expanding working classes in Europe and middle-class obsessions with family organization, sexual standards, medical care, and moral instruction.[47] More broadly, many of the intellectual underpinnings of the

American belief in racialized cultural hierarchies rested upon a European foundation.[48] Within this shared mental universe, there was a real porousness between the domestic and Orientalist categories Americans employed to understand the Vietnamese. The ensemble of assumptions underlying the American belief in cultural hierarchies, whether posed in Social Darwinian, neo-Lamarckian, or Orientalist terms, reveals the circularity of ideas that informed the intertwined American and European discourse on Vietnam and the colonial world.

From Singing *Nhaques* to Selfish *Colons*

While American attitudes toward the Vietnamese remained remarkably constant during the interwar period, the perceptions of French colonialism formed by American journalists, scholars, travelers, missionaries, and consuls underwent a sharp transformation—from the largely benign images of the 1920s to the harsh criticism of the 1930s. Throughout the 1920s, most Americans held a favorable view of French colonialism and its impact on Vietnam. Percy Standing's admiring account of "French progress" in Vietnam illustrates the positive attitudes shared by many American observers toward French administrative, economic, and social policies. French efforts to develop Vietnam into one of the world leaders in rice production as well as to promote the development of coal and rubber were lauded, as was French "progress" in expanding educational opportunities for the indigenous population. "The colony," Standing concluded, was "ably and humanely administered."[49]

The supportive outlook that characterized these accounts was reinforced by the publication of works by French journalists and travel writers in the United States in the 1920s that presented a bucolic picture of French colonialism, complete with "singing *nhaques*," or peasants, toiling happily in rice fields.[50] A few commentators and the reports of American consuls from Saigon foreshadowed some of the critiques Americans would later offer of French colonialism, particularly the use of tariffs to protect French economic interests in Vietnam and the expense of lavish public works projects initiated by the French. But even these dissenters believed, as Gertrude Emerson argued, that France would "carry forward the commercial and financial development" of Vietnam with eventual success.[51]

Beginning in the 1930s, however, American observers became increasingly critical of French colonial policies and their apparent disregard for the welfare of the Vietnamese. By the end of the interwar period, most U.S. commentators on Vietnam would have endorsed Mona Gardner's contention in 1939 that "French colonization is poor, uneconomical, and inordinately selfish." Almost all aspects of French colonial rule came under sharp American censure in the 1930s. The French administrative structure in Vietnam was criticized for its overcentralization and financial disorganization, as was the "excessive growth" and inefficiency of colonial bureaucrats. Colonial bureaucrats, particularly local administrators, were reproached for a lack of administrative skills and facility in indigenous languages. The French settler population, or *colons*, also drew American scorn. Thomas Steep's characterization, in a 1934 article for the *American Mercury*, of besotted and whoring French *colons* who lived with a "maximum of ease" and a "minimum of exertion" typified the common American view.[52]

The efforts of French administrators and *colons* to develop the Vietnamese economy attracted particular U.S. criticism in the 1930s. Many Americans contended that the French had been unsuccessful in increasing the production of rice, long the central element of the Vietnamese economy, to meet rising demand both within Vietnam and in international markets. A disorganized French colonial administration, they argued, had done very little to better the selection of seeds and plants, improve cultivation practices, increase sources of needed capital, or standardize marketing and distribution structures. Similar problems, Americans suggested, impaired French efforts to develop pepper, cotton, timber, and silk cultivation. American observers did point out French success in rubber production. But they believed the dependence of colonial rubber planters on state subsidies and the lack of organized projects of research and experimentation common among Dutch and British planters elsewhere in Southeast Asia would hinder the future competitiveness of Vietnamese rubber in the world market. Along with the failure to develop the Vietnamese economy, Americans argued, plans by France to use Vietnam as a market for its own goods and to gain entrance to the market of China went unfulfilled, given the continued poverty of most Vietnamese and the failure of French efforts to promote trade with China.[53]

American observers also criticized the administrative mismanagement and flawed policies they believed had undermined a number of the major public works projects launched by the French in Vietnam. Although some commentators admired the ambitious scope of French efforts to build a network of rail lines and roads throughout Vietnam, most Americans were critical of how French infrastructure projects were designed, constructed, and operated. Transportation routes, Americans contended, were chosen for political rather than economic reasons, with rails and roads built through deserted areas instead of regions with larger populations and greater economic potential. French engineers unfamiliar with local terrain placed rail and road lines on unstable ground that proved expensive to maintain. Graft and corruption often doubled the cost of initial construction estimates, profiting investors and contractors but draining the colonial government's finances as it sought to pay back loans at high rates of interest. Once in operation, U.S. commentators argued, rail lines were seldom profitable as much of the colonial economy remained underdeveloped, indigenous trade remained highly localized, and the lines were inefficiently managed. The upkeep of vast roadways was viewed as a "terrific burden" on colonial finances. As Americans like Virginia Thompson contemptuously observed, French transportation policy in Vietnam reflected a fundamental misconception. Rail and road networks, she argued, were only the "means" rather than the "creators" of wealth. The French, with what Thompson termed typical "unreflecting enthusiasm and a wanton lack of foresight," appeared to believe the reverse, basing their policies on the mistaken assumption that rails and roads would create wealth "merely by their passage through a country."[54]

Diplomats and other American observers directed particularly vociferous criticism at the tariff structure the French had imposed on the Vietnamese economy. Throughout the 1930s, U.S. consuls in Saigon despaired of French efforts to do "everything in their power to keep out foreign competition" in Vietnam. Through a tariff structure that protected French shipping and markets from foreign competition, numerous consular reports from Saigon contended, France became the destination for almost all of Vietnam's exports and the source for most of its imports, crowding out potential U.S. trade and investment in the colony. American criticism of French tariffs, however, was not limited to their impact on American business in Vietnam. For U.S. diplomats and other observers, the tariff system was symptomatic of the inadequacies of French colonial rule. The tariff, which many Americans argued was the result of political pressure by individual industrialists, suggested that the French lacked confidence in their own competitive abilities and were incapable of framing an economic policy for Vietnam that looked after the best interests of the colony as a whole. There were several inevitable results, many argued, of these misguided tariff policies. As tariffs put a premium on Chinese imports and Vietnamese rice exports to Japan, observers pointed to a substantial reduction in French commerce with China and the rest of East Asia, undermining what many Americans believed to be one of the chief French goals for colonial rule in Vietnam. Tariffs, others argued, produced a sharp rise in the cost of living for both the Vietnamese and the French settler population and, some ominously hinted, threatened continued French colonial control of Vietnam.[55]

In addition to their criticisms of French administration and the colonial economy, interwar American observers of Vietnam devoted significant attention to what they perceived as the unfavorable impact of French political, economic, and social policies on Vietnamese society. Many Americans noted that colonial administrative positions were held by an "inordinate" number of Frenchmen, leaving the Vietnamese little role in the operation of the colonial bureaucracy. Vietnamese who did enter the civil service, they argued, were often paid a "pittance," with salaries far below those of their French counterparts. Efforts to promote indigenous representation in colonial governing counsels were criticized as insubstantial. Unwilling to provide training and experience in government for substantial numbers of Vietnamese, the French colonial order, as Gardner suggested, was "sowing no seeds of patriotism in order to reap a harvest of loyal citizens one to two generations from now."[56] U.S. observers were also critical of the excessive tax burden placed on the Vietnamese by the French. American consuls accused France of levying taxes on the Vietnamese to pay for "expenses [that] depend properly on France," including the salaries of the colonial bureaucracy and the costs of "unproductive" public works projects. The regressive head and land tax rates were very high and often arbitrarily increased, Americans argued, and French monopolies on salt, opium, and alcohol served as indirect taxes that added substantially to the "burdens of an already tax-ridden people."[57]

Along with their critiques of excessive taxation and French exclusion of the Vietnamese from colonial government, American observers voiced disapproval of many aspects of French education, labor, and medical policies in Vietnam. French efforts to establish an educational system for the Vietnamese, Americans believed, were largely ineffective. French plans to establish a nationwide network of rural elementary schools, they argued, went unrealized, and those schools that were established seemed "small and unsanitary." Teachers were reportedly in short supply, received inadequate training, and were poorly paid. Textbooks were "nonexistent" or "inappropriate." The use of French as a primary language of instruction, many argued, was particularly unsuited to a predominantly rural population. The unfortunate result of these ill-conceived policies, observers suggested, was continuing high rates of illiteracy. U.S. commentators were also critical of the educational opportunities the French provided for Vietnamese elites. Americans contended that French lycées, or secondary schools, admitted only a handful of Vietnamese students, reserving the majority of places for French children. The French-established University of Hanoi appeared to have low standards, mediocre students, and "appallingly few graduates." Other observers noted that the French set up serious obstacles for Vietnamese who wished to attend university in France. A "dubious" future awaited the limited number of Vietnamese who received secondary and university degrees, Americans argued, as few graduates were taken into the colonial administration while the majority were left unemployed.[58]

French labor and medical policies in Vietnam also received strong American criticism. Most observers noted that labor standards in colonial Vietnam were far below those of other colonized territories. Many commentators focused on the ill treatment and dangerous working conditions of Vietnamese mine and plantation workers, detailing incidents of "the worst kind of torture" by French overseers, the prevalence of disease, and meager salaries and inhuman living conditions. Noting the lack of French social legislation and recurrent Vietnamese labor strikes in 1936, several observers claimed there was "a wide-spread feeling among the masses that a New Deal [was] not only due, but overdue."[59] Americans did praise aspects of French medical policies, applauding the French-built hospitals in major Vietnamese cities. But most commentators noted that the mass of rural Vietnamese remained "isolated" from all medical attention as the French made few efforts to construct hospitals and infirmaries in the countryside. Americans were also critical of the French for limiting funds needed to expand the number of trained Vietnamese doctors and for setting low salary levels for indigenous medical personnel.[60]

The transformation of the relatively benign American images of French rule in the 1920s into the vociferous critiques of the 1930s was in part related to broader changes in the international system as the political and economic stability of the mid- to late 1920s gave way to worldwide economic depression and the rise of Hitler's Germany in the 1930s. Franco-American relations were far from harmonious in the 1920s, but substantial bilateral agreement emerged over disarmament and the international economy. In the more difficult global environment of the 1930s, however, Franco-American discord and mutual suspicion were the norm.[61] At one level, changing American perceptions of the French in Vietnam were part of this broader negative turn in Franco-American relations. American critiques of French tariff and trade policies in Vietnam, for instance, quite closely matched U.S. criticisms of French trading practices in France itself.

The changed perspective on French colonialism in the 1930s was also the result of quite different economic conditions in the colony itself. American perceptions in the 1920s were formed at a time when the French enjoyed considerable economic return from the colonial economy. The 1920s marked the culmination of an economic boom for the French in colonial Vietnam. Investment capital flowed freely from Paris and Lyon, agricultural and commodity exports increased rapidly, and the Vietnamese provided a reliable and inexpensive labor pool. Symbolic of French success were the profits of the Bank of Indochina, which multiplied forty times between 1895 and 1922. With the coming of the Great Depression, however, colonial economic fortunes precipitously declined. Export markets for rubber and rice evaporated, landowners defaulted on bank loans, once-prosperous companies entered bankruptcy, and many thousands of Vietnamese farmers and workers were left unemployed.[62] While U.S. views in the 1920s severely underestimated the problems French colonialism posed for Vietnamese society, the world-

wide economic depression meant the conditions Americans encountered in colonial Vietnam during the 1930s were measurably worse than they had been in the
previous decade.

If these larger forces conditioned American commentary on French colonial
rule in Vietnam, the sharp critiques of the 1930s tended to focus on the failure of
the French approach to colonialism. U.S. observers believed the French had not
met what they viewed as the responsibilities and obligations of a colonial power
to better the lives of its colonized subjects whose own racial characteristics and
physical environment made self-improvement improbable, if not impossible. Few
Americans attacked colonialism in the abstract, reflecting Virginia Thompson's
somewhat uneasy but pragmatic sentiment that it was "idle speculation to debate
whether or not the Annamites were better off spiritually before the French conquest. Sooner or later they would have been forcibly drawn into the modern world,
and in the sense that it was inevitable, French colonization is beyond good and
evil." [63] Rather, Americans argued, French policies in Vietnam had unfortunately
been governed largely by the principle of assimilation, a process disparaged by
American observers because it made "a clean sweep of all native traditions" and
brought "into existence a group of social half-breeds" who had "lost the feeling of
kinship to their old past yet [were] not completely at home in their new present."
Instead, Americans championed the principle of association, which they approvingly regarded as maintaining "native individuality" while promoting "native development." The rule of colonized peoples by association, many contended, was
"as little odious" as it was possible for colonialism to be.[64]

The insistence of American observers on the virtues of colonial rule by association emerged against what might be seen as an internal process of colonization at
home as white Americans sought to define the relationship between a burgeoning
immigrant population and its proper place in American society. For the first decades of the century, the assimilationist policies Americans found so troubling in
Vietnam shaped immigration policy in the United States. The Americanization
efforts of the Progressive era aimed at speedily teaching immigrants English, the
essentials of American citizenship, and faith in American values. During World
War I, a more coercive approach emerged in the 100 percent American campaigns
that sought to suppress foreign political and cultural traditions that might nurture
anti-American sentiments. In the racially charged climate of the postwar period,
these efforts persisted in a variety of forms and finally culminated in the passage
of a race-based system of immigration quotas in 1924 that sharply curtailed subsequent immigration to the United States.[65]

Although historians of American immigration policy have not directed sustained attention to the late 1920s and 1930s, the associationist models Americans

advocated in Vietnam and for colonial rule more generally resonate with broader contours of domestic immigration policy. The assimilationist, hyper-Americanism approach gave way in this period to a sense that gradual acculturation rather than rapid coercion would eventually transform immigrants into American citizens. The widely influential writings of sociologist Robert Park argued that all immigrant groups underwent a "race relations cycle," a slow but "natural" process of advancement through which "the culture of . . . a country is transmitted to an adopted citizen." At the level of popular culture, the multiethnic celebrations organized by civic leaders and educational officials throughout the interwar era offered ethnicity as a sideshow of folk cuisine, dance, and dress to tell the story, as one scholar argues, of "an inevitable and painless transformation of diverse folk cultures into a unified American culture."[66] Both Park's writings and the multiethnic celebrations closely paralleled the beliefs in cultural hierarchies and gradualism favored by American writers on colonial Vietnam, presupposing a static, Anglo-American core of political and cultural norms that would eventually transform the immigrant population.[67]

Along with this domestic shift in the making of immigrants into Americans, the faith of American observers in the virtues of colonial rule by association was also intimately connected to their insistence that Vietnamese and other Asian societies were fundamentally different from and inferior to those in the West. Only gradually, Americans argued, could a Western colonial power correct the deficiencies that climate and race had imposed on colonized peoples and develop indigenous competence in responsible self-government. Yet much of French rule appeared to Americans to ignore the essential differences between Western and tropical Oriental societies such as Vietnam, as well as the importance of gradualism for effective and permanent reform of Vietnamese society. The French policy of assimilation, Americans argued, introduced Western norms and values that "bewildered" Vietnamese society. To the Vietnamese, one observer noted, French law "was dispensed in a secular, harsh and almost inhuman manner." Another commented that French education prompted "the Annamite . . . to grow up unstable and unbalanced." While French policies undermined the political and social traditions of the Vietnamese, Americans contended, the French also prevented substantial Vietnamese participation in the newly created French colonial order. Unlike the British and the Dutch in Southeast Asia, observers argued, the French insisted on almost complete control of Vietnamese political affairs by French officials and functionaries, making only "half-hearted efforts . . . to hand over responsible positions to the native and create deliberative assemblies."[68]

The comparison with European policies elsewhere in Southeast Asia was a common practice in interwar writings on Vietnam. If a latent Orientalism infused perceptions of indigenous societies in Southeast Asia, they nonetheless emerge as superior to the Vietnamese. Mona Gardner, whose analysis of Vietnam was presented in the context of her encounters with other states and peoples in the region, conveyed much more favorable impressions of Thailand, the Dutch East Indies, and British Malaya as did the most important American interwar studies of the region. The fundamental difference almost all of these works pointed to was the form of colonial rule or, in the Thai case, what was often considered the nature of its guided self-colonization. Unlike French colonial rule, interwar observers argued, the Dutch, the British, and the Thai monarchy (using British and American models) approached the development of backward and primitive populations through the principles of association. As Amry Vandenbosch, who would play a role in American policy deliberations during World War II about the fate of postcolonial Vietnam, approvingly commented in his 1931 study of the Dutch East Indies,

> The cardinal principle of Dutch colonial policy is association. . . . The Indonesians had lost whatever distinctively indigenous political and cultural life they had possessed, and . . . it could not be revived. . . . The chief function of colonial administration, . . . while always respecting the Indonesian religious institutions . . . , is the protection and strengthening of native society: . . . widening out of the social horizon, collaboration of the native elite, differentiation according to needs inside the frame of unity, connecting up nationalism with the work of construction, and finally the transformation of the mechanical structure into an organic dispensation . . . to prepare them for full participation in Dutch political and national life.[69]

These affinities for Dutch and British colonial policies reflected U.S. self-perceptions as an exceptional colonial power in the Philippines whose progressive policies of association offered constructive models for reform. Interwar writings on the American colonial project in the Philippines, sometimes authored by former officials in the colonial regime, unanimously celebrated the salutary effect of gradual American approaches to political tutelage, education, and social welfare reform. The passage of the Tydings-McDuffie Act in 1934, which provided a timetable for Philippine independence, was often pointed to as evidence that U.S. policies had provided even better results than those of the British and the Dutch.[70] Most American observers would have agreed with the conclusions of a report by Philippine governor general Dwight F. Davis on his 1931 visit to Vietnam that implicitly contrasted the success of American colonial policies in the Philippines with the selfishness and incompetence of the French: "The poverty of the average native . . . is very apparent. . . . The native people are considered useful for the purpose of labor and, with that end in view, their welfare is not entirely neglected but little effort is made to improve their mental condition or to give them any real voice in government. . . . The underlying principle of all governmental activities is to develop the country economically for the benefit of France."[71]

U.S. interwar critiques of French colonialism were not expressions of anticolonial sentiments. No Americans in the interwar period suggested that improvements in Vietnamese society would come without the firm guidance of a Western power. But not only did they believe the French had gone about their colonial endeavors in Vietnam in the wrong way; American commentators were also deeply pessimistic that French colonial policy might shift to the more progressive associative principles they favored. Some observers did praise what they viewed as the associationist administrative and social reforms launched by French governor generals such as Albert Sarraut and Alexander Varenne during the interwar period. But they noted that most promised reforms proved ephemeral in the face of powerful assimilationist pressures that better reflected the French "passion for *ordre*" and certainty that their "civilization was the highest and most perfect on earth." As Virginia Thompson commented in a view shared by a number of Americans, "The balance sheet of French Indo-China up to now has registered . . . more destructive than constructive change."[72] Convinced of the tenacious hold of assimilationist doctrines on French policies, most American observers in the 1930s abandoned the previous decade's more optimistic assessment of French colonialism, viewing the potential for reform in French colonial rule of Vietnam as highly unlikely.

Of Bandits, Jealousies, and Imported Radicalism

Interwar American discourse on Vietnamese political behavior, filtered almost entirely though French colonial informants, conveyed none of the dynamism of indigenous anticolonial thought. Instead, assessments of the nature and significance of Vietnamese nationalism rested on unfavorable perceptions of the Vietnamese under French colonialism. U.S. observers were struck by the manifestations of anti-French and nationalist sentiment in Vietnam during the interwar period, but they usually attributed it to outside, often Soviet, direction.

American commentators noted the organization of a range of indigenous political parties in the 1920s, from the moderate Constitutionalists in the south to the more radical National Party, modeled on China's Kuomintang, and the ICP in the north. Observers also remarked on the rise of an indigenous nationalist leadership, with a few interwar accounts providing the first American discussion of the role played by Ho Chi Minh in Vietnamese anticolonialism. But Americans focused

on the increasing instances of anticolonial political agitation and violence between 1925 and 1931 and, again, in the late 1930s. Incidents that attracted particular attention included numerous assassination attempts against French officials,
the student strikes of 1926 and 1927 in Hanoi and Saigon, the 1930 Yen Bai uprising
in northern Vietnam led by the Nationalist Party, the peasant rebellion of 1930–
31 in the north central Vietnamese provinces of Nghe An and Ha Tinh organized
by the communists, and labor and student unrest in Saigon after 1936.

To most Americans, the rise of anticolonialism and nationalism in Vietnam
was the inevitable result of the failed French policies of assimilationist rule. "The
policy of assimilation," Thomas Ennis argued in a sentiment widely shared by
many observers, "means native unrest." French policies, many Americans contended, had plunged the mass of rural Vietnamese peasants into the "black
misery" of poverty. Through discriminatory tariffs, the excessive tax burden, the
mistreatment of plantation and mine workers, the failure to improve rural education and health care, and the "wanton extravagance" of colonial public works
projects, observers such as *Christian Science Monitor* correspondent Marc Greene
believed the French had created "an economic state not far from servitude" that
stimulated widespread peasant and worker discontent. French colonial rule,
Americans contended, had also frustrated the ambition of Vietnamese elites. Not
only were educational opportunities limited, but many persons educated in
French lycées and universities often found themselves unemployed or underpaid
as the colonial bureaucracy remained dominated by higher-paid French officials.
These unrealized aspirations and accumulated grievances, observers like Thomas
Ennis argued, underlay the increasingly vocal opposition to French colonial rule:
"The disturbances have been led by high-school and college graduates, unable to
find worthy employment in a land where formerly their talents as 'scholars' would
have procured for them official posts. These 'disinherited,' as they consider themselves, feel that the French regard them only as clerks, fit for petty responsibility
provided foreign chiefs constantly supervise every act. . . . Antagonisms will continue until all barriers regarding native ambition are removed."[73]

If Americans were critical of the French policies that had produced indigenous
discontent, they were far from championing Vietnamese nationalism. In part,
these views were conditioned by a broader antipathy toward revolutionary forms
of political change that shaped American perceptions of the earlier Mexican, Chinese, and Russian revolutions.[74] But the beliefs in racialized cultural hierarchies
through which Americans came to their disparaging perception of the Vietnamese
as an inferior and primitive people were also critical to their unfavorable assessments of Vietnamese nationalism. Most U.S. observers were highly skeptical of
the competence of nationalist leaders. Reflecting the common American percep-

tion that selfishness, dishonesty, and vanity were embedded in the "oriental psychology" of the Vietnamese, observers contended that "mutual jealousies" and "the mismanagement of funds" characterized the behavior of most indigenous anticolonial elites and presented almost insurmountable obstacles to the emergence of capable nationalist leadership. In the absence of a "constructive" nationalist agenda and effectively organized political parties to promote indigenous well-being, Americans disapprovingly argued, Vietnamese nationalist leaders resorted all too often to acts of isolated political violence. Many incidents of anticolonial agitation were rendered by Americans as "acts of terrorism," "brutal murders," or "acts of banditry."[75] American observers also cautioned against overestimating mass support for indigenous nationalist leaders. Most of these observers would have agreed with the comments of Foster Rhea Dulles in a 1927 article for *Current History* that the "vast masses of people" never thought of "nationalist aspirations." Even with the burdens imposed upon Vietnamese peasants and workers by French colonial rule, many commentators suggested, the lethargy induced by Vietnam's climate proved far "too fatiguing for revolutionary feelings."[76]

American observers wrongly attributed the emergence and organization of most large-scale anticolonial protest movements in Vietnam to the work of external agents. Drawing on their derisive perception of Vietnam's permeability to foreign influence, Americans believed that any successful effort to surmount what they termed the "natural" obstacles to effective anticolonial nationalist organization had to come from exogenous forces. The emergence of Vietnamese nationalist sentiment in the early part of the century, Americans suggested, reflected increasing exposure to intellectual currents in France, Japan, and China. By the 1920s, they argued, Marxism had become the more important external influence on Vietnamese nationalism. Many Americans contended that most incidents of anticolonial agitation in Vietnam during the interwar period were directed by Soviet or Chinese agents. In analyzing the anticolonial strikes, insurrections, and uprisings of the late 1920s and early 1930s in Vietnam, Thomas Ennis argued that they were "set in motion" and "controlled" by the Soviet Union as "part of the Soviet plan to concentrate upon the remote regions and rouse the peasantry." In a long report on "communistic activities" in Vietnam prepared in 1930, Henry I. Waterman, an American consul general in Saigon, attributed anticolonial violence to "the influence of revolutionary ideas imported from communistic China." Virginia Thompson, while acknowledging the nationalistic element of Vietnamese anticolonial agitation, emphasized its subordination to Moscow.[77]

The direct links that interwar observers identified between incidents of Vietnamese anticolonialism and the Soviet Union were often more imagined than real. Thomas Ennis argued that Comintern agent Michael Borodin directed the

1930 Yen Bai uprising even though Borodin had left Asia for the Soviet Union in 1927. Other observers provided biographical sketches of Ho Chi Minh that emphasized his close association with Moscow in the 1930s at a time when Ho's links with Stalin and the Comintern were at their lowest ebb.[78] But inaccuracies in U.S. observations are less important for understanding perceptions of Vietnamese nationalism than for gaining an appreciation of the continuing American insistence that external forces were a necessary precursor for substantial change in Vietnamese society. Just as the Chinese had shaped Vietnamese society some thousand years earlier, Americans believed, communism found fertile ground in an imitative and unreflective society.

Given the American dismissal of Vietnamese nationalism as an effective indigenous force, assessments by interwar observers of the future course of nationalism in Vietnam focused on the nature of French policy. Although alarmed by the brutality of Vietnamese anticolonial violence, U.S. commentators were critical of the "swift and ruthless" repressive tactics employed by the French to restore order, pointing to instances of torture, secret trials, bombing of villages, and destruction of crops.[79] Rather than relying on repression, some Americans suggested, France should seek a modus vivendi with the Soviets as they had brought the Vietnamese "pot to boil." An agreement with the Soviets, they argued, would give the French time to implement needed colonial reforms. A number of observers, reflecting the U.S. preference for associationist forms of colonial rule, urged the French to promote the gradual development of "responsible" and "moderate" nationalist sentiments by making available places in the colonial administration for educated Vietnamese elites, providing a larger indigenous role in governing the colonies, and undertaking projects to improve rural socioeconomic well-being. Most commentators, however, remained pessimistic that the French would attempt the substantial political and social reform Americans believed were necessary to create a climate of moderate indigenous nationalism. Many Americans believed armed force rather than reform would probably continue to characterize future French responses to radical Vietnamese nationalism.[80]

Clearly U.S. images of colonial Vietnam, and the assumptions that sustained them, contained internal contradictions, unsuspected ironies, and misperceptions. Interwar American observers devoted scant attention to the systemic effects of French colonial policies on the living conditions and political behavior of the Vietnamese. Although U.S. critics of French colonial rule were vociferous, the prism of racialized cultural hierarchies that shaped their perceptions of the Vietnamese prevented them from understanding indigenous responses to colonialism. For instance, because they viewed the Vietnamese as hopelessly lazy, it did not occur to Americans that everyday Vietnamese behavior under the French colonial regime might be a subtle form of anticolonial rebellion, a defensive reaction to a colonial system that provided little hope for political or economic advancement. And although unknown to U.S. observers, important aspects of their deprecatory assessment of Vietnamese society were shared by scholar-gentry and radical elites in Vietnam, particularly in the Reform Movement's embrace of Social Darwinism. But even if Americans had been better informed about Vietnamese political thought, the means through which indigenous actors believed society could be transformed, whether by Confucian virtue, revolutionary heroism, or Leninist organization, and their ultimate aims of a neo-Confucian peace or a Marxist classless society had little resonance in an American discourse shaped by misperceptions of Vietnamese responses to colonialism and an abiding faith in the superiority and universal applicability of U.S. ideals.

The certainty of interwar observers that American approaches to colonial tutelage differed sharply from French ideas and practices also obscured essential commonalities between American self-perceptions of what President William McKinley termed "benevolent assimilation" and French conceptions of themselves as "fathers" to their Vietnamese "children." The French *mission civilisatrice* and the contention of French governor generals that "a father does not abandon his children" may have been unconvincing to contemporary U.S. observers. But their own unwavering assertion in the 1930s that Vietnam needed a New Deal implied that Vietnamese society did not so much require independence as a new father in the American image.[81] The sharp dichotomy American observers posed between assimilation and association obscured the essential similarities between the two forms of colonial rule. As scholars of French colonialism have recently noted, both approaches were fundamentally variations on the colonial exercise of power over subject peoples and rested on the notion that the backward nature of colonial peoples required French tutelage.[82] Notwithstanding the claims of contemporary American observers, the embrace of associative forms of colonial rule and the rendering of the Vietnamese through the framework of racialized cultural hierarchies exposes their deeper complicity in what they preferred to see as European colonial norms. Even the critique Americans offered of French rule and the exceptionalist claims they made for their success in the Philippines belie the affinity of U.S. practices with the broader Western colonial project and its inherent nationalism. Just as Americans were infused with an unwavering belief in the superiority of their political, economic, and social models in the Philippines, the British, the Dutch, and the French simultaneously celebrated their own colonial achievements, and denigrated the practices of Americans and other European powers, to promote an exceptionalist national identity at home.[83]

American policy makers during World War II and its aftermath often pointed to the exceptionalism of the U.S. approach to the Vietnamese and other non-Western peoples, a claim that has gone largely unchallenged by many historians of U.S. relations with the postcolonial world. Yet the interwar assumptions about the backward nature of the Vietnamese and the proper forms of colonial rule, which so closely parallel those of the European colonial powers from which Americans sought to distance themselves, would continue to frame perceptions of the Vietnamese during World War II and beyond. As U.S. policy makers began to construct their own vision of Vietnam's postcolonial future and confronted the rise of Ho Chi Minh's Viet Minh in the early 1940s, the contradictions and tensions between these persisting commonalities in Euro-American colonial assumptions and self-perceptions of American exceptionalism powerfully influenced their deliberations and shaped the contours of Vietnamese-American relations.

3 TRUSTEESHIP AND THE AMERICAN VISION OF POSTCOLONIAL VIETNAM

At the 11 November 1943 meeting of the State Department's Subcommittee on Territorial Problems, Kenneth P. Landon, as he listened to a discussion of the future role of the Great Powers in determining the postwar political status of Vietnam, remarked that he "could not help thinking of the colored gentleman in the Civil War who had been chided for not enlisting. In reply, he asked his interlocutor whether he had ever seen a dog fight and if so whether he had ever seen the bone take sides. . . . As the colored people had been the bone in the case of the Civil War it was assumed by many that the Oriental peoples were the bone of contention in the controversy under discussion." Landon, a member of the State Department's newly formed Division of Southwest Pacific Affairs, questioned whether this was actually the case, suggesting that postwar planning for Vietnam give more attention to "the oriental point of view." It was Landon's impression that many members of the subcommittee "assumed that the bone could be disposed of quickly and easily, but this was a dangerous assumption on which to act." Landon added, "While it might be true temporarily it was nevertheless possible that the bone might have feelings about itself and might at some later date even become a dog."[1]

Most of those present at the meeting were either confused by Landon's analogy or rejected it altogether. One subcommittee member asked Landon who "was the bone in this case." Another member, assuming Landon saw the Chinese rather than the Vietnamese as the "bone" in question, attacked the notion that "European powers were dogs" and "Orientals were bones" as "fallacious," adding, "There was in fact no greater dog in this part of the world than the Chinese themselves." Several other subcommittee members assented.[2]

Landon's effort to draw attention to the role of the Vietnamese in shaping their postcolonial future was unusual among wartime American policy makers. But the attention accorded to Vietnam and the racialist lens through which its future development was viewed were not. As the 1930s came to a close, Vietnam began to take on an unprecedented geostrategic importance for the United States. American policy makers viewed the Japanese challenge to the balance of power in Asia with considerable alarm throughout the 1930s in the wake of the Japanese occupation of Manchuria and the outbreak of the Sino-Japanese war. After 1937, American concern with Japanese intentions increasingly shifted from China to Southeast Asia as Vietnam proved to be a key staging area for Japan's southward movement in the region.[3] The Japanese decision to station troops in northern Vietnam in September 1940 was particularly alarming to American policy makers. Any further advances threatened continuing access to critical strategic raw materials in British Malaya and the Dutch East Indies that provided the majority of the U.S. supply of tin and rubber.[4] When the Japanese moved to occupy southern Vietnam in July 1941, President Franklin D. Roosevelt issued a potentially debilitating freeze order on Japanese assets in and trade with the United States, which remained significant despite escalating Japanese-American tensions in Asia. The dangers Japanese aggression in Vietnam posed to U.S. perceptions of regional stability in Southeast Asia, numerous scholars have argued, were among the most important precipitating factors in the coming of the U.S. war with Japan in December 1941.[5]

The outbreak of the Pacific war in 1941 and the continuing challenge Japanese occupation of Indochina presented for French colonial control of the region provided the United States with the opportunity to shape the creation of an independent postwar Vietnamese state. Throughout the war, the Japanese allowed Vichy France to administer Indochina, but the strong Japanese military presence in the colony severely damaged French colonial authority.[6] To many American policy makers, Vietnam appeared to be a bone that required their advice and guidance. Just a few months after the Japanese attack on Pearl Harbor, President Roosevelt expressed doubts about French colonial rule in Indochina and initiated plans to place Vietnam under some form of international trusteeship. By mid-1942, discussions were under way within the State Department on possible forms of international supervision for the development of indigenous political and civil society in postwar Vietnam. From 1942 onward, Roosevelt vigorously pressed members of the wartime alliance to support trusteeship, winning the endorsement of Chiang Kai-shek and Stalin. At the same time, U.S. officials in southern China were increasingly drawn into discussions about trusteeship for Vietnam. By the spring of 1945, however, the United States had retreated from these efforts, abandoning plans for the international supervision of Vietnam's transition to independence and acquiescing to the return of the French to Indochina.

Franklin Roosevelt's dogged pursuit of trusteeship for Indochina during World War II has often been viewed as a peculiarly quixotic personal crusade.[7] While scholars debate Roosevelt's culpability for the quiet death of trusteeship in the spring of 1945, most wistfully agree that postwar American diplomacy toward Vietnam marked a sharp break with FDR's wartime plans for Indochina. But if Roosevelt's advocacy of trusteeship ended in failure, its significance lies not in a story of what might have been. Rather than a didactic parable of a pacific alternative to the increasingly bellicose character of subsequent Cold War diplomacy in Vietnam, trusteeship marked the full articulation of a persisting American vision that transcended FDR's personal crusade.

Roosevelt's certainty that trusteeship was the best tool to realize America's imagined postcolonial Vietnam and his optimism that the European colonial powers would support the venture were not shared by all U.S. policy makers. But the assumptions that underlay his larger vision were. Central to these wider aims was the American construction of Vietnam that had first emerged in the interwar period. For Franklin Roosevelt and the diplomats, military officials, and intelligence operatives in Washington and East Asia who framed the U.S. vision of postwar Vietnam, the interwar critiques of Vietnamese society and French colonialism were the starting point for outlining the problems they perceived in colonial Vietnam. Wartime American policy makers believed the Vietnamese were innately incapable of self-government, French rule had done almost nothing to correct these deficiencies, and the dislocations of the Pacific war offered the opportunity to arrest the stagnation of Vietnam's civil society by providing the Vietnamese with tutelage in U.S. political, economic, and social models. Even more important, the assumptions of racialized cultural hierarchies and the superiority of the American colonial project in the Philippines along with the reliance on French reporting about Vietnam that drove interwar perceptions remained critical to wartime policy deliberations. If the transformation of the incipient American vision of Vietnam's future into policy encountered serious and ultimately insurmountable obstacles, these efforts and the assumptions that guided them would continue to powerfully shape and constrain U.S. policy toward Vietnam in the aftermath of World War II.

Benefiting the Owner: Franklin Roosevelt and Trusteeship

At a 21 July 1943 meeting of the Pacific War Council, the interallied working group that oversaw military operations in the Pacific theater, President Roosevelt addressed the members of the council assembled in the Cabinet Room of the White House:

> Indo-China should not be given back to the French Empire after the war. The French had been there for nearly one hundred years and had done absolutely nothing with the place to improve the lot of the people. . . . Probably for every pound they got out of the place they put in only one shilling. . . . We ought to help these 35,000,000 people in Indo-China. Naturally they could not be given independence immediately but should be taken care of until they are able to govern themselves. . . . In 1900 the Filipinos were not ready for independence nor could a date be fixed when they would be. Many public works had to be taken care of first. The people had to be educated in local, and finally, national governmental affairs. By 1933, however, we were able to get together with the Filipinos and all agree on a date, namely 1945, when they would be ready for independence. Since this development worked in that case, there is no reason why it should not work in the case of Indo-China. In the meantime, we would hold Indo-China as a trustee. This word cannot even be translated into some languages. It means to hold for the benefit of the owner.[8]

Roosevelt's remarks before the Pacific War Council were not his first mention of plans for international trusteeship in Indochina. But the sentiments they conveyed aptly characterize his approach to the creation of a postcolonial Vietnamese state and the powerful linkages between interwar American commentary on Vietnam and wartime policy making. Roosevelt saw French rule in Vietnam as a particularly egregious example of colonial failure. Traveling with his son Elliott to Casablanca in 1943, a journey that brought him intimate views of poverty and disease in French Morocco, Roosevelt reflected on French colonial rule in Vietnam: "Why was it a cinch for the Japanese to conquer that land? The native Indo-Chinese have been so flagrantly downtrodden that they thought to themselves: Anything must be better than to live under French colonial rule!" In his remarks before the Pacific War Council, Roosevelt argued the French acted solely in their own economic self-interest in Vietnam and had done nothing to "improve the lot of the people." It was a refrain that he would repeat many times in wartime discussions of trusteeship for Indochina with the Chinese, the British, and the Soviets. In a meeting with Stalin at the Tehran conference in November 1943, where he won the support of the Soviet leader for trusteeship, for instance, Roosevelt told Stalin "that after 100 years of French rule in Indochina, the inhabitants were worse off than they had been before."[9]

Underlying Roosevelt's hostility toward French policy in Indochina, just as it had underlain the attitudes of interwar American observers of Vietnam, was not so much opposition to colonial rule itself as a sense that the French had not upheld the obligations of a colonizing power. In one of his earliest statements on French colonialism in Vietnam, Roosevelt observed in May 1942 that "the French did not seem to be very good colonizers." French conduct in Indochina, he suggested, "was at considerable variance with the general practice of Great Britain and the United States to encourage natives to participate in self-government to the limit of their abilities."[10] Roosevelt made explicit some ten months later the critical role French failure to reform Vietnamese society played in his assessment of Indochina's future, arguing "that we must judge countries by their actions and that in that connection we should all avoid any hasty promise to return French Indo-China to the French."[11]

Roosevelt was also certain that the Vietnamese were unable to govern themselves, an assumption that rested in part on his belief that the failed policies of the French had left the Vietnamese unprepared for independence. But his use of the word "naturally" to introduce his assertions before the Pacific War Council that the Vietnamese were not yet ready for self-government and required external improvement suggests that his perception of Vietnam's political immaturity was also refracted through the prism of racialized cultural hierarchies. Roosevelt's direct knowledge of indigenous Vietnamese society was extremely limited. In one of the few instances in which he described the Vietnamese, Roosevelt called them "people of small stature, like the Javanese and Burmese," who were "not warlike," a comment that recalls the negative interwar U.S. perception of Vietnam as a feminized and weak society amenable to outside influence.[12] In presenting to the Pacific War Council Vietnamese society as analogous to the Philippines before American colonial rule, Roosevelt also linked his vision of Vietnam to the broader and more familiar American beliefs that posed a natural division between the stasis of non-Western societies and the dynamism of the West. The reductionist analogy Roosevelt used to join Vietnamese and Filipino societies may have seemed particularly compelling because he viewed Vietnam as another backward Asian society in need of development on more progressive Western lines.

The interconnections Roosevelt drew between Vietnam and the Philippines were central to his conception of Vietnamese development under trusteeship. Roosevelt's brief before the Pacific War Council that the success of American policy in the Philippines demonstrated that there was "no reason why it should not work in the case of Indo-China" illustrates his oft-expressed faith in the universality of American models in the Philippines and the ease of their cross-cultural transfer. In a November 1942 radio address on American policy toward colonial territories, for example, Roosevelt argued, "I like to think that the history of the Philippine Islands . . . provides . . . a pattern for the future of other small nations and peoples of the world. It is a pattern of what men of good-will look forward to in the future—a pattern of a global civilization."[13]

But Roosevelt's emphasis on gradual evolution toward full independence in the Philippines suggests that he saw the process of political and social development in Asia as very slow. In Roosevelt's view, some forty-five years would elapse between the coming of U.S. rule to the Philippines and independence. Roosevelt argued that in 1900, not only were the Philippines unprepared for independence, but a date could not "be fixed when they would be." Even after thirty-three years of efforts to build public works and provide education in "local, and finally, national governmental affairs," Roosevelt continued, both American and Philippine elites agreed that the Philippines would not be "ready for independence" until 1945. As Roosevelt suggested in his November 1942 radio address, only after the "fulfillment of physical and social and economic needs" and tutelage in "the various steps to complete statehood" could the Philippines enjoy self-government.[14]

Given Roosevelt's perception of the universality of the Philippine model as well as the particular parallels he saw between Vietnam and the Philippines, his description of American efforts to guide the Philippines toward independence at the Pacific War Council indicates that he envisioned the transformation of Vietnamese society under international trusteeship would be marked by the same gradualism and moderation that had characterized U.S. colonial policy in the Philippines. These lessons from the American experience in the Philippines informed Roosevelt's presentation of a timetable for trusteeship in Vietnam. In conversations with Chiang Kai-shek and Stalin later in 1943, for instance, Roosevelt raised the Philippine analogy to suggest that trusteeship "would have the task of preparing the people for independence within a defined period of time, perhaps 20 to 30 years." As he told a group of reporters accompanying him on his return from the Yalta conference in 1945, "The situation there [in Indochina] is a good deal like the Philippines were in 1898. It took fifty years for us to . . . educate them for self-government."[15]

Roosevelt's emerging vision of postcolonial Vietnam was not, however, as sharp a departure from prevailing colonial norms as his rhetoric sometimes suggested and he himself appeared to believe. The easy links Roosevelt drew between his plans for Vietnam and American policy in the Philippines should not obscure the failure of the U.S. colonial project in its own terms. As one leading scholar of

American colonialism in the Philippines argues, the three central policies undertaken to transform Philippine society in the U.S. image—preparing the Filipinos to exercise governmental responsibilities, providing primary education for the masses, and developing the economy—"failed . . . to bring about fundamental change," challenging "the widely held myth . . . of the United States as an essentially successful colonial power." [16] Nor did Roosevelt's views, shared by many who would make wartime American policy on Vietnam, acknowledge the inherent similarities in U.S. and European colonial aims and practices. What the United States celebrated as "benevolent assimilation" in the Philippines both sanitized the violence of colonial conquest and presumed the backwardness and inferiority of Filipino beneficiaries. If U.S. colonial tutelage in the Philippines was a transitional stage to independence, as another scholar recently argued, "self-rule was not the product of a social compact among equals but the result of sustained disciplinary measures requiring the colonized to submit unstintingly to a pedagogy of repression and mastery." [17] Despite Roosevelt's belief that trusteeship in Vietnam marked a revolutionary break from the colonial past, the shared Euro-American beliefs that underlay the U.S. approach to the Philippines and Vietnam belied his exceptionalist claims.

Unaware, or unconcerned, about these contradictions, Roosevelt was optimistic that the French could be prevented from returning to Indochina and that the British and Chinese could be induced to support U.S. plans for the area. By the time the Pacific War Council met in July 1943, FDR had repeatedly demonstrated his willingness to act on his critique of French rule in Indochina and to challenge French policy. In the winter and spring of 1942, Roosevelt reacted forcefully to reports that the French had entered negotiations with the Axis powers to permit their use of French commercial ships, including French merchant vessels in Indochinese ports. Calling the potential use of French ships by the Japanese and other Axis powers "furtherance of their acts of aggression," he demanded that the French withdraw from negotiations. Eventually Japanese forces unilaterally seized the French vessels in Indochina, but the incident, marked by bitter exchanges between American and French diplomats that reinforced prevailing distrust of France's intentions, demonstrated Roosevelt's willingness to contest French strategic initiatives he believed were inimical to U.S. interests.[18]

On other occasions, Roosevelt expressed his strong belief that U.S. promises since the outbreak of war in Europe to work toward the liberation of France and its empire from the Axis powers did not imply the postwar American support for the return of French rule in Indochina. At a meeting with the Joint Chiefs of Staff at the White House in January 1943, Roosevelt was particularly exercised by recent written pledges given by Robert Murphy, his personal representative to the

Vichy French authorities in North Africa, that provided assurances of U.S. support for the restoration of the French colonial empire. Roosevelt told the Joint Chiefs that Murphy "had exceeded his authority." Some "colonial possessions," Roosevelt argued, should "not be returned to [the] French," and he expressed "grave doubts as to whether Indo-China should be." [19] Later in 1943, in an effort to foreclose any French involvement in military planning against the Japanese in Indochina, Roosevelt prevented France from becoming a member of the Pacific War Council despite the keen desire of the French to join. Responding to a memorandum from Acting Secretary of State Edward R. Stettinius that recommended French requests to join the council be "put off," as they stemmed from France's desire to "protect French interests in Indochina," Roosevelt replied, "Yes, defer." [20]

As part of his broader strategy to build up China as one of the postwar great powers, Roosevelt was particularly confident that the Chinese would follow the lead of their U.S. patron on Indochina policy. In part, Roosevelt's successful attempt to gain Chiang Kai-shek's support for international trusteeship in Indochina at wartime summits with the leaders of the Great Powers was a symbolic effort designed to connote the equivalence of China with the Soviet Union and Great Britain in deliberations over the postwar world. But Roosevelt also sought to involve the Chinese in his Indochina policy because he believed that China "had no desire to annex Indo-China," preferring to serve as a disinterested party in preparing the area for independence. His certainty that the Chinese would play a benign role in the future of postwar Indochina emerged in American support for Chinese proposals to invade northern Vietnam that emerged in late 1942 and 1943. Despite vigorous protests from France, the State Department and the War Plans Division of the War Department, with Roosevelt's apparent assent, supported China's plans. Neither the War Department's nor the State Department's assessment of Chinese intentions raised the possibility that the invasion might be linked to wider Chinese political ambitions in the region. U.S. analysts accepted China's arguments that it "had absolutely no territorial design on Indo-China" and commented favorably on Chinese willingness to contribute to broader Allied military objectives in Asia. [21]

With Chinese as well as Soviet support for U.S. policies in Indochina, Roosevelt hoped that any potential British objections to international trusteeship could be neutralized. He was aware of opposition to trusteeship from the British Foreign office, suggesting "they fear the effect it would have on their own possessions." But his meetings with British foreign secretary Anthony Eden in 1943 were a source of cautious optimism that the British would accede to American wishes. According to a memorandum by Secretary of State Cordell Hull summarizing a White House meeting between FDR and Eden in March 1943, Eden told the president he was "favorably impressed" with trusteeship proposals for Indochina. In a memorandum prepared by Roosevelt's assistant Harry Hopkins on the same meeting, Hopkins reported, "The President and Eden seemed to be much closer together than they were at the beginning of their conferences" on trusteeship policies.[22]

While both Roosevelt and Churchill refrained from discussing trusteeship in their meetings and correspondence in 1943 and 1944, Roosevelt forcefully made his views known to the British through other channels. In a January 1944 memorandum to Secretary of State Hull, Roosevelt told Hull of his recent conversation with Lord Halifax, the British ambassador to Washington:

> I saw Halifax last week and told him quite frankly that it was perfectly true that I had, for over a year, expressed the opinion that Indo-China should not go back to France but that it should be administered by international trusteeship. France has had the country—thirty million inhabitants for nearly one hundred years—and the people are worse off than they were at the beginning. . . . The case of Indo-China is perfectly clear. France has milked it for one hundred years. The people of Indo-China are entitled to something better than that.[23]

With this apt characterization of his motivations for promoting international trusteeship, Roosevelt entered the final years of the war certain that the U.S. vision of postwar Vietnam would prevail.

Debating the Instruments of Change:
Postwar Planning and Vietnam

As President Roosevelt worked in 1943 to advance his plans for international trusteeship in Indochina, members of the State Department's postwar planning staff and its Divisions of Far Eastern and Western European Affairs began to craft their own proposals to prepare Vietnam for independence and self-government. The final recommendations of State Department planners favored a more limited role for the United States in Vietnam's future development than the one envisioned by Roosevelt and reflected a somewhat different assessment of the geopolitical forces acting on Indochina. But their deliberations on the necessity for political, economic, and social change in Vietnam revealed the broader assumptions that guided Roosevelt's plans for trusteeship as well as his insistence that U.S. models could best direct Vietnam's future development.

The most sustained wartime discussion in Washington of Indochina policy took place in the Subcommittee on Territorial Problems, one of many committees in the State Department's labyrinthine postwar planning apparatus. In meetings held in November 1943, the subcommittee took up the question, "Should Indo-China be restored to French sovereignty, with or without conditions?" For these discussions its regular membership was supplemented with representatives from the Division of Far Eastern Affairs and several members of the policy planning research staff who were to serve as area specialists.[24] None of these specialists had particular training on Vietnam, but three of them—Kenneth P. Landon, Amry Vandenbosch, and Melvin K. Knight—did bring some knowledge of Southeast Asia and French colonialism. Landon, a former missionary in Thailand for ten years, had recently joined the State Department's Division of Southwest Pacific Affairs. Vandenbosch, a University of Kentucky political scientist who was the leading American scholar on the Dutch East Indies, and Knight, an economic historian who had published works on French colonial rule in North Africa, were members of the research staff. The subcommittee was chaired by Isaiah Bowman, a noted Johns Hopkins geographer and an important adviser to President Roosevelt on colonial issues.[25]

The subcommittee initially took up a review and discussion of working papers prepared by Vandenbosch and Knight on French colonial practices in Indochina and the capabilities of indigenous peoples to govern themselves. In their critical assessments of French colonialism and Vietnamese society, which met with general agreement among the members of the subcommittee, Vandenbosch and Knight echoed the views of President Roosevelt and the thrust of interwar U.S. commentary on Vietnam.[26] Subcommittee members believed that French practices in Vietnam "fell short of the standards set by most of the other Western European powers." French bureaucracy in Indochina, Knight told the committee, was marked by "inefficiency" and "corruption": "High officials were all appointed as a result of political considerations and had no intimate knowledge of the country which they administered . . . whereas the lower bureaucrats were under paid and were in no way equal to the tasks that faced them. . . . Corruption was rife everywhere. . . . The use of alcohol and opium by the lower officials was so common it attracted no attention and many of their practices were unprintable."[27]

French economic policies in Indochina were also criticized as selfishly serving "the interests of the mother country" rather than "the colonies." Although Knight noted that efforts to build railroads and other public works projects "had contributed greatly to the prosperity of the area," he argued that indigenous peoples had seen little of the benefits as they were burdened by ever higher tax burdens to support the development of the French export economy. Recalling interwar American critiques of French tariffs in Indochina, Knight also suggested that the injustices of French protectionist policies undermined both the development of the colonial economy and the improvement of indigenous economic welfare:

"As an importer chiefly of manufactures, Indo-China paid French protectionist prices. . . . As an exporter chiefly of crude material, Indo-China received little protection but sold mainly at world-market prices. . . . Indo-Chinese rice and corn remained cheap in the 1930's while France was guaranteeing high prices to her wheat farmers at home by means of tariffs and quotas. Thus Indo-China sold cheap and bought dear within a tariff partnership designed by and for the other partner." [28]

Along with its critique of French administrative and economic practices, the subcommittee also shared the views of Roosevelt and interwar U.S. observers of French Indochina that the Vietnamese were not yet ready for independence. Their impressions of Vietnamese political immaturity, like those of FDR, were partially grounded in perceptions of the failures of French colonial rule. Vandenbosch told the subcommittee that the French had made no effort to prepare the "natives" under their rule for self-government: "French administration of Indo-China was not directed toward developing colonial self-government. . . . French policy . . . deliberately restricted the opportunity for native participation in government. The French claimed that the natives did not possess the requisite qualifications to assume the responsibilities of self-government, but they did not encourage the development of those qualifications. French educational policy, for instance, emphasized advanced training for a comparatively few natives." Knight, revealing his own limited knowledge of colonial Vietnam, noted his surprise that "the native population had no knowledge of the French language and apparently did not have any understanding of France and the French." [29]

France's unwillingness to prepare the Vietnamese for eventual self-government, subcommittee members argued, represented a sharp departure from what they believed to be prevailing colonial norms. Vandenbosch told the subcommittee that the "Dutch had done much better by their colonies than had the French" as "the Indonesians had made more rapid progress in the direction of self-government under the Dutch than had the populations of Indo-China under the French." A sense of the superiority of U.S. policies in the Philippines also shaped the subcommittee's perception that France's failure to guide Vietnamese political development had violated a fundamental obligation of colonizing powers. Assistant Secretary of State Adolph A. Berle, another subcommittee member, observed that "self-government, as was indicated by our experience in the Philippines, depended . . . on the policy which the government pursued." [30]

The subcommittee's perceptions of Vietnamese political immaturity also rested on assumptions guiding interwar American characterizations of Vietnam as an inferior and imitative "little China," although this impression emerged more elliptically in their deliberations. In a discussion of Vietnam's "backward political development," Knight told subcommittee members that "it was doubtful whether the Annamites . . . would have been any better off had the French not taken them in hand." Vandenbosch called French rule the "glue" that held Vietnam together, adding that "it would not be possible to conduct any government in this area" without it.[31] Many members of the subcommittee assumed the Chinese had dominated Vietnam's precolonial history and political customs, reinforcing their sense that Vietnamese society lacked traditions of indigenous governance. Beyond "the patriarchal family which had been the dominating social force up to the time of the French arrival," Knight argued, there had been "no organized system of government . . . to establish public order." When asked if the Vietnamese had put up any opposition to French conquest, Knight, unaware of vigorous if unsuccessful Vietnamese efforts in the late nineteenth century to oppose the French presence, replied that "these areas had been protectorates of China and it was . . . from the Chinese that the main objections had come." Other committee members, such as Adolph Berle, believed the Vietnamese "were Chinese for the main part."[32]

The subcommittee's contemptuous perceptions of Vietnamese nationalism did not reassure them that Vietnam was capable of self-government. Members of the subcommittee expressed sympathy with the frustrations that had produced nationalist sentiment in Vietnam as they believed French colonial policy had done little to advance Vietnamese political or socioeconomic welfare. But their unfavorable impressions of nationalist politics reinforced their sense that the Vietnamese lacked the abilities necessary to govern themselves immediately. As Vandenbosch told the subcommittee, the nationalist movement was "limited" to a small number of educated elites who were unable to win the support of the peasant masses. Nationalist leaders, he observed, were "split by factional strife and [an] inability to formulate a constructive program acceptable to a wide following." Reflecting the interwar American emphasis on the innate deficiencies of the Vietnamese character, Vandenbosch suggested that "violence, mismanagement of funds, dishonesty and petty bickering . . . characterized most of the nationalist organizations."[33]

The idea that indigenous political traditions or abilities might permit the Vietnamese to govern themselves in the postwar period was almost inconceivable to the members of the subcommittee, as a revealing exchange between Melvin Knight and the subcommittee chair, Isaiah Bowman, illustrates. Despite his derisive portrait of Vietnamese political culture, Knight somewhat timorously suggested that the Vietnamese might be capable of self-government without external direction. Bowman, with the apparent assent of the committee, immediately encouraged Knight to elaborate. Did Knight really believe the chances of self-government in Vietnam were good? When Knight replied that "it would be a good bet," Bowman questioned him further. Under Bowman's continuing pres-

sure, Knight began to back away from his initial assertion, suggesting "it was probably difficult for an old culture to be reformed along modern lines." But he added
that the "case was still open as to whether it was governable." Not satisfied, Bowman pressed him again. Finally, Knight conceded that "while at some future time
Indo-China might be made self-governing," the time had not yet arrived.[34]

Both the subcommittee's critique of French colonial rule and its perceptions
of Vietnamese political immaturity informed its approach to deliberations over
the postwar status of Indochina at its 11 November 1943 meeting. The subcommittee quickly ruled out full independence. "The elements necessary for the early
establishment of an independent Indo-China are lacking," the subcommittee observed, because of French failure to prepare the Vietnamese for self-government
and the "weak" and "disorganized" character of Vietnamese nationalism. The subcommittee also voiced its unanimous opposition to the full restoration of French
sovereignty, given that "the French had not done a good job of administering Indo-
China." In view of past French behavior, the subcommittee suggested, "it would
appear that unconditional restoration of French sovereignty would provide no
guarantee for the improvement of native welfare."[35]

There was considerable debate and disagreement, however, over the appropriate policy to promote Vietnam's eventual movement toward independence, with
advocates of international trusteeship pitted against supporters of a vaguer international accountability for the restoration of some form of French colonial rule. A
minority of the subcommittee embraced President Roosevelt's proposal for international trusteeship in "recognition of the failure of France to provide adequately
for the welfare of the native population." Proponents of trusteeship were particularly pessimistic about the likelihood of reforming French colonial practices. Only
through international administration, they argued, could Indochina develop "the
basis for eventual political . . . independence and for a rising standard of living."
Given prevailing views of the inability of Vietnam to govern itself, they suggested
a trusteeship period in Indochina of "considerable and unforseeable duration."[36]

A majority of the subcommittee members raised a number of objections to
international trusteeship for Indochina. Several members questioned the efficacy
of employing an international administrative agency to effect reform in an indigenous society. Trusteeship, one member argued, would be "experimental in character and of doubtful effectiveness." Although French administration "was maintained at a low level of competence," he continued, "the long experience of the
French in the colony could be utilized to good advantage during the period of
postwar development." Several members also asked how France could be required
to relinquish its sovereignty over Indochina when the British and the Dutch were
likely to maintain their colonies in Southeast Asia. Advocates of trusteeship argued

that France was a special case as it had not been able to protect itself and its colonies at the outset of the war. Moreover, they suggested, "the difference of physical strength was so great between France on the one hand and Great Britain and the United States on the other" that France could only retake Indochina with the assistance of Allied military forces and would thus be bound by the wishes of the other powers.[37]

But most of the subcommittee believed the situation faced by France was more ambiguous. One member reminded his colleagues that the French believed they "had never lost the empire," as Indochina was occupied but not administered by the Japanese. The French could also "make the case," he suggested, "that the collapse of France was due to the misbehavior of all the European powers and not the French alone." Several members observed that a "moral equality existed between the various allies," suggesting that if the French played any military role in the liberation of Indochina, they were entitled to a voice in its postwar development. To insist on trusteeship in this event "might sacrifice the possibility of French cooperation after the war."[38]

The majority of the subcommittee also pointed to British colonial policy and the uncertainty of future Allied military strategy in Indochina as potentially critical factors undermining plans for international trusteeship. Unlike FDR's more optimistic assessment of British policy in 1943, subcommittee members argued that British support for trusteeship was unlikely because of the dangers it posed to Britain's own colonies. "It was clear," one member argued, "that we could not ask France to give up its sovereignty over Indo-China without asking the same of the British." Other subcommittee members pointed out that while the future course of Allied military campaigns in Southeast Asia remained unsettled, several possible scenarios made trusteeship unlikely. As one member suggested, France might regain control of Indochina "without reliance on allied aid" and make it impossible to impose international trusteeship in the region.[39]

While the uncertainties of the wartime situation prompted it to reject international trusteeship, the subcommittee remained sympathetic to its goals of reforming French colonial practices and preparing the Vietnamese for eventual self-government. In place of international trusteeship, the majority of the subcommittee supported three proposals aimed at placing postwar French colonial rule in Indochina under "international accountability." First, the committee recommended the establishment of a regional commission to oversee the decolonization of Southeast Asia. Commission members would include the United States, Great Britain, France, China, the Netherlands, the Soviet Union, and the Philippines. The new commission, modeled on the Anglo-American Caribbean Commission established in 1942, would oversee efforts to promote indigenous political, economic, and social development. Second, the subcommittee called for the formulation of a colonial charter in which the colonial powers pledged to provide "for native welfare," including provisions for the "training of the local population in self-government." Finally, the subcommittee recommended that each colonial power submit to the regional commission an annual report on political and socio-economic progress made during the year. If France was amenable to these three proposals, it would be permitted to return to Indochina in the postwar period.[40]

Confident of the powers of international suasion, the subcommittee believed that the combination of incentives and constraints offered by the regional commission, a colonial charter, and the preparation of annual reports would reform French colonial practices in Indochina and hasten the emergence of a self-governing Vietnamese state in a more realistic manner than the "idealism" of international trusteeship. The subcommittee was particularly optimistic of British support, observing that "if we and the British could agree on some such conditions . . . it might be possible to bring the French around to our point of view." Noting that the British had recently mentioned a desire to "extend and develop" the Anglo-American Caribbean Commission, the subcommittee suggested that Great Britain might be willing to support a regional commission for Southeast Asia. Since the British had accepted regional commissions, one subcommittee member noted, "it would not be unreasonable to ask the British government . . . to go one step further and agree" to a colonial charter. With British participation as well as that of the other European powers in the Southeast Asian regional commission, the French would be much less likely to raise the objections subcommittee members anticipated in response to international trusteeship. As one committee member put it, "Regional commissions probably represented the highest common denominator of willingness to accept sovereignty restrictions on the part of the colonial powers."[41]

The differences in approach to the postwar development of Vietnam within the Subcommittee on Territorial Problems reflected wider debates within the State Department on postwar planning for Indochina that emerged in late 1943 and early 1944. Among the wartime State Department entities concerned with Indochina were the Divisions of Western European and Southwest Pacific Affairs and two other postwar planning committees, the CAC and the Committee on Colonial Problems. While all four groups took as a starting point the same unfavorable perceptions of French colonial rule and Vietnamese capacities for immediate self-government that had animated discussion in the Subcommittee on Territorial Problems, they were divided on the principles that should guide postwar Indochina's political development. The Division of Western European Affairs and the Committee on Colonial Problems supported a return of French colonial rule to Indochina under the supervision of a regional commission. The Division of Southwest Pacific Affairs favored international trusteeship. The members of the CAC were almost evenly divided between the two proposals, but the committee eventually supported the restoration of French rule under a regional commission.[42]

More important than the debates over the mechanisms by which to guide Indochina toward postwar independence, however, were the common assumptions that informed proposals for international trusteeship and for regional commissions. Both proposals shared Roosevelt's unwavering belief in the applicability of U.S. political values and institutions for organizing the postwar Vietnamese state and tutoring the Vietnamese people in principles of self-government as well as the moderation Roosevelt believed had marked America's successful policy in the Philippines. Advocates within the State Department for international trusteeship wholly reflected this Rooseveltian vision. The fullest extant outline of U.S. plans for trusteeship in Indochina, contained in a 10 March 1944 CAC working paper drafted mainly within the Division of Southwest Pacific Affairs, went far beyond Roosevelt's somewhat cryptic vision of how trusteeship would actually work. Its calls for the establishment of an executive, a legislative, and a judicial branch under joint control of the Vietnamese and international trustees; for the creation of a civil service board to oversee training in local and national governmental affairs; for immediate voting rights for indigenous peoples; and for a constitutional convention demonstrate the depth of U.S. faith in the cross-cultural transfer of its political institutions. The twenty-year period of trusteeship before granting Vietnam full independence recommended in the working paper also suggests the persistence of the gradualist Philippine model in shaping State Department policy toward Indochina.[43]

But the combination of a regional commission, a colonial charter, and annual reports that increasingly dominated State Department planning for postwar Indochina also firmly rested on the use of U.S. models to correct slowly the perceived weaknesses in French colonialism and Vietnamese society. Discussions of how a colonial charter and annual reports would serve as conditions for a return of French colonial rule most fully reflected the American vision of political and economic liberalization in Vietnam. State Department planners suggested that France be required to establish local and national representative institutions, to provide for indigenous suffrage, to expand educational and occupational opportunities, to allow tariff autonomy, and to develop local industries. Indicative of the confidence in U.S. models was a proposal by members of the Subcommittee on Territorial Problems to include "freedom of the press from foreign newspapermen" as one of the components of the colonial charter. Committee members argued that if "a good American newspaperman could be sent into . . . these areas with freedom to publish his finding [*sic*] it would probably have a very beneficial effect on the administrative system." The value of annual reports as a tool to monitor French progress in Indochina also appealed to department planners in part because they somewhat self-righteously recalled the salutary "habit" of furnishing the report of the Philippine governor general to the League of Nations.[44]

The differences separating Roosevelt and State Department proponents of trusteeship from advocates of regional commissions, colonial charters, and annual reports were not over the conceptual framework guiding their recommendations but represented variances in some of their assessments of the geopolitical context in which U.S. policy toward Vietnam operated. As their critiques of international trusteeship suggest, many State Department planners were both more willing than Roosevelt to acknowledge the legitimacy of a future French role in Indochina and less confident that U.S. policy aims could be realized over British objections. But even in analyses of the geopolitical dimension of Indochina policy, there were important similarities, particularly regarding judgments of Chinese intentions. Although a few State Department planners raised the possibility of Chinese political ambitions in postwar Southeast Asia, most shared Roosevelt's view that China had no territorial ambitions in Indochina and would work with the United States to effect orderly change in the region.[45]

But if the shared assumptions that joined Roosevelt's advocacy of trusteeship and the deliberations of State Department planners marked the emergence of a fully articulated vision of Vietnam and its future, how the United States would finally choose to affect political, economic, and social change in Vietnam, as well as its ability to do so, would depend on developments in Vietnam and southern China.

Subservient Annamites and Duplicitous Chinese: Wartime American Reporting on Vietnam from Southern China

In a December 1942 cable to Washington, American ambassador to China Clarence E. Gauss reported that he had seen a letter protesting the arrest by Chinese authorities of a Vietnamese nationalist leader. A year would pass before Gauss and his embassy staff realized whom the Chinese had arrested. Gauss relayed a letter in a December 1943 dispatch to the State Department from the Central Committee of the Indochina Section of the International Anti-Aggression Association. The letter asked Gauss for assistance in the "immediate and unconditional" release of "Hu Chih-ming . . . in order that he may lead the members of the Association in activities against the Japanese." The "Annamite" in question, Gauss told the department, "was apparently" the same person whose arrest he had reported the previous December.[46]

Gauss's December 1943 dispatch, the first mention by any U.S. policy maker of Ho Chi Minh, reveals the limitations on American wartime reporting on Vietnam from the field and its dismissive perceptions of Vietnamese nationalism. The embassy staff did make inquires into the reasons for Ho's continued detention, apparently unaware that he had been released by the Chinese some four months earlier. But the name Ho Chi Minh meant nothing to Gauss and the embassy's political officers. Nor did Gauss see the need to reply to the "Annamite organization" or further investigate its activities. The French delegation at Chungking, the primary source of information about the Vietnamese for American officials in southern China, had assured him it "was of little importance," probably one of the "Annamite organizations under the auspices of the Kuomintang," representing nothing "more than an attempt by the Chinese to make a show of their friendly feelings for subject peoples in Asia." [47]

Gauss and the American embassy in Chungking were one of several critical sources of U.S. political reporting on Vietnam from wartime China. While Indochina remained occupied by the Japanese, American diplomatic, military, and intelligence personnel responsible for following developments in Vietnam did so from Chungking or Kunming in southern China. Along with the embassy in Chungking, the most important sources were the consulate in Kunming, the American military command in the China theater, and representatives of the oss, the Office of War Information, the U.S. Naval Group in China, Army Intelligence, and the GBT Group, a nongovernmental intelligence-gathering organization led by Laurence Gordon, who had served as Texaco's agent in French Indochina before the war.[48]

What these Americans learned about Vietnam came largely through conversations with the French and, to a lesser extent, the Chinese. Only after mid-1944 did U.S. personnel in the field begin to encounter the Vietnamese themselves. Both before and after 1944, U.S. operatives filtered their perceptions through the same ensemble of assumptions and suppositions that guided wartime analyses in Washington and the observations of interwar American writers on Vietnam. The particular reliance of these officials on French informants, at the same time that they were strongly critical of French colonial practices, mirrors the interwar deference to the French in apprehending the nature of Vietnamese society and the broader complicity of Americans with French notions of the backward and inferior Vietnamese. But in this case, French views, refracted through the reporting of

U.S. officials in southern China, were also influential in shifting the more benign view held in Washington of Chinese intentions in Vietnam, eventually prompting efforts to reassess U.S. policy toward Indochina.

OSS planning documents for Morale Operations (MO) in Indochina, designed to discredit the Japanese and disseminate pro-American propaganda to the Vietnamese, offer appraisals from the field of Vietnamese society and its perceived receptivity to U.S. models that were typical of the tenor of American reporting from southern China in this period. Because MO planners saw their task as an extension of psychological warfare, they sought to identify what they termed "Annamite mentality." Like interwar U.S. studies of "Annamite psychology," their analyses were informed by the division between Western and Asian thought processes inherent in the belief in racialized cultural hierarchies. The starting point for their work was the assumption that "Annamite reasoning" was fundamentally different from "our own." As one member of the MO planning team for Indochina remarked, "The stimuli from . . . reality can and do produce stereotypes in the minds of the natives quite different from those produced in our own minds."[49]

In the discussions of the Vietnamese role in American psychological warfare strategies by MO planners, the characteristics most commonly ascribed to the "Annamite mind" were almost always negative and condescending. One MO report noted that it was "futile" to attempt to win over the Vietnamese to the Allied cause by "propagandizing" them that a Japanese defeat would ultimately benefit Vietnam, as it was "part of the fundamental psychology of Annamites to be interested only in ventures which promise a quick turnover." Reports that presented the "individual Annamite" as "a rather vain person" and urged MO campaigns to "flatter the pride of the Annamites by telling them that without their co-operation the Japs would not be able to do a thing" were lauded by MO senior planners as raising "an excellent, and well-taken, point."[50]

Another MO planning document suggested that the "subservience" and "mercenary proclivities" inherent in Vietnamese society were barriers to the successful establishment of an indigenous underground organization:

The Annamites have been a subject race for so many years, by the French, and the Chinese before them, that they have no organizing ability or initiative. . . . They are quite incapable of developing an organization of any kind, certainly not an underground. Being suspicious of each other and practicing trickery among themselves, any organization they have ever attempted to create has always broken down from the incapacity of its members to pull together. An underground organization would fall apart before it ever got going. . . . The mercenary proclivities of the Annamites is another hindrance to the development of a successful underground. The Annamites will do anything for money but they cannot be expected to take risks from ideological motives.[51]

Propaganda leaflets were potentially more effective strategies, MO planners argued, because "Annamites love to talk," "enjoy lengthy discourses or lectures," and responded best to "emphatic" or "exaggerated words which qualify force."[52]

These deprecatory images of Vietnamese society also shaped the assertions by MO planners for the OSS that Vietnam would be highly receptive to U.S. direction. "The Annamites are used to obeying," one MO report argued. "Instructions, advice, pleas or recommendations coming from Americans would be effective because they are authoritative. The Annamites recognize authority." Another report suggested that because the "Annamites are very much impressed by physical strength, courage and skill," they particularly enjoyed American films about "cowboys" and "test pilots." The report also stressed that "they are *very much impressed by mechanical perfection*, such as frigidaires, reconditioning units, guns, plants, etc., and for them the word 'American' is synonymous with perfection in all that is modern industry."[53]

The text of a leaflet prepared for distribution in Vietnam illustrates how these assumptions were translated into MO policy:

> Annamites. Prior to 1940 you were able to judge by the movies you saw the physical strength of Americans and the might of their industry. You have been able to judge the perfection of their products once imported into French Indo-China. Their war materials are more perfected yet, their men stronger and better trained than those you saw in the movies. You know the results in Europe of the might of the Allies which will bring in a few weeks the rout of the German armies. You have been able to judge the effectiveness over Indo-China of the few airplanes that we have. So far we have not busied ourselves with the Japanese in Asia, but we are going to take care of them now and bring over thousands of airplanes, men, ammunition. . . . You know then that Japan will be crushed by us. Do not work for Japan. By working for them . . . you delay the moment when you will enjoy the products of the mighty industries of the Allies.[54]

Drawing on their image of the Vietnamese as a simple, almost childlike people, MO planners urged that the leaflet use "brightly colored" pictures presenting "some of the de-classified inventions (American) which might possibly be . . . of use to the Annamites" as well as drawings or photos that depicted "the relative sizes of American soldiers vs Japanese."[55]

Reports from the other branches of the OSS and from the American consul in

Kunming suggest that the perceptions of the Vietnamese that emerge in the OSS MO campaign for Indochina resonated throughout American dispatches from the field on Vietnam in 1943 and 1944. One OSS research and analysis report drew attention to the "backward" nature of indigenous society, commenting that pre-colonial Vietnam was "a strongly localized society founded on the Oriental type of village community. . . . Family organization took care of a great variety of economic, political and other social functions. . . . There was not a compact state of our sort, but rather a system of almost treaty types of obligations between center and periphery."[56]

Reflecting pervasive American assumptions of Vietnamese subservience and susceptibility to external control, reports in early 1944 on Vietnamese nationalism in southern China from Arthur R. Ringwalt, the U.S. consul in Kunming, stressed the central role of the Chinese in organizing and controlling any effective Vietnamese political grouping. In a revealing 21 January dispatch, Ringwalt discussed the "veritable reign of terror" unleashed by what he termed the "Annamite Revolutionary Alliance" against Vietnamese living in and around Kunming who might be sympathetic to the French.[57] The alliance, Ringwalt had argued in previous dispatches, was "sponsored," "subsidized," and "trained" by the Kuomintang. Its current "regime of terror," he reported, had also been launched at the insistence of the Chinese. Nonetheless, Ringwalt argued, these tactics were likely to be successful. "The Annamite population," he suggested, "has fundamentally neither the courage nor the conviction to withstand the reign of terror which has recently been inaugurated." Unable to grant initiative or agency to the Vietnamese as independent political actors, he told the department that "mass defections" from the French to the Chinese-sponsored "Annamite Revolutionary cause may confidently be anticipated."[58]

The character of U.S. diplomatic, military, and intelligence reporting from China also highlights the critical role of the French agents operating in southern China as informants for American assessments, reinforcing the distance that separated U.S. observers from developments in wartime Vietnam and their responsiveness to French perceptions of Vietnam despite their strong critique of French colonial rule. As late as June 1944, William R. Langdon, the new American consul at Kunming, wrote to the Division of Southwest Pacific Affairs to explain that continuing wartime dislocations rendered Indochina largely inaccessible to most outside observers:

> You no doubt get the idea that I am favorably placed for observing Indochina . . . by looking at the map. The map, however, doesn't give the true physical picture. The former railroad to Haiphong comes to a dead end at Pishihchai, 180

kilometers from the Indochina rail head Laokay. Between Pishihchai and the frontier is a rugged belt of country without good roads—even if there were road there would probably be no busses because of the gas and motor transport shortage. So if someone wants to have a physical contact with Indochina, he must ride a wretched military train to Pishihchai and thence hoof it 120 miles to Laokay, eluding the vigilance of the French border patrols and their Japanese supervisors. There is no direct mail or telegraphic communication with Indochina, and the French Consul tells me he hasn't seen an Indochina paper for two years. The frontier is closed tight except for a little protected smuggling. . . . There is secret communication with Indochina. . . . [But] the intelligence one gets in Kunming will be second-hand and colored by the divergent interests in Indochina of each source: the French, their sovereignty and imperial interests, with which the British are in sympathy; the Allied military forces, an exclusively bombing target and military intelligence interest; the Chinese, a half-baked, not clearly defined Chinese or anti-imperialist interest.[59]

Despite the considerable expatriate Vietnamese population in Kunming, Vietnamese contacts were conspicuously absent from Langdon's list of potential intelligence sources. Like OSS MO planners who cautioned against using Vietnamese agents to build an underground organization, most U.S. diplomats and military intelligence personnel in this period would have agreed with Laurence Gordon, the leader of the GBT network, who commented that he did not "bother with natives . . . on the grounds that they would be ineffectual and dangerous."[60]

As Langdon's June 1944 report suggested, American observers in southern China called upon the French or the Chinese for the raw intelligence information that informed their reports to Washington. Without exception, U.S. embassy and consular reporting on Vietnam before mid-1944 was derived from either French or Chinese sources, with Chinese materials often passed on to the Americans by the French. Dispatches from Chungking or Kunming were almost inevitably introduced with phases such as, the "information on which this report is based has been obtained from the French consul at Kunming" or "members of the French military mission." U.S. intelligence reporting on Vietnam also relied predominantly on French and Chinese connections. French military and diplomatic personnel were frequently cited as sources for OSS research and analysis reports on Vietnam. The GBT network that provided intelligence for the OSS on Vietnam utilized French agents only, as did one of the odder U.S. intelligence-gathering operations run by the navy. In a partnership with Chinese intelligence services, Milton E. Miles, the commander of the U.S. Naval Group in China, organized an intelligence mission for Indochina in 1943. Miles selected Robert Meynier, a young

French naval officer, to run the operation with the assistance of his Eurasian wife, whose maternal relations were part of a Vietnamese mandarin family. Despite the reputed connections of his wife, the limited clandestine operation put into place by Meynier was almost completely dominated by French agents.[61]

The growing reliance on French sources for U.S. diplomatic and military intelligence reporting, however, did not prompt a fundamental shift in U.S. attitudes toward French rule in Indochina. American observers continued to remain sharply critical of French colonial practices. Echoing the sentiments of most American diplomats and intelligence personnel in China, one OSS report noted in 1944, "Indo-China has certainly seen very little development during the last seventy years. . . . It has been exploited in many ways contrary to the interests of the native peoples." A State Department dispatch referred to the "French record of unconscionable exploitation of the Annamite people."[62] Nor did a reliance on French intelligence sources produce new U.S. sympathy for the full restoration of French rule. American diplomats and military figures remained extremely wary about the political motivations underlying French eagerness to join the Allied war efforts in Indochina. A proposal in early 1944 by the head of the French military mission in China to drop leaflets promising reforms of French rule in postwar Indochina, for instance, was vigorously opposed by both the State Department and the U.S. military command in China because it would have involved the "political commitment of the American armed forces."[63]

Mutual animosity rather than friendly cooperation marked the Franco-American relationship in southern China. In a November 1943 letter describing a dinner he hosted for two French officers, Laurence Gordon voiced the exasperation of many Americans who worked with the French: "Where the hell do they get the shells? They disgusted me. They sat there, in American made uniforms and ran down the States, or rather talked condescendingly about it."[64] French representatives in southern China also spoke disparagingly of their American counterparts and were highly suspicious of U.S. intentions. In a typical report, the French ambassador in China observed in August 1944 that while American activities in China were "disorganized" and "amateurish," they were conducted in a "dangerous . . . spirit entirely unfavorable to maintaining our position in Indochina."[65]

Despite mutual antagonisms and suspicions, the continuing use of French informants by U.S. diplomatic and military personnel in China betrays the underlying similarities between American assessments of Indochina and prevailing colonial norms. The oft-repeated assertion in reports from China, one that echoes the views of American interwar observers and wartime policy makers in Washington, that French rule had played a central role in Vietnam's political and socioeconomic underdevelopment rested on a sense of French failure to uphold what the

Americans defined as the obligations of a colonizing power. The uncritical absorption of many French views on Indochina in American reports from the field, particularly their unfavorable analyses of indigenous society and Vietnamese nationalism, also suggests that American observers shared a number of French colonial assumptions. Many Americans in China, again like interwar observers and policy makers in Washington, fully accepted the premises of the French and other European colonial powers that the weaknesses of colonized peoples were the result of the inferiority inherent in non-Western societies.

In the late summer of 1944, Americans in southern China did begin to encounter representatives of the Viet Minh, the organizational vehicle through which Ho Chi Minh and the Vietnamese communists would seize power in Vietnam in August and September of 1945. Although Americans began to report more fully on developments within Vietnam without the use of intermediary French informants, their perceptions of the Vietnamese remained extremely unfavorable. A Viet Minh delegation in Kunming met with Americans in August and September 1944 and provided the basis for the first U.S. reports on the existence of the Viet Minh, its organizational structure, and its program for national independence. Their American audience was unimpressed with what it learned. William Powell, the representative of the Office of War Information in Kunming, reported on several meetings with the Viet Minh and called them "rather naive politically" and "not too well organized." Commenting on a history of Vietnamese anticolonialism that representatives of the Viet Minh had given him along with appeals for U.S. assistance, Powell patronizingly remarked,

> The whole document . . . certainly is a touching appeal. Any coherent appeal from an oppressed people who wish to rule themselves is touching. However, from conversations with these leaders themselves and with well-informed foreigners here, I think there is little doubt but what they are not ready for complete independence. They've had little experience in modern government . . . and probably will require quite a bit of tutelage before they can completely run their country themselves in as responsible a manner as a modern post-war government must be run.

The reactions of the OSS to its meetings with the Viet Minh were similar, suggesting "while they might be filled with zeal and enthusiasm for the Cause, they were more or less amateurs and did not have the qualities of leadership which a movement of this kind if it is to succeed . . . would require." The OSS was also skeptical of the Viet Minh's claim that its active membership exceeded 200,000 in northern Vietnam. Relying on French sources, they claimed the numbers were much smaller. And while OSS observers were the only Americans to note the presence of the ICP among the member organizations of the Viet Minh, they drew no particular conclusion other than the brief comment that the communists "no longer received aid from the Russians."[66]

William Langdon was even more critical of the Vietnamese, dismissing the Viet Minh as a group of "no real importance in the Indochina question" after a 9 September 1944 meeting with several representatives of the organization. Langdon reported to Washington that they "lacked the spirit and aggressiveness one would expect of revolutionaries" and "did not impress [him] as having proper knowledge of the world or a sufficient grasp of the international situation." They were not, he argued, "far enough advanced politically to maintain a stable society or familiar enough with administration, jurisprudence, science, industry, finance, communications operation, and commerce to run a state on modern lines." Ironically, Langdon's assessment of the Viet Minh mirrored aspects of his own quite critical summary of prevailing French sentiment toward the Vietnamese. In a subsequent cable, he observed that the French "dismissed . . . the attitude of the Annamite people . . . with a wave of the hand saying the Annamites did not count and were no factor whatsoever in the political situation as they were all corrupt, backward, incompetent and unreliable."[67]

The French were also instrumental in shifting American attitudes toward Chinese intentions in Indochina. Initially, U.S. observers in China perceived Chinese intentions in Indochina with the same benign attitude that characterized Franklin Roosevelt's views in Washington. In several dispatches to Washington from Chungking in 1942, American ambassador Gauss reported that "the Chinese had a very positive interest in the future status of Indo-China" and downplayed the possibility of "Chinese imperialism . . . in the Far East."[68] The French, however, perceived the Chinese as a significant threat to their aims of regaining Indochina. In an August 1944 memorandum, General Zinovi Pechkoff, the Russian-born French ambassador in China, summarized the fears that had informed French perceptions of China since the outbreak of the Pacific war. "The Chinese government . . . has not recognized the legitimacy of French rule" in Indochina, he contended. At the urging of the United States, it had "declared itself favorable to independence for the peoples of Southeast Asia." Even more alarming, the French ambassador suggested, were Chinese professions of support for Indochinese independence that masked their desire for indirect or direct control of the region. By "supporting and funding Annamite revolutionary groups in China," Pechkoff argued, the Chinese hoped to have a "predominant political influence" in any postwar independent Vietnamese state. He also pointed to fears of the "territorial ambitions" of Chinese provincial military leaders, suggesting that planning continued for a Chinese invasion of northern Vietnam, or what he termed "the pillage of Tonkin." Even if the central government opposed these plans, he suggested, it was powerless to stop them, as it had ceded "almost complete autonomy to the provinces."[69]

Certain that the Americans underestimated the dangers China posed to Indochina, French diplomatic and military missions took every opportunity to present the Chinese in a duplicitous light to the U.S. observers in southern China. In meetings with American officials in 1943 and 1944, the French relayed information they hoped would demonstrate Chinese domination of Vietnamese nationalist groups in China and Chinese plans for the invasion of Indochina aimed at long-term hegemony in the region. French reports initially concentrated on the organization and funding of Vietnamese nationalist groups by the Chinese, but they tended to reinforce U.S. perceptions of Vietnamese susceptibility to external control rather than raise alarms about Chinese intentions.[70]

French reports in December 1943 of a possible Chinese invasion to permanently occupy portions of Vietnam had a much greater impact on U.S. observers. Reporting from Kunming, Arthur Ringwalt relayed the concerns of the French consul that China planned to annex northern Vietnam and "set up in the rest of Indochina a regime nominally by and for Annamese but actually in the interests of and dominated by the Chinese." Ringwalt argued there was "substantial evidence to substantiate the French belief" and called Chinese plans "opportunistic." The response to Chinese plans from the American embassy in Chungking was extremely critical, marking a significant shift in U.S. field reporting on Chinese intentions in Vietnam:

> Chinese policy with regard to Indochina is ill-defined. It appears to rest, as do so many other Chinese policy questions, on a shifting basis of political opportunism. . . . One of the principal aims of present Chinese policy is . . . the recovery of "lost territories," and Chinese national opinion (insofar as it exists in China) is therefore in an expansionist mood. It may accordingly be expected that action based on the premise that such areas as Indochina . . . are "lost territories" might be considered if thought expedient by the leaders of the Kuomintang and the Government. In other words, judging from the present temper of China, it is probable that no opportunity will be lost to establish and increase Chinese influence and control in Indochina to as great a degree as circumstances render practicable.[71]

This more critical tone in U.S. assessments of Chinese policy began to characterize diplomatic and intelligence reporting in 1944 as the French continued to pass along evidence of what they perceived as Chinese duplicity. William Langdon, whose first reports from the consulate in Kunming suggested that the Chinese had "no concrete wishes for Indochina after the war," grew increasingly suspicious of China's intentions. Reporting on the minutes of a meeting between Vietnamese nationalists and a Chinese military leader he had received from the French consulate, Langdon drew attention to Chinese insistence that the Vietnamese should not seek out "the support of any 'third power' (vis., the United States)" as evidence of "Chinese political ambitions."[72]

In the summer of 1944, the French provided oss and Office of War Information representatives with a history of Indochina prepared by a Chinese general affiliated with the secret police, which further increased U.S. suspicions. It argued that Vietnam was historically, geographically, and culturally a part of China and should, for its own benefit, again become part of China. An oss summary and comment on the book, noting the author's reliance on statements of Chiang Kai-shek to support his argument, suggested it "may reflect in some degree the Chinese official attitude." William Powell observed, "We cannot assume that this is anything approaching an official view, but I do think he expressed the true sentiments of many Chinese leaders. . . . It is no secret that the Chinese have definite territorial designs upon at least a portion of Indo-China (Tonkin) and entertain dreams of at least exercising the dominant foreign influence throughout the entire country. . . . The French . . . feel this way, which accounts for much of their . . . fear of post-war China."[73]

Broader U.S. perceptions of China were of course shifting in 1944 without any influence from the French. The assessments of Chiang Kai-shek's government by the American embassy in Chungking were increasingly negative, reporting on Chinese military weakness, rampant corruption and inefficiency in the Chinese government, and popular discontent with the Kuomintang. Aware of the rise and vitality of the Chinese communists, embassy reports advised Washington to rethink its long-term commitment to Chiang.[74] Given prevailing U.S. attitudes in the field, French efforts to influence American perceptions of Chinese intentions fell on receptive ears. But in almost every case, it was evidence provided by the French that pushed U.S. observers in southern China to translate their broader suspicions of the Chinese into more specific concerns about Chinese intentions in Indochina.

The changing sense of Chinese policies toward Vietnam by American diplomats in the field also had a subtle impact on their policy recommendations. In the summer of 1944, William Langdon began to advocate a conditional restoration of French rule in Indochina. The tenor of Langdon's recommendations fully reflected prevailing American assumptions of French colonial failure, Vietnamese inadequacies, and the promise of U.S. models. But his evaluations of the mechanisms by which to implement the American vision of postwar Vietnam reflected heightened suspicions of Chinese intentions. While Langdon reiterated the familiar American view that "the Annamites are not yet materially or politically prepared for independence," he added, in a clear reference to Chinese political ambitions, that an independent Vietnamese state would be incapable of "resisting aggression from neighbors." He also lauded trusteeship as "ideal at this stage for Indochina" but questioned if it was "within the realm of practical politics," as "it would be most certain to be opposed and obstructed" not only by France and Great Britain but by China as well. The "only logical proposition for Indo-China," Langdon argued, was a period of tutelage under continued French rule. Reflecting the confidence of the United States in its abilities to reform both French colonialism and Vietnamese society, Langdon suggested the "commanding position" of the United States ought to make it possible to impose "certain conditions" on the French "to obtain for the Annamites some substantial political rights." Langdon presented his recommendations with considerable urgency, suggesting Chinese "political designs on Indo-China" were "likely at any moment to require important political judgments on our part."[75]

The American embassy in Chungking shared Langdon's concerns. Ambassador Gauss expressed his alarm over Chinese intentions in Indochina and its implications for U.S. policy in a late July 1944 dispatch to Washington:

> There have not been lacking in the past year indications that Chinese Government is toying with hope that developments in respect to Indo-China will be such that China can gain political ascendancy of at least northern part of Indo-China after Japs are driven out. Lack of a clear-cut American policy in regard to Indo-China has undoubtedly encouraged Chinese in this hope. . . . Although we must continue to work for a strong and unified China, there is little question that this country will be one of the big four in name only, that its military and political weakness will but add to our burden and responsibility and that it can be expected to take every possible advantage of our own altruism to further Chinese economic and political interests in adjacent areas such as Indo-China.

The time had come, Gauss told Washington, to "formulate a clear and definite policy" for Indochina.[76]

Trusteeship's Denouement

Warnings from American observers in southern China of possible aggressive Chinese intentions were not the only evidence U.S. policy makers received in the summer and fall of 1944 that geopolitical realities in Indochina were shifting in ways that could challenge the mechanisms through which they hoped to advance their vision of postcolonial Vietnam. In August the State Department in Washington received a British aide-mémoire asking for U.S. approval of an enhanced French role in future military operations in Indochina, including the establishment of a French military mission under SEAC in India and the development of a French expeditionary force for use in the liberation of Indochina. The British voiced their full support for these proposals.[77] In an 8 September memorandum to Roosevelt, Secretary of State Cordell Hull presented the aide-mémoire as evidence that "British policy has swung behind restoration of French authority" in Indochina, suggesting that the French proposal came at "British instigation." Noting that Indochina was not at present in the SEAC theater, Hull argued that British support for the French was aimed at extending the boundaries of the SEAC command to strengthen their position in regaining their colonies in Southeast Asia and Hong Kong. Hull also expressed concerns over Chinese intentions in Indochina, telling the president that there were "persistent reports that the Chinese hope for political ascendancy in northern Indochina."[78]

Throughout the fall of 1944, Washington continued to receive reports outlining British efforts to support French military conquest of Indochina. In a 10 October memorandum to Roosevelt, Hull commented on the imminent arrival of the French military mission at SEAC in Ceylon and British promises of "full collaboration." Undersecretary of State Stettinius passed on a dispatch to Roosevelt in early November from the American consul in Colombo detailing further incidents of Franco-British collusion. The dispatch included a portion of an OSS report that argued, "There can be little doubt that the British and Dutch have arrived at an agreement with regard to the future of Southeast Asia, and now it would appear that the French are being brought into the picture. It would appear that the strategy of the British, Dutch and French is to win back and control Southeast Asia, making the fullest use possible of American resources, but foreclosing the Americans from any voice in policy matters."[79] Later that month Patrick Hurley, the new American ambassador to China, cabled FDR to confirm OSS reports that the British, French, and Dutch had joined forces at SEAC. "Bound together by a vital, common interest namely repossession of their colonial empires," Hurley argued, you may expect them to "disregard the Atlantic Charter and all promises made to other nations by which they obtained support in the earlier stages of the war."[80]

But if assessments of British, French, and Chinese policies represented a new awareness of the potential geopolitical obstacles to the implementation of trusteeship, U.S. policy at the end of 1944 remained bounded by the broader prism through which Americans had viewed wartime developments in Indochina. In his

8 September memorandum to Roosevelt in response to the British aide-mémoire, Hull argued that American policy could thwart French, British, and Chinese ambitions in Indochina. He admitted trusteeship would be "difficult to insist upon . . . if similar declarations could not be secured" from the other colonial powers in Southeast Asia. Reflecting the preferences of State Department planners for the conditional restoration of French rule in Vietnam, he advocated "dramatic and concerted announcements" of a specific timetable for independence and the steps to be taken "to develop native capacity for self-rule."[81]

Although Roosevelt did not respond directly to Hull's proposal, in a series of notes commenting on British and French machinations at SEAC he reiterated his belief that the United States should play a central role in postwar Vietnam's future. But unlike the British, who continued to press Roosevelt for approval of their aide-mémoire throughout the fall of 1944, Roosevelt attached no particular urgency to removing the ambiguities in Allied military policy affecting Indochina. He told Edward Stettinius on 1 January 1945, "I still do not want to get mixed up in any Indochina decision. It is a matter for post-war. By the same token, I do not want to [get] mixed up in any military effort toward the liberation of Indochina from the Japanese. You can tell Halifax that I made this very clear to Mr. Churchill. From both the military and civil point of view, action at this time is premature."[82] At the Yalta conference in February 1945, Roosevelt renewed his advocacy of trusteeship in conversations with Stalin. Emphasizing his unwillingness to assist French military objectives in Vietnam, Roosevelt told Stalin that Charles de Gaulle had recently asked him for ships to transport French forces to Indochina. He added, somewhat impishly, "that up to the present he had been unable to find the ships."[83]

Back in Washington the following month, Roosevelt initiated an extended conversation with Charles Taussig, an influential adviser on colonial issues, that suggested British and French pressures to revise Allied military strategy in Indochina had begun to affect FDR's trusteeship plans. Taussig asked the president "if he had changed his ideas on French Indo-China." Roosevelt initially said no, but, Taussig continued, "the President hesitated a moment and then said—well if we can get the proper pledge from France to assume for herself the obligations of a trustee, then I would agree to France retaining these colonies with the proviso that independence was the ultimate goal. I asked the President if he would settle for self-government. He said no. I asked him if he would settle for dominion status. He said no—it must be independence."[84] Roosevelt's remarks were a significant departure from his oft-stated opposition to France's return to Vietnam, but they did not so much represent his abandonment of trusteeship or his larger vision of postcolonial Vietnam as a shifting perception of the geopolitical forces acting on Indochina and the necessity to adjust the mechanisms by which to implement trusteeship. Moreover, Roosevelt continued to resist British and French efforts to play a larger military role in Indochina.

Two days after his conversation with Taussig, Roosevelt received a cable from British prime minister Winston Churchill asking that SEAC commander Louis Mountbatten be allowed to undertake operations in Vietnam. Churchill's cable reflected a long-standing British aim to extend its military efforts into territories such as Indochina and Hong Kong that had been designated a part of the American-dominated China theater. The British position had drawn objections first from Chiang Kai-shek and, later, from Roosevelt and U.S. military commanders in China. Throughout late 1944, Roosevelt resisted British proposals to shift the boundaries of SEAC, viewing British intentions as a subterfuge to liberate Indochina themselves and return it to French sovereignty. By March 1945, relations between Admiral Mountbatten and Albert Wedemeyer, the American commander in the China theater, had sharply deteriorated as Wedemeyer forcefully represented Roosevelt's opposition to British operations in Vietnam.[85]

Churchill's cable of 17 March 1945 to Roosevelt, though couched in terms of improving military coordination and relations between Mountbatten and Wedemeyer, was a renewed effort to exert British control in Vietnam and bolster the French position. Roosevelt's response, insisting that all operations in Indochina remain within the sphere of the American-dominated China theater, gave little encouragement to British designs, suggesting that FDR remained hopeful of molding the region's geopolitical forces in a manner favorable to implementing his vision of postwar Vietnam. Churchill tried again in an 11 April cable that more explicitly urged U.S. support for the French position in Indochina.[86] Roosevelt never responded. He died the following day.

With Roosevelt's death came the end of U.S. advocacy of international trusteeship in Vietnam. When Harry Truman moved into the Oval Office at the White House, he replaced the paintings by Frederick Remington that had hung above the fireplace during Roosevelt's tenure with portraits of Simon Bolívar, Miguel Hidalgo y Costilla, and José de San Martín, whom Truman had long admired as eighteenth-century liberators of Latin America from Spanish colonial control.[87] In the spring and summer of 1945, however, Truman's respect for Latin American anticolonialism did not extend to the promotion of independence for colonial Vietnam. Deliberately kept away from such critical wartime diplomatic and military developments as the Manhattan Project while he was vice-president, Truman undoubtedly knew little, if anything, of American postwar planning on Vietnam. Confronted by a host of more pressing issues, Truman only nominally oversaw two decisions that severely limited U.S. ability to influence postwar developments in

Vietnam. In May, Truman offered no opposition to State Department assurances to France that the United States recognized French sovereignty over Indochina. In July, at the Potsdam Conference, Truman endorsed the expansion of SEAC's borders. Northern Vietnam remained in the China theater, but Vietnamese territory south of the sixteenth parallel became the responsibility of SEAC. By early September, French troops had joined British forces in occupying Saigon and accepting the surrender of Japan.[88]

Despite the U.S. decision to move away from trusteeship, a number of contemporary French and British observers in the spring and summer of 1945 viewed U.S. support for the French return to Indochina with caution, remaining uneasy about future American intentions in Vietnam.[89] While the European powers were right to be skeptical of a fundamental transformation in U.S. thinking about Vietnam, their lingering suspicions should not obscure the critical commonalities that united American and European perceptions and policies toward Vietnam. Much of the existing scholarship on trusteeship minimizes or ignores those similarities. Along with viewing trusteeship as Roosevelt's personal crusade, these works often ruefully render it as a lost opportunity for acting on U.S. historical identification with the principle of self-determination.[90] The few departures from this approach, which depict trusteeship as an example of a peculiarly American manifestation of empire, also remain bounded by this exceptionalist explanatory framework for wartime U.S. policy in Vietnam.[91] But whether mourning declension from U.S. anticolonial ideals or recovering a suppressed empire with uniquely American values and forms, these works emphasize essential U.S. differences from European colonial norms and the historical novelty of an American approach to colonialism. Like the policy makers they analyze, they do not interrogate critically the contradictions in U.S. self-conceptions as an anticolonial power. Nor do they explore the revealing ways in which American discourse on colonized peoples closely followed that of most European colonial powers.

The central place of time in American thinking about trusteeship for Vietnam is particularly revealing of the shared Euro-American norms out of which U.S. policy arose as well as how it would complicate relations with the French and the Vietnamese after 1945. Whether posed as the almost half-century of U.S. colonial rule in the Philippines or the quarter-century of trusteeship envisioned for Vietnam, the virtually unanimous perception among wartime American policy makers of the necessity for an exceedingly long period of tutelage in U.S. political, social, and cultural models signaled an underlying certainty of the vast chasm that separated the stasis of backward Vietnam from the dynamism of the United States.

The conscious ordering of time in plans for trusteeship in Vietnam—premised on a gradual, unilinear, and progressive path to human development—sought to provide a temporal framework to guide the Vietnamese toward political and social change in the American image. By attempting to engineer the processes of change in Vietnam through the manipulation of the meaning and passage of time, trusteeship represented a variation, rather than a sharp departure, from the hierarchical conceptions of racial difference and the exercise of power at the heart of European colonialism.[92] In this sense, European suspicions about U.S. intentions in Vietnam might be seen not so much as fears that a crusading U.S. anticolonialism sought to overturn the colonial order but as a more nationalistic reaction against the emergence of a powerful rival who sought to challenge Europeans' own efforts to control colonial time and space.[93]

Significantly, however, the temporal order embedded in trusteeship was also an effort to retard the passage of time, indicating the doubts that lurked beneath the supreme confidence through which Americans and Europeans appeared to approach the colonial project. The compression of time was an essential element in the dual character of the conceptions of modernity that animated Euro-American understandings of their own societies and those they encountered in the colonized world. On one hand, the embrace of modernity reflected assurance of the universal and enduring virtues of contemporary Western society. But the telescoping of time, an inevitable result of the competitive and speculative rhythms of capitalism that accompanied the rise of modernity, also produced an overwhelming fear of fragmentation, transience, and chaotic change.[94] This prevailing sensibility was reinforced for both American and European policy makers of the World War II era, whose historical experience was shaped by two world wars, the rise of fascism, and the worldwide economic depression. For Americans, these dislocations had a domestic dimension, too, in interwar concerns about immigration and the orderly arrangement of the internal spaces of the nation.

The palpable doubts and fears over what the uncontrolled acceleration of time could produce framed the temporal order that informed U.S. plans for trusteeship in Vietnam. The dislocations of World War II quickened the pace toward decolonization in Vietnam and much of the colonized world, producing a sense among both the colonizers and the colonized of time rushing forward. For both the French and the Americans, the quickening pace of change was viewed with alarm. If the French would have preferred to arrest completely the temporal movement toward decolonization, U.S. plans for trusteeship, with their twenty-year timetable for Vietnamese independence, were also profoundly conservative. Emblematic of the fears upon which the faith in modernity rested, trusteeship aimed to retard the passage of time in order to wrest control over temporality and re-assert the centrality of rational, orderly, and gradually progressive paths to Vietnam's future development.[95]

With the movement away from trusteeship, and the related notions of colonial commissions and charters, Americans abandoned their efforts to manipulate so closely the processes of change in Vietnam. Moreover, the accelerating movement toward decolonization in Vietnam made an extended period of tutelage in advance of independence moot. Ironically, the Vietnamese revolutionaries who joined Ho Chi Minh in proclaiming Vietnam free of French colonial rule in September 1945 enthusiastically embraced the modernist conception of quickening time. But in the aftermath of World War II, innate suspicions of the Vietnamese capacity for self-government and the claims of the superiority of U.S. models of political, economic, and social development that had framed the broader American vision of postcolonial Vietnam persisted. They would fundamentally shape the policy of the Truman administration toward Vietnam and set the United States on a course that sparked bitter tensions with both Vietnam and its wartime European allies.

SELF-EVIDENT TRUTHS?
Vietnam, America, and the August Revolution of 1945

On 2 September 1945, a clear and hot Sunday afternoon, Ho Chi Minh mounted a wooden podium in Hanoi's central Ba Dinh Square. Before an enthusiastic crowd of almost 400,000 supporters, he proclaimed Vietnam free of French colonial rule, marking the successful culmination of the August Revolution, which brought to power the leadership of the first postcolonial independent Vietnamese state, the Democratic Republic of Vietnam. Ho began his speech in this way: "All men are created equal. They are endowed by their Creator with certain inalienable rights; among these are life, liberty, and the pursuit of happiness. This immortal statement was made in the Declaration of Independence of the United States of America in 1776. In a broader sense it means: All peoples on earth are equal from birth, all peoples have a right to live, be happy and be free."[1]

The Jeffersonian echoes in Ho Chi Minh's declaration of Vietnamese independence were not the only symbolic representations of the United States present during independence day celebrations in Hanoi. As Ho delivered his address, the attention of his audience was at one point diverted by several low-flying American P-38 planes that suddenly dipped down over the crowd. Their presence above Hanoi was purely accidental and their decision to fly lower was probably the result of the pilots' curiosity about events on the ground. But many people in the crowd took the planes and their movement downward as a prearranged U.S. salute to Vietnam's independence, an interpretation the Vietnamese leadership apparently did little to discourage.[2]

After Ho had completed his address, Vo Nguyen Giap, the minister of the interior in the new Vietnamese government, spoke to the crowd of the principles animating the government's plans for the development of the nation and the conduct of its diplomacy. Referring to the United States, Giap said, "America . . . is a democratic country which has no territorial ambitions. Yet it bore the greatest burdens in defeating our enemy, fascist Japan. Therefore we consider America a good friend." With the speeches completed, Ho, Giap, and the other members of the cabinet walked across the street to what had been the residence of the French *gouverneur-général* in Indochina. From the grand stairway of this imposing structure, they watched and waved to a parade of well-wishers. Among them were groups of men and women carrying placards with a photograph of Harry Truman and a caption that read, "Vietnam Honors Truman" as well as banners that proclaimed, "America Supports Vietnamese Independence." [3]

The central symbolic place of an imagined America at the independence day ceremonies in Hanoi rested upon the legacies of the radical anticolonial discourse of the 1920s and 1930s in which the United States had played such an important role. As the Vietnamese revolutionaries around Ho Chi Minh worked throughout World War II to overthrow the French colonial order in what would culminate in the August Revolution of 1945, they constructed a vision of postcolonial Vietnam that drew on this supple and fluid prewar discourse that had simultaneously valorized the revolutionary heroism and voluntarism that young radicals favorably equated with the United States, embraced the ideals of socialist internationalism, and looked beyond Stalin and the Soviet Union to Chinese communist thought and practice to indigenize Marxism-Leninism. These varying strands of interwar thought and perceptual experience infused the voluntarist vision of revolutionary nationalism through which Vietnamese revolutionaries sought to gain mass support at home and diplomatic assistance abroad for Vietnamese independence. But with the rise of the United States during World War II to a hegemonic place in shaping the contours of postwar international order, America was no longer solely an imagined actor in Vietnamese anticolonial politics but one Vietnamese revolutionaries believed could powerfully influence their postcolonial future. The subtle interplay between the extrinsic demands of a rapidly shifting wartime global environment and the symbolic vocabularies of indigenous anticolonial discourse framed the wartime quest for power by Vietnamese revolutionaries, and the place of the United States in it. [4]

The imagined postcolonial Vietnam of U.S. wartime policy makers also became considerably more real during the August Revolution and its aftermath in ways Americans had not fully anticipated. With the Vietnamese presenting their independence as a virtual fait accompli, and with increasing efforts by the French to reclaim their colonial control of Indochina, the gradualist vision of sustained tutelage through trusteeship or colonial commissions no longer held much meaning in the Vietnamese context. The August Revolution also brought the first sustained contact between U.S. officials, generally intelligence and military operatives who had been sent to Vietnam to oversee the Japanese surrender, and Vietnamese revolutionaries. But as Americans in both Vietnam and Washington apprehended the transformative events of the August Revolution and the conflicting demands of the Vietnamese and the French that arose in its wake, their responses remained bounded by the hierarchical notions of Vietnamese incapacities for self-government and claims of the superiority of U.S. models for postwar Vietnamese development that had become almost axiomatic to U.S. conceptions of postcolonial Vietnam.

More Friends and Fewer Enemies:
Wartime Visions of Vietnamese Independence

The leadership of the ICP Central Committee gathered at Pac Bo in the mountainous northern Vietnamese province of Cao Bang near the Chinese border for the party's Eighth Plenum on 10 May 1941. For those meeting at Pac Bo, the German defeat of France in June 1940 and the Japanese military occupation of Indochina offered new opportunities for advancing the revolutionary anticolonial agenda.[5] In the resolutions adopted at the Pac Bo Plenum, the party began to articulate the vision of voluntarist revolutionary nationalism that would bring it to power at the end of World War II and shape the dynamics of its wartime diplomacy with the United States.

Preparations for the plenum reunited the former leadership of the 1920s-era Revolutionary Youth League, including Ho Chi Minh, Vo Nguyen Giap, Pham Van Dong, and Truong Chinh, who would lead the party throughout the wartime period and guide its victory in the August Revolution.[6] The plenum brought the return of Ho Chi Minh to Vietnam after an absence of almost ten years. Although officially attending the plenum simply as a Comintern representative, Ho dominated the proceedings as he had the party's preparatory activities in southern China since his arrival in Yunnan in 1940. Truong Chinh also played a major role at the conference. Vo Nguyen Giap and Pham Van Dong, although not present at the conference itself, joined Ho in Yunnan in 1940 and were active in the preparations leading to the plenum. Significantly, the internationalist leadership of the 1930s, particularly from southern Vietnam, was not present at the conference as the French had executed and imprisoned many of them in harsh campaigns of repression in 1939 and 1940.[7] Most of the other members of the party's Central Committee present at Pac Bo were, like Truong Chinh, Pham Van Dong, and Vo

Nguyen Giap, northern and central Vietnamese whose formative political experiences had been in Vietnam or southern China rather than Moscow or France.

The plenum also marked the resurgence of the revolutionary heroism and voluntarism that had animated interwar radical anticolonial discourse as well as its developing appreciation for Maoist thought. Focusing on national liberation rather than the strategy of class struggle that had characterized the party's approach through much of the 1930s, the plenum's chief resolution, titled "New Policies of the Party," argued, "The Indochinese revolution is at present no longer a bourgeois-democratic revolution that solves the anti-imperialist and agrarian problems. Rather, it is a revolution to solve only one urgent problem, national liberation. The Indochinese revolution during this period is, therefore, a revolution of national liberation."[8] The plenum's focus on national liberation and the absence of the internationalist faction of the party at Pac Bo did not mean that the ICP and its leadership had abandoned Marxism-Leninism. But the new direction of the ICP did reflect the predominant influence of Ho Chi Minh and the Youth League leadership in shifting party objectives to address the changed circumstances in Vietnam after the outbreak of World War II.

A short poem titled "Majestic Pac Bo," composed by Ho Chi Minh several months before the Eighth Plenum, illustrates the fusion of revolutionary nationalism and internationalism that came to dominate wartime revolutionary discourse and strategy:

> Distant mountains, distant water
> Each immense they must be named anew
> This stream Lenin, that mountain Marx
> Two sides united into one country (son ha).[9]

The imagery of Ho's poem, particularly the identification of mountains and water with Marx and Lenin, consciously linked radical articulations of Vietnamese patriotism to a new internationalist order. Mountains and water were commonly used in elite and popular cultural texts as symbols to express the mythological origins of Vietnamese identity. In the best-known story of the origins of Vietnamese civilization, a prince of the sea, Lac Long Quan, and a princess of the mountains, Au Co, are regarded as the progenitors of the Vietnamese race.[10] By equating Marx with mountains and Lenin with water, Ho skillfully linked the leaders of modern internationalism with these mythical Vietnamese cultural heroes. Just as marriage between Lac Long Quan and Au Co was believed to have given birth to the dynasty that first ruled Vietnam in the third millennium B.C., Ho's poem suggested that the uniting of Marxist mountains and Leninist water would produce the new

Vietnamese nation. Ho's choice of language further emphasized these parallels. By using the noun *son ha*, literally translated as "mountains and rivers" but commonly used in classical writings to mean land or country, Ho denoted both the nationalist and the internationalist components of the Viet Minh vision.[11]

These imaginative ties between nationalism and internationalism received more concrete expression in the resolutions of the Eighth Plenum. Party leaders at Pac Bo took great care to emphasize that the renewed focus on national independence in no way marked the abandonment of the party's commitment to social revolution: "To put aside the bourgeois-democratic revolution and put forward the national liberation revolution does not mean that the Indochinese proletariat neglects the agrarian tasks, and it also does not mean that it takes a step backward. It means only to take a shorter step in order to take a longer one."[12] The realization of Vietnamese independence through broad class and international alliances, the plenum resolutions continued, was a necessary precursor to the subsequent pursuit of a socialist revolution: "At the moment if we are not able to resolve the questions of national liberation and do not demand independence and freedom for the entire nation, then not only will all our peoples continue to live like cattle; we will not be able to demand what is in the class interest for ten thousand years."[13]

If the radical discourse of the 1920s played a more critical role in party deliberations at Pac Bo than the Stalinist models of the 1930s, the internationalist dimension of the wartime strategy of revolutionary nationalism also underscored the continuing influence of Chinese communist political and military thought. One of the plenum's most important resolutions called for "a new democratic Vietnam following the spirit of the new democracy."[14] The term "new democracy" first emerged in Mao Tse-tung's published writings in *The Chinese Revolution and the Chinese Communist Party* (December 1939) and *On the New Democracy* (January 1940) as the Chinese communists struggled to build a united front with the Kuomintang against the Japanese.[15] In these works, part of what Mao called the "sinification of Marxism" that aimed to transform the nature of Marxism by drawing on Chinese historical experience, he described three types of state systems: republics under bourgeois dictatorships, republics under the dictatorship of the proletariat, and republics under the joint dictatorship of several revolutionary classes. The latter, Mao suggested, was the preferred form "in the revolutions of the colonial and semi-colonial countries," as it promoted cooperation from a broad spectrum of political groups outside the Communist Party itself. Within the context of Sino-Japanese war, Mao argued that membership in the new democracy should be based on attitudes toward the Japanese presence in China. Those who resisted Japanese aggression were to be regarded as members of the revolutionary classes and should enjoy democratic rights, while individuals and classes who wavered in their resistance or whose interests allied them with Japanese imperialism were to be subjected to the dictatorship.[16]

The explicit use of the ideas surrounding the new democracy in framing the party resolutions at the Pac Bo Plenum suggests that radical interest since the late 1930s in Chinese communist responses to the outbreak of the Sino-Japanese war continued to play a significant role in Vietnamese efforts to develop the notion of revolutionary nationalism within an internationalist idiom. Persisting interest among the ICP leadership in Maoist models may have resulted from several factors. The plenum took place during the period of the Nazi-Soviet pact, when guidance from the Soviet Union, never extensive during the course of World War II, was at a minimum. Along with memories of the failure of the Stalinist revolutionary line in Vietnam during the early 1930s, Soviet disinterest may have pushed party leaders to look for alternative internationalist models to guide the Vietnamese revolutionary struggle. Moreover, the similarities of the Chinese and Vietnamese wartime situations would have increased the attraction of Mao's approach to revolution. If his articulation of the new democracy was less a theoretical innovation than a restatement of Leninist discussions of a bourgeois revolution led by a proletariat vanguard, well-known to Ho and the ICP leadership, Mao's willingness to draw upon indigenous experiences to reshape apprehensions of internationalism may have emboldened Vietnamese radicals to do the same.

While Chinese models were perhaps most important in shaping the guerrilla warfare strategy of the army that the party sought to establish in the aftermath of the Pac Bo Plenum,[17] they also played a role in the creation of the Independence League of Vietnam (Viet Nam Doc Lap Dong Minh), more commonly known as the Viet Minh. Central to realizing the vision of revolutionary nationalism, the Viet Minh was established at the May 1941 plenum to unite all "revolutionary forces," regardless of class background, that opposed Vietnam's principal wartime enemies: the "counterrevolutionary forces" of "French oppressors" and the "Japanese fascists" and their "lackeys." Potential members of the Viet Minh included "patriotic workers, farmers, rich peasants, landlords and local bourgeoisie" who would be organized into a series of interlocking national salvation associations (cuu quoc hoi) to represent various professional, ethnic, and religious groups in society. They were to form the basis of Vietnam's new democracy.[18]

With the establishment of the Viet Minh came a renewed emphasis on indigenous traditions of patriotic resistance, particularly efforts to draw upon the revolutionary heroism that had animated expressions of Vietnamese anticolonialism. In ways that echoed the voluntarist celebration of American and European figures as guides to revolutionary action in the radical discourse of the 1920s, the manifesto of the Viet Minh made particular reference to such patriotic heroes as the Trung Sisters, Ngo Quyen, and Le Loi, who had led celebrated efforts to resist Chinese occupation, as well as the leaders of the Aid the King movement in the 1880s against the French. Even more explicit was Ho Chi Minh's *History of Our Country* [*Lich Su Nuoc Ta*],[19] written and disseminated in early 1942, which consciously drew on reform generation leader Phan Boi Chau's well-known verse histories of Vietnamese patriotic leaders to call forth a renewed spirit of voluntarism. Ho employed similar rhetorical devices as the editor of *Vietnam Independence* [*Viet Nam Doc Lap*], a handwritten, two-page weekly newspaper established after the Pac Bo Plenum to win support for the Viet Minh, that was widely circulated in northern Vietnam.[20]

The resurgence of the radical voluntarist visions of the 1920s in the resolutions of the Pac Bo Plenum and the formation of the Viet Minh also had important implications for the broader principles that would govern the ICP's wartime diplomacy. Party leaders viewed domestic policies and diplomacy as interconnected. If wartime Vietnam posed opportunities for the realization of national independence, party leaders recognized that their international isolation and continuing French colonial control under Japanese auspices presented difficult obstacles for the fledgling Viet Minh vision. Calling for the adoption of a policy of "more friends and fewer enemies" (*them ban bot thu*), the plenum's resolutions argued that the renewed emphasis on national rather than social revolution would encourage necessary and valuable external alliances: "If at the present we promote the slogan of overthrowing the landlords and redistributing the land to the tillers not only will we throw away an Allied force, a supporting force in the revolution to overthrow the French and the Japanese, but what is more, that force will go over to the side of our enemy and become the rear guard of our enemy."[21]

The inclusive and flexible organizing principles of the Viet Minh were also brought to bear in assessing potential external allies that were seen as variable depending on the course of the war. At the time of the Pac Bo Plenum, party assessments of the "balance of forces" included the Chinese nationalists and the Soviet Union as the "direct rear guard," with a vaguer "indirect rear guard" made up of the antifascist forces fighting in Europe and the Pacific. Over time, as party leaders perceived changes in the balance of wartime forces, Great Britain and, increasingly, the United States would be seen as particularly important potential allies. At this point, the discourse of revolutionary heroism and voluntarism would join with strategic imperatives in fostering closer relations. As Ho Chi Minh suggested in *History of Our Country*,

The Chinese, Americans, Dutch, and English,
Are causing the Japanese trouble by fighting them everywhere
This is a good opportunity for us,
To rise and restore the country of our ancestors.[22]

Although the United States remained on the periphery of Vietnamese aims in 1941 and 1942, both the strategic and the voluntarist components of the vision of revolutionary nationalism that emerged at Pac Bo set the parameters of the Viet Minh's future diplomacy with the United States.

Encountering Faulkner and American Pilots: Vietnamese Revolutionary Diplomacy in a World at War

Despite the importance of the May 1941 plenum in shaping the domestic and diplomatic strategies that brought the ICP to power at the close of World War II, the Viet Minh enjoyed only a very limited immediate success. In the aftermath of the plenum, Ho Chi Minh, Pham Van Dong, and Vo Nguyen Giap remained in the isolated northern mountainous region of Vietnam surrounding Pac Bo, known as the Viet Bac, to organize revolutionary bases and expand the influence of the Viet Minh. They worked to build mass organizations, local militias, and an alternative administrative system. Truong Chinh returned to the Red River delta around Hanoi to undertake clandestine party organizing and to act as the editor of another Viet Minh newspaper, *National Salvation* [*Cuu Quoc*], published just outside Hanoi. Continuing French repression, however, frustrated party efforts in both the Viet Bac and the Red River delta. In particular, French military campaigns from the summer of 1941 through the spring of 1942 destroyed many of the base areas and other party organizations created in the Viet Bac.[23]

Vietnamese diplomacy in the wake of the Pac Bo Plenum also encountered serious obstacles. While party leaders continued to follow international developments closely, devoting substantial attention to news about the war in Europe and Asia in the Viet Minh newspapers, they remained isolated from channels of communication that would have brought them into closer contact with events beyond northern Vietnam.[24] The limited diplomatic initiatives launched by party leaders focused almost entirely on promoting closer relations with the Chiang Kai-shek regime in China. But Ho Chi Minh's frequent efforts after the plenum to win support from the Chinese military authorities in southern China for the fledging Viet Minh came to an end with his arrest in southern China in August 1943.[25]

During his fourteen-month incarceration, Ho wrote a series of poems, known collectively as his *Prison Diary [Nhat Ky Trong Tu]*, while he moved through a shifting series of Chinese jails and underwent significant hardships similar to those faced by many ICP leaders in French prisons during the 1930s. Several poems from the *Prison Diary* evoke the continuing international isolation faced by wartime Vietnamese revolutionaries; they also reveal Ho Chi Minh's appreciation of the geopolitical dimensions of the Pacific war. In "News Report: Willkie Given a Warm Reception," Ho contrasted the visit in 1942 of Franklin Roosevelt's unofficial envoy, Wendell L. Willkie, to the headquarters of Chiang Kai-shek's government in Chungking with his own forced sojourn in southern China:

Both you and I are China's friends.
We both are heading for Chungking.
You're sitting in the seat of honor —
meanwhile I'm lying low in jail.
Both you and I speak for our countries —
why don't they treat us the same way?
Coldness towards one, warmth towards another —
so goes the world as streams flow to the sea.

A subsequent poem, "A British Delegation in China," reinforced these themes of isolation and marginalization:

Americans had left, then Britons came.
They're lionized and feted everywhere.
I was sent over, too, as China's friend.
A special kind of welcome I've received.[26]

Beginning in 1943, international developments began to shape a more favorable revolutionary environment for the ICP's domestic and diplomatic initiatives. The victories of the Soviets at Stalingrad and the British at El Alamein and the success of U.S.-led invasions of North Africa and Guadalcanal in late 1942 marked a serious reversal in Axis military power in Europe and Asia. In Vietnam the growing realization of an eventual Japanese defeat began to undermine the prestige and authority of the increasingly isolated Japanese-backed Vichy French colonial government under Admiral Jean Decoux.

In February 1943 the Standing Committee of the ICP Central Committee met to formulate new strategies to take advantage of these developments. With Ho Chi Minh still in prison in China, the meetings were led by Truong Chinh. The resolutions adopted at these meetings, second in importance only to the Pac Bo Plenum, would guide ICP policy and the direction of the Viet Minh until the August Revolution of 1945. Along with renewed calls for developing revolutionary bases and military forces in the countryside, the February 1943 resolutions also devoted particular attention to launching a "cultural front" (mat tran van hoa) and forming new assessments of the impact of the changing international environment on the party's potential external allies. Both developments would shape the increased attention the Vietnamese accorded to diplomacy with the United States after 1943.[27]

The cultural front was designed to foster support for the Viet Minh from radical and progressive members of the urban intelligentsia, many of whom had been active in the student radical movements of the late 1920s but had distanced themselves from the class-based mass politics of the 1930s. Urban organizing efforts, though hampered by continuing French surveillance and repression, were among the most successful wartime Vietnamese initiatives and an important contributing factor to the widespread urban support the Viet Minh received in the August Revolution of 1945. The establishment of cultural front organizations in cities such as Hanoi, Hue, and Saigon intensified the renewed emphasis on voluntarism. Truong Chinh set the tone as the editor of the new party newspaper *Banner of Liberation* [*Co Giai Phong*], which was published clandestinely near Hanoi beginning in 1944. In one of the first issues, Truong Chinh published a poem titled "To Be a Poet" ["La thi si"] under the pseudonym Song Hong, or Red Wave, that enjoined Vietnamese writers and artists to celebrate the revolutionary heroism of traditional patriotic resistance figures to "bring the courage of Spring to the people's dark winter." Other newspapers ran stories on particular historical figures who had successfully led Vietnamese troops into battle against precolonial Chinese invaders.[28]

The cultural front also brought a resurgence of the search for external models in which the United States had played such a prominent role in the 1920s. In Hanoi a group of leading intellectuals associated with the cultural front regularly contributed to the journal *Impartial Opinion* [*Thanh Nghi*].[29] Among them was Dao Duy Anh, the likely author of the 1928 pamphlet *European and American Civilization* that had depicted the United States as an ideal for the revolutionary transformation of Vietnam. Illustrating the tenor of revolutionary urban wartime thought and the resurgence of an imagined America within it, *Impartial Opinion* looked toward eventual Vietnamese independence and gave particular attention to foreign models for the construction of the state and civil society. Articles investigating the structure and organization of European parliaments and banking systems were common, as were stories on the drafting of the Chinese constitution and nineteenth-century Chinese efforts at economic self-strengthening. Reflecting the legacies of the materialist conception of U.S. society in the anticolonial discourse of the 1920s, the United States played a role in discussions focused around the promotion of agriculture, manufactured products, and industry.[30]

Vietnamese translations of Western literature appeared alongside these investigations of American, European, and Chinese approaches to the organization of state and society. Although the works of European authors were more commonly featured, several issues from the summer of 1944 contained a serialized translation of William Faulkner's short story "Smoke." It is difficult to know how Vietnamese readers might have perceived a story that tells of the protracted fight between a poor southern farmer, Anselm Holland, and his two sons over land and inheritance. But the decision to publish a Vietnamese translation of a work by Faulkner was not accidental, belying the persisting French prism through which perceptions of the United States by many Vietnamese revolutionaries continued to be formed. Faulkner was one of the few American authors popular with French elites, and a number of his writings were available in Vietnam in French translations. Moreover, as Jean-Paul Sartre has suggested, reading Faulkner became a symbol of resistance in Vichy France during World War II. For the editors of *Impartial Opinion* who worked under close French censorship, the decision to publish "Smoke" might have represented a veiled criticism of the Vichy colonial regime. The narrative of "Smoke" itself and its focus on money and property likely reinforced Vietnamese perceptions of the materialist base of U.S. society.[31]

Although not directly related to the cultural front, the wartime period saw a substantial increase in the accessibility of U.S. culture for urban Vietnamese elites. A Vietnamese-language catalog published in 1940 of recordings from RCA Victor indicates that American jazz and big band music were available to a Vietnamese audience, as were readings of famous American political orations by Washington, Lincoln, and Wilson. Phrase books and self-study guides, sometimes published by presses associated with the radical urban intelligentsia, also appeared for the first time to help Vietnamese speakers learn English. The availability and use of such publications suggest a broader awareness of changing wartime conditions and the potential future role the United States and Great Britain might play in Vietnamese affairs. The dialogues and essays in these self-study guides included references to U.S. agriculture, industry, and technology, reinforcing existing images of the United States.[32]

If the organization of the cultural front shaped relations with the United States in informal ways, reassessments of the international context facing Vietnam at the meeting of the Standing Committee of the ICP Central Committee in February 1943 had a more direct effect on the future course of Vietnamese wartime diplomacy. Party leaders undertook a sustained discussion of the future military strategy of the Chinese, British, and Americans in Asia, arguing it would play a critical role in realizing Vietnamese national independence. The resolutions adopted by the Standing Committee emphasized the importance of building alliances with the Allied powers:

> Because the Japanese fascists employed Indochina as the base of their struggle against Britain, America, and China, a counter-offensive will take place to advance the democratic side in the Far East: the British, American, and Chinese army will enter Indochina to destroy the Japanese. When this happens, we must use the opportunity to our best advantage to lead a nationalist revolt and seize political power. At the same time we must foster good relations with Great Britain, America, and China in order that they recognize the freedom and independence of the Indochinese people and begin to withdraw from Indochina after we have together defeated the Japanese and French fascists.[33]

In the winter of 1943, these predictions remained somewhat optimistic. While a full-scale Allied military invasion of Indochina never took place, in 1945 the three powers did occupy an increasingly prominent role in bringing Japanese occupation of Vietnam to an end. As they did, the February 1943 resolutions provided the overarching framework for the Viet Minh's response.

In the meantime, party leaders sought to lay the groundwork in 1943 and 1944 for improved relations with China and the United States. These initiatives were particularly important for the Viet Minh, as the organization of revolutionary bases and the military within Vietnam continued to encounter severe and effective French repression. The Viet Minh's initial diplomatic efforts in this period focused on China. While Ho Chi Minh's continuing imprisonment in China remained a significant impediment to better relations with the nationalist Chinese government, the Viet Minh press exhibited a more conciliatory attitude toward the Chinese as early as the spring of 1943. In an article in *National Salvation* commemorating the anniversary of the Vietnamese defeat of a Chinese military invasion in 1789, the author admonished readers that Vietnamese pride "in one of the most brilliant pages of our history" should not obscure the importance of the contemporary relationship with China: "We feel proud of it, but we won't allow the enemy to make use of the hostility between us and the Chinese people. . . . We should not be angry with the Chinese. On the contrary, we must unite with them to fight against the common enemy."[34]

With Ho Chi Minh's release from prison in September 1943, Sino-Vietnamese relations improved substantially. Ho remained in southern China, entering negotiations with Chinese authorities to bring increased Viet Minh control of Vietnamese nationalist groups in exile in southern China that had enjoyed substantial

Chinese patronage, such as the Vietnam Revolutionary League (Viet Nam Cach Menh Dong Minh Hoi). In an effort to win further assistance and support from Chinese military authorities, Ho also sought to portray the Viet Minh as the most important potential indigenous ally for the Chinese in their struggle against the Japanese in Indochina. Little was known within Vietnam of these developments until Ho's return in September 1944. A special fall issue of *National Salvation* devoted to foreign relations focused on the promise of the Sino-Vietnamese relationship. The lead article, signed "Viet-Anh" but likely written by Ho Chi Minh, argued, "It is imperative to safeguard relations between the Chinese and Vietnamese peoples. The Chinese, following Sun Yat-sen's policy of creating a united front of oppressed Asian nations, are the vanguard of the Asian peoples' struggle against the Japanese aggressor." Along with the need to foster bilateral ties, the article also proposed a broader alliance with China and the Western powers to promote independence movements in India and Southeast Asia:

> The Vietnamese people call upon the Chinese Resistance Government under Chiang Kai-shek to convene an inter-Asian conference on Chinese territory. The conference should foster cooperation between the Asian nations and the Allies to defeat the Japanese imperialists; advance toward full independence for all Asian nations, big and small; and counter Japan's deceitful pan-Asian policy. Vietnam, represented by the Viet Minh, is ready to participate together with China, India, Korea, the Philippines, the Indonesian archipelago, etc., at this genuine pan-Asian conference.[35]

Although calls for Asian unity and increased inter-Asian diplomacy would form a substantial component of Vietnamese diplomacy after 1945, little came of these utopian proposals during the war. Moreover, the Sino-Vietnamese relationship remained fragile despite improvements in bilateral ties with China. Given the long Vietnamese historical memory of repeated Chinese invasions and the Viet Minh's own efforts to celebrate former leaders of the patriotic resistance against the Chinese, Viet Minh propaganda had to go to considerable lengths to justify cooperation with China. One contributor to *National Salvation*'s issue on foreign policy claimed that Vietnamese resistance to the Mongol invasions of the thirteenth century was not really anti-Chinese as the Mongols were the shared enemy of both the Vietnamese and the Chinese. While admitting China had once been Vietnam's enemy, the author argued that these struggles had been against "feudal China whereas contemporary China was in a process of democratization and would therefore no longer oppress small nations." Another contributor reiterated these benign views of Chinese intentions, arguing, "The Chinese would not do any harm if they entered Vietnam. They did not intend to colonize the country and would not come to loot, only to cooperate in fighting the Japanese. There might be a few corrupt officers and also some cruel soldiers in the Chinese army, so the Chinese should improve the discipline of its troops before they entered Vietnam. On our part, we Vietnamese should play the role of hosts in welcoming the Allied troops."[36] Party leaders were privately both more skeptical and fearful of Chinese intentions but appear to have hoped their overtures to China would reassure the Chinese government of Vietnam's good intentions and forestall Chinese interference in Vietnamese domestic affairs in ways that would prove inimical to the interests of the Viet Minh.[37]

Whatever the difficulties of the Sino-Vietnamese relationship, Viet Minh efforts to cultivate improved relations with China did result in providing the Vietnamese with wider access to the other Allied powers who maintained operations in southern China, including the United States. Pham Van Dong made use of these contacts to petition for the release of Ho Chi Minh from his Chinese prison in late 1943, directing requests not only to the Chinese authorities but also to the American ambassador in Chungking.[38] Of greater long-term significance for Viet Minh relations with the United States was Chinese permission to maintain a delegation in Kunming, which allowed the Vietnamese to foster ties with U.S. military, diplomatic, and intelligence operatives headquartered there. While Ho Chi Minh and Pham Van Dong supervised the Viet Minh activities in Kunming, the delegation itself initiated the most intensive contacts with Americans before 1945. It was led by Pham Viet Tu, a northerner in his early thirties who, as a secondary school student in Hanoi, had come of age during the time of the radical student protests of the late 1920s and later wrote for a variety of radical newspapers before joining the Viet Minh and coming to Kunming in 1943.[39]

In August 1943, Pham Viet Tu presented the American consul in Kunming, William R. Langdon, with a letter requesting U.S. recognition of the Viet Minh and the provision of arms and advisers to help the Vietnamese defeat the Japanese. Tu framed the Viet Minh appeal in this way:

In view of the possible collaboration between us, an oppressed people, and the United States, friend of the feeble, for the common cause of destroying Japanese fascism, we formulate these vows with all the sincerity at our command, counting on America, upholders of justice, who are fighting for the equality of peoples, to help our movement of national liberation which has been fiercely and patiently fought for so long alone. In the name of those principles of freedom for which the United States stands, we beseech American aid, both moral and material. We now ask such aid from you, generous America! All the people of Indochina are ready to assist America and will receive her as a liberator. We hope America will not disappoint them in their cry for help by her indifference. . . . Loyal to the common cause, we address this appeal to you, will you not hear it?[40]

The rhetorical excesses of Tu's letter were in part a conscious exercise in diplomatic flattery and represented the supplicant tenor of formal Vietnamese approaches to its potential external allies. This discourse of supplication recalls the practices common to Sino-Vietnamese relations before the French colonial period, which provided the only indigenous model for the formal conduct of diplomacy. In the official tributary relationship guiding exchanges between the Chinese and the Vietnamese emperors, the language and behavior of Vietnamese emissaries to the Chinese court were carefully prescribed to reflect the superior power and authority of the Chinese.[41] Tu's letters also revealed the imagined commonalities that framed Viet Minh images of the United States. Such an appeal to the United States made sense for geostrategic reasons, but expectations that Americans might actually act on behalf of Vietnamese as well as the qualities Tu ascribes to the United States recall the persisting voluntarism that shaped young radicals in the 1920s.

In a meeting in early September with William Langdon that marked the first direct encounter between the Viet Minh and an American official, Pham Viet Tu drew on these assumptions about U.S. ideals and power to argue forcefully for assistance from the United States. But as a summary of the sometimes tense exchange between Langdon and Tu suggests, the initial American response to Viet Minh requests may not have reinforced Vietnamese perceptions of the United States:

Mr. Langdon said . . . American friendship with France was too ancient and firm for the United States to act in an unfriendly way. . . . Mr. Pham replied that Annamites are well aware of the long-standing Franco-American friendship and that his League had no intention of fighting the French but wishes to range its members on the side of the Allies to fight the Japanese; also that the League had a plan of action for this purpose if the United States would provide arms and assistance. Mr. Langdon interrupted at this point to say that this aspect of the Annamite question was military and that the League ought properly to discuss it with the Allied military commands. Mr. Pham said he would stick to the political aspects of the matter and accordingly ask Mr. Langdon to recommend to the American Government that it insist upon autonomy for the Annamite people. . . . Mr. Langdon said the normal course would be to deal directly with the French, as France was a democracy and was morally bound to heed the wishes of all the elements of the nation. Mr. Pham countered that in theory this was the proper procedure of course, but to advocate it in the case of Indochina was fatuously to ignore the realities of the situation, as there was only repression and no democracy in Indochina. How could America, the champion of justice, he asked, on theoretic grounds blandly close its eyes to the wrongs done to a suffering branch of the human family.[42]

Despite the reticence of the American consul to accede to Tu's requests, the Viet Minh continued its efforts in the fall and winter of 1944 and 1945 to win U.S. confidence and support. In November 1944, Viet Minh guerrillas in northern Vietnam under the direction of Pham Van Dong met an American pilot whose plane had been shot down by the Japanese. Providing him with food and shelter, they eventually ensured his safe passage out of Vietnam and escorted him to U.S. military officials in Kunming. The rescue and return of the pilot not only illustrates continuing Viet Minh efforts to court U.S. favor but also reveals the place of the United States in its domestic strategy and the misperceptions that sometimes informed Vietnamese images of America. A special issue of *Vietnam Independence* in February 1945, edited by Pham Van Dong, was designed as a large poster using the format of an eight-panel cartoon that told of Viet Minh efforts to rescue the American pilot. Telling the story in pictures with a minimum of words fit the broader editorial policy of *Vietnam Independence*, which under the editorship of both Ho Chi Minh and Pham Van Dong used simple language and pictorial representations to communicate Viet Minh appeals to a broad rural audience, many of whom had minimum levels of literacy.[43]

The special issue was a conscious effort to boost Viet Minh prestige among its Vietnamese audience by linking the movement to the United States. The issue's banner headline proclaimed, "The American Army Is Our Friend," a sentiment that was pictorially reinforced by juxtaposing the stars and stripes of the American flag against the yellow star and red background of the Viet Minh banner. Pham Van Dong did not identify the national origins of the U.S. flag or explicitly discuss why the Viet Minh–American friendship was significant, suggesting a degree of certainty among the party leadership that the bulk of the Vietnamese population was already aware of U.S. military power and the potential status it accorded to the Viet Minh.

The cartoon figure used to depict the American pilot, on the other hand, suggests that both the authors and the readers of the special issue retained a physical image of Americans largely undifferentiated from those of other Westerners. The bespectacled American pilot with his small mustache looked much like earlier Vietnamese caricatures of Frenchmen, a conclusion reinforced by the pilot's hat and uniform, which resembled French rather than U.S. military dress. Such images betrayed the limited direct contact between Vietnamese and Americans and the imagined quality of Vietnamese wartime representations of the United States.

The special issue of *Vietnam Independence* also pointed to interconnections between Viet Minh foreign and domestic policies. If in part the issue was intended to impress its readers with the external allies of the Viet Minh, it also sought to mobilize the population in support of its foreign initiatives. The issue promised that "whoever saves American pilots will be generously rewarded by the Viet Minh." The significance of these sorts of activities, and the emphasis on orality rather than the printed text in reaching rural peoples, was also reflected in a play titled "Rescue of American Pilots," organized by the Viet Minh and presented in villages in the Viet Bac in this period.[44]

At the same time that the Viet Minh attempted to demonstrate their good offices to the United States through the rescue of American pilots, Ho Chi Minh was introducing himself to U.S. military and intelligence operatives in Kunming. In early 1945, Ho became OSS agent 19, or Lucius, and used his reports from Vietnam on the Japanese to emphasize the common struggle of the Viet Minh and the Americans against Japan. Many of his reports articulated Vietnamese grievances against French colonialism and subtly called for U.S. support of the Viet Minh in their struggle against both Japanese and French imperialism. In one report, dated February 1945, Ho discussed Vietnamese attitudes toward the Allied powers employing language that again recalled the radical voluntarism of the late 1920s. Ho argued that the Vietnamese "liked America best because of her generous promise to give the Philippines independence, her friendly attitude with the small and weak nationalities and her liberal help to those who fight Fascism." Ho's language reflected a rhetorical strategy that would come to play an increasing role in official discourse. Reminders of U.S. promises of independence for the Philippines and French unwillingness to do the same for Vietnam helped to explain to a domestic audience how potentially valuable Viet Minh efforts to seek U.S. support for Vietnamese independence might be.[45]

Party leaders also promoted a more materialistic rationale for America's willingness to support the Viet Minh cause. One party newspaper in the south suggested that the United States and Great Britain were imperial powers that did not necessarily think about the "best interests of Indochina." But because the United States was intent on becoming the world's supreme economic power and the British sought to preserve their economic interests in China, they were "favorable to the idea of Annamite independence because they wanted the assurance of our collaboration." For this reason, the article suggested, "to profit from the divergence of interests between the world powers and notably between Great Britain and the

United States, we should sign an economic treaty with these countries that would be profitable to both of them. In this way, they will not have any reason to refuse to recognize the independence of Indochina."[46]

Although the returns on the Viet Minh's diplomatic initiatives to China and the United States in 1943 and 1944 were modest, party leaders were increasingly optimistic that continuing Allied military successes in Europe and Asia confirmed the assessments of the February 1943 Standing Committee that had called for the development of a partnership between the Viet Minh and the Allies to defeat the Japanese and bring Vietnam independence. The liberation of Paris in August 1944 and the U.S. naval victory against the Japanese at the battle of Leyte Gulf in October 1944, along with the defeat of the Japanese in the Philippines and Japanese reverses on the island of Okinawa in early 1945, suggested the imminent collapse of the Germans and Japanese to many Vietnamese observers.[47]

At the beginning of 1945, party leaders began to believe that conditions would soon be favorable for an Allied invasion and the launching of an insurrection for national rebellion. As *National Salvation* proclaimed in January 1945, "Insurrection! This spring must be the spring of insurrection. . . . The world revolution is moving fast, urging us into action. In Indochina the Japanese and French are going to kill each other. The Allied troops will soon move in. The enemy ranks will be confused. The opportunity for insurrection is at hand." Similarly, Pham Van Dong argued in *Vietnam Independence*, "The purpose of the Allied attack on Indochina is to fight and drive out Japan, which is to say the Allied forces will free our country from Japanese aggression. This will be an opportunity for the Viet Minh to make every effort together with the Allied forces in fighting Japan. . . . Then our rights will be recognized and supported by the Allies."[48]

The Japanese coup of 9 March 1945 in Indochina appeared to confirm Vietnamese hopes. Within days, most French military and civilian authorities were imprisoned, and Vietnam became a Japanese colonial possession. More than eighty years of French colonial rule had come to an end. Although the Japanese installed a puppet government in Hue led by conservative Vietnamese elites, the new administration's nominal authority, a devastating famine in northern and central Vietnam, and perceptions of declining Japanese military fortunes elsewhere in Asia meant the coup opened a power vacuum in Vietnam.[49]

The leaders of the Viet Minh were quick to seize on the potential implications. An ICP Central Committee meeting a few days after the coup issued what has been termed the "historic directive" that formally guided the Viet Minh seizure of power in August 1945. While the authors of the document argued that a general insurrection could take place even without an Allied invasion, they expected one and devoted a substantial portion of the document's resolutions to preparations for it. Titled "Be Ready to Rally to the Allied Powers," the directive urged the organization of "demonstrations to welcome" the Americans, British, and Chinese and the formation of people's militias to fight the Japanese "side by side with the Allied Powers."[50] As the Viet Minh prepared for the general insurrection in the spring and summer of 1945, the rhetoric and practice of revolutionary nationalism that had first reemerged at the Pac Bo Plenum in May 1941, and the place of the United States within it, would continue to shape Vietnamese strategies.

America in the August Revolution and Its Aftermath

The long-anticipated Allied invasion of Indochina through which the Viet Minh had hoped to defeat the Japanese and achieve national liberation never materialized. Instead, as one leading scholar of the August Revolution has argued, the insurrections in Hanoi, Hue, Saigon, and provincial capitals throughout Vietnam in the last weeks of August that brought the Viet Minh to power on 2 September were the results of "historical fortuity and revolutionary ability."[51] With the U.S. decision to drop atomic weapons on Hiroshima and Nagasaki in early August and the subsequent Japanese capitulation, the vacuum of political power opened by the March coup widened, and the Japanese position in Indochina became ever more precarious. In this favorable situation, the Viet Minh was able to effectively realize its wartime revolutionary nationalist vision and employ its facility at organization and popular mobilization to launch successfully the insurrections that made up the August Revolution.

Although the United States played a less central role than Vietnamese revolutionaries had expected in fostering the conditions that would allow them to seize power and establish an independent Vietnamese state, the leaders of the Viet Minh continued to look to America for support during the August Revolution and its aftermath. They focused on the U.S. intelligence and military operatives in southern China and those posted to Vietnam after the Japanese capitulation. Shortly after the Japanese coup, Ho Chi Minh met with General Claire Chennault, the U.S. Air Force commander in China, and representatives of the oss in Kunming, offering to provide more extensive intelligence information on Japanese operations in Indochina and seeking support for the Viet Minh's anti-Japanese activities in Vietnam. Just as he had earlier, Ho also used the reports he prepared for the oss to discuss the aims of the Viet Minh and their efforts to obtain military and administrative control of northern Vietnam. Impressed with the quality of the intelligence provided by the Viet Minh and their organizational abilities, Archimedes Patti, who headed the oss Secret Intelligence operations for

Indochina in Kunming, gained approval for the use of the Viet Minh in several planned anti-Japanese missions in Vietnam. On 16 July, several members of the OSS "Deer" team under the command of Allison K. Thomas parachuted into Vietnam near the Chinese border and were met by Ho Chi Minh, Vo Nguyen Giap, and some two hundred members of the Viet Minh militia. In the first weeks of August, the Deer team provided the Viet Minh with a modest number of weapons and supervised a strenuous series of training exercises. With the news of the imminent Japanese surrender in mid-August, the OSS officers and Viet Minh forces made their way to the provincial capital of Thai Nguyen, where the Viet Minh engaged the Japanese in a five-day street battle.[52]

Meanwhile, Patti arrived in Hanoi on 22 August at the height of the August Revolution. He was immediately greeted by representatives of the Viet Minh and serenaded by a military band that played the U.S. national anthem. Although Patti was sent to Vietnam as a neutral observer of the Japanese surrender, the leadership of the Viet Minh attached particular importance to his presence. Patti provided the only official conduit to the United States, and he was already known to Ho Chi Minh, who viewed him as sympathetic to the Viet Minh cause. Patti met several times with Ho and Giap in the final weeks of August, dining with both of them on the eve of Vietnamese independence and providing a translation of the U.S. Declaration of Independence for use in Ho's speech. Ho and Giap used their meetings with Patti to boost U.S. confidence in the ability of the Vietnamese to undertake the administration of an independent state, to seek recognition of the Viet Minh–led provisional government, and to receive economic, educational, and technical support for the future development of the Vietnamese state. Ho and Giap also prevailed on Patti to send a message to President Truman, via U.S. authorities in Chungking, that asked for the Viet Minh to be a part of any future Allied discussions of Vietnam's postwar status.[53]

The aftermath of the August Revolution and the celebrations of Vietnamese independence ushered in a period of increasing instability in Vietnam. At the Potsdam Conference in July 1945, the Allied powers agreed that Chinese forces would take the surrender of the Japanese in northern Vietnam while the British would do the same in the south. Against the coming of Chinese and British forces and French military efforts to regain French sovereignty in Indochina in the fall of 1945, the leadership of the newly established DRV intensified its efforts to maintain relations with representatives of the U.S. government newly posted to Vietnam. General Philip E. Gallagher arrived in Hanoi in mid-September as the senior U.S. military adviser to the Chinese forces occupying northern Vietnam and served as the highest-ranking American officer in Vietnam until his departure in December. Ho Chi Minh and Gallagher met four or five times in private sessions that Ho used to repeat his calls for U.S. material and moral support for the DRV. As one sign of the status he accorded Ho's government, on several occasions Gallagher included Ho in regular meetings with the leaders of Chinese and French military delegations in Hanoi to discuss problems arising during the occupation period.[54]

Along with Gallagher, Ho encountered several other U.S. officials in the fall and winter of 1945, including Arthur Hale, who led a two-week fact-finding mission for the State Department in October, and Frank M. White, who served as the representative in Hanoi of the Strategic Services Unit (the former OSS) between December 1945 and March 1946. Reports of these meetings by White and Hale suggest Ho Chi Minh continued to seek American assistance, mainly for economic development and opportunities for Vietnamese students to study in the United States. More subtly, Ho also sought to differentiate Vietnamese attitudes toward the United States from those of the other Allied powers. One evening, on very short notice, Ho invited Frank White to join him at a dinner to honor French and Chinese military authorities in Hanoi. White, a major, already uneasy about the "glacial" reception he received from a group made up of officers that far outranked him, was particularly embarrassed to be seated next to Ho. When he suggested there was some resentment over the table arrangement, Ho replied, "I can see that. But who else could I talk to?"[55]

Just as Ho Chi Minh had used Archimedes Patti as a conduit for sending messages to Washington, he asked General Gallagher and other Americans posted to Hanoi to transmit a series of letters to President Truman and Secretary of State James F. Byrnes in late 1945 and early 1946. As one letter to President Truman suggests, Ho appealed to U.S. pledges of self-determination and the model of Philippine independence to underscore calls for U.S. promises of support for the DRV: "It is with this firm conviction that we request of the United States as guardians and champions of World Justice to take a decisive step in support of our independence. What we ask has been graciously granted to the Philippines. Like the Philippines our goal is full independence and full cooperation with the United States." In a letter to Secretary Byrnes urging the establishment of cultural relations, Ho suggested that the Vietnamese were "keenly interested in things American," particularly "modern technical achievements." He asked to send a delegation of fifty Vietnamese students to the United States to undertake training in agriculture, engineering, and other applied sciences; in another message he requested humanitarian relief for food shortages in northern Vietnam.[56]

Ho Chi Minh's efforts to contact Americans posted to Hanoi were accompanied by similar initiatives on the part of the leaders of the Viet Minh in the south, who had established a provisional government in Saigon during the August Revolution. Most important was Pham Ngoc Thach, one of the leading members of the Viet Minh executive committee in the south. Thach was born to a southern middle-class family, studied medicine in France, and became active in Viet Minh efforts to mobilize students in Saigon at the close of World War II. Designated as commissioner for foreign relations, he served as the Viet Minh liaison with the OSS "Embankment" mission to Saigon led by Peter Dewey in the fall of 1945.[57]

Thach met frequently with members of the OSS mission in Saigon, providing information about the history of Vietnamese anticolonialism and the aims of the new provisional government. He echoed Ho Chi Minh's requests for material and moral support from the United States, often mentioning the case of the Philippines as a potential model for Vietnam in his conversations with Americans. Thach's appeals to the OSS mission also drew on Viet Minh perceptions of the linkages between revolutionary nationalism in Vietnam and the United States. As the report of one OSS officer on his meetings with Thach in September 1945 suggests, the Viet Minh claimed to view the United States differently from the other European powers: "Americans are considered to be a separate people, and the Viet Minh leaders expressed the hope that Americans would view favorably their bid for independence, since we ourselves fought for and gained our independence under a situation considered to be similar to that as exists in Indo China to-day. The Viet Minh leaders were especially desirous of gaining our friendship and often expressed the hope that we would sponsor their bid for independence." Finally, Thach's appeals reflect the materialist conceptions that contributed to Viet Minh perceptions of the United States. Thach often suggested the commercial possibilities for the United States in Vietnam and stated that the Vietnamese government looked forward "to the opportunity of cooperating with American industrial and businessmen in the sphere of common progress and for the reconstruction of Vietnam."[58]

Despite these intensive efforts during and after the August Revolution, the leadership of the DRV was unable to achieve real advances in Vietnamese-U.S. relations. None of Ho Chi Minh's letters to Washington was ever acknowledged. Nor were U.S. military and intelligence operatives, sent to Vietnam under instructions of strict neutrality to broker the Japanese surrender and the Allied occupation, able to offer more than individual expressions of generalized support for Vietnamese independence. Yet Vietnamese efforts in Hanoi and Saigon to obtain U.S. material and moral support persisted throughout the fall of 1945 and in early 1946. In part, any connection with American prestige, no matter how modest, would have been important for the fledgling Vietnamese government, not only as a mark of international legitimacy but to impress its domestic constituency. The interest by the leaders of the DRV in symbolic as well as substantive aspects of their relations with the United States—not only on independence day but in its aftermath—

suggests that the psychological boost of an association with the United States remained an important motivation in sustaining efforts to foster ties with America.

The DRV's diplomacy with the United States must also be appreciated against the larger geopolitical forces acting on Vietnam in this period. The regime's U.S. initiative mirrored its tactics toward the occupying Chinese forces in the north. Concerned with preserving Vietnam's independence and with forestalling postwar French efforts to reclaim Indochina, the DRV sought to use both the Chinese and the Americans as buffers against the French. DRV relations with local Chinese military authorities were not always smooth, and much of the leadership worried that the Chinese intended to dominate Vietnam politically and militarily. But although the situation in the north was delicate and potentially volatile, DRV leaders went to great lengths to court the Chinese officials in Hanoi and skillfully manipulate the intense antagonism that emerged between the local Chinese and French military authorities.[59]

Beyond their contacts with the Chinese and the Americans, the leaders of the DRV struggled to establish an independent Vietnamese state in virtual international isolation. Neither the Soviet Union nor the Chinese communists, who played an insubstantial role in the immediate postwar period in Vietnam, offered the DRV any form of material support. Ho Chi Minh sent a series of cables to Stalin, very much like those he sent to Truman (and in some cases identically worded), asking for Soviet recognition and technical support. None of them met with a response from Stalin. In fact, the comment made by a diplomat in the Soviet foreign ministry on one message read, "to be left unanswered."[60]

The international dynamics of the situation in the south were even more difficult for the DRV. Here America's apparent official neutrality, while far less than the DRV may have hoped to receive from the United States, stood in sharp contrast to what the Vietnamese perceived as the overt hostility of the British occupying forces and their efforts to promote the return of the French. Initially, the Viet Minh leadership in the south sought out British military personnel and diplomats much as they had U.S. OSS officers, publicly praising the British troops as "liberators from Japanese and French domination." At the same time, Ho Chi Minh cabled London to request British support for flood relief efforts in the north.[61]

But as French troops, with what the Vietnamese increasingly viewed as British acquiescence, tried to expel the provisional Vietnamese government from Saigon and the surrounding areas, tensions with the British increased markedly. Ho Chi Minh immediately lodged a letter of protest with the British prime minister, accusing the British of "smokescreening French aggression." The Viet Minh also undertook a propaganda campaign aimed at the Indian troops who made up a large portion of the British military force in Saigon. Arguing that ties of anticolonialism bound Indians and Vietnamese troops, it urged Indian troops to lay down their arms. Although the campaign had little practical effect, it intensified British-Vietnamese hostilities. Pham Ngoc Thach met with British officials on several occasions in early October in an effort to resolve their differences, including meetings with General Douglas Gracey, who led the British occupying forces in southern Vietnam, and representatives of the British Foreign Office. But neither side was inclined to view the other sympathetically. Gracey, who in his internal reports called the Viet Minh a "puppet government" made up of "a very large hooligan element," demanded that the Vietnamese give up their arms and recognize French military authority. Pham Ngoc Thach, along with the other leaders of the Viet Minh's provisional government in Saigon, insisted that the British restore Vietnamese authority in the south. By mid-October, formal contact between the two sides had ceased, and the military struggle in the south intensified.[62]

If the DRV's sustained appeals to the United States in the aftermath of the August Revolution rested in part on their psychological impact within Vietnam and the forbidding international context in which the new government operated, the lingering potency of interwar radical discourse on Vietnamese perceptions of the United States was also essential to how the leaders of the DRV framed their petitions to the United States and the persistence by which they were advanced. In both his letters to officials in Washington and his meetings with Americans in southern China and Hanoi, Ho Chi Minh drew on a vision of the United States and its imagined ties with Vietnam shaped by the radical discourse of the 1920s. Perceptions of the voluntarist heroism of U.S. patriots in the eighteenth century and selfless leaders such as Abraham Lincoln, as well as the materialist base and technological advances of American society, provided common points of reference for Vietnamese revolutionaries and influenced both their expectations of the United States and the sorts of appeals they believed were most likely to elicit a positive response from U.S. officials. These shared sentiments were further underscored by the critical place of radical discourse in the revolutionary nationalist vision that animated the Viet Minh's wartime domestic and diplomatic outlook. Without these real or imagined ties between the United States and Vietnam, which received renewed attention in urban areas through the Viet Minh's wartime cultural front, it is unlikely that the more symbolic efforts to accord American prestige to the new Vietnamese state would have resonated so deeply with the regime's domestic audience.

How these perceptual legacies joined strategic imperatives to shape Vietnamese diplomacy toward the United States is best illustrated by the establishment of the Vietnamese-American Friendship Association (Hoi Viet-My Than Huu) in Hanoi in the fall of 1945. The association, which operated with the approval and encouragement of the central government, aimed to promote improved economic and cultural relations with the United States through public lectures, the translation of books, language courses, and the publication of a monthly magazine. Several thousand Hanoi residents became contributing members within the first two months of the association's founding. Its leaders came from Hanoi's commercial community with ties to the new government, including Trinh Van Binh, the director of the DRV's customs service, who served as president, and Tran Luu Dy, a leading import-export merchant, who acted as general secretary. U.S. military personnel and intelligence operatives in Hanoi, some of whom had developing working relationships with the group's leaders and had encouraged the founding of the association, were invited to attend events as observers. General Gallagher, along with the former Vietnamese emperor Bao Dai, were among the two hundred guests at the association's high-spirited first meeting. Trinh Van Binh's opening address, with its emphasis on the "importance of American science in our thoughts and activities," and Gallagher's response, which conveyed his hopes for future educational exchanges, not only set the tone for the association's broader objectives but appeared to lend official U.S. prestige to its endeavors. With the formal speeches out of the way, several Vietnamese women sang a medley of traditional Vietnamese songs, followed by Gallagher, who delivered a "lively performance" of American songs, which ushered in several hours of singing and dancing.[63]

As the subjects of the articles that make up the three extant issues of the *Vietnamese-American Friendship Association Review* [*Viet-My Tap Chi*] suggest, the materialist views of U.S. society that emerged at the association's first meeting shaped both its members' perceptions of the United States and the aspects of Vietnam they believed would be of greatest interest to Americans. The nature of these perceptions emerges most strongly in an article speculating on the future of Vietnamese-American relations that concentrated on U.S. commerce, mass culture, and technology. In discussing economic relations, one author asserted,

We shall adopt an "open door" policy in the economic field. The American products are overflowing the world, the American plants have taken the place of those of the whole world. So, there is no reason why we should not consume American-made goods as the British, the French and everybody in the world is doing now. Vietnam will be a new market for American manufactured goods, and what is more, we do not see any reason why the Americans should not build up a Ford plant in our own country. Moreover, Vietnam will also be a source of supply for the American industry. Our country is potentially rich. By insuring the Vietnam market, the Americans have nothing to lose, and everything to gain.

Reflecting Vietnamese perceptions of the applied rather than purely intellectual character of American thought, the author continued,

> In the field of thought we have much less to learn from the U.S. than in the field of technique. . . . It is only in the field of technique that we must take our hats off . . . to the U.S., the master of modern science. In that respect, our students will learn from the U.S. innumerable and precious things which are to improve the material life of our people, the wealth and efficiency of our country. . . . We shall look to the U.S. for a sincere and effective help: from that country we shall ask for teachers, engineers and technicians of all kinds; to it we shall send our students.[64]

These materialist sentiments reflected the analysis that informed most of the *Review*'s articles. English-language features focused on commercial issues, including articles on industrialization, Vietnamese handicrafts such as silver and lace-making, and manufacturing of raw materials such as wood oil. Some attention was also directed to Vietnamese culture and criticisms of French colonial rule as well as toward stories that emphasized the shared anticolonial aims of Vietnam and the United States during World War II. Among the articles in Vietnamese, most focused on commercial developments in the United States, including considerations of Franklin Roosevelt's economic policies.[65]

Unlike more official Vietnamese approaches to the United States, the rhetoric of the Vietnamese-American Friendship Association achieved more tangible and immediate results. The association played host in 1946 to several leading U.S. firms with interests in Vietnam's postwar economic development. The American-owned Standard Vacuum Oil Company (Stanvac), which had established significant oil refining and marketing operations in the Dutch East Indies before World War II, sent agents to Hanoi, as did California-Texaco, which was represented by Laurence Gordon, who had organized the GBT group and acted as a Texaco agent before the war. Stanvac representatives and Gordon met with ministers in the DRV government, including Vo Nguyen Giap. General Motors, Milwaukee motorcycle producer Harley-Davidson, and several New York–based insurance underwriters also sent agents to Hanoi and Saigon. Even before U.S. firms began to send representatives to Vietnam, American films, which had been among the most popular and substantial U.S. exports to Vietnam before World War II, were showing again in movie houses in major Vietnamese cities. One contemporary observer estimated that U.S. releases accounted for 70 percent of the films shown in Vietnam in the immediate postwar period. The trend was inaugurated in October 1945 with the screening of *Blondie Goes to Town* in Hanoi, which suggested to one Vietnamese writer for the *Review* that "the U.S.A. . . . is a grand and lovely country and the Americans a nice people."[66]

Despite these advances in forging unofficial commercial and cultural links, the perceptual underpinnings of Vietnamese diplomacy with the United States began to show signs of wear in late 1945 and 1946. Contemporary U.S. observers reported a gradual decline of American prestige in Vietnam, suggesting that U.S. officials were encountering new obstacles in their efforts to meet with members of the DRV's cabinet.[67] In part, Ho Chi Minh's extended absences from Vietnam during much of 1946 while he conducted negotiations with the French closed the most important channel of communication with Vietnamese authorities. But the reticence of other members of the DRV cabinet to meet with U.S. officials does suggest a certain disillusionment over America's unwillingness to act in ways Vietnamese revolutionaries thought it might.

The period also marked the emergence of a muted internationalist discourse in internal government and party memorandums that warned of "imperialist collusion of the British and Americans in aiding the French." These private musings and internationalist influences received more public expression with the publication by radical presses in 1946 of Vietnamese translations of books originally authored by figures associated with Chinese communism as well as some of the writings of Ho Chi Minh from the prewar period. Among these publications was the section of Ho's 1927 *Road to Revolution* on the American revolution in which he praised American heroism in the war for independence against the British and in the civil war, but he also cautioned that "America today is not like America of this older time." The republication of *Road to Revolution*, and with it Ho's claim that America was an imperfect revolutionary model because U.S. workers remained oppressed by industrialists such as Henry Ford, was a reminder of the internationalist register that continued to shape the views of Vietnamese revolutionaries.[68]

But these developments do not so much challenge the sincerity of continuing Vietnamese appeals to the United States as illustrate the varied strands of revolutionary thought and the tensions between them that continued to make up the broader outlook of the DRV's leaders. Moreover, as Franco-Vietnamese relations deteriorated throughout 1946 and the two sides moved ever closer to armed conflict, internationalist sentiments remained muted. When the DRV leadership again turned to the United States for assistance after the outbreak of war with the French in December 1946, the wartime postcolonial vision of revolutionary nationalism, and the place of America in it, continued to animate its diplomacy.

Coda: America Confronts the August Revolution and Postcolonial Vietnam

The U.S. military and intelligence operatives in Kunming, Hanoi, and Saigon who met with Ho Chi Minh and observed the events of the August Revolution offered the first sustained official observations from the field on the efforts by Vietnamese revolutionaries to establish an independent Vietnamese state. Like accounts of Roosevelt's wartime plans for the establishment of an international trusteeship in Indochina, memoirs and scholarly works on this encounter have posited that it, too, represented a lost opportunity for Vietnamese-American relations. The memoirs of Archimedes Patti, who led the OSS delegation to Hanoi in late August and September 1945, have been particularly influential in shaping this interpretation, arguing that the favorable impressions that he and other U.S. operatives developed of the Viet Minh as sincere and effective nationalists who sought a working relationship with the United States never received careful attention in Washington. With Patti's memoirs as a starting point, journalists and scholars have suggested that a significant gap emerged in this period between the admiration of the Vietnamese by Americans in the field and the concerns of policy makers in Washington, who, preoccupied with emerging Cold War tensions in Europe and fostering stronger ties with France, ignored or downplayed the reports of Patti and like-minded field operatives.[69]

The perceptual gap between Washington and the field, however, was considerably narrower than these widely accepted interpretations suggest. Just as the legacies of Vietnamese radical discourse in the 1920s and the Viet Minh's revolutionary nationalist ideology framed the DRV's diplomacy toward the United States, the American wartime vision of Vietnam provided a common frame of reference that linked the deliberations of policy makers in Washington with the observations of Americans in the field on the August Revolution and its aftermath. Patti's memoirs, so central to existing interpretations of American policy toward Vietnam in this period, often obscure these essential commonalities. While perhaps an accurate representation of his private attitudes toward the Viet Minh, they do not always reflect the nature of his contemporary reporting from the field. For instance, Patti characterized a 27 August 1945 meeting between himself, Vo Nguyen Giap, and the senior French representative in Hanoi, Jean Sainteny, in his memoirs in this way: "Despite his efforts to appear civil, he [Sainteny] set the tone by cutting Giap short with a paternal lecture. . . . Giap, in perfect French and with absolute self-control, said he had not come to be lectured. . . . For the first time in his life Sainteny was meeting face to face a Vietnamese who dared to stand up to a Frenchman. . . . Sainteny had been outplayed and was visibly annoyed."

But in a cable sent to Kunming the day after the meeting, Patti analyzed the encounter quite differently, suggesting it "was apparent from the start that French had upper hand and that during the course of negotiations Annamites lost considerable ground mainly due to their inferiority complex when confronted by a European."[70]

The sensibility of Patti's 1945 cable was not an isolated phenomenon. Its more ambiguous and critical tone, which belied the pervasive influence of broader U.S. unfavorable judgments about the Vietnamese, characterized not only much of Patti's contemporary reporting but many of the dispatches prepared by other U.S. military and intelligence operatives in Vietnam. As these reports were summarized and disseminated to the State Department and the White House, they offered little that would have surprised most readers in Washington. Indeed, the common perceptual framework that joined field observers and policy makers in Washington ensured that field impressions would confirm rather than challenge a central supposition that had animated the U.S. wartime vision of Vietnam: the inadequacies of the Vietnamese themselves posed one of the greatest obstacles to the realization of independence and effective self-government in Vietnam. Along with continuing tensions with the French and faith in the utility of U.S. models for Vietnamese political and socioeconomic development, these unfavorable perceptions shaped the contours of Washington's Vietnam policy in the immediate postwar period.

As U.S. field operatives observed the events before and after the August Revolution, their assessments of the Viet Minh and its capacity for independent self-government both reflected and reinforced prevailing assumptions of Vietnamese political immaturity and susceptibility to outside direction. Although OSS representatives in Kunming had been willing to involve the Viet Minh in intelligence-gathering operations in Indochina in the spring of 1945, they were often critical of the reports provided by Ho Chi Minh on the Japanese and the activities of the Viet Minh, calling them "exaggerated and distorted." They were also increasingly skeptical of undertaking psychological operations in the area. As James R. Withrow, who headed these efforts for the OSS in the China-Burma-India theater, argued in a May 1945 memorandum, psychological operations in Vietnam "would be a wasted effort" because of what he perceived as the innate incapacities of indigenous peoples:

> The natives . . . cannot be inspired to resistance by an ideological appeal. They are apathetic as to who rules them, nationalistic movements to the contrary notwithstanding. What nationalist agitation there is, has been instigated by individuals seeking mainly to serve their self-interests rather than those of their countrymen. . . . An Annamite's services are at the disposal of him who pays

the best. . . . There is no sense of solidarity among the natives, and hence no sense of nationalism. They are in consequence always divided and thus subject to foreign rule. . . . The natives . . . are naturally lazy. . . . Such a background of life-long habits of indolence, is another obstacle to zeal for a cause.[71]

These sentiments also underlay criticisms offered by U.S. observers in Hanoi of Viet Minh activities during and after the August Revolution. In one typical cable from late August 1945, Archimedes Patti questioned whether the Vietnamese were up to the task of self-government:

> Provisional government groping in the dark. After series of talks with leaders of provisional government I am convinced that they are not politically mature. . . . They have no knowledge of meaning of terms such as nationalization, Congressional Assembly, Liberalism, democracy, etc.; words which they use quite freely, but during course of conversations they planned exactly opposite. Pillaging and looting has begun. . . . Provisional government is now preparing to requisition the Bank of Indo-China as it has already requisitioned the Yunnan railroad from Lao Kay to Hanoi. It has similar plans for electric company, water works and all transportation facilities. They call this "nationalization." They state "they are essential to the livelihood of the new government."

Along with his dismissal of the ability of the Vietnamese to conduct their own political affairs, Patti emphasized the probable role of external direction in Viet Minh activities. "I am convinced that they are . . . being misled by Japanese agent-provocateur and Red elements," he argued. The "whole business had misleading misguided Soviet tinge assisted by well organized fifth column activity."[72] Such an analysis would have resonated with the conclusions of U.S. wartime observers of Vietnam in southern China and policy makers in Washington who had pointed to Vietnam's susceptibility to foreign influence as both further evidence of Vietnamese political immaturity and an explanation of the emergence of nationalist agitation in a society they believed was incapable of independent sustained political action.

U.S. accounts of the administrative and military capacities of the DRV in the fall of 1945 conveyed a continuing skepticism of Viet Minh abilities and a sense of its permeability to foreign influences. Suggesting the government "lacked executive ability," General Philip Gallagher argued that the Vietnamese "were not yet ready for self-government and in full-fledged competition with other nations would 'lose their shirts.'" On military matters, Gallagher believed the Vietnamese to be "too enthusiastic and too naive," arguing that Vietnamese perceptions of its own military prowess were more a matter of bravado rather than substance. "They

are strong on parades and reiterate their willingness 'to fight to the last man,'"
Gallagher continued, but in an armed conflict with the French "they would be
slaughtered." The few instances in which Gallagher was impressed by aspects of
the Viet Minh he usually ascribed to external forces; for instance, he saw the "ear-
marks of some Russian influence" in what he termed their "excellent organization
and propaganda techniques."

The reports of Arthur Hale, the State Department representative who visited
Hanoi in the fall of 1945, revealed similar perceptions of innate indigenous incapacities, commenting that while the "political doctrine of the independence
movement has borrowed slogans and formulae from mature revolutionary and
democratic movements in the West, its expression of these techniques is often
mawkish and childish." Hale also pointed to external, largely Soviet, influences
on the new Vietnamese state. Robert H. Knapp, a political warfare specialist with
the OSS mission in Hanoi, provided perhaps the most dismissive account of the
new Vietnamese regime as made up of "pure imports from Moscow" or ministers
"hiding their real personality under an assumed name":

> Summing up the regime, it seems pretty obvious that in spite of its camouflage
> it is predominantly that of a party well trained in revolutionary technique ap-
> plied to a simple minded people completely devoid of critical sense. Its motto
> might be "destruction and obstruction"—if judged by results. Personal ambi-
> tions and xenophobia are becoming more and more apparent. In its efforts to
> appear plebiscited by the people, who up to the present has shown very little
> enthusiasm for any kind of politics, its propaganda has turned them into a pack
> of snarling jackals by appealing to the mob's lowest criminal instincts and upset-
> ting all standard tradition. Will all this double crossing, deceit, hatred, violence
> and crimes lead to independence? . . . Someone is going to get Indochina, and
> I don't think it will be the Annamites.[73]

Not all of the reports from Vietnam took this critical tone. U.S. perceptions
of Ho Chi Minh were a notable exception. OSS and military observers in Hanoi
who encountered Ho in the summer and fall of 1945 were almost uniformly impressed by his abilities and political acumen. Allison K. Thomas, the leader of the
OSS Deer team who met Ho shortly before the August Revolution, termed him
"sincere and able" in a September 1945 report summarizing the work of the Deer
mission. In a dispatch to Kunming on the eve of Vietnamese independence following an extensive series of conversations with Ho, Archimedes Patti reported,
"He impresses me as sensible, well balanced politically minded individual. His demands are few and simple namely independence." William D. Borrowes, another
OSS officer who met with Ho in Hanoi several times in September 1945, reported,

"My personal opinion is that Ho Chi Minh is a brilliant and capable man, completely sincere in his opinions." Arthur Hale argued that Ho was "the outstanding personality in the Annamite government. A cultured, well-educated man of international experience, he has given the government a certain dignity." The U.S. commander of the China theater search detachment in Vietnam who came to know Ho Chi Minh in this period conveyed similar sentiments to Kunming. His comments suggest that he brought largely unfavorable assumptions into his first meetings with Ho. But his perceptions were transformed by their encounters: "A photograph which I saw of Mr. Ho gives one the impression of a wild-eyed revolutionary who has spent most of this time either in the jungle or starving in a garret. Face to face however, he makes an entirely different impression. He is mild in manner, kindly in expression, and his eyes are soft and gentle. He does not rant. . . . I honestly believe that he is willing to die for the freedom of Viet Nam."[74]

Not only did these favorable impressions of Ho Chi Minh stand in stark contrast with U.S. criticisms of the Viet Minh; they were also quite different in tone from the reports on encounters with other Vietnamese revolutionaries. According to most American observers, the qualities they attributed to Ho were not shared by other leaders of the DRV they met in Hanoi and Saigon. Hale commented that "Ho's manner" made a "more favorable impression" than that of "his less cosmopolitan, and in some instances more radical, associates." There was a "sharp difference," Hale continued, between "Ho's suavity" and the "rougher, more doctrinaire behavior of the heads of departments." Many Americans found it difficult to take members of Ho's government seriously. Patti's dismissive comments about Vo Nguyen Giap at their meeting with Jean Sainteny shortly before the August Revolution were echoed by Frank White, who confused Giap with a waiter. "He came and he stood quietly at one juncture when I was talking to Ho," White reported in an account of a DRV reception in early December 1945. "He was wearing a sort of an open shirt and shorts. . . . the garb that houseboys often wore and it wasn't until later . . . that Ho turned to him to clarify . . . a point that I realized he wasn't a waiter." White's mistake—Giap was then serving as the DRV's minister of interior—suggests that the derisive U.S. prism that shaped perceptions of the Vietnamese continued to exert a powerful influence.[75]

The favorable images of Ho Chi Minh held by OSS and military operatives in Hanoi, however, were not a complete departure from this larger American vision of the Vietnamese and the nature of Vietnamese society. The genuine admiration U.S. observers expressed for Ho Chi Minh did rest in part on the appeal and force of his personality. Without doubt, Ho consciously used his meetings with Americans to distance himself from his internationalist past and frame Viet Minh nationalism and the struggle for independence within what he perceived as the broader ideals of the United States. American observers, who were increasingly aware of his connections to Moscow and the Comintern, would have been unlikely to accept Ho's claims unless they had believed in his sincerity. But if Ho's persuasive abilities were a contributing factor in shaping the favorable impressions of him formed by field operatives, the susceptibility of Americans to Ho's appeals was also conditioned in important ways by the suppositions of Vietnamese political immaturity and susceptibility to foreign influences that guided more negative assessments of the Viet Minh. Ho's extensive experiences outside Vietnam—what one observer referred to as Ho's "cosmopolitanism"—helped Americans explain why he appeared to behave so differently from other Vietnamese revolutionaries. Although a few Americans expressed concern over his connections to international communism, Ho's overseas training, even if it took place in Moscow, did not seem particularly dangerous to most contemporary observers. Rather, it allowed them to appreciate and recognize his abilities without disturbing their broader assessments of the innate Vietnamese incapacity for effective political organizing.[76]

The willingness of American observers to accept Ho Chi Minh's professed embrace of U.S. ideals also reflected the limitations they continued to ascribe to indigenous political thought. Few Americans believed the Vietnamese held deep political convictions or that they grasped the principles underlying either socialist or democratic values. In their assessments of "Red" influences within the Viet Minh, Americans seldom referred to firm ideological commitments, focusing instead on the role of Marxism-Leninism in shaping short-term tactics and strategy. Despite Ho's unusual background, Americans believed that he, like other Vietnamese, would not find it difficult to turn from leftist to democratic ideals and institutions with a little prodding from the United States in a society they perceived as so pliable to external influences. Given such assumptions, the U.S. field operatives who came to admire Ho had little trouble seeing him as a potentially committed democrat. As one member of Gallagher's military mission argued, "If Americans . . . were to indicate displeasure at their communist background . . . [a] more democratic organization would probably evolve." An OSS report suggested that although Ho "formerly favored Communist ideals, he now realized that such ideals were impracticable for his country, and that his policy now was one of republican nationalism." One OSS research and analysis report went even further, arguing that Ho "was a convinced Democrat who has always rallied around himself all the revolutionary forces of the country for winning of independence under the aegis of democracy."[77]

The apparent eagerness of some U.S. observers in the field to use Ho as a vehicle to transfer American values and aims onto the Vietnamese movement for independence did prompt clashes with their superiors in southern China and

Washington. Colonel Richard Heppner, who supervised OSS activities in Vietnam from southern China, cabled various OSS officers in Hanoi several times in the fall of 1945 ordering them to halt what he viewed as improper interventions in Vietnamese domestic affairs. In a dispatch on 3 September he told Patti, "You will not rpt not act as mediator, go between or arranger of meetings . . . between French, Annamite or Chinese." Heppner responded in a similar fashion to a plan by Carleton Swift Jr., an OSS officer in Hanoi, to use American influence with Ho Chi Minh to moderate the policies and personnel of the DRV government. Swift had reported to Kunming in October that "if approached informally, but firmly, it is considered possible that Ho Chi Minh might be willing to eliminate extremists from his cabinet and . . . substitute moderates." He argued that such an initiative could be undertaken through the auspices of the Vietnamese-American Friendship Association, which, he added, had been "organized under OSS supervision" and was "willing to follow our propaganda directive." Because Heppner was away from Kunming, Swift's cable was relayed directly to the OSS headquarters in Washington. Alarmed by Swift's suggestions, Washington reminded Heppner that the initiative exceeded the OSS brief in Vietnam: "If such an activity is going on . . . it must be stopped immediately. If Swift has submitted himself to such ill advised action you should recall him at once and take the necessary steps to clear our people from any political action." Upon his return to Kunming, Heppner responded immediately, recalling Swift and telling Washington that Swift's proposal "merely outlines a plan which I have emphatically vetoed as being unwise and inadvisable."[78]

These incidents did not so much reflect a widening chasm in perceptions of the Vietnamese or a shift in broader U.S. hopes for postwar Vietnam as illustrate the tensions that resulted from the delicate and precarious position of U.S. observers in Vietnam. The OSS and military operatives serving in Hanoi and Saigon in this period arrived with strict instructions to limit themselves to military and intelligence matters and to adopt a posture of absolute neutrality in their dealings with the Vietnamese, Chinese, French, and British. Given the escalating levels of tensions between these four groups, suspicions of U.S. objectives, the political ramifications of the August Revolution, and an official U.S. policy that both acquiesced to French efforts to regain their sovereignty of Indochina and called for eventual Vietnamese independence, it is not surprising that some U.S. observers found it difficult to maintain strict neutrality in such a complex situation. The line between efforts to serve as a neutral, disinterested broker and appearances of partisanship was very narrow. Yet, as Heppner's efforts suggest, U.S. commanders in southern China continued to insist that it should not be crossed.[79]

The difficulties facing U.S. observers in Vietnam were also compounded by their own squabbling and jealousies, a development that was well known to their superiors in southern China. Archimedes Patti was a particular target of criticism. Several of the OSS officers serving in northern Vietnam expressed their strong dislike of Patti. These included members of the Deer team mission, one of whom called Patti "an egotist of almost psychopathic degree." In a less vituperative but still critical vein, an American military representative in Hanoi reported to Kunming that "Captain Patti . . . has handled his contacts with . . . Annamese rather badly . . . [and] he was overly patronizing toward the Japs and Annamese. . . . Some statements made by Captain Patti were ill-considered and not in accord with the understood policy." Such criticisms had more to do with clashes of personality and judgments of professional conduct than with any real differences in attitudes toward the Vietnamese. General Gallagher, who had lent his prestige to the cultural aims of the Vietnamese-American Friendship Association and involved Ho Chi Minh in his meetings with Chinese military authorities, engaged the Viet Minh in a manner similar to that of Patti but viewed his own actions quite differently. In a letter of 20 September, Gallagher told Robert B. McClure, the deputy commander of American forces in the China theater, "Confidentially, I wish the Annamites could be given their independence, but, of course, we have no voice in this matter." Skeptical of Patti's ability to represent U.S. interests effectively, Gallagher cautioned McClure that Patti might not appreciate the importance of that distinction:

> Patti talks too much and is ingratiating to the Annamites, the French and the Japs. . . . He has got a great deal of information . . . [but] we have found that in many instances he has been off the track completely. He loves to appear mysterious, and is an alarmist. He always gets me into the corner of a room and whispers into my ear. When I enter a room, I expect to see him come out from under a rug. . . . I don't think much of him personally, believe he is trying to build an empire and appear important. Would just as soon he be relieved at an early date by someone a little less spectacular.[80]

Despite the significance of these internecine tensions in shaping the experience of some U.S. operatives in Vietnam, they had very little impact on how field observations of the August Revolution and the establishment of the DRV were conveyed to Washington. The reports on Vietnam that William J. Donovan, the director of the OSS, prepared for President Truman and the State Department accurately reflected the ambiguous and often critical perspectives offered from the field. Drawing primarily on the observations contained in Patti's dispatches, Donovan informed Truman and the State Department that "the Annamites" suffered from "an inferiority complex in relations to the Europeans" and that "the leaders of the Annamese Provisional Government" were "not politically mature" but were "misled by . . . communist elements" and "seem to have no knowledge of the meaning of terms they frequently use, including . . . liberalism, democracy."[81] These conclusions were reinforced in meetings held in December 1945 and January 1946 between representatives of the State Department and various U.S. field officers who had served in Hanoi at the time of the August Revolution, including Patti and Gallagher. In the course of their conversations, field observers did express their admiration for Ho Chi Minh as "an able and respected person" but usually did so within the broader context of their uncertainty that his regime could master the challenges of self-government.[82] Had President Truman or the State Department undertaken a substantial review of U.S. policy toward Vietnam in the aftermath of the August Revolution, the reports of OSS and military operatives from the field would not have provided them with much evidence that prior U.S. assessments of the Vietnamese had been misguided. Even in their admiration for Ho Chi Minh, the attitudes of field observers reflected and reinforced prevailing U.S. perceptions of the political immaturity of the Vietnamese and their susceptibility to external direction.

Policy makers in Washington, however, had no intention of radically shifting U.S. policy toward Vietnam. Although Vietnam was far from central to American diplomacy in the immediate postwar period, policy initiatives continued to be guided by essential tenets of the broader wartime vision of Vietnam that saw the influence and ideals of the United States, rather than the actions of the Vietnamese or the French, as essential to establishing the conditions that would foster lasting political and socioeconomic change in Vietnam. Along with their unfavorable perceptions of the DRV and Vietnamese nationalism, policy makers retained considerable suspicion regarding the direction of French policy in Vietnam. As one State Department internal policy memorandum in November 1945 stated, while the United States did "not question French sovereignty in Indochina," it did favor a "voluntary initiative on the part of the French in the development of a government to be run for, and increasingly by, the Indochinese themselves." Skeptical of French sincerity in acting as a trustee for the Vietnamese, the memorandum suggested that the French needed to show a "more positive indication" of their efforts to promote "self-government." It also expressed particular alarm at the escalating conflict between the Vietnamese government and the French.[83] The policies of the French and the fractious character of Franco-Vietnamese relations, along with the unease with which Americans viewed the capabilities of the Vietnamese, led policy makers to believe that the United States should continue to play an important role as a tutor and mediator in realizing the construction of a postcolonial independent Vietnamese state. It was a role that the Vietnamese might have welcomed, but one that the French often deplored.

Efforts to provide U.S. tutelage to the Vietnamese in this period centered on the establishment of a reading room and library by the USIS in August 1946 in a building adjacent to the American consulate in Saigon. It was intended to provide a venue for instructing urban Vietnamese in American ideals, institutions, and achievements. The library contained magazines and books with a particular focus on U.S. politics and technology. The reading room was surrounded by a series of shifting pictorial panels that illustrated, as the director of the library noted in one monthly report, "the Philippine Republic, the Bikini experiments, science and technological developments in the United States, . . . the post-war world organization, the modern American home, and American cities." A regular series of films on American education, technological ingenuity, and health care was also shown at the library, including such gripping titles as *Autobiography of a Jeep,* and a series of broadcasts of American music was initiated on a local Saigon radio station. Attendance records suggest that several thousand Vietnamese used the library each month during the last half of 1946, with a slightly higher number attending the film series.[84]

Although the aims of this cultural diplomacy were modest, they provoked vociferous criticism from the French, who despite formal U.S. support for their return to Vietnam, were suspicious of what they viewed as continuing American efforts to subvert French authority. U.S. diplomats posted in Saigon reported with exasperation on French efforts to "use all possible procrastinating means" to prevent the opening of the reading room in the summer and fall of 1946, including an unwillingness to make available necessary office space, harassment of the Vietnamese translators who worked for the USIS, and the misuse of customs regulations and duties to impound American books, journals, and films sent from Washington. One U.S. diplomat in Saigon interpreted French intransigence this way: "Many French in FIC believe US favors natives over French and that US does so to gain advantages in this area. Accordingly any display of the American way of life by USIS is considered as basically anti-French."[85]

Most U.S. policy makers would have disputed the accuracy of this analysis, but it aptly captured French perceptions. In their reports on developments in Vietnam during this period, the French devoted careful and critical attention to the activities of American intelligence operatives, businessmen, and diplomats. The French were particularly alarmed by the return to Vietnam of some former OSS personnel whom they had bitterly criticized during the August Revolution for their anti-French sentiments. To the French, their interest in the postwar development of the Vietnamese economy betrayed a particularly sinister connection between U.S. commercial penetration and official designs on Vietnam by the United States. American diplomats, these reports suggested, were also prone to anti-French comments and interested in fostering U.S. commercial ties to Vietnam. French reports viewed the activities of the USIS in a similar light, suggesting that "the exaltation of American power and ideals of democracy" were an effort to bring Vietnam "into the American orbit. They promise independence and prosperity in exchange for strictly economic advantage."[86]

Along with the cultural mission of the USIS reading room, American diplomats also sought to serve as mediators in the escalating conflict between the DRV and France over the terms of Vietnamese independence. Despite their awareness that the French distrusted U.S. impartiality, policy makers continued to believe that the United States could act as a disinterested broker in Vietnam. As Abbott Low Moffat, the head of the State Department's Division of Philippine and Southeast Asian Affairs who would lead the most substantial U.S. efforts at mediation in 1946, later recalled, "I always felt that we could see the situation . . . more objectively . . . because we could . . . analyze problems without the handicap of self-interest, prejudice, pride or domestic politics."[87] U.S. policy makers, of course, did bring preconceptions with them as they watched the protracted negotiations between Ho Chi Minh and French authorities in the spring and fall of 1946 fail to resolve the differences between them. The reports of U.S. diplomats who met with French officials and representatives of the DRV, including Ho Chi Minh and Vo Nguyen Giap, in Paris and Hanoi throughout 1946 displayed severe doubts about Vietnamese capabilities and French intentions. In a cable to Secretary of State Byrnes on 12 December written shortly after he completed an intensive, weeklong round of meetings with French and Vietnamese officials in Hanoi, Moffat summarized prevailing American views. He argued that three "basic troubles" separated the Vietnamese and the French: "complete mutual distrust," the "failure of the French" to make adequate provisions for eventual Vietnamese independence, and the "almost childish Vietnamese attitude and knowledge on economic questions and vague groping [about] independence and sovereignty." Without continued "neutral good offices," Moffat warned, no settlement could be reached. As a result, the "French position will steadily deteriorate and possibility even French influence vanish leaving area to Chinese-Soviet competition."[88]

There was little opportunity for Americans to act on Moffat's suggestions. Twelve days after his cable, on 19 December 1946, full-scale war broke out in Hanoi between France and the DRV. Moffat's hints at future Soviet and Chinese influence in Vietnam, however, presaged a new American concern in Vietnam. The State Department first began to raise concerns about the DRV's possible subservience to Moscow in September 1946, asking diplomats in Paris, Hanoi, and Saigon to keep Washington informed of any evidence to support such a conclusion. Those concerns were heightened in late November when the American ambassador in Paris, Jefferson Caffery, informed the Secretary of State that the French had "positive proof that Ho Chi Minh is in direct contact with Moscow and is receiving advice and instructions from the Soviets." The French themselves had conveyed similar reports to the U.S. consul in Saigon in hopes of undercutting any pro-Vietnamese sympathy among U.S. policy makers.[89]

Among the instructions Acting Secretary of State Dean Acheson issued to guide Moffat during his work in Hanoi was a reminder that he should "keep in mind . . . least desirable eventuality would be establishment Communist-dominated, Moscow oriented state Indochina." Moffat's observations did not confirm the department's apparent worst fears. While he argued that the DRV was controlled by a "small communist group possibly in direct touch with Moscow . . . and Yenan," Moffat suggested that attempts to "communize country [were] secondary and would await successful operation of nationalist state." Echoing the sentiments of many U.S. field operatives in 1945, Moffat believed that Vietnamese leaders were "most familiar" with "communist party techniques and discipline" rather than ideology.[90] But Moffat's comments did not close the matter. Given American perceptions of Vietnamese political immaturity and susceptibility to external direction, the potential threat remained. As the United States struggled to influence postcolonial Vietnam after 1946, mistrust of Soviet and Chinese intentions in Vietnam joined persisting suspicions of Vietnamese incapacities and French policies to shape the course of U.S. conduct.

IMPROBABLE OPPORTUNITIES
Vietnamese and American Diplomacy in the Postcolonial Moment

Shortly after the outbreak of war between the Vietnamese and the French, Ho Chi Minh's Democratic Republic of Vietnam (DRV) launched a four-month diplomatic initiative in the spring and summer of 1947 designed to secure the support of the Truman administration. Centered in Thailand, the Vietnamese effort was led by Pham Ngoc Thach, now deputy minister in the Office of the President and one of three men who directly advised Ho Chi Minh. From April to June, Thach presented a series of substantive proposals to representatives of the U.S. government and business communities in Bangkok aimed at winning American confidence and assistance. Thach's agenda included calls for recognition of the DRV and mediation of the war with the French, requests for economic rehabilitation loans and promises of economic concessions to U.S. businesses, and appeals for technical assistance and cultural exchange.

The Vietnamese initiative inspired the Truman administration's only sustained internal reexamination of its relationship with the DRV. The drive prompted efforts to reestablish direct diplomatic contact with the DRV as well as a comprehensive evaluation of Ho Chi Minh's government and its willingness to accept advice and guidance from the United States. Nonetheless, the DRV's initiative ended in failure. Like Ho Chi Minh's efforts to win U.S. support in the aftermath of the August Revolution, these Vietnamese proposals ultimately met with official silence from administration policy makers in Washington.

Despite its failure, the DRV initiative and the reactions of the Truman administration to it reveal the forces shaping Vietnamese and American diplomacy in the newly emerging and fragile postcolonial world. For the Vietnamese revolutionaries who led the DRV, the first years of the war with France brought sustained military defeat and escalating administrative chaos, putting the continued survival of Ho Chi Minh's government in jeopardy. With Soviet diplomacy focused on Europe and the Chinese communists preoccupied by civil war, the DRV also faced almost complete isolation from the communist world. In large measure, the wartime vision of revolutionary nationalism informed the DRV's efforts to address this crisis, prompting not only appeals to the Truman administration but a wider series of domestic and diplomatic initiatives. On the domestic front, the Vietnamese government launched a series of internal reforms aimed less at socialist revolution than at boosting its popular legitimacy and developing military and economic self-sufficiency. With the possibility of external assistance from the communist world foreclosed, the DRV's initiative to the United States was accompanied by renewed diplomatic efforts with the Nanking government in China and a sustained campaign among the newly independent states of South and Southeast Asia that emphasized shared bonds of nationalism and anticolonialism.

The Truman administration remained largely unaware of the larger forces shaping the DRV's U.S. diplomacy. For policy makers in Washington and American diplomats in Hanoi, Saigon, and Paris, the uncertainties of the postwar geopolitical situation in Western Europe and East Asia combined with the assumptions that had guided wartime U.S. policy toward Vietnam to shape the administration's response to the DRV initiative. Fears of Vietnamese subservience to Moscow that first had emerged in 1946 intensified with the escalation of Soviet-American tensions in Europe and increasing pessimism over the ability of the Nanking government to prevail against the communists in the Chinese civil war. Moreover, the commitment of the United States to maintain French political and economic stability in Western Europe complicated its abilities to challenge French policies in Vietnam directly.

Against this more immediate context, most U.S. policy makers continued to view the Vietnamese as politically immature, innately susceptible to outside direction, and victimized by misguided French colonial policies. These assumptions sharply heightened fears that French colonialism in Vietnam might not be replaced by a postcolonial state modeled on U.S. ideals and institutions but by one molded in the Kremlin's image. It was a chance few Americans were willing to take. But if Cold War fears lent heightened urgency to U.S. policy toward Vietnam, as the geostrategic dislocations of World War II had for Franklin Roosevelt and proponents of trusteeship, the perceptual legacies of the U.S. wartime vision of postcolonial Vietnam continued to frame the broader context of Washington's policies toward the DRV in 1947.

Vietnam and the Diplomacy of Revolutionary Nationalism

After nine months of often acrimonious diplomatic negotiations over the terms of Vietnamese independence, war broke out between France and the DRV in December 1946. The Vietnamese government's national authority quickly eroded as the DRV army faltered under the strong French military challenge. French armed forces took most of the provincial capitals of northern and central Vietnam in January 1947. By early February, the imperial capital of Hue had fallen to the French after a six-week siege. In mid-February, after two months of sporadic fighting, Vietnamese forces withdrew from Hanoi, which once again fell under French control.[1]

The adverse military situation prompted Ho Chi Minh to move his government from Hanoi to a shifting series of jungle headquarters in the mountainous northern regions of the country, where it remained until the French defeat in 1954. Although the government retained loose control over rural northern Vietnam, the fragile central state apparatus constructed by the DRV leadership in 1945 and 1946 largely ceased to function. As one contemporary critic noted in the DRV newspaper *Truth* [*Su That*], "plans were slow in coming out" and "orders and instructions were not complete." Each rural community, this critic continued, "simply followed its own developments concerning tactics and organization. At the same time the way our cadres worked was also poor so that each time an order to set something in motion needed coordination it seemed to be too difficult."[2] Communication beyond northern Vietnam was even more challenging. Some use was made of wireless radios, but more commonly governmental decisions were transmitted by couriers who made the two- to three-month trip between Hanoi and Saigon partly by boat and partly by foot.[3]

The crisis precipitated by military defeat and the collapse of the government's administrative structure was compounded by the DRV's isolation from its potential allies in the communist world. There is little evidence of sustained contact or of financial and technical assistance from the CCP, the Soviet Union, or the French Communist Party in the early years of the war against the French.[4] Support from the CCP, increasingly important to the DRV after 1949, was insignificant during this period. The CCP, preoccupied with fighting the Nanking government in Manchuria and northern China in early 1947, served as a model for Vietnamese military strategy but offered almost no financial or technical assistance. Nor did the Soviet Union extend substantial guidance or assistance to the Vietnamese. Concerned with events in Europe, including the communist struggle for power in France, the Soviets expressed sympathy for the Vietnamese cause but remained noncommittal about the specific levels of assistance the Vietnamese might receive.[5] The French Communist Party remained aloof from the DRV until its ejection from the French ruling coalition in the spring of 1947; even then, however, members were able to offer little more than internal party resolutions to secure the withdrawal of French troops.[6]

In this difficult domestic and international environment, the DRV sent Pham Ngoc Thach to Bangkok in the spring and summer of 1947 to seek the Truman administration's support. Two elements comprised the DRV initiative: efforts to convince the administration of the moderate and independent character of the Vietnamese government and calls for U.S. political, economic, and cultural assistance. Thach's contacts with the American embassy in Bangkok between April and May were directed at the former. In frequent conversations with Lieutenant Colonel William Law, the assistant military attaché to the Bangkok embassy, and with American businessmen, Thach sought to inform the U.S. government of developments in Indochina from the DRV's perspective, demonstrate the moderate character of the Vietnamese regime, and convey the DRV's capability and seriousness of purpose.

During this initial phase of the DRV initiative, Thach submitted two Vietnamese documents to the U.S. government that illustrated the nature of his efforts. The first was a series of answers Thach gave on 9 April to questions formulated by Law and Edwin F. Stanton, the American ambassador to Thailand. Thach's responses stressed the inclusive composition of the Vietnamese government and the nationalist orientation of communism in Vietnam. "The actual government," Thach said, "is . . . of broad national makeup, comprised of men from all three regions of the country." The cabinet ministers "are not associated with a particular party," he continued; rather, the "choice of ministers has been made in consideration of their worth and popularity." Emphasizing its nationalist program rather than a commitment to socialist revolution, Thach argued that communism in Vietnam since 1932 had embodied "the spirit of national resistance against French colonialism" and "is nothing more than a means of arriving at independence." Thach also sought to reassure the administration about the DRV's economic program, claiming that "the government" and "the communist ministers . . . favor the development of capitalist autonomy and call on foreign capital for the reconstruction of the country."[7]

In a second Vietnamese document, Thach endeavored to translate these broader appeals into concrete proposals aimed at increasing U.S. confidence in the DRV's capabilities. This document, a memorandum to representatives of the American International Engineering Group in Bangkok, is one of several Thach prepared and distributed to U.S. firms in Thailand. It offered a quid pro quo:

guarantees of monopolistic economic concessions to American business in return for agricultural, industrial, and military equipment as well as $10 to $20 million in U.S. rehabilitation loans. Of particular interest are what Thach termed the "economic privileges" the DRV was willing to grant to U.S. firms. The strangest, perhaps, was tourism. At a time of political and socioeconomic turmoil, Thach called Vietnam "an ideal country for tourists." More serious were promises of tax-free monopolies for American imports and for the rice export trade, potentially the largest in Asia, as well as calls for establishment of small U.S. manufacturing plants in Vietnam. Significantly, in view of Thach's efforts to demonstrate conciliation toward the French, an American rubber concession was specifically excluded from the proposal. "The majority of rubber fields' owners are French," Thach said, "so we cannot guarantee the monopoly of export because it is necessary to give some economic interests to the French." [8]

The moderate image Thach wanted to convey to the Truman administration in the first phase of the DRV's initiative was reinforced by his own appointment and a subsequent reshuffling of the DRV cabinet. By selecting Thach to represent the DRV to the Truman administration, Ho Chi Minh hoped to communicate a conciliatory message to the Americans. The choice of Thach, who had been the Viet Minh's commissioner for foreign affairs in the south and served as the Vietnamese liaison to the U.S. intelligence operatives posted to Saigon in the fall of 1945, to meet American officials in 1947 may be seen as an effort to capitalize on what the Vietnamese viewed as a positive encounter with the United States.[9] Ho Chi Minh may also have hoped to influence favorably U.S. perceptions of his government through his appointment of Hoang Minh Giam, the leader of the Vietnamese Socialist Party, as foreign minister in March and a shift in the composition of his cabinet in July. Three communist ministers were dismissed in the July cabinet reshuffle, including Defense Minister Vo Nguyen Giap (who continued to run the army), and were replaced by noncommunists who supported Ho's policies.[10]

Thach's calls for direct assistance from the United States to the Vietnamese government in late May and early June opened the final phase of the DRV initiative. The requests were preceded on 8 May by Foreign Minister Giam's appeal to the Truman administration for U.S. diplomatic recognition, a policy Giam claimed "would increase United States prestige and influence . . . and establish peace in Southeast Asia."[11] The substance of Thach's message was more pragmatic: "We recognize the world-politics of the U.S. at this time does not permit taking a position against the French." Instead, Thach appealed for political, economic, and cultural assistance from the Truman administration. He sought U.S. mediation of the Indochina war to guarantee a settlement with France either through tripartite discussion or the presentation of the Vietnamese case before the United Nations by the Philippines. Thach explicitly disavowed any interest in American weapons, repeating the request he had made of U.S. businessmen for a substantial loan to provide capital and technicians for economic reconstruction and development. He also expressed concern that the Vietnamese had "seen U.S. culture only through the French 'prison' [sic]" and proposed the establishment of joint scientific organizations, funding for a chair in American literature at the University of Hanoi, and scholarships for Vietnamese students at American universities to foster enhanced mutual understanding.[12]

The DRV initiative to the Truman administration and the context from which it emerged reveal the persisting importance of the wartime vision of revolutionary nationalism and the place of the United States in it in framing Vietnamese efforts to preserve and protect the independence of the postcolonial state against the French military challenge.[13] The urgent sense of domestic crisis, limited diplomatic options, the careful selection of Thach to meet with U.S. diplomats in Bangkok, and the character of the messages he delivered convey a seriousness of purpose on the part of the DRV to develop a closer relationship with the Truman administration. In particular, Thach's appreciation for the constraints acting on U.S. policy and his interest in economic and cultural, as well as political, assistance indicated both persisting materialist conceptions of the United States and the DRV's interest in developing a realistic and long-term alliance with the Americans.

The DRV's American diplomacy and the revolutionary nationalist vision that inspired it were also closely linked to the Vietnamese government's other efforts to address the crisis it faced in 1947. Much of the DRV's diplomacy between 1946 and 1949 was directed at winning recognition and support in Southeast Asia and India. After World War II, the common experiences of anticolonialism and decolonization promoted the development of a supra-national consciousness and increased indigenous efforts to promote regional cooperation. These developments marked a sharp departure from the colonial period. Before 1945 the colonial powers in South and Southeast Asia had consciously kept communications among colonized peoples at a minimum. In large part French Indochina followed this pattern, with the vast majority of Vietnamese elites in the colonial period influenced by France or China rather than developments in Southeast Asia or India.[14]

Ho Chi Minh was an exception. Not only did he spend a year working with the overseas Vietnamese community in Thailand in 1928 after the collapse of the Youth League in Canton; Ho also served in 1930 and 1931 as the head of the Comintern's Far Eastern Branch in Hong Kong, where he prepared detailed reports on revolutionary nationalist developments in the Philippines, the Dutch East Indies, Malaya, and Burma and played a role in the formation of the Malay Communist Party.[15] Ho Chi Minh's experiences left the DRV well placed to build on postwar sentiment for regional cooperation. Consciously drawing upon these historical legacies and shared nationalist ties, the leaders of the DRV actively sought support for their struggle against the French through regional diplomacy, including the development of bilateral relations, participation in regional conferences, and establishment of clandestine arms networks throughout Southeast Asia.

The DRV enjoyed widespread pledges of moral support from nationalist leaders and groups in India and Southeast Asia in the first year of the war against the French. Pandit Nehru, who at the time served as vice-president of the Indian interim government and minister for external affairs, sent several messages to Ho Chi Minh in late 1946 expressing his hopes for "the beginning of close and friendly relations between our two countries." On 7 January 1947, Nehru issued an appeal to France to "revert to peaceful methods in Indo-China," arguing that "the attempt of France to crush the spirit of freedom in Indo-China has deeply moved the Indian People who have always stood for the freedom of every part of Asia. . . . Their sympathies inevitably go to the people of Indo-China." In early January the Congress Party sent a resolution of support to the DRV. In February members of the Indian legislative assembly voiced "the feeling of sympathy felt by all sections of our people for the Viet Namese people in their fight for freedom." The *National Herald* praised Ho Chi Minh as "one of the most outstanding personalities the new revolutionary Asia has produced," while the *Hindustan Times* argued that "the awakened peoples of Asia cannot afford to look on while the infant Republic of Viet-Nam is being brutally murdered." In April, Gandhi issued a statement of "full sympathy" with the Vietnamese cause. Some Indian nationalists went further, attempting to organize a volunteer Indian army to fight alongside the DRV against France. Although Indian troops never reached Vietnamese soil, efforts to organize Indian medical teams to serve in Vietnam were realized.[16]

In a 6 January 1947 statement in Burma, nationalist leader Aung San expressed support for the DRV and contended that it was "necessary for all the states of Asia to assist" the Vietnamese in their struggle against the French. Efforts were also made to join the Indians in sending a volunteer force to Vietnam, though factionalism within the Burmese nationalist movement was a contributing factor to the ultimate failure of these plans. Beginning in 1947, Burmese newspapers and political parties such as the Burmese Socialist Party and the League of Young Burmese Muslims initiated an annual practice of marking the 2 September anniversary of Vietnamese independence with praise for the DRV's war effort. From the fledgling Indonesian republic engaged in its own struggles with the Dutch came promises of moral support that emphasized the strong parallels between the Vietnamese and Indonesian revolutions. In British Malaya the general secretary of the Malay National Youth Corps organized a Support Viet Nam Volunteer Corps to provide arms and manpower. One trade union asked its members in Malaya and Singapore to boycott French ships from and to Indochina.[17]

While much of the support the Vietnamese received from India and Southeast Asia was a spontaneous outpouring of shared postcolonial nationalist sentiments, the DRV also worked from their mission in Bangkok to develop bilateral ties in the region. Several historical, geographical, and political factors accounted for the location of the DRV mission in Thailand. Ho had sojourned there in 1928, and Thailand had a substantial overseas Vietnamese population in the northeast, many of whom supported the DRV's goals and policies. Given the DRV's international isolation, Thailand also provided critical access to Western and Asian states, most of whom posted diplomatic representatives in Bangkok, as well as air, sea, and communication links to the world beyond Asia. Perhaps most important, the Thai government led by Pridi Phanomyong was sympathetic to the DRV and broadly supportive of regional anticolonial cooperation. While the Thai government hesitated to accord full diplomatic relations to the DRV, it did offer a form of unofficial recognition by permitting the Vietnamese to open the Representational Office of the Democratic Republic of Vietnam (Van Phong Dai Dien Viet Nam Dan Chu Cong Hoa) in late summer of 1946.[18]

In addition to its efforts to promote closer relations with the Thai government, the DRV mission in Bangkok became the center for Vietnamese attempts to promote the diplomacy of revolutionary nationalism in Southeast Asia and beyond. Propaganda activities were a central part of the mission, which established the Vietnam News Service to disseminate the DRV's point of view on developments in Vietnam to Western and Asian diplomats in Bangkok through a weekly English-language mimeographed information sheet. The English-language *Bangkok Post*, edited by Alexander MacDonald, who had been an operative with the OSS mission in Thailand during World War II, reprinted many of these releases, further broadening the audience for the DRV's positions. In addition, MacDonald published a number of booklets prepared by the mission that sought to place the DRV's diplomatic and domestic policies in a nationalist and anticolonial context. The DRV mission in Bangkok also worked to establish linkages elsewhere in Asia that built upon the professions of moral support the regime had received following the outbreak of war with the French. Special representatives, some of whom had been trained in English at a small foreign-language college established by the DRV in one of the northern resistance zones, were sent to India, Burma, Singapore, Malaya, and Indonesia in an effort to foster more expansive official and unofficial bilateral ties.[19]

The operations of the DRV mission in Bangkok were broadly supervised by Ho Chi Minh and Vo Nguyen Giap from the resistance zones of northern Vietnam, but the difficulties of communication meant the mission was largely autonomous in its day-to-day activities. To get from northern Vietnam to Bangkok, for instance, required a three-month journey on foot through treacherous and war-ravaged terrain. Pham Ngoc Thach, who traveled most frequently between Thailand and Vietnam as Ho's emissary, provided an important link between the mission and the central government. The leading figures within the permanent mission appear to have been selected for their personal loyalties and their ability to represent the DRV effectively abroad. The latter criterion often resulted in the appointment of more cosmopolitan southerners who had strong linguistic skills and were not openly associated with the Communist Party. The head of the mission, Nguyen Duc Quy, was from central rather than southern Vietnam but otherwise fit these parameters. He had been Vo Nguyen Giap's private secretary in 1942 and a close associate of Pham Ngoc Thach in 1945; was proficient in French, English, Thai, and Chinese; and was a member of the noncommunist Democratic Party (Dan Chu Dang). Le Hy, who supervised the mission's intelligence-gathering and information services, was a southerner who had edited a resistance newspaper during World War II and spoke English and French. Tran Van Luan, a roving diplomat associated with the delegation, was a southern-born member of a middle-class family who had come of age in the radicalized climate of the late 1920s, studied in France, and worked with Pham Ngoc Thach in Saigon in 1945.[20] A final leading member of the delegation, Tran Van Giau, was also a southerner who had studied in France, but he had much closer and overt ties with the Communist Party, suggesting the presence of a muted internationalist dimension within the DRV's broader diplomatic strategy of revolutionary nationalism.[21]

With the November 1947 coup that toppled the Pridi regime in Thailand and the gradual establishment of a military authoritarian regime less supportive of the DRV's aims, the operation of the mission in Bangkok became more precarious. In March 1948, Pham Ngoc Thach undertook negotiations in Rangoon to establish a new base of operations in Burma. Although Aung San had been assassinated the previous year, the civilian government under U Nu remained sympathetic to the DRV. Like the Thais in 1946, the U Nu government did not offer formal diplomatic recognition to the DRV but permitted the Vietnamese to establish a representational office in Rangoon, provided some funding for its operation, and made available a radio transmitter to send news back to Vietnam. While the mission in Bangkok remained important in facilitating a clandestine trade in arms (discussed below) that was critical for the resistance in southern Vietnam, Rangoon became the central point between 1948 and 1950 for establishing contact between the central government in the resistance zones of northern Vietnam and the wider world. The mission in Burma was headed by Tran Van Luan, who coordinated continuing efforts to foster bilateral ties in the region. Intelligence-gathering and information activities were also shifted to Rangoon, where the DRV news bulletin continued to be produced under the direction of Hoang Nguyen, a northerner, who was a talented student of English at the regime's foreign-language college and a young protégé of Truong Chinh. Both Luan and Hoang Nguyen traveled extensively within Burma as well as in India, Indonesia, and Malaya throughout the late 1940s.[22]

Beyond these efforts to forge regional bilateral ties, the DRV was active in the Asian Relations Conference in India and the negotiations leading to the establishment of the Southeast Asia League in Thailand, both aimed at promoting regional cooperation by formalizing political, economic, and cultural linkages. The Asian Relations Conference, held between 23 March and 2 April 1947 in New Delhi under the auspices of the Indian government, aimed to address the common problems facing Asian countries in the postcolonial era.[23] The conference opened with calls to Asian unity by Pandit Nehru, who drew particular attention to the contrast between the isolation of Asian countries from one another under European colonial rule and the economic and cultural interchange that had characterized inter-Asian relations in the precolonial period. He suggested that these historical legacies served as a starting point for renewed regional cooperation, a sentiment echoed by Mahatma Gandhi, who addressed the closing session of the conference before an audience of more than 25,000.[24]

For most of the ten-day conference, delegates were organized into working groups to discuss and prepare reports on movements for national independence, racial issues, postcolonial economic transitions, cultural problems, and the status of women. Twenty-eight Asian and Middle Eastern states were represented by more than 190 delegates at the conference, including the DRV, whose delegation included Tran Van Giau and Tran Van Luan from the mission in Bangkok and Mai The Chau, the DRV's representative in India. Viewing the conference as an important opportunity to break Vietnam out of its international diplomatic isolation, the DRV representatives were an active presence in almost all of its proceedings.[25]

Despite the socioeconomic and cultural agenda that conference organizers had hoped would shape the meetings, political issues dominated the discussions in working groups. The Burmese and Indonesian delegations, which were among the largest at the conference, often played a leading role. Together with the DRV representatives, the Burmese and Indonesian delegations used the working group on national movements for freedom and other forums to seek assistance for their anticolonial struggles beyond pledges of moral support. The Indonesian delegation, led by Prime Minister Sutan Sjahrir, whose government had just received de facto recognition from the Dutch over parts of the archipelago, called for the development of an Asian press agency to speed regional communication on nationalist movements, the withdrawal of all colonial armies from Asian countries, and a series of concrete measures to accelerate the full independence of Asian peoples. Their proposals met with vocal support from the Vietnamese and Burmese delegations.[26]

The DRV delegates, keen on boosting support within Southeast Asia, India, and China for the war against the French, offered a plea for diplomatic recognition and a more activist regional diplomacy. In a call for regional support at a 30 April session that included reference to the hemispheric solidarity engendered by the United States through the Monroe Doctrine, Tran Van Giau argued

> that sufficient help was not rendered to the country by the democratic countries when the French set up a puppet government in Cochin China. On the other hand arms and ammunition manufactured in these countries were being used against Indo-China. While he was grateful to all countries and especially to India for their sympathy, this was not sufficient help in their struggle for independence. He wanted the Indian delegates to approach their Government to accord recognition to the Government of Vietnam. In addition, he wanted them to use their influence to get the United Nations Organization to take up the question. He also wanted steps to be taken to stop French reinforcements. . . . What was needed in Asia was not a neutrality bloc but a fighting federation. There can be no national union between the French and the Viet Namese even as there can be none between the Dutch and the Indonesians, or the British and the Indians. America has the Monroe Doctrine and there are attempts at a federation of Europe. We in Asia should form one great federation, not against Europe, nor against America, but to fight and protect our freedom.[27]

The Indonesian and Burmese delegations fully supported these Vietnamese sentiments, "hoping that the freedom gained by the Viet Namese people would not be allowed to be lost but preserved by all the Asian countries."[28]

If such exchanges promoted increased inter–Southeast Asian cooperation at the conference, the less effusive Indian and Chinese responses to DRV proposals belied the fragility of pan-Asian postcolonial unity and the complexities of inter-Asian diplomacy. Nehru reiterated India's "sympathy with Viet Nam's struggle for freedom" but envisioned a more limited role for Asian diplomacy: "Nehru said that he did not see how the Indian Government could be expected—or for that matter, other Asian countries—to declare war on France. That was not the way to proceed, and by such precipitate action they were likely to lose in the long run.

Any wise government would try to limit the area of conflict. It would, however, bring sufficient pressure to bear but that could not obviously be done by governments in public meetings."[29] The Chinese delegation, made up of Kuomintang party leaders and academics, supported Nehru's position.

These moderate declarations fell far short of what the DRV delegation might have liked. But despite their disappointment and privately voiced suspicions of Indian and Chinese designs in Southeast Asia, the Vietnamese, like other delegations from Southeast Asia, were nonetheless quick to express publicly their gratitude for the "kindness" India and China had shown the region's nationalist struggles. Two British observers at the conference commented on the resulting tensions that emerged in the diplomatic line pursued by the Southeast Asian delegations:

> The South-East Asia group . . . were conscious that they were not strong enough to stand on their own feet either economically or politically but there were filled with a deep mistrust, both of China and India. This was apparent at all times and it was only their even greater if more sentimental dislike of imperialism that persuaded them to accept Chinese or Indian leadership as the lesser of two evils. There was a particularly close association between the Indonesian and Viet Nam delegates. They were both keenly interested in the possibility of support amounting to positive assistance from their great neighbours.[30]

In a further show of support for Indian policies that illustrated continuing Vietnamese hopes for pan-Asian support and cooperation, Tran Van Luan, the leader of the DRV delegation, joined the governing council for the establishment of an Asian relations organization that the Indian government hoped would carry on the work of the conference until its next planned meeting in China in 1949.[31]

The founding of the Southeast Asia League in September 1947 in Bangkok intentionally sought to draw upon the inter–Southeast Asian unity forged at the New Delhi conference. The league's idealistic constitution declared that "the peoples of South East Asia are convinced that their freedom, their well-being and their security will be more effectively assured by uniting their efforts for the achievement of their common ideals and aspirations." League members pledged themselves to the realization of full independence and the rise of economic and social standards in the region. The league was intended as a nongovernmental organization, aiming to promote the study, research, and exchange of ideas on Southeast Asia as the foundation for the ultimate establishment of a Southeast Asian federation that would join member states into an official regional group. Among those who were part of the league's formation were political figures, intellectuals, and students from Thailand, Indonesia, Burma, Malaya, and Laos.[32]

The DRV mission in Bangkok was an important presence in the establishment of the league, reflecting Ho Chi Minh's strong interest in regional solidarity and organization. As early as November 1945, Ho had written to the president of Indonesia urging the adoption of a joint declaration calling for the creation of a regional federation to promote "liberation and independence from foreign domination."[33] In addition to participating in the deliberations over the league's constitution, the DRV mission offered the resources of the Vietnam Information Service to the fledgling organization. Following the adoption of the constitution, three members of the DRV mission were elected to the league's executive committee: Tran Van Giau served as vice-president; Le Hy, as treasurer; and Tran Van Luan, as a member-at-large. In part, the league provided the DRV with another front to advance its regional diplomacy and gain support for the war against the French. The DRV was instrumental in continuing discussions in the fall and winter of 1947 aimed at putting into place the more official Southeast Asian federation. The league may also have appealed to the Vietnamese as a way of forging closer ties with the Pridi government in Thailand. While the Thai government did not lend official backing to the league, several close supporters of Pridi played a critical role in its organization; one proponent served as the president of the league's executive committee. League members hoped over time to receive official endorsement from Pridi or his government.[34]

Although the DRV's bilateral diplomacy in Southeast Asia and its diplomatic initiatives through the Asian Relations Conference and the Southeast Asia League brought few material rewards, these connections fostered ties of nationalism and anticolonialism that made possible the organization of clandestine regional networks to obtain arms, military supplies, and medicines needed for the war against the French. By 1947, Bangkok had become the center for an underground network that sent arms and supplies into southern Vietnam. The organization and operations of this network, as they emerge in contemporary French and British intelligence reporting, were complex and far reaching. The DRV mission in Bangkok and military officials in the Vietnamese base areas in northeastern Thailand organized land and sea routes across and around Cambodia that brought rice, fish, poultry, pepper, and opium produced in the resistance zones in central and southern Vietnam to Thailand. Using these commodities as well as financial contributions and tax receipts from the overseas Vietnamese community in northeastern Thailand, the mission purchased arms, radio equipment, and medical supplies that were sent back to southern Vietnam through the same overland and sea routes. Ironically, much of the military equipment purchased by the DRV in Thailand was American-made surplus from World War II that had been given to the Free Thai resistance movement against the Japanese led by Pridi Phanomyong during World War II.[35]

Thai naval officers and several leading Thai politicians and government min-

isters formerly associated with the Free Thai resistance movement provided official and unofficial support for these operations. The Thai navy, closely allied with
the Pridi government, showed public support for the DRV on several occasions, including the presentation of gifts of arms at celebrations honoring Ho Chi Minh
in Bangkok in July 1947. More important, the Thai navy often provided logistical
support for the DRV's sea transport routes. Former Free Thai agents still active in
northeastern Thailand helped facilitate the operation of the DRV land routes into
Cambodia; the ministers of finance and industry in the Pridi government may also
have assisted in arranging for the transport of arms across the Thai-Cambodian
border. The Vietnamese were also able to garner unofficial support from opponents of the Pridi regime. One of the most important Thai firms involved in the
arms trade was owned by Khuang Aphaiwang, the leader of the Democratic Party
who opposed the Pridi government. Joining forces in an uneasy alliance with Field
Marshall Phibun Songkhram and the other army leaders who led the November
1947 coup that toppled the Pridi regime, Aphaiwang served as prime minister in a
short-lived postcoup civilian government. Aphaiwang, whose family had lost substantial lands in western Cambodia under French colonial rule, was a supporter
of the broader resistance against France throughout Indochina. Aphaiwang's company helped to establish lines of credit for the DRV with Bangkok banks and facilitate the purchase of arms and other military supplies.[36]

The DRV's clandestine arms procurement networks were not limited to Thailand. The Vietnamese used Bangkok as a base from which to expand their arms
purchasing that eventually included clandestine arrangements with sellers in
Burma, Singapore, and the Philippines. After April 1948, when Phibun ousted
the Aphaiwang government and gradually initiated a crackdown on the forces in
Thai politics sympathetic to the DRV, Vietnamese operations in Thailand became
somewhat more difficult. While Bangkok and northeastern Thailand remained a
crucial link in the DRV's arms procurement efforts, the Philippines increasingly
became an important center for arms trafficking in a network that involved former
British and American intelligence operatives who traded surplus U.S. military
goods through Philippine firms. These materials reached DRV resistance zones
through either China or a complicated sea and land route that went through Singapore, Thailand, and Cambodia before entering Vietnam. Though less extensive
than the Southeast Asian network, China, too, became an important source of
DRV military supplies for troops fighting in the resistance zones of northern Vietnam. Using agents in Hong Kong and Canton as well as overseas Chinese commercial firms located in northern Vietnam, the DRV arranged for arms purchases
from nationalist Chinese military commanders in southern China. Entering Vietnam through land and sea routes, they were often U.S., Italian, or Swedish arms

that had been sent to the Chinese by the United States for use during World War II or in the Chinese civil war.[37]

The military equipment obtained by the DRV through these clandestine networks was substantial. Contemporary French intelligence reports claimed that the arms traffic was "continuous and significant." In 1946 the mission in Bangkok oversaw the transport of 20 tons of arms through overland routes. Between 1949 and 1950 some 156 tons were transported each year. Arms may have reached southern Vietnam by sea routes in even larger quantities. In the last four months of 1947, for example, the French navy seized 250 tons of contraband arms that were probably only a small fraction of the arms getting through to Vietnam by sea. Shipments of arms from the Philippines intended for Vietnam captured in 1948 and 1949 were valued at over $100,000. Estimates of the value of the arms trade between northern Vietnam and the Kuomintang in southern China in 1947 were between 300,000 and 900,000 piasters in a two-month period. Although available evidence makes it difficult to draw precise conclusions about the larger significance of the arms traffic, DRV documents captured by the French in this period suggest that the arms traffic was vital to the war effort against the French. With the exception of arms produced in local armament factories and those captured from the French, the DRV's arms networks were the only major external source of military supplies until diplomatic recognition of the DRV in 1950 by the Chinese communists opened a new source of military assistance. From 1946 to 1949 the clandestine arms networks in Southeast Asia and southern China played a critical role in the ability of the Vietnamese to hold their own against the French in a period of international isolation.[38]

The arms trade in southern China was accompanied by more official DRV efforts to promote relations with the Nanking government, an initiative that resulted less from efforts to build on shared nationalist sentiment than the centuries-old Vietnamese diplomatic practice of maintaining favorable relations with China to forestall possible intervention in Vietnam's domestic affairs. Despite the predatory actions of the Chinese occupation forces in Hanoi in the fall and winter of 1945, the DRV made strenuous efforts to protect Chinese refugees caught in the crossfire of initial skirmishes between French and Vietnamese troops in Hanoi and Haiphong at the outbreak of the war with the French. In February 1947 the DRV planned to send a four-man delegation to Nanking, a mission its leader Nguyen Duy Thanh, the China hand in the DRV's small foreign ministry, termed an effort "to get rid of the French, with the help of the Chinese." While a French offensive in February in northern Vietnam forced the abandonment of the mission, the DRV renewed its efforts in the spring of 1947. At the Asian Relations Conference held in New Delhi in March and April, both Tran Van Luan and Tran Van Giau held extensive talks with delegates from the Nanking government. No substantive agreements were reached, however, and the Vietnamese remained disappointed about the lack of public Chinese support for the DRV at the conference.[39]

The DRV's efforts to foster a relationship with China continued into the summer of 1947 at a time when many observers believed Chiang Kai-shek's armies would shortly defeat the CCP's main force. To some extent this was an exercise in propaganda. In a July interview, Ho sought to draw an ideological link between the DRV and the Nanking government, claiming, "We are realizing the People's Three Principles of Asia's great revolution, as stated by Dr. Sun Yat-sen, though the French reactionary colonialists mistook them for the 'class principles' of Karl Marx." But other efforts had a more substantive intent. Vo Nguyen Giap traveled to Canton to meet with representatives of the Nanking government in May 1947. A seven-man delegation led by Nguyen Duy Thanh entered China in October only to be arrested by local Nanking authorities and held until the following February. Despite Chinese disavowals of the actions of its local representatives, Thanh returned to Vietnam after his release rather than continue on to Nanking. Although Thanh's aborted mission marked the last major effort at establishing official ties with Nanking, the clandestine ties forged with the government's military continued to provide an important source of arms, military supplies, and medicines for the resistance in northern Vietnam until the fall of 1948.[40]

Far-reaching internal reforms accompanied the DRV's diplomatic initiatives in India, Southeast Asia, and China, suggesting that the DRV's leadership was prepared to develop domestic autonomy if its efforts to win assistance in Asia and from the United States failed. In April 1947 a central party cadre conference issued a directive calling for an immediate shift to guerrilla techniques in order to regain the initiative against the French. As part of this shift, all villages under the DRV's control were instructed to establish self-defense militia units, and training in guerrilla warfare began in newly liberated areas. Domestic weapons manufacturing also increased, with the construction of major factories at Phu-Tho in northern Vietnam and the establishment of local arms workshops producing bazookas, grenades, pistols, rifles, and machine guns.[41] The DRV also renewed efforts to launch moderate forms of socioeconomic reform begun during the August Revolution, including calls for increased food and industrial production, revived efforts to reduce land rents by 25 percent, and intensified literacy drives. The government's policy toward the reduction of land rents illustrates the character of these efforts. Rather than undertaking full-scale land reform to achieve a socialist transformation of the countryside, the DRV sought to alleviate rural distress by reducing rents while maintaining existing landownership patterns to keep local notables and rich peasants in the nationalist coalition against the French.[42]

To the leadership of the DRV, the policies of revolutionary nationalism at home and abroad were closely intertwined. Whether building military and economic self-sufficiency and undertaking moderate socioeconomic reform within Vietnam or fostering psychological and material support through ties with the United States, China, India, and the newly independent states of Southeast Asia, the DRV drew upon the perceptual legacies of the colonial period and World War II to fashion a policy that would preserve and maintain Vietnamese independence against the French military challenge. The Truman administration would come to perceive Vietnamese aims quite differently.

The United States Faces the Democratic Republic

The DRV's overtures to the Truman administration in the spring and summer of 1947 came at a time of increasing resolve in American policy toward Europe and of continued indecision and growing frustration in East Asia. With the announcement of the Truman Doctrine in March and the Marshall Plan in June, U.S. efforts to contain Soviet expansionism in Western Europe began to find full expression. Among policy planners in Washington, the political and economic stability of France was a particularly high priority.[43] But policy toward East Asia, particularly China, remained fluid. Throughout 1947 the administration debated the efficacy of continued support to Chiang Kai-shek in the civil war between the Nanking government and the Chinese communists.[44] The Chinese issue was particularly acute for George Marshall, who returned from a failed effort to mediate the civil war shortly before he became secretary of state in February 1947.

While resolve in Europe and indecision in East Asia would in part frame the immediate context of the U.S. response to the DRV, the persistence of the broader American wartime vision of Vietnam shaped and constrained the reactions of the Truman administration. Despite its support for the position of France in Western Europe, the administration remained uneasy about French colonial policies in Vietnam. Moreover, unfavorable notions of the Vietnamese capacity for self-government became an increasing concern with the rise of fears that the Vietnamese might be susceptible to external Soviet direction. At the same time, the administration continued to hope that the United States could realize its vision of a postwar Vietnamese state in the American image.

Yet as Secretary of State Marshall suggested a month before the Vietnamese began their campaign to win U.S. support, these interlocking assumptions and aims were increasingly difficult to reconcile:

We have only very friendliest feeling toward France and we are anxious in every way we can to support France in her fight to regain her economic, political and military strength and to restore herself as . . . one of the major powers of the world. In spite any misunderstanding which might have arisen in minds French in regard to our position concerning Indochina they must appreciate that we have fully recognized France's sovereign position in that area. . . . At same time we cannot shut our eyes to fact that there are two sides this problems and that our reports indicated the lack French understanding of other side . . . and continued existence dangerously outmoded colonial outlook and methods in area. Furthermore, there is no escape from fact that trend of times is to effect that colonial empires in XIX Century sense are rapidly becoming a thing of past. . . . On the other hand we do not lose sight fact that Ho Chi Minh has direct Communist connections and it should be obvious that we are not interested in seeing colonial empires administrations supplanted by philosophy and political organizations emanating from and controlled by Kremlin.

Marshall concluded by declaring that "we do have a vital interest in political and economic well being this area." But he added, "Frankly we have no solution of the problem to suggest." [45] In its deliberations over the DRV's diplomatic initiative, the Truman administration sought in part to resolve the policy dilemmas posed by its unfavorable perceptions of the Vietnamese and the French and the role it believed U.S. ideals should play in shaping postcolonial Vietnam.

The Truman administration's response to the efforts of the DRV in March and April 1947 to demonstrate its moderate character was initially quite favorable, prompting Secretary Marshall's approval of plans by U.S. diplomats in Southeast Asia to reestablish direct diplomatic contact with Ho Chi Minh's government. In response to Hoang Minh Giam's appointment as foreign minister in March, James O'Sullivan, the American vice-consul at Hanoi, cabled Washington: "Giam is a 'moderate' with whom the French might deal." [46] The American ambassador to Thailand, Edwin F. Stanton, favorably characterized Pham Ngoc Thach as "a man of intelligence and very considerable energy." Moreover, Stanton commented that the "disillusionment felt by members of the Vietnamese government with the French communists" in large measure explained Thach's "desire to contact the American authorities" and "enlist our support." [47]

On 24 April, O'Sullivan cabled Secretary Marshall and proposed that he meet directly with Pham Ngoc Thach in Bangkok. O'Sullivan had met Thach in Hanoi before the outbreak of the Indochina war had forced Ho's government into the jungles of Thai Nguyen. While O'Sullivan did not share Stanton's favorable impression of Thach, calling him "a very shifty character," O'Sullivan was convinced that Thach was "close to Ho Chi Minh" and that "conversations with him would probably result in his revealing more information than he realized." Concerned about allaying what he termed "French suspicions," O'Sullivan suggested that official connections with this initial visit could be avoided by authorizing him leave to travel to Bangkok at his own expense.[48] Within a week, Marshall cabled his approval, both for the meeting itself and the arrangements O'Sullivan had proposed. Of particular interest to Marshall were the answers Thach might give to questions about the "extent of communist control" in the DRV and "the degree of subservience to Moscow to be expected of communist leaders."[49]

O'Sullivan's proposed meeting, however, was soon abandoned. Ambassador Stanton cabled Marshall on 7 May, informing him that Thach had left Bangkok. At the same time, he mentioned that Tran Van Giau remained in Bangkok and could serve as a "useful contact." Stanton recognized Giau as the former head of the Viet Minh's provisional government in the south in late summer and early fall of 1945 and more recently as a member of the Vietnamese delegation to the New Delhi Asian Relations Conference. But Stanton expressed doubts about O'Sullivan meeting any Vietnamese representative, suggesting that such an encounter "would certainly come to the attention of the French legation officials who might attach undue significance" to it.[50] Two days later, Marshall cabled O'Sullivan to withdraw his approval for the meeting with Thach; without reference to the possibility of initiating contact with Giau, Marshall cited Thach's absence and concerns over French reaction as reasons for the change.[51]

In part, O'Sullivan's failure to meet Thach in Bangkok reveals the importance that the Truman administration attached to its commitment to the French in Vietnam. O'Sullivan's caution, Stanton's doubts, and Marshall's reversal reflect U.S. sensitivity to French opinion. Stanton's efforts to keep Thach's contacts with the American embassy in Bangkok outside regular diplomatic channels reinforce this conclusion. Appreciating what he called the "delicacy of the situation in Indochina," Stanton argued that "utmost discretion is essential in dealings with Vietnamese officials." Stanton used his assistant military attaché, Lieutenant Colonel William Law, as an intermediary in all of the Bangkok embassy's dealings with Thach. Law, who had served a tour of duty in Kunming near the Sino-Vietnamese border during World War II, had established contact with local representatives of the DRV shortly after his appointment in May 1946.[52] At no time did Stanton acknowledge in writing any communication from Thach, saying, "It is better for Law to make informal contact . . . even though these contacts are well known to the French."[53]

The Truman administration's hesitancy to reestablish direct contact with the

DRV was also influenced by the administration's shifting perceptions of Chiang Kai-shek's government in China. In April 1947, while Thach sought to win U.S. confidence in Bangkok, the DRV renewed its efforts to foster Chinese support in meetings between Tran Van Giau and representatives of the Nanking government at the Asian Relations Conference in New Delhi. At the same time, the Truman administration was expressing repeated concern over the Nanking government's policy toward the DRV. As Secretary Marshall told Charles S. Reed, the American consul at Saigon, shortly after he approved O'Sullivan's meeting with Thach, "The Chinese cannot be expected to follow a clear and simple policy, but the Department assumes any Vietnamese government acceptable to the Chinese . . . may be considered free of predominant connections to the Communist International." Marshall added, however, that the evidence of Chinese attitudes and policy toward the DRV was "so far conflicting."[54]

At issue were two contradictory views of Chinese intentions in Indochina, a debate that reflected sharp divisions within the American embassy in China on the nature of the Nanking regime.[55] John Leighton Stuart, a former missionary and president of Yenching University who became the U.S. ambassador to China in 1946, was a vocal champion of Chiang Kai-shek and took a sympathetic view of Chiang's policy toward Vietnam. As he confidently told Secretary Marshall in a May 1947 cable, even the French ambassador to China agreed that the Chinese had abandoned their designs on Indochina in 1946 and now supported French policy in the region.[56] Against Stuart's favorable assessment, W. Walton Butterworth, a career Foreign Service officer and counselor to the American embassy in China, represented the view of most professional diplomats in the embassy. Butterworth insisted that Chiang was corrupt and untrustworthy and intended to place Indochina under Chinese influence or direct control. As early as March 1947, Butterworth told Marshall that the Chinese believed "no consideration is due France." Warning that Nanking's calls for the protection of ethnic Chinese in Vietnam could serve as a pretext for military intervention, Butterworth raised "the likelihood that the Sudeten pattern would be followed" by the Chinese in Indochina, an ominous reminder of Hitler's policy toward Czechoslovakia in 1938.[57]

Between Marshall's approval of O'Sullivan's meeting with Thach in Bangkok on 2 May and the reversal of his decision seven days later, the debate over Chinese intentions reemerged in reports from Reed in Saigon and O'Sullivan in Hanoi on the attitudes of the Chinese consul generals in Vietnam toward the DRV. Echoing Stuart's view of Chinese policy, Reed reported that the Chinese consul general to Saigon, Ing Fong Tsao, supported French policies. Ing believed, Reed's report claimed, that the DRV was "completely controlled by Communist elements whose idea of a nationalist state is but a prelude to an eventual communist state." Ing's willingness to work with Bao Dai and other Vietnamese non-communist nationalists, Reed suggested, demonstrated Chinese willingness to mediate the Franco-Vietnamese conflict.[58] O'Sullivan's report on the attitude of Yuen Tse Kien, the Chinese consul general in Hanoi, reinforced Butterworth's less favorable assessment of Chinese intentions. Commenting that Yuen's support for the DRV against the French "ha[d] never wavered" since his appointment in the fall of 1945, O'Sullivan reported that Yuen "reasons that if Vietnam were independent and began to play the Moscow game too strongly the Chinese would be able to handle the situation."[59]

Had the Truman administration accepted one view of Chinese intentions in Indochina, the significance of the DRV's appeals to the Nanking government might have been clearer. If the Chinese had been seen as intent on wresting control of Vietnam from the French, Ho Chi Minh's efforts to win the assistance of the Nanking government might have provided the administration with evidence that the DRV was too closely tied to a government hostile to U.S. commitments in the region. Or, had the Chinese been viewed as sympathetic to the French, perhaps even willing to mediate Franco-Vietnamese differences, the DRV's appeals to Nanking might have appeared to U.S. policy makers as confirmation of conciliation and moderation on the part of the Vietnamese. In the event, the Truman administration was left with the sense that the Nanking government was "playing Vietnam so that China will have two strings to her bow."[60] Just as sensitivity to French opinion prompted caution in the administration's response to the DRV, continuing uncertainty over Chinese intentions shaped its ambiguous perceptions of the DRV's Chinese initiatives and contributed to Marshall's hesitancy to reestablish diplomatic contact with the Vietnamese.

With the possibility of direct contact between the Truman administration and the DRV foreclosed, the administration's attention to the DRV initiative waned until Thach's June appeal for U.S. support and assistance was conveyed to Washington. In mid-July, Marshall asked American diplomats in Saigon and Hanoi for an appraisal of the DRV should events force the French to recognize the DRV as the legitimate government in Vietnam. Marshall's request, the only intensive effort by the Truman administration between 1946 and 1949 to examine the nature of Ho Chi Minh's government, raised five broad questions: Did communist influence in the DRV put Vietnam in the Soviet camp? What was Ho Chi Minh's connection to Moscow? Did most Vietnamese understand the meaning of communism? Would the DRV, without French pressure, permit "free expression" or become a "police state under one-party rule"? And finally, what was the attitude of the Vietnamese people toward the United States?[61]

In the view of Charles S. Reed, the American consul in Saigon, Ho Chi Minh's direct ties to Moscow were extremely limited. Nonetheless, Reed suggested that Ho's forceful leadership, along with the inability of the majority of the Vietnamese population to understand Western notions of self-government, might prompt the emergence of a communist state in Vietnam antithetical to U.S. interests. "Soviet policy toward Vietnam," Reed told Marshall, "appears to be one of remote control rather than of open support." Reed argued that "there is no proof that he [Ho] has renounced his communist training. . . . A wily opportunist, Ho will take any aid coming his way to gain his ends without disclosing his ultimate intentions." Reed asserted that Ho's leadership represented an "aggressive minority" who "could bring about the evolution of a communist state even if the majority of the Vietnamese are not particularly interested in the communist message."

Unfavorable perceptions of the Vietnamese capacity for self-government underlay Reed's analysis. Reed viewed the capabilities of the Vietnamese through a prism of racial stereotypes. "Few of the Annamites are particularly industrious," Reed reported, nor were they noted for their "honesty, loyalty or veracity." And while he added that the Vietnamese national character may be "a direct and pernicious result of decades of French maltreatment," Reed insisted that "the great bulk of the population was not prepared for self-government." Despite France's previous record, Reed concluded that the removal of "French pressure and the absence of Western democratic control" would make it impossible to prevent a "police state" with "Communist leanings."[62]

Writing from Hanoi, Vice-Consul James O'Sullivan voiced a more moderate view of Ho Chi Minh's communist connections and the aims of the DRV. Echoing some of the themes that arose in Pham Ngoc Thach's portrayal of Ho's regime, O'Sullivan contended that the

> influence of the Communists in the present government would not be sufficient to put Viet Nam squarely in the Soviet camp although there would be pull in that direction. . . . Ho's very great reluctance to admit that he is Nguyen Ai Quoc or to show any connection whatsoever with Russia is indicative of his realization that he must deal with the West. Ho wrote twenty-five years ago that national revolution must precede Communist revolution in Indochina and it is obvious his first concern is to get rid of the French here. He is trying to obtain aid wherever he can and will tend to be oriented toward the source from whence the assistance came.

Patriotism and nationalism, O'Sullivan suggested, formed the basis of the DRV's appeal. "Most Vietnamese," O'Sullivan asserted, "do not really understand" the meaning of communism "as an international form," nor would "they care if it was thoroughly explained to them." Like Reed, although without his racial rhetoric,

O'Sullivan argued that the Vietnamese had "no democratic tradition" and speculated on the possible "danger of a police state under one-party rule."[63]

Although Marshall had limited his request to reports from Reed and O'Sullivan, Jefferson Caffery, the American ambassador to France, also cabled his views of the DRV to the secretary. Far more alarmed than American diplomats in Vietnam about Ho Chi Minh's relationship to the Soviet Union, according to Caffery,

> [The] absence of any widespread belief in or sympathy for Communism among the masses of Ho Chi-Minh's admirers and their apparent apathy towards Communist teachings cannot seriously be regarded in these times as potent factors against the establishment of a government which would follow Moscow's directions. Recent experiences have shown only too well how a relatively small, but well-trained and determined, minority can take over power in an area where democratic traditions are weak. Nor can remoteness of Moscow be regarded as an adequate safeguard. From Ho Chi-Minh's past career there can be little doubt but that he maintains close connections in Communist circles.[64]

Caffery's perceptions were also shared by William C. Bullitt, the American ambassador to the Soviet Union in the mid-1930s and, later, to France before the outbreak of World War II. In a series of conversations with the State Department's Division of Philippine and Southeast Asian Affairs in the spring of 1947, Bullitt claimed that if Vietnam were "liberated under the present government," the DRV "would immediately be run in accordance with dictates from Moscow." To Bullitt's suspicions about Vietnamese communism was also added the same unfavorable notion of Vietnamese capabilities that Reed reported from Saigon. "The Annamese are attractive and even lovable," Bullitt claimed, but "essentially childish."[65]

Only Marshall's query about Vietnamese perceptions of the United States yielded a uniform response, suggesting that all of these observers viewed the Vietnamese through the prism of superior notions of U.S. political culture. O'Sullivan's sentiment that "Vietnamese people here still regard the United States as a promised land and earthly paradise" resonates throughout these reports. Reed did interject a cautionary note, suggesting that "if American advice and action run counter to what" the Vietnamese "think is the full sum of their desiderata, the U.S. might not be so popular." But the others shared O'Sullivan's view that the Vietnamese were "exceedingly sensitive to United States opinion and unquestionably would accept American advice."[66]

Although the reports Marshall received did not result in any immediate change in U.S. policy toward the DRV, they illustrate the factors that shaped the administration's perceptions of Vietnamese communism and its rejection of the DRV initiative. The reports of Caffery and Bullitt reveal how French views forcefully made their way into U.S. policy discussions. Both of their reports, far more strident than those of American diplomats in Vietnam on the extent of Soviet influence over the DRV, paralleled French efforts to shift international perceptions of the Indochina war from a colonial struggle to an anticommunist crusade.[67] American diplomats in Vietnam often dismissed French claims. As O'Sullivan told Marshall in a July 1947 cable, "It is curious that the French discovered no Communist menace in the Ho Chi Minh government until . . . it became apparent that the Vietnamese . . . would not bow to French wishes."[68] But with Caffery and Bullitt, both influential senior diplomats, presenting similar arguments, the French position gained enhanced legitimacy in U.S. policymaking circles. Caffery, sixty-one in 1947, had served in the Foreign Service since 1913 with high-level postings in Japan, Latin America, and Western Europe. Bullitt, fifty-six in 1947, was also an experienced diplomat. O'Sullivan's junior status may have encouraged the administration to disregard his more moderate portrait of the DRV. O'Sullivan, thirty-one in 1947, had joined the Foreign Service just five years earlier; his appointment as vice-consul to Hanoi was his first significant post.[69]

These reports also reflect how little information American diplomats had on which to base their evaluations of the DRV. No new information is presented in these cables, nor are their characterizations of the DRV backed by any systematized sets of evidence. Particularly significant is the absence of any discussion of the internal crisis facing the Vietnamese government, how Soviet influence might be brought to bear on the Vietnamese, or the character of the DRV's efforts at internal reform. The differences between these reports—more of tone than substance— are better accounted for by individual temperament or the geographic setting of the authors' posts. Reed, who doubted the existence of strong ties between the DRV and Moscow but remained skeptical of Vietnamese ability to maintain an independent communist state, spent most of his professional life in colonial enclaves, first as a representative of a U.S. rubber company in Sumatra during the 1920s, later as a young Foreign Service officer in Shanghai and Beijing in the 1930s, and finally as American consul in Saigon just before and immediately after World War II. Reed's post in Saigon, the center of French power and where the DRV had always been weakest, would have provided him with easy access to French views. O'Sullivan's post in Hanoi and his access to high-ranking members of the DRV's cabinet before the outbreak of the Indochina war would have increased his exposure to DRV viewpoints and helps to account for his more nuanced view of Vietnamese communism.

Caffery's and Bullitt's sympathy to French perceptions of the DRV reflects their willingness to rely on French judgments of Vietnamese politics as well as their individual backgrounds. Caffery, a Louisiana Catholic of French ancestry who held an honorary degree from the University of Lyon along with other French honorific awards, was popular with the French government. Bullitt's personal ties to France were also very strong. After he left his post as ambassador to France, he enlisted in the French army in 1944 and served as an infantry major. Later he was made a commander in the French Legion of Honor. Moreover, Bullitt was an outspoken anticommunist; his experiences as American ambassador to the Soviet Union at the high point of Stalin's purges had convinced him of "Soviet fanaticism bent on world domination."[70]

A unanimous distrust of the Vietnamese capacity for self-government and a sense of the superiority of U.S. political culture emerges from these reports as well, suggesting that the U.S. wartime vision powerfully shaped the administration's perceptions of Vietnamese communism and its rejection of the DRV initiative. Whether expressed in racial terms, such as Bullitt's characterization of the Vietnamese as children, or in the confident assumption of Vietnamese deference to U.S. advice and models, all of these reports view the majority of the Vietnamese population as passive, uninformed, and vulnerable to outside control. For policy makers like Marshall, concerned with the extent of Soviet influence over the DRV, these images of the Vietnamese must have been particularly disturbing. If the Vietnamese were unfit for political independence and self-government, as all of these reports appeared to confirm, the potential for an independent and moderate communist government under DRV auspices surely seemed remote. As one State Department analyst put it, "It may be certain that Ho and Co will succeed in setting up a Communist State if they get rid of the French." But, he continued, "let me suggest that from the standpoint of the security of the United States, it is one hell of a chance to take."[71]

Despite the importance the Vietnamese attached to relations with the United States in the immediate postcolonial period, the likelihood that the encounter between the Vietnamese revolutionaries who made up the leadership of the DRV and policy makers in the Truman administration in the spring and summer of 1947 would produce a substantial shift in Vietnamese-American relations was always improbable.[72] In part, U.S. and Vietnamese misperceptions of the aims and meaning of the DRV initiative contributed to the obstacles that blocked the development of closer relations between the United States and the DRV. If the revolutionary nationalist aims of DRV policy held an internal logic for the Vietnamese, they were not always perceived in the same way by the Americans. From the Vietnamese perspective, assistance from both the Truman administration and the Nanking government to mediate the Indochina war would be mutually reinforcing, as were their efforts to win support for the newly independent states of Southeast Asia and India. For the U.S. government, however, suspicious of Nanking's intentions in Indochina and uncertain about its East Asia policy, the DRV's appeals to China heightened administration fears of the Vietnamese susceptibility to outside control. The broader aims of the DRV's Asian diplomacy appear never to have permeated the consciousness of the Truman administration.

There were also misperceptions on the Vietnamese side. Thach and the leadership of the DRV may have perceived as normal the channel of communication with the U.S. government in Bangkok through Lieutenant Colonel Law. Law, Thach's only direct American contact, held a position similar to those of the American OSS officers who worked with the DRV in 1945. In view of Thach's favorable experiences with the OSS mission to Saigon and Ho Chi Minh's successful interactions with the OSS and U.S. military personnel in Hanoi, the administration's selection of Law as an intermediary with the Vietnamese might have initially been interpreted by the DRV as an encouraging sign of U.S. interest in its appeals. But for the Americans, the use of Law, an assistant military attaché, suggests the relatively low priority initially accorded to Thach's mission and demonstrates the extent of administration efforts to keep contacts with the Vietnamese out of normal diplomatic channels.

The institutional mechanisms that shaped the Truman administration's perceptions of Vietnamese communism also significantly reduced the possibility that policy makers in Washington would see the situation in Vietnam as a place to implement what John Lewis Gaddis termed the "wedge strategy" of America's emerging containment doctrine.[73] Aimed at reducing Soviet influence and power by promoting fragmentation in what was perceived as a Soviet-backed international communist movement, the wedge strategy produced U.S. support for Josip Tito's break with the Soviet Union in 1948 and encouraged "Asian Titoism" by leaving open the possibility of U.S. cooperation with the PRC in 1949. Unlike the State Department's political reporting on Mao's China, the administration's assessments of Ho Chi Minh and the DRV came from two major sources: U.S. diplomats in Vietnam and in France. In this way, the pessimistic accounts of Soviet influence in the DRV from the American embassy in France made their way into policy discussions along with the somewhat more moderate reports of U.S. diplomats in Vietnam. By contrast, American diplomats in China reported directly to the secretary of state without significant challenge from their colleagues in Western Europe. Moreover, many of the Foreign Service officers who staffed the department's Division of Philippine and Southeast Asian Affairs in Washington had minimal training in area studies and language, leaving them unprepared to question the reports they were receiving from the field or the broader assumptions guiding U.S. policy.[74]

Perhaps the most important factors in shaping the failure of the DRV's initiative, however, were the shared assumptions between diplomats in the field and policy makers in Washington that made up the U.S. vision of postcolonial Vietnam. The persisting construction of the Vietnamese national character through the prism of racialized cultural hierarchies dominated American perceptions of the encounter with the DRV in 1947, prompting not only innate distrust of the Vietnamese capability for independent government but significantly heightened fears of the DRV's susceptibility to Soviet control.[75] After the Truman administration's rejection of the DRV initiative, these perceptions, which never again received any serious re-examination, would serve as the starting point for subsequent policy discussions on Vietnam. In this sense, the Vietnamese-American encounter in 1947 was of enduring significance.

In June 1948, representatives of the Departments of State, the Army, and the Navy posted in Southeast Asia met in Bangkok to discuss U.S. policy in the region. In their extended conversations about Vietnam, the familiar, unfavorable U.S. descriptors of the Vietnamese quickly emerged. As one American diplomat argued, the "average Annamite is extremely credulous and tends to be easily influenced. . . . Unfortunately, even the most intelligent natives appear to be more willing to believe the latest fantastic rumor . . . than to absorb . . . fundamental principles." In their assessments of the nature of Ho Chi Minh's government, none of the conference participants challenged George Abbott, then serving as the U.S. consul general in Saigon, who argued that "there seems to be little doubt as to [Ho Chi Minh's] allegiance to Moscow. . . . He is surrounded by a small but able group of Annamese Communists and with them effectively controls the Viet Minh government and its army." Although Abbott admitted there was no evidence of "direct contact with Moscow," he assumed "an old Communist with the background of Ho Chi Minh does not need much direction."[76]

The conclusions reached by Truman and his policy makers as they deliberated over the DRV initiative in 1947 also directly informed the Department of State's policy statement on Indochina issued on 27 September 1948 that would guide future conduct toward Vietnam. It suggested that a major goal of U.S. policy was to

eliminate so far as possible Communist influence in Indochina and to see installed a self-governing nationalist state which . . . will be patterned upon our conceptions of a democratic state as opposed to the totalitarian state which would evolve inevitably from Communist domination. . . . We have not urged the French to negotiate directly with Ho Chi Minh, even though he probably is now supported by a considerable majority of the Vietnamese people, because of his record as a Communist and the Communist background of many of the influential figures in and about his government.[77]

U.S. policy makers now explicitly recognized that Ho Chi Minh and the DRV were inappropriate partners for efforts to realize U.S. plans for a postcolonial independent state in Vietnam. But suspicions of Vietnamese capabilities, criticisms of French policies, and the certainty that U.S. ideals would best shape postwar Vietnam still framed the American vision of postcolonial Vietnam and continued to pose difficult dilemmas for the Truman administration. The September policy statement reiterated that an "increased effort should be made to explain democratic institutions, especially American institutions and American policy, to the Indochinese." It admitted, however, that the French continued to view such activities as "inimical to their own long-term interests." According to the statement, the French "have never understood . . . the strength of the nationalist movement with which they must deal."[78] As the United States increasingly moved after 1948 to support the French-backed indigenous regime led by the former Vietnamese emperor Bao Dai as an alternative to Ho Chi Minh's government, these perceptual tensions along with the persisting assumptions of Vietnamese political immaturity would condition and inhibit any future alliance between the French, Bao Dai, and the United States.

If the assumptions of racialized cultural hierarchies embedded in the American vision of postcolonial Vietnam remained a critical framework within which the new exigencies of the Cold War were viewed, one might ask why the Truman administration recognized an independent Indonesia in 1949. After all, the character of indigenous Indonesian society had been rendered in the same derisive terms as that of the Vietnamese by interwar observers and wartime policy makers. Moreover, the prevailing scholarly explanation for the divergence in the Truman administration's approaches to Vietnam and Indonesia is the Cold War itself, a defense that initially appears to offer more internal consistency. In this view, the Indonesian nationalists, unlike the Vietnamese revolutionaries around Ho Chi Minh, showed themselves capable of remaining independent from the forces of international communism, demonstrated most forcefully by their execution of the indigenous communist leadership in 1948. They increasingly seemed to offer a regime more likely to reduce the future danger of Soviet subversion in the region than did continuing Dutch rule. At the same time, this interpretation suggests that the far greater significance U.S. policy makers accorded to France over Holland in the emerging Cold War strategy of containment meant that opposition to Dutch colonialism was much less likely to affect negatively the balance of forces on what the United States perceived as the central Cold War battleground in Western Europe.[79]

But a plausible case can be made that elements of the wartime postcolonial vision central to U.S. policy making on Vietnam were of vital importance in framing the U.S. approach to Indonesia and providing an interpretative prism for viewing the emerging pressures of the Cold War. If the United States viewed the innate capabilities of both the Vietnamese and the Indonesians unfavorably, wartime policy makers, including Franklin Roosevelt, saw Dutch policy following U.S. norms and ideals much more closely than did French colonial practices in Vietnam.[80] These careful distinctions between forms of colonial rule and the significance attached to them meant Americans interpreted the potentialities for self-determination in Vietnam and Indonesia in somewhat different ways. French colonial policies were viewed as further evidence of the complete inability of the Vietnamese to govern themselves. But Dutch policies were perceived as addressing and correcting innate weaknesses in Indonesian society, enough to assure the Truman administration that Indonesian self-government was a viable proposition whose postindependence development could take place through continuing tutelage in U.S. models.[81]

Moreover, U.S. policy makers did not reach this decision quickly. The hesitation and gradualism by which the administration embraced an independent Indonesia also bear strong similarities to the Vietnamese case. Indonesian nationalists, like the Vietnamese, declared their independence in the fall of 1945 and sought U.S. support. But just as American perceptions and policies toward the Vietnamese resulted in tacit support for the French, Truman's policy toward Indonesia favored Dutch colonial interests for much of the late 1940s despite the administration's own insistence on its neutrality. Uncertain about the viability of Indonesian independence, until mid-1949 the administration promoted gradual liberalization and tutelage under Dutch rule rather than Indonesian self-determination.

The conservative response to the situations in Indonesia and Vietnam reinforces the powerful influence of derisive assumptions about non-Western societies in shaping U.S. conceptions of the postcolonial world. As Thomas Borstelmann argues in his study of postwar U.S. support for the apartheid regime in South Africa, the "members of the Truman Administration were products [of] a racially hierarchical culture whose values they shared and celebrated. . . . Their own experiences before coming to power trained them to identify with Europeans rather than with other peoples in international affairs." [82] A note from George Kennan to Secretary of State Dean Acheson in 1949 exemplified the predominance and persistence of hierarchical thinking among the administration's chief foreign policy figures. The governments of the non-West, Kennan told Acheson, were "states with colored populations . . . unsteadied by tradition" who were "the neurotic products of exotic backgrounds and tentative western educational experiences, racially and socially embittered against the West."[83] The domestic dimensions of these sentiments, like their interwar and wartime articulations, were reflected in the administration's policy toward African Americans. Pushed by rights claims of African Americans that paralleled key aspects of Vietnamese and Indonesian demands, Truman's symbolic gestures on race in the late 1940s were not quickly translated into action, and the institutionalized racial discrimination of the prewar era and assumptions of white superiority remained firmly rooted in domestic society.[84]

The influence of the Cold War in Europe on the divisions between the U.S. approaches to Indonesia and Vietnam might also be viewed somewhat differently. If Holland held less geopolitical significance than France for Cold War policy, it was also relatively more stable, not just in terms of the lack of communist strength in domestic politics but in broader socioeconomic terms as well.[85] The deep concern of U.S. policy makers with the weaknesses of France was made pressing by fears of Soviet intentions in Western Europe. But it also reflected their commitment to making a liberal, capitalist order in postwar Europe, an undertaking whose central aims and planning long predated the Cold War.[86] In this sense, the DRV's entreaties to the United States forced U.S. policy makers to choose between rebuilding postwar France or creating the postcolonial state in Vietnam. In the Indonesian case, on the other hand, differing perceptions of Holland in the postwar order never forced the United States to make such a stark choice. Posed in this way, the decision to let postcolonial Vietnam wait most certainly reflected Cold War imperatives, but it also betrayed the continuing significance of the prism of cultural hierarchies that joined the Euro-American vision of postwar international order.

In the wake of their failed initiative to the United States in 1947, the DRV did not immediately abandon the diplomacy of revolutionary nationalism. In a continuing effort to shift U.S. perceptions of the Vietnamese government, Pham Ngoc Thach approached Lieutenant Colonel Law in Bangkok in February 1948 about the possibility of sending an official U.S. observer to the jungle headquarters of the DRV in northern Vietnam to gain firsthand impressions of the Vietnamese regime. The Truman administration declined. The Vietnamese also sought to maintain and expand their official ties and clandestine networks in Southeast Asia.[87]

But the Vietnamese recognized the difficulties posed by the Truman administration's rejection of their initiative and by the signs that the United States was moving to support the French-backed Bao Dai regime. As one internal party memorandum in 1948 suggested, "There exists certain contradictions between the French and the Americans. . . . But if . . . [they] hold together we will have to face the opposition of two strong powers." A directive to southern cadres, which reflected the DRV's concern with U.S. intentions in this delicate period, stated, "The foreign policy of our government toward the United States . . . demands that we must not take any action that would attract American animosity. . . . We now put into place a plan that strictly prohibits the writing of any document, journal or book, neither a word or a line, that might have harmful repercussions for our government's relations with the United States." Ho Chi Minh's very public efforts to convey the DRV's continued interest in relations with the United States through interviews with the American press that emphasized Vietnamese nationalism and the opportunities Vietnam presented for the investment of U.S. capital reflect this strategy and the concerns that underlay it.[88]

But as Mao's victory in China looked more certain in 1948, the muted internationalist discourse that had emerged in the aftermath of the August Revolution intensified, with the nationalistic and voluntarist sentiments that underlay Vietnamese appeals to the Truman administration and within Southeast Asia superseded by the rhetoric of anti-imperialism and anticapitalism. Internal party memorandums were increasingly critical of the United States after the summer of 1947, a development that culminated in Truong Chinh's speech before the Sixth Cadre Conference of the Central Committee in January 1949. In this speech, Truong Chinh devoted substantial attention to the "failure of American imperialism," contrasting it to "the glorious success of the Chinese liberation troops." If the United States continued to help the French, Truong Chinh argued, "it would be defeated in Indochina as it had been in China."[89] But while DRV attitudes toward China and the Soviet Union warmed, the perceptual legacies of the past would continue to animate and complicate Vietnamese policy. Tensions between indigenous conceptions of nationalism and internationalism forged under colonialism and during World War II, historical memories of the failure of Soviet-directed party activities in the early 1930s, and Ho's own tense relations with Stalin, along with historical Vietnamese suspicions of Chinese intentions in Vietnam, did not necessarily augur a harmonious beginning to the imminent embrace of Vietnam by Stalin and Mao.

CONCLUSION
Becoming Postcolonial in a Cold War World

The Cold War came to Vietnam at the end of January 1950. On 15 January, Hoang Minh Giam, the minister of foreign affairs of the DRV, announced the Vietnamese decision to recognize the PRC and requested the establishment of formal diplomatic relations. On 19 January, the PRC recognized the Vietnamese government. And on 30 January, the Soviet Union joined China in announcing its recognition of the DRV. Within weeks, Vietnam had been accorded diplomatic recognition by Poland, Romania, Czechoslovakia, Hungary, Bulgaria, Albania, and Yugoslavia. With Chinese recognition also came military advisers and substantial amounts of military equipment and supplies for the war against the French.

The U.S. response was swift. On 3 February 1950, the Truman administration announced its recognition of the French-backed Associated States of Vietnam led by former Vietnamese emperor Bao Dai. In May the administration allocated $15 million in military and economic aid to the French and the Bao Dai government for their fight against the DRV and, as Washington saw it, the forces of international communism; the figure had increased to $100 million by the end of the year. By the end of 1952, the United States had assumed 40 percent of the costs of the war and maintained a substantial presence of military and economic development advisers. By the close of the war in 1954, the United States had contributed more than 75 percent of the cost of the conflict and provided economic aid to the Bao Dai government at levels exceeded only by U.S. assistance to South Korea.

The coming of the Cold War to Vietnam—what had been a virtually unimagined contingency for Vietnamese revolutionaries and U.S. policy makers at the end of World War II—would exert a powerful influence on the subsequent course of Vietnamese-American relations and the construction of the postcolonial Vietnamese state, shaping the division of Vietnam into north and south at the Geneva Conference in 1954; the increasing centrality of Vietnam for U.S. policy makers in the 1960s and 1970s; and the approaches that informed DRV foreign relations and domestic policy in northern Vietnam during the U.S. war. To insist that Vietnamese and U.S. conceptions of postcolonial Vietnam and the larger ideational forces that shaped them fully explained the meanings of the U.S. war in Vietnam, a war that claimed the lives of some 57,000 Americans and more than 3 million Vietnamese, would be extreme. But so, too, is the insistence in most accounts of Vietnamese-American relations that these developments can *only* be understood in relation to the Cold War. Rather, the rise of the Cold War in Vietnam in the 1950s and its intensification in subsequent decades intersected with the visions and assumptions of the imagined Vietnam and America of Vietnamese revolutionaries and U.S. policy makers in a mutually constitutive fashion. And in the aftermath of the Cold War, the lingering influences of these imaginings, and the tensions and contradictions within them, remain central to how Vietnamese and Americans conceive of one another and Vietnam's place in the global order.

The seeming decisiveness with which the Truman administration embraced the French-backed Associated States government led by Bao Dai and with which the DRV entered its alliance with the Soviets and the Chinese in January 1950 belied the ambiguities that shaped both decisions. U.S. policy was accompanied by continuing derision for its new Vietnamese allies and sharp tensions with the French over the construction of the new Vietnamese state that reflected the overarching U.S. vision of postcolonial Vietnam. The administration had greeted with considerable skepticism French moves beginning in 1947 to put forward Bao Dai as a credible nationalist alternative to Ho Chi Minh. These French efforts, which became known as the Bao Dai solution, culminated in the Elysée Agreement of March 1949, through which the French pledged to grant eventual Vietnamese independence but continued to hold responsibilities for such essential matters as foreign relations and defense. The agreement did not specify when Vietnam would receive its independence; in the meantime it stipulated that Vietnam would join Laos and Cambodia as "associated states" within a broader French union that was controlled from Paris. Bao Dai returned to Vietnam in July 1949 to lead this nominally independent Vietnamese state.

Throughout the late 1940s, many American diplomats were critical of Bao Dai and the terms by which the French intended to organize his new government. In their assessments of Bao Dai, Americans in part believed that the former emperor lacked popular legitimacy, a recognition that Ho Chi Minh retained a commanding nationalist following in Vietnam despite their own objections to him. As Charles S. Reed, the U.S. consul in Saigon, argued, "Unfortunately, the majority of natives stoutly maintain that Ho Chi Minh is the man, and the only one, who represents them and they will oppose the putting forward of any other candidate as the creating of but another puppet and the erecting of a smoke screen of France's real intentions."

But U.S. diplomats also judged Bao Dai and part of his cabinet through the same unfavorable prism by which they had judged Vietnamese revolutionaries. Bao Dai and his compatriots appeared to most U.S. observers as naive and incapable of governance. As one diplomat commented from Hanoi in June 1948 on the installation of the Nguyen Van Xuan government in what was an initial phase of the Bao Dai solution, the "expressions on the faces of both the participants and the spectators gave one the impression that the whole thing was a rather poorly managed stage show, with the actors merely going through the motions. The appearance of Xuan, his stocky figure clothed in mandarinal robes which he quite obviously did not know how to handle, almost succeeded in introducing a note of low comedy. Gilbert and Sullivan came to mind."[1]

American diplomats were also critical of the continuing limitations the French imposed on Vietnamese independence, reflecting a continued belief that U.S. political ideals and institutions rather than French colonial models best served the development of the postcolonial state. In 1948 and 1949, many policy makers in Washington along with diplomats in Paris, Hanoi, and Saigon argued that French plans for the Bao Dai solution were a "continuation of parade puppets such as French have produced over past two years." They insisted that France should provide assurances for full Vietnamese independence "to dispel Vietnamese distrust of the French, split off adherents of Ho," and "materially reduce hostilities." Only "with concrete evidence [that the] French [are] prepared [to] implement promptly creation [of] Vietnam as free state . . . with all attributes of free state," Secretary of State Marshall contended, could a potential Bao Dai government succeed. In the face of persisting French unwillingness to accede to these American views, many policy makers in 1948 and 1949 believed that the United States should not "be committed in any way to approval" of the Bao Dai solution until the French undertook a "liberal and enlightened policy." As late as December 1949, Secretary of State Acheson continued to question the viability of the Bao Dai regime, arguing that the French must provide a "timetable leading to independence" and immediately show evidence of a mechanism to implement it.[2]

Strongly felt Cold War pressures blunted the salience of these concerns in 1950 and brought U.S. recognition of Bao Dai and the Associated States government. In the immediate aftermath of recognition, there was a brief period of optimism that the Bao Dai government would finally fulfill U.S. aspirations for postwar Vietnam. For those Americans most favorably inclined toward Bao Dai, however, this initial enthusiasm was usually tempered by a lingering disdain for Vietnamese capabilities. As Edmund Gullion, the chargé d'affaires in Saigon, reported to Washington in June 1950,

> It would be a mistake to underestimate Bao Dai. . . . For all his faults he is intelligent, patriotic and easily dominates type of politician Vietnamese Government possesses. . . . With any stranger he freezes into traditional impassivity of an Annamite Emperor combined with oriental diffidence. . . . He is also a thoroughly unhappy man with no friends. . . . His nervous constitution does not stand isolation he imposes on himself and his all night jeep hunts after tigers are escapades of man possessed. Yet until his country gets some kind of democratic set up he remains, for that part of it which Commies have not suborned, its constitution, spiritual leader, substitute for parliaments, for popular consent and national sovereignty. This is hard job for man brought up as puppet Viceroy and not as Thomas Jefferson.[3]

Even as Gullion put forward his somewhat curious defense of Bao Dai, skepticism of Vietnamese political abilities, objections to French policies, and the broader assumptions underlying the U.S. vision of postwar Vietnam were beginning to reemerge in the Truman administration's policy making. These concerns would come to animate the increasingly fractious partnership between Bao Dai, the French, and the Americans throughout the early 1950s.

If the U.S. decisions of 1950 are not fully explicable within a Cold War framework, those of the DRV should not be seen, as one scholar put it, as evidence that the Vietnamese state was well on its way to becoming a "model satellite" of the Soviets and the Chinese.[4] The circumstances surrounding Soviet and Chinese recognition of Ho Chi Minh's government are more usefully understood within the larger and more fluid context of Vietnamese radical discourse and the revolutionary nationalist vision of the DRV's leadership. Under strong military pressure from the French, unable to meet their own military needs from domestic sources, and facing continuing isolation in the international arena, the DRV saw Mao's victory in China as a welcome avenue for external assistance and support in its war against the French. But more than circumstances or crude ideological affinities conditioned Vietnamese interest in Chinese military supplies and advisers. The revolutionary nationalist vision that had guided the leaders of the DRV since 1941 was in part framed by Mao's ideas of the "new democracy" as well as his military tactics and strategies. Unlike the failure of Stalin's revolutionary line in the early

1930s, the application of these principles by the DRV in their political and military struggle against the French after 1946 had proved workable within a Vietnamese context.

But if the Vietnamese were anxious to gain Chinese support after 1949, they still hoped to retain the flexible revolutionary nationalist character of their foreign policy and to remain apart from the emerging bipolar structure of the international system. Available Vietnamese evidence suggests that the Chinese set the terms of their new relationship with the DRV, insisting on the exchange of formal diplomatic recognition as the price for Chinese military assistance. Moreover, for public consumption, the Vietnamese were instructed to send a note to the PRC initiating the request for diplomatic ties to suggest that they had set the process in motion. The Vietnamese, who were keen on military assistance, appeared to prefer a less formal relationship. At the same time, Mao sought to facilitate Soviet recognition of the DRV by working to arrange a rapprochement between Ho Chi Minh and Stalin, whose relationship had been cool since Ho fell from favor within the Comintern in the mid-1930s. The Vietnamese, with few other options before them, acquiesced to the terms of the Chinese, but the incident foreshadowed how Vietnamese and Chinese interests would often prove inimical in the future.[5]

One indication that the DRV maintained its interest in a diplomacy that at least partially transcended the boundaries of the international communist world was the continuing salience of Southeast Asia and India for both Vietnamese and U.S. policy makers. The Truman administration put intense pressure on the newly independent states in the region to recognize the Bao Dai government. Despite a concerted U.S. effort in India, Indonesia, Burma, the Philippines, and Thailand to influence regional perceptions of Bao Dai, most of these states remained unconvinced. Even the leadership of the former U.S. colony in the Philippines resisted, prompting Secretary of State Acheson to remark, "This general indifference or lack of understanding may prove to be disastrous for those nations as Communism relentlessly advances. It is impossible for the United States to help them resist Communism if they are not prepared to help themselves." India and most Southeast Asian states continued to see the conflict in Vietnam as a nationalist struggle against colonialism, finding it considerably less easy than the Truman administration to overlook French unwillingness to grant Vietnam full independence. As one American diplomat in the region argued, "Basic reason is detestation by these countries of colonialism and their repugnance voluntarily to recognize any regime which in their mind represents perpetuation of colonial rule." Only Thailand bowed to U.S. pressures in 1950, although the Thai decision to recognize Bao Dai provoked a severe schism within the government that led to the resignation of the foreign minister. Most leaders in the region would have agreed with Carlos P. Romulo, the Philippine representative at the United Nations, who argued that Bao Dai "was and is regarded throughout Asia as a French puppet."[6]

Despite their unwillingness to embrace the Bao Dai government, the newly independent states in Southeast Asia and India also hesitated to extend formal diplomatic recognition to the DRV. The Indonesian parliament did debate a motion calling for recognition proposed by the Socialist Party in the spring of 1950, but the measure fell well short of passage. A stance of official neutrality, however, did not mean these states were unresponsive to continuing efforts by DRV diplomatic representatives to win more informal manifestations of psychological and material support. The Burmese foreign minister attended a reception sponsored by the DRV mission in Rangoon in September 1951 to honor the sixth anniversary of Vietnamese independence, an occasion that also produced substantial support for Ho Chi Minh's government in the Burmese press. In a more substantive way, the DRV was able to maintain its clandestine arms traffic both in the Philippines and, despite official Thai support for Bao Dai, in Thailand as well. These continued linkages, and the refusal of most states in the region to accord legitimacy to Bao Dai, not only suggest that the anticolonial and national premises on which the Vietnamese had based much of their diplomacy in the late 1940s were far from ephemeral concerns in the region; they also reinforce the sincerity of Vietnamese interest in maintaining the diplomacy of revolutionary nationalism even as the DRV welcomed Soviet and Chinese support.[7]

Although the military support the DRV received from the Chinese was vastly more important than the weapons it continued to obtain from clandestine networks in Southeast Asia for the Vietnamese war against the French, the persistence of the Vietnamese revolutionary nationalist vision conditioned the escalating and persistent conflict that marked the Sino-Vietnamese relationship after 1950. At the most basic level, the massive influx of Chinese advisers, weapons, and supplies often seemed to overwhelm the Vietnamese. After 1951, a Chinese political advisory group also sought to involve itself in the making of DRV domestic policy. The fragile and underdeveloped Vietnamese state apparatus underwent a serious strain as the leadership of the DRV worked to absorb Chinese supplies and advisers. Disputes over military tactics and strategy quickly emerged, particularly after the failure of Chinese-inspired military campaigns in 1951. Personal antipathies between Chen Geng, the senior CCP military adviser and representative to the DRV, and Vo Nguyen Giap, who commanded the DRV's army, only accentuated these tensions. In his diary Chen Geng described Giap as "slippery and not very upright and honest." More broadly, Chen castigated the Vietnamese for "their fear of letting other people know their weakness" and lacking "Bolshevist self-criticism." Chen noted in his diary, seemingly without irony, that he pointed out these failings to Giap and other Vietnamese revolutionaries but never received a reply.[8]

By 1954 the Sino-Vietnamese relationship was under severe strain. Just before the battle of Dien Bien Phu that brought final Vietnamese victory over the French, Vo Nguyen Giap, after heated debates with his Chinese advisers, finally rejected a Chinese battle plan that would probably have ensured a Vietnamese defeat.[9] At the same time, the Chinese delegation led by Chou En-lai at the Geneva Conference, organized to bring a peaceful resolution to the Franco-Vietnamese conflict, was urging DRV delegate Pham Van Dong to moderate Vietnamese demands for full control of the country. Unable to resist Chinese pressures, the DRV acquiesced to a final settlement that gave them immediate control over a portion of the country smaller than what they had initially believed their victory at Dien Bien Phu would entitle them.[10] If they suppressed their resentment at Geneva, the experience left a lingering bitterness and suspicion of the Chinese. The disastrous land reform campaign launched by the DRV in northern Vietnam between 1954 and 1956 with Chinese encouragement and support further strained Sino-Vietnamese relations.[11] As the Vietnamese turned once again to Chinese as well as Soviet support in their war against the United States in the 1960s, the perceptual legacies of these tensions with China, along with significant disagreements with the Soviets in the late 1950s over the timing and nature of revolutionary activity in southern Vietnam, joined the difficulties of navigating the treacherous shoals of the Sino-Soviet split to ensure that the revolutionary nationalism that had animated the radical vision of the postwar Vietnamese state would continue to frame and complicate Vietnam's diplomacy in the communist world.[12]

The broader U.S. vision of postcolonial Vietnam also continued to frame American perceptions of the Vietnamese and the often acrimonious Cold War partnership between the United States and its Vietnamese and French allies in the post-1950 period. A State Department Policy Planning Staff report on Vietnam from mid-1950 captures prevailing sentiments about the U.S. encounter with Vietnamese society and the persisting assumptions that framed U.S. perceptions of Vietnam's backward character:

We sometimes tend to forget that the majority of Asians is a peasant [sic] steeped in Medieval ignorance, poverty and localism. Preoccupied with extracting a meager livelihood, his horizon barely extends beyond the next village. . . . They are insensitive to invocations on our part of the bonds of democratic ideology—which do not exist for them—or of the desirability of preserving Western civilization—which at worst has rankling memories for them or at best is a sort [of] mail order house for technological skills and capital goods.[13]

As U.S. perceptions of the DRV in this period suggest, these attitudes had become almost unshakable. The ability of the DRV to hold its own against the French on the battlefield in the late 1940s, as well as a series of Vietnamese military victories beginning in 1950, might have prompted U.S. observers to modify their conceptions of the Vietnamese as a backward, lazy, and incompetent people unable to rise to the challenges of constructing and maintaining an independent state.[14] American perceptions of the Chinese communists in this period did undergo a transformation. At the beginning of the Korean war, many U.S. policy makers saw the Chinese as an "unaggressive, nonmechanical and unmartial" people whose "comic opera warriors" were no match for sophisticated Western armies. But after Chinese intervention in the Korean conflict, these images shifted quite radically. The Chinese became a fierce and threatening mass whom Americans such as General Douglas MacArthur, in a speech before Congress in 1951, termed "excellent soldiers, with competent staffs and commanders."[15]

A similar reassessment of the Vietnamese communists never took place. Despite considerable evidence of Vietnamese communist military prowess and strategic sophistication, American diplomatic reporting was refracted through the prism of unfavorable assumptions about the Vietnamese and the French that denied any real agency to the Vietnamese. In their comments on the substantial victories gained by the Vietnamese communist military in a series of campaigns launched against French positions near the Chinese border in the fall of 1950, American diplomats and intelligence operatives emphasized the critical role of the Chinese communists and the French. Reflecting the persistence of the idea that Vietnamese society was particularly permeable to external control, many analysts argued that Vietnamese military victories reflected Chinese communist military direction of their Vietnamese puppets. An assessment prepared by the Central Intelligence Agency in late December 1950, for example, claimed, "The Chinese Communists have been training and equipping large numbers of Viet Minh [Vietnamese communist] troops in China and are supplying . . . considerable amounts of matériel. . . . [They] give the Viet Minh a distinct superiority over present French forces." American observers also suggested that Vietnamese victories provided further evidence of the failure of French policies in Vietnam rather than signs of Vietnamese capabilities. According to another American analysis of the border campaigns, the French "have failed in Indochina to provide adequate political and military leadership, to develop sound military plans, and to utilize properly their military resources."[16]

Within months of the Truman administration's decision to recognize the Bao Dai government, tensions quickly emerged over the political, economic, and social construction of the new Vietnamese state. In the fall of 1950 the administration began to voice doubts about the capabilities "of the Vietnam Govt and its leadership to inspire support." A National Intelligence Estimate prepared by the Central Intelligence Agency somewhat dryly suggested that Bao Dai's "qualities of leadership" were "hitherto unrevealed." Exercised about Bao Dai's extended absences from Vietnam and his indifferent leadership, Secretary of State Acheson instructed the U.S. diplomats in Saigon to inform him that the "US Govt does not regard him as indispensable to contd existence and growth in stability" of Vietnam and that he must "display an unusually aggressive leadership and courage." Policy makers also expressed dissatisfaction with the French regime, including "deficient French generalship" and colonial controls of the economy that deprived Vietnam of its "economic liberty." But a larger problem, most Americans agreed, was that "concessions to nationalist sentiment, leading toward full sovereignty for the Bao Dai Government, have been forthcoming so slowly and with such seeming reluctance on the part of the French" that the government had not "won a strong nationalist following in any quarter."[17]

Persistent dissatisfaction with the Bao Dai government and French policies toward Vietnam continued to animate U.S. discussions of Vietnam after 1950. American diplomats maintained their unfavorable assumption of the Vietnamese capacity for self-government. Writing from Hanoi in 1952, one exasperated U.S. diplomat in Hanoi characterized Bao Dai's new prime minister, Nguyen Van Tam, as a "puppet, 'cop' and sadist" and the rest of his cabinet as composed of "reactionaries, criminals, assassins," and "men of faded mental powers."[18] As increasing amounts of U.S. military and economic aid entered Vietnam, American scorn for French colonial methods and the assurance that U.S. models would best guide the construction of the Vietnamese state also intensified and provoked bitter disputes between French and American officials on how U.S. aid dollars in Vietnam would be spent. The organization and command of the Vietnamese national army was a particular concern of the Americans who supported Vietnamese control against strong French opposition. From the U.S. perspective, a Vietnamese-controlled army presented an institutional basis and a disciplinary mechanism to develop ties of loyalty to the Bao Dai government and, under the supervision of U.S. military advisers, to instill the notions of political community and citizenship Americans believed were essential for a viable postcolonial state.[19]

With the French defeat at Dien Bien Phu in 1954, the Eisenhower administration was free to pursue the realization of the American vision for Vietnam without interference from the French. As it did so, unfavorable perceptions of the Vietnamese and the certainty that U.S. political ideals and institutions served as universal models continued to shape the perceptions of the newly organized Ngo Dinh Diem government in the mid-1950s. The administration faced its first test in what is known as the sect crisis in the spring of 1955. In late March 1955, the Cao Dai and the Hoa Hao, sectarian religious movements with substantial popular support in southern Vietnam, joined the gangster-like Binh Xuyen organization that controlled Saigon's police force in a United Front to demand the reorganization of Ngo Dinh Diem's government. In the confrontational style that characterized many of his responses to his political opponents, Diem refused to consider the front's demands. Eisenhower's personal envoy in Vietnam, General J. Lawton Collins, acting on instructions from Secretary of State John Foster Dulles, insisted that the only solution to the crisis was for Diem to broaden his cabinet, but he despaired at Diem's intransigence. As Collins reported to Dulles in a cable from Saigon, "I told Diem that he must learn how to handle strong men who disagree with him since the knack of governing consists largely in that skill."[20]

For American observers, Diem's unwillingness to emulate U.S. models of governance to solve the sect crisis was a continuing reflection of Vietnamese political immaturity. As Collins told Dulles, "We are not dealing here with fully rational, educated, unbiased Westerners. The Prime Minister of this country must know how to direct men who are highly venal, and who have not learned to subordinate their selfish interests for the good of the country." Many Vietnamese, he added "simply cannot handle these mental adjustments." To Collins and other American diplomats, these weaknesses were a result of the "oriental psychology" of Diem and his ministers.[21] Collins's assessment of Diem eventually prompted him to recommend to Dulles that the United States withdraw its support of the Diem government. Initially the Eisenhower administration resisted, but in late April 1955 Dulles cabled the American representatives in Saigon to inform them of U.S. plans to replace Diem and reorganize the South Vietnamese government. The policy reversal was short lived. Faced with Diem's decisive victory in late April battles with United Front troops, Dulles once again shifted U.S. policy, cabling the Saigon embassy in early May to reaffirm U.S. support for Diem.

Like J. Lawton Collins, U.S. policy makers in the postwar period seldom paused to explicate the premises that lay behind their perceptions of the Vietnamese and the role they believed U.S. models should play in the construction of a new political community in Vietnam. Nor were these ideas ever fundamentally challenged. Americans continued to classify and define the Vietnamese in a way that signaled U.S. power and superiority. At the same time, the growing American sense of mission to remake Vietnamese society in its own image continued to join U.S. policy in Vietnam to the broader Euro-American project to transform the immutable, stagnant, and primitive "oriental."

The American vision of postcolonial Vietnam that first emerged during the interwar and World War II periods remained an essential starting point for U.S.

attitudes toward its South Vietnamese allies in the 1960s, which were often as fractious and strained as they were with the French, Bao Dai, and Diem in the 1950s, and its policies for the development of the South Vietnamese state.[22] After 1954 the idiom of modernization rather than cultural hierarchies informed U.S. discourse and policy toward the postcolonial world, including Vietnam. In its conceptual underpinnings, however, modernization theory reflected many of the central assumptions of the racialized cultural hierarchies that had shaped U.S. efforts to identify and manipulate social change in non-Western societies throughout the century, including a sharp distinction between the "backward" and the "modern" and the insistence that "stagnant societies" ought to move in a gradual, linear path toward the universal evolutionary endpoint represented by the United States.[23]

The significance of these ideas in mediating and framing the Cold War imperatives that brought Vietnam to a central position for U.S. foreign policy in the 1960s is perhaps best revealed in Lyndon Johnson's thinking about Vietnam at the time of his decision to send U.S. ground troops to South Vietnam. Johnson's attitude toward Vietnamese society was derisive, as his often-expressed sense of North Vietnam as a "piss-ant" nation or "a raggedy-ass little fourth-rate country" suggests.[24] But for Johnson, the escalating war in Vietnam held meanings beyond the need for Soviet containment. In a key speech on Vietnam delivered at Johns Hopkins University in April 1965, Johnson coupled his expression of U.S. resolve against communism with an offer of $1 billion to support an immense project under the auspices of the United Nations to build dams along the Mekong River in Thailand, Laos, Cambodia, and Vietnam to foster regional economic development, a project Johnson believed could include Ho Chi Minh's government. "The vast Mekong River," Johnson said in the speech, "can provide food and water and power on a scale to dwarf even our TVA."[25] The connection Johnson made to the New Deal Tennessee Valley Authority, a project one scholar of Johnson's policy in Vietnam has aptly termed the internal colonization of a backward America, suggests that the interconnections between U.S. models of development and their universal applicability continued to exert a powerful hold on America's imagined Vietnam.[26] As Johnson said after the speech, "I want to leave the footprints of America in Vietnam. I want them to say when the Americans come, this is what they leave—schools, not long cigars. We're going to turn the Mekong into a Tennessee Valley. . . . Old Ho can't turn me down."[27]

If the Cold War in Vietnam began in 1950, it ended not in April 1975 with the victory of the Vietnamese revolutionaries over the South Vietnamese regime but in August 1995. Along with the decision by the Vietnamese to embark on a series of market economic reforms in the late 1980s and the collapse of the Soviet Union, the establishment of formal diplomatic relations between Vietnam and the United States in August 1995 brought the Cold War in Vietnam to an end. In its aftermath, the central issues that animate the contemporary Vietnamese-American relationship, and the underlying assumptions that shape them, remain embedded in the tensions, ambiguities, and interconnections that framed the Vietnamese and U.S. visions of the postcolonial world. In the early 1990s, as American business leaders began to pressure the Bush and Clinton administrations to reopen trade and diplomatic ties with Vietnam, the Vietnamese character appeared to undergo an almost complete transformation in the American mind, with the business community arguing that Vietnam's "well-educated, disciplined, hardworking labor force" would transform the country into the next Asian tiger. But with the lifting of the U.S. trade embargo against Vietnam in February 1994, this initial optimism quickly gave way to allegations of Oriental somnolence, widespread corruption, and bureaucratic ineptitude that recalled the more familiar critiques of Vietnam the United States had offered.[28]

Secretary of State Warren Christopher traveled to Hanoi in August 1995 for the ceremonies to formalize the establishment of diplomatic relations. Christopher's speech was a manifestation of the post–Cold War triumphalism through which many Americans now used globalization, rather than modernization or racialized cultural hierarchies, to evoke the transformative power of U.S. political, economic, and cultural models for the postcolonial world.

> The main story of the late 20th century is the ascendancy of open societies and open markets in country after country, which has the effect of lifting the lives of hundreds of millions of people. If Vietnam is to find an important place in the community of nations . . . it should move beyond just opening its doors. The key to success in this rapidly changing world is the freedom to own, to buy, to sell; and the freedom to participate in the decisions that affect our lives. . . . There are many different models of market economies. But whether you go to New York, or Tokyo, or Bangkok, you will find most of the fundamentals are the same. . . . In each, efficiency, hard work, and imagination are rewarded, not discouraged. . . . But I believe sustained economic development is more likely where additional factors are present—where courts provide due process, where newspapers are free to expose corruption, and where businesspeople can make decisions with free access to accurate information. The foundation of market economies . . . can only be fully guaranteed by the rule of law.[29]

But this at least publicly deracialized restatement of non-Western backwardness and the efficacy of U.S. political and economic models brought its own share of contradictions and tensions in the Vietnamese context, from the sweatshop conditions of Nike factories in Vietnam to the currency crises that gripped Southeast and East Asia in 1998.[30] The hidden hand of globalization, so central to U.S. claims for the global market and political liberalism, has obviously failed to promote either reform in these developing economies or mechanisms of public welfare for the people at the bottom of society, for whom the crisis has had its most devastating effects.[31] Meanwhile in U.S. domestic society, which served as the pattern according to which Americans often defined the proper ordering of national space abroad, the gap between rich and poor has widened inexorably under the new global order, and exclusionary answers to the question of who can fully participate in the national community at home in debates over affirmative action and immigration have been increasingly embraced.[32]

The postcolonial visions of Vietnamese revolutionaries, and the place of the United States in them, also cast a long shadow in contemporary Vietnam. The decision of the Vietnamese Communist Party in 1986 to undertake renovation (*doi moi*) brought the economic reforms that had captured Secretary of State Christopher's imagination. The market reforms, adopted to arrest the economic stagnation and poverty that had engulfed the country in the wake of its victory in the American war, called for opening the economy to foreign investment.[33] While the largest foreign investors in Vietnam in the 1990s have been from Asia, Australia, and Western Europe, the Vietnamese state has attached particular importance to U.S. trade and investment as well as assistance from U.S.-dominated international economic institutions such as the World Bank and the World Trade Organization. In framing an approach to the United States, the Vietnamese state's initiatives resonate with the revolutionary nationalist discourse of the August Revolution and its aftermath, particularly efforts by the DRV to seek U.S. economic assistance and the materialist conceptions of the United States that underlay those efforts. A 1945 issue of the *Vietnamese-American Friendship Association Review* contained the comment, "Vietnam will be a market for American manufactured goods, and what is more, we do not see any reason why the Americans should not build a Ford plant in our new country." This sentiment was recalled and reinscribed by the presence of a giant, inflated replica of a Pepsi-Cola can that hovered over the major thoroughfares of Ho Chi Minh City in 1994 the morning after President Clinton announced that the United States would lift its decades-long trade embargo against the Vietnamese.[34]

But if the reforms have brought a sharp increase in the level of Vietnamese economic growth in the late 1980s and 1990s, Vietnamese reactions to the arrival of the market and its state patronage have been profoundly ambivalent. In a short story titled "The General Retires" ["Tuong ve huu"] by Nguyen Huy Thiep, perhaps the leading author in contemporary Vietnam, perceptions of the corrosive effect of the market on human relationships and the moral void at the heart of the state-sponsored market system received their most dramatic expression. One of the story's central characters is the general's daughter-in-law, a doctor who works at a maternity clinic in Hanoi. At home, to supplement the family's income, she raises a pack of Alsatian dogs to sell to wealthier Hanoi households as guard dogs, a practice which suggests the everyday presence of the market reforms in the rhythms of Hanoi life and the fraying of social relations that they produced. Over time the general realizes that his son's wife takes home aborted fetuses from the maternity clinic to feed to the dogs. Appalled, the general confronts his son and demands he put a stop to this practice. His son, who emerges in the story as an impotent figure powerless to resist the moral transgressions of the market his wife has introduced into the household, remarks, "I had known about it but dismissed it as being a matter of no significance."[35]

These critiques of the market economy, and implicitly of the Vietnamese state, are often expressed in ways that recall and reshape central elements and tensions in the fluid postcolonial imaginings of Vietnamese revolutionaries, and the place of the United States in them. In "The General Retires," the general himself, a decorated veteran of the French and the American wars, emerges as a valorized figure of moral probity in sharp contrast to the almost banal immorality and greed that surround him. The corrosive venality the story sets the general against betrays the continuing suspicion of capitalist materialism equated with the United States in some of the radical discourse of the interwar period. The story's portrayal of the general uses other dimensions of this symbolic vocabulary for more subversive purposes. The approving qualities ascribed to the general recall the revolutionary heroism at the heart of much of Vietnamese anticolonial discourse. This image is perhaps most vividly captured by Phan Chu Trinh's depiction of the noble and virtuous George Washington in his 1917 *Rare Encounters with Beautiful Personages*, in which Washington's exemplary behavior brought a radiant peace and security to the new American nation. In setting the probity of the general against the immorality of his daughter-in-law, "The General Retires" seeks in part to reveal the contemporary Vietnamese state's inability to realize its own ideals.

The pervasive and profound disillusionment with the state and the market reforms in "The General Retires" is replicated in recent novels, films, and poetry produced in northern Vietnam. This sensibility is captured in the words of the narrator of Bao Ninh's novel *Sorrows of War* [*Noi buon chien tranh*], one of the most popular of these works among Hanoi readers. The narrator's disillusioning experiences as a soldier and veteran reveal the emptiness at the core of the state's assurances of a socialist revolutionary transformation at the end of the war and the new promises of the market: "The future lied to us, there long ago in the past. There is no new life, no new era nor hope for a beautiful future." [36]

These critiques of the market economy are not ubiquitous in contemporary Vietnam. Over half the population of Vietnam in the 1990s is under twenty-one, and many young people have fully embraced the market economy. The Vietnamese revolution and the symbolic meanings it held for those who lived through it are far from the consciousness of individuals born after 1975. The differences in generational sensibilities emerge starkly in Le Hung's 1992 play *Fable for the Year 2000* [*Huyen thai nam 2000*]. In one critical scene, an old man and a student are involved in a standoff on a bridge. The old man insists he should go first because his generation produced everything in society: houses, roads, the contested bridge, even the young student. The student, angry and impatient that old men "occupy all the most important positions except in homes for the aging," proclaims that he cannot wait until the old man "has walked his last step" and criticizes the "pathetic" legacy the older generation has left. This generational divide, and the individualistic sensibilities of the young protagonist, recalls the more personal dimension of Vietnamese radicalism in the 1920s, its generational tensions and the desire of young radicals, as they learned more about societies in the United States and Europe, for individual freedom and moral autonomy. The turn to collectivist paths of political and social action in Vietnamese anticolonialism after the 1920s foreclosed this dimension of revolutionary discourse until recently. But its contemporary rearticulation among Vietnamese youth holds potentially transformative implications for Vietnamese conceptions of the proper ordering of domestic society.[37]

In 1992 a short story by a young author titled "The Prophecy" ["Linh Nghiem"] appeared to great interest in Hanoi. It told the tale of a young man named Hinh, the son of a mandarin, who longed to acquire the magical powers that would one day enable him to lead his countrymen to their future destiny. The destiny itself does not particularly concern Hinh, but he is intent upon leading the Vietnamese people to it. In a dream one evening, Hinh meets a messenger from the gods who tells him to seek out a small flower garden. Once he reaches the garden, Hinh is told, he should walk slowly with his eyes fastened on the ground to "look for this." It will only take a moment, the messenger tells Hinh, and as a result he will "possess the world." When he awakens, Hinh finds the flower garden and begins to pace, looking downward. Slowly a crowd gathers, first children, then the disadvantaged of society: unemployed workers, farmers who had left their poor rural villages to find work in the city, cyclo drivers, prostitutes, beggars, and orphans. Watching Hinh, they ask in turn, "What are you looking for?" And he replies, "I am looking for this." Hopeful of turning up a bit of good luck, they join Hinh, and soon multitudes of people are crawling around in the garden. Hinh looks around at the crowd searching with him and believes the prophecy has been fulfilled: he possesses the world. With that realization, Hinh goes home.

To Vietnamese readers, the story was immediately recognized as a parable with Hinh representing Ho Chi Minh and the prophecy seen as coming from a secular god, Karl Marx. "This" was the promise of the socialist future, but as the story suggests, the prophecy was hollow. Socialist ideals did enable Vietnamese revolutionaries to develop a mass following and an independent state, but despite the sacrifices of some thirty years of war against the French and the Americans, the promises of a more egalitarian and just society remained unfulfilled. "Looking for this" might more broadly be taken as the ongoing Vietnamese search for meaning in the postcolonial present. As "The Prophecy" concludes,

> The crowd continued on, like a torrent of water in a stream that never runs dry. . . . They had no idea what "this" was they were looking for, but still they hoped. A full stomach, a warm bed . . . no matter that it was a nebulous future possibility, it was still alluring enough that they poured after it like a stream of water.
> Noon.
> Then evening.
> And still the multitude pushed and jostled in the midst of the flower garden called Spring.[38]

In all of these varying senses, the postcolonial world and the American order-building projects of the twentieth century, of which the imagined Vietnam and America of Vietnamese revolutionaries and U.S. policy makers provide one articulation, remain in the process of becoming.

NOTES

In addition to the abbreviations in the text, the following abbreviations
are used in the notes.

AOM
Dépôt des Archives d'Outre Mer, Archives Nationales, Aix-en-Provence, France

AOM-CD
Conseiller Diplomatique, Dépôt des Archives d'Outre Mer, Archives Nationales,
Aix-en-Provence, France

AOM-CP
Conseiller Politique, Dépôt des Archives d'Outre Mer, Archives Nationales,
Aix-en-Provence, France

CMCD
Tran Huy Lieu et al., eds. *Tai Lieu Tham Khao Lich Su Cach Mang Can Dai Viet
Nam* [Research materials on the history of the contemporary Vietnamese revolution].
12 vols. Hanoi: Nha Xuat Ban Van Su Dia, 1955–58

FDR-MR
Map Room File, 1941–45, Franklin D. Roosevelt Papers As President,
Franklin D. Roosevelt Library, Hyde Park, New York

FDR-PS
President's Secretary's File, 1933–45, Franklin D. Roosevelt Papers As President,
Franklin D. Roosevelt Library, Hyde Park, New York

FRUS
Foreign Relations of the United States (Washington, D.C.: U.S. Government Printing
Office, 1955–90)

HST
Harry S. Truman Library, Independence, Missouri

IO
> India Office Library and Records, Orbit House, London, England

MAE
> Archives du Ministère des Affaires Étrangères Diplomatiques, Paris, France

MB
> Papers of Earl Mountbatten of Burma, Hartley Library, University of Southampton, Highfield, England

Notter Files
> Records of the Advisory Committee on Post-War Foreign Policy, Records of Harley A. Notter, 1939–45

PRO
> Public Records Office, Kew, England

PSA
> Records of the Philippine and Southeast Asia Division, 1944–52

RG 38
> Record Group 38, Records of the Office of the Chief of Naval Operations, National Archives, Washington, D.C.

RG 59
> Record Group 59, Records of the Department of State, National Archives, Washington, D.C.

RG 84
> Record Group 84, Records of Foreign Service Posts, National Records Center, Suitland, Maryland

RG 226
> Record Group 226, Records of the Office of Strategic Services, National Archives, Washington, D.C.

VKD
> Ban Chap Hanh Trung Uong Dang Cong San Viet-Nam (Executive Board of the Central Committee of the Communist Party of Vietnam). *Van Kien Dang, Tap III, 1930–1945* [Party documents, vol. 3, 1930–45]. Hanoi: Ban Nghien Cuu Lich Su Dang Trung Uong Xuat Ban, 1977

INTRODUCTION

1 *L'Avenir du Tonkin*, 19 March 1887. The most complete contemporary discussion of the 1887 colonial exhibition in Hanoi and the uses to which *Liberty* was put is a series of articles in *L'Avenir du Tonkin*, the official organ of the French regime in northern Vietnam, from 19 March to 23 April 1887.

2 My discussion of the placement of the statue at the Place Neyret and the spatial geography of colonial Hanoi relies on Nguyen Van Uan, *Hanoi Nua Dau The Ky XX, Tap 1* [Hanoi in the first half of the twentieth century, vol. 1] (Hanoi: Nha Xuat Ban Hanoi, 1994), 126, 154, 323–58; Andre Masson, *Hanoi pendant la périod héroïque, 1873–1888* (Paris: Librairie Orientaliste Paul Geuthner, 1929); Jacques Betz, *Bartholdi* (Paris: Minuit, 1954), 217; and Ernest Hébrard, "L'Urbanisme en Indochine," in *L'Urbanisme*

aux colonies et dans les pays tropicaux, ed. Jean Royer (La Charité-sur-Loire: Delay-ance, 1932), 282–86. For penetrating discussions of the broader relationship between architectural forms and power in French colonialism, see Paul Rabinow, *French Modernism: Norms and Forms of the Social Environment* (Chicago: University of Chicago Press, 1989), and Gwendolyn Wright, *The Politics of Design in French Colonial Urbanism* (Chicago: University of Chicago Press, 1991).

3 Ho Chi Minh, "Tuyen Ngon Doc Lap" [Declaration of independence], in *Ho Chi Minh Toan Tap, Tap 3, 1930–1945* [Ho Chi Minh's collected works, vol. 3, 1930–45] (Hanoi: Nha Xuat Ban Su That, 1983), 387. Archimedes Patti, who led the American OSS delegation to Hanoi in September 1945, discusses his involvement in the drafting of Ho's speech in his memoirs; see Patti, *Why Viet Nam? Prelude to America's Albatross* (Berkeley: University of California Press, 1980), 223–24. For a fascinating comparative discussion of the translation and reception of the Declaration of Independence in a variety of national contexts, see the contributors to "Interpreting the Declaration of Independence by Translation: A Round Table," *Journal of American History* 85, no. 4 (March 1999): 1279–1460.

4 The *Statue of Liberty*, of course, played a critical symbolic role more recently in East Asia during the student protests at Tiananmen in 1989. For an insightful analysis of the multiple meanings accorded to it by Chinese students, see Joseph W. Esherick and Jeffrey N. Wasserstrom, "Acting Out Democracy: Political Theater in Modern China," *Journal of Asian Studies* 49, no. 4 (November 1980): 835–65, and Tsao Tsing-yuan, "The Birth of the Goddess of Democracy," in *Popular Protest and Political Culture in Modern China*, ed. Jeffrey N. Wasserstrom and Elizabeth Perry (Boulder, Colo.: Westview Press, 1994), 140–47.

5 "France's Gift Accepted," *New York Times*, 29 October 1886, cited in Albert Boime, *Hollow Icons: The Politics of Sculpture in Nineteenth-Century France* (Kent, Ohio: Kent State University Press, 1987), 131. On the meanings accorded to the original *Liberty* in both France and the United States at the time of its installation in New York Harbor, see Boime, *Hollow Icons*, 111–39, and Marvin Trachtenberg, *The Statue of Liberty* (New York: Penguin, 1976).

6 Lydia H. Liu, *Translingual Practice: Literature, National Culture, and Translated Modernity: China, 1900–1937* (Stanford: Stanford University Press, 1995), 27.

7 My approach to the making of Vietnamese and American postcolonial visions is informed by what has sometimes been termed practice theory that sees political and social structure and human agency as mutually constitutive forces. The key texts include Pierre Bourdieu, *Outline of a Theory of Practice* (Cambridge: Cambridge University Press, 1977); Anthony Gidden, *Central Problems in Social Theory* (Berkeley: University of California Press, 1979); and Michael de Certeau, *The Practice of Everyday Life* (Berkeley: University of California Press, 1984). For one important statement of the potentialities of this approach for analyzing colonial and postcolonial relations in the European context, see Ann Laura Stoler and Frederick Cooper, "Between Metropole and Colony: Rethinking a Research Agenda," in *Tensions of Empire: Colonial Cultures in a Bourgeois World*, ed. Frederick Cooper and Ann Laura Stoler (Berkeley: University of California Press, 1997), 1–56.

8 See Gary R. Hess, *The United States' Emergence As a Southeast Asian Power, 1940–*

1950 (New York: Columbia University Press, 1987); Andrew J. Rotter, *The Path to Vietnam: Origins of the American Commitment to Southeast Asia* (Ithaca: Cornell University Press, 1987); Lloyd C. Gardner, *Approaching Vietnam: From World War II through Dienbienphu, 1941–1954* (New York: Norton, 1988); Michael Schaller, *The Origins of the Cold War in Asia: The American Occupation of Japan* (New York: Oxford University Press, 1985); William S. Borden, *The Pacific Alliance: United States Foreign Economic Policy and Japanese Trade Recovery, 1947–1955* (Madison: University of Wisconsin Press, 1984); and Robert M. Blum, *Drawing the Line: The Origins of the American Containment Policy in East Asia* (New York: Norton, 1982).

9 The presumed autonomy of American developments in much of the postwar historiography, as Dan Rodgers has recently argued, was itself tied to the political exigencies of the Cold War, particularly the need to differentiate completely the American experience from that of the Soviets. But it also more broadly reflected what Peter Novick termed "the mood of affirmation and consensus" that marked American historical writing in the immediate postwar period, a mood that persisted longer among many diplomatic historians than it has elsewhere in the discipline. See Daniel T. Rodgers, "Exceptionalism," in *Imagined Histories: American Historians Interpret the Past*, ed. Anthony Molho and Gordon S. Wood (Princeton: Princeton University Press, 1998), 21–40, and Peter Novick, *That Noble Dream: The "Objectivity Question" and the American Historical Profession* (Cambridge: Cambridge University Press, 1988), 415.

10 While recent works have immensely enriched understanding of Soviet and Chinese policy toward Vietnam, their limited analysis of Vietnamese policy tends to refract the aims and policies of the Vietnamese through available Soviet and Chinese sources. Among the most important of these works are Mari Olsen, *Solidarity and National Revolution: The Soviet Union and the Vietnamese Communists, 1954–1960* (Oslo: Norwegian Institute for Defence Studies, 1997); Chen Jian, "China and the First Indo-China War, 1950–54," *China Quarterly*, no. 133 (March 1993): 85–110; Qiang Zhai, *China and the Vietnam Wars, 1950–1975* (Chapel Hill: University of North Carolina Press, 2000); and Ilya V. Gaiduk, *The Soviet Union and the Vietnam War* (Chicago: Ivan R. Dee, 1996).

11 On the nature of Vietnamese archival materials and continuing limitations on access, see my *Vietnamese Archives and Scholarship on the Cold War*, Cold War International History Project Working Paper No. 7 (Washington, D.C.: Woodrow Wilson International Center for Scholars, 1993). On the problems of sources and interpretations for scholars of Soviet foreign policy despite their far greater access to party and government primary materials, see Melvyn P. Leffler, "Inside Enemy Archives: The Cold War Reopened," *Foreign Affairs* 75, no. 4 (July/August 1996): 120–34, and the contributors to "Symposium: Soviet Archives: Recent Revelations and Cold War Historiography," in *Diplomatic History* 21, no. 2 (Spring 1997): 215–305.

12 Robert Latham, *The Liberal Moment: Modernity, Security, and the Making of Postwar International Order* (New York: Columbia University Press, 1997).

13 Melvyn P. Leffler, *A Preponderance of Power: National Security, the Truman Administration, and the Cold War* (Stanford: Stanford University Press, 1992).

CHAPTER ONE

1 For a full text of the "Revendications," see Alain Ruscio, ed., *Ho Chi Minh: Textes, 1914–1969* (Paris: L'Harmattan, 1990), 22–23; the letter accompanying the proposal of the Groupe des Patriotes Annamites to the conference secretariat at Versailles is reprinted in Ho Chi Minh, *Ho Chi Minh Toan Tap, Tap 1, 1920–1925* [Ho Chi Minh's collected works, vol. 1, 1920–25] (Hanoi: Nha Xuat Ban Su That, 1980), 480. The origins and drafting of the "Revendications" are discussed in Bui Lam et al., *Souvenirs sur Ho Chi Minh* (Hanoi: Éditions en langues étrangères, 1965), 25; *Chu Tich Ho Chi Minh o Phap* [Ho Chi Minh in France] (Hanoi: Nha Xuat Ban Thong Tin Ly Luan, 1988), 44–51; Daniel Hémery, *Ho Chi Minh de l'Indochine au Vietnam* (Paris: Gallimard, 1990), 42–45; and Nguyen Khanh Toan et al., *Avec L'oncle Ho* (Hanoi: Éditions en langues étrangères, 1972).

2 The recent discovery in the French colonial archives of a letter from Ho Chi Minh to the French *résident supérieur* in central Vietnam posted from New York City in 1912 provides confirmation of long-standing undocumented claims of Ho's sojourn in the United States during this period. See "Lettre de Nguyen Tat Thanh [Ho Chi Minh's given name] au Résident Supérieur de l'Annam, New York, 15 décembre 1912," in Daniel Hémery, "Jeunesse d'un colonisé, genèse d'un exil: Ho Chi Minh jusqu'en 1911," *Approches-Asie* 4, no. 11 (1992): 134.

3 On the conservative nature of the examination system in nineteenth-century Vietnam, see Alexander B. Woodside, *Vietnam and the Chinese Model: A Comparative Study of Vietnamese and Chinese Government in the First Half of the Nineteenth Century* (Cambridge: Harvard University Press, 1971), 169–233.

4 "Cau Hu Lau Van" [Indictment of corrupt customs], in *Hop Tuyen Tho Van Viet-Nam, 1858–1930* [A collection of Vietnamese poetry and prose, 1858–1930], ed. Vu Dinh Lien et al. (Hanoi: Nha Xuat Ban Van Hoa, 1963), 613–18, originally published in *Dang Co Tung Bao* [Old lantern miscellany] in 1907; translated in David G. Marr, *Vietnamese Anticolonialism, 1885–1925* (Berkeley: University of California Press, 1971), 176.

5 On Vietnamese interpretations of Social Darwinism, see Hue-Tam Ho Tai, *Radicalism and the Origins of the Vietnamese Revolution* (Cambridge: Harvard University Press, 1992), 20–22.

6 For a penetrating discussion of the place of Social Darwinism in the Chinese context, see Prasenjit Duara, *Rescuing History from the Nation: Questioning Narratives of Modern China* (Chicago: University of Chicago Press, 1995), 139–44. On the broader transnational flow of ideas within Asia during this period, of which the Vietnamese reformers were a part, and its transformative potential, see Rebecca E. Karl, "Creating Asia: China in the World at the Beginning of the Twentieth Century," *American Historical Review* 103, no. 4 (October 1998): 1096–1118, and Xiaobing Tang, *Global Space and the Nationalist Discourse of Modernity: The Historical Thinking of Liang Qichao* (Stanford: Stanford University Press, 1996).

7 On the ways in which the Nguyen state's rigid control over publishing contributed to the static character of Confucian thought in nineteenth-century Vietnam, see Woodside, *Vietnam and the Chinese Model*, 186–88.

8 *Nam Quoc Vi Nhan Truyen* [Stories of Vietnam's great men], quoted in Dang Thai Mai, *Van Tho Cach Mang Viet-Nam Dau The Ky XX* [Vietnamese revolutionary poetry and prose in the early twentieth century] (Hanoi: Nha Xuat Ban Van Hoc, 1964), 96; translated in Marr, *Vietnamese Anticolonialism*, 166.

9 *Van Minh Tan Hoc Sach* [The civilization of new learning], in Dang Thai Mai, *Van Tho Cach Mang Viet-Nam Dau The Ky XX*, 208–228.

10 Except where noted, the following discussion of the Reform Movement's activities and leadership that set the broader context through which reformist images of America emerged relies on Marr, *Vietnamese Anticolonialism*; Vuong Tri Nhan, ed., *Phan Boi Chau and the Dong-Du Movement* (New Haven: Yale Southeast Asia Studies, 1988); Dang Thai Mai, *Van Tho Cach Mang Viet-Nam Dau The Ky XX*, 11–204; and Tran Van Giau, *Su Phat Trien Cua Tu Tuong o Viet Nam tu The Ky XIX den Cach Mang Thang Tam, Tap II* [The development of ideas in Vietnam from the nineteenth century to the August Revolution, vol. 2] (Hanoi: Nha Xuat Ban Khoa Hoc, 1975).

11 *A-te-a* [Asia ballad], sometimes known as *De Tinh Quoc Dan Ca* [Ballad to awaken countrymen!], in Dang Thai Mai, *Van Tho Cach Mang Viet-Nam Dau The Ky XX*, 308–16.

12 Among the most enduring of Phan Boi Chau's writings were *Hoa Le Cong Ngon* [An appeal bathed in tears] and *Viet-Nam Vong Quoc Su* [History of the loss of Vietnam]. The former is reprinted in *Nghien Cuu Lich Su* [Historical studies] 56 (1963): 41–44; the latter, in *Phan Boi Chau Toan Tap* [Phan Boi Chau's collected works], 2 vols. (Hue: Nha Xuat Ban Thuan Hoa, 1990), 2:95–182.

13 Phan Chu Trinh, "Thu Gui Toan Quyen Beau" [A letter to governor general Beau], in The Nguyen (Nguyen Ba The), *Phan Chu Trinh* (Saigon: Nha Xuat Ban Tan Viet, 1956), 81–100, originally published in *Nam Phong* in 1906.

14 Several of Phan Chu Trinh's prison poems are reprinted in Dang Thai Mai, *Van Tho Cach Mang Viet-Nam Dau The Ky XX*, 342–43. Among his essays written in Paris is *That Dieu Thu* [Seven-point letter] (Hue: Anh Minh Xuat Ban, 1958), a denouncement of the reigning Vietnamese emperor, Khai Dinh, originally written in 1922.

15 Dong Kinh Free School text, ca. 1907, cited in Dang Thai Mai, *Van Tho Cach Mang Viet-Nam Dau The Ky XX*, 76.

16 *Van Minh Tan Hoc Sach*, 210, 224–25.

17 On the ambivalence of Liang Ch'i-ch'ao's perceptions of the United States, see Hao Chang, *Liang Ch'i-ch'ao and Intellectual Transition in China, 1890–1907* (Cambridge: Harvard University Press, 1971), 193, 221–22, 239–45, and Michael H. Hunt, *The Making of a Special Relationship: The United States and China to 1914* (New York: Columbia University Press, 1983), 263–65. For an English translation of one of Liang's essays on America, see "The Power and Threat of America," in *Land without Ghosts: Chinese Impressions of America from the Mid-Nineteenth Century to the Present*, ed. R. David Arkush and Leo O. Lee (Berkeley: University of California Press, 1989), 81–95. The Chinese reformer K'ang Yu-wei, whose writings were as influential as Liang's for the Vietnamese reform generation, remained admiring of American models but questioned their immediate relevance to China given contemporary levels of development; see Hsiao Kung-ch'üan, *A Modern China and a New World: K'ang Yu-wei, Reformer and Utopian, 1858–1927* (Seattle: University of Washington Press, 1975), 209, 387–88, 524–

33, 575–78, and Jung-Pang Lo, "Sequel to the Chronological Autobiography of K'ang Yu-wei," in *K'ang Yu-wei: A Biography and a Symposium*, ed. Jung-Pang Lo (Tucson: University of Arizona Press, 1967), 195, 198–201. On Japanese perceptions of America in this period, see Akira Iriye, *Pacific Estrangement: Japanese and American Expansionism, 1897–1911* (Cambridge: Harvard University Press, 1972).

18 *Mei-kuo*, or "Beautiful Country," became the standard term for the United States in Chinese court documents by the late 1850s, in sharp contrast to the continued use of more derogatory traditional terminology for Western European states. *Hua-chi'i-kuo*, or "Flowery Flag Country," a term that also connoted beauty and respect, was a more colloquial mid-nineteenth-century usage from southern China; it reflected Chinese perceptions that the stars of the American flag, often seen atop U.S. ships in coastal port cities, looked like flowers. On the etymology of these Chinese terms, see Earl Swisher, *China's Management of the American Barbarians: A Study of Sino-American Relations, 1841–1861, with Documents* (New Haven: Far Eastern Publications, 1953), 616–17; Hsü Chi-yü, *Ying-huan chih-lüeh* [A brief survey of the maritime circuit] (1848), 9:8, 10, translated in Fred W. Drake, *China Charts the World: Hsü Chi-yü and His Geography of 1848* (Cambridge: Harvard University Press, 1975), 161–62; and Hunt, *Making of a Special Relationship*, 43.

19 Phan Boi Chau, "Ke Chuyen Nam Chau" [Telling the stories of the five continents], in *Phan Boi Chau Toan Tap*, 1:251.

20 *A-te-a*, 313.

21 Phan Boi Chau, "Ke Chuyen Nam Chau," 1:251–52.

22 Hsü Chi-yü, *Ying-huan chih-lüeh*, 9:10a–b, 30, in Drake, *China Charts the World*, 165. On the role Hsü's account played in shaping representations of Washington by Chinese reformers, see Drake, *China Charts the World*, 196; Hsiao Kung-ch'üan, *Modern China and a New World*, 90; and Joseph R. Levenson, *Liang Ch'i-ch'ao and the Mind of Modern China* (Berkeley: University of California Press, 1970), 17. On the importance of Chinese geographical works in nineteenth-century Vietnam, see Woodside, *Vietnam and the Chinese Model*, 44, 236–39.

23 Fred W. Drake, "A Nineteenth-Century View of the United States of America from Hsü Chi-yü's *Ying-huan chih-lüeh*," *Papers on China* 19 (December 1965): 48–49; Susan Wilson Barnett, "Protestant Expansion and Chinese Views of the West," *Modern Asian Studies* 6, no. 2 (1972): 129–49. In another odd reversal, American missionaries in China presented an inscribed stone tablet to the American government in 1862 that was placed in the newly constructed Washington Monument; the text contained the quote from Hsü cited above. See Drake, *China Charts the World*, 195.

24 "Nhan Chi Em Ban Gai" [Advice for fellow sisters], in Dang Thai Mai, *Van Tho Cach Mang Viet-Nam Dau The Ky XX*, 335. At the same time that Washington became a part of Phan Boi Chau's symbolic vocabulary in Vietnam, the leadership of the Tung-menh hui in China, including Sun Yat-sen and Chang Ping-lin, were devoting attention to Washington as well. For instance, the first issue of *Min-pao*, the organization's most important periodical, in November 1905 included a picture of George Washington on the front page as one of the world's greatest revolutionary nationalists. Phan Boi Chau came to know both Sun Yat-sen and Chang Ping-lin at this time in Toyko, and the ideology and structure of the Tung-menh hui in part shaped Phan's later establish-

ment of the League for the Restoration of Vietnam. On the use of Washington by the Tung-menh hui, see Michael Gasster, *Chinese Intellectuals and the Revolution of 1911* (Seattle: University of Washington Press, 1969), 39–40, 104, 196–99. On Vietnamese awareness of *Min-pao* and the influence of the Tung-menh hui on Phan Boi Chau's visions of Vietnamese anticolonial politics, see Marr, *Vietnamese Anticolonialism*, 124, 216.

25 Hoang Trong Mau, *Loi Tuyen Cao cua Viet-nam Quang Phuc Hoi* [Proclamation of the League for the Restoration of Vietnam], and Hoang Trong Mau and Tran Can Kien, *Thu Gui Dong Bao Nghe-Tinh Trong Dip Thanh Lap Viet-nam Quang Phuc Hoi* [Letter sent to our fellow countrymen in Nghe An and Ha Tinh provinces on the occasion of the establishment of the League for the Restoration of Vietnam], in Dang Thai Mai, *Van Tho Cach Mang Viet-Nam Dau The Ky XX*, 372, 257.

26 The impact of the commitment to independence and liberty evident in the Chinese novel on Phan Chu Trinh and his contemporaries is conveyed in his 1905 poem "On Reading *Rare Encounters with Beautiful Personages*" [Doc *Giai nhan ky ngo*]:

> The scramble for survival is jolting all the world.
> Hearts broken, heroes and heroines gather at the Liberty Bell.
> Even though his hair is gray, a man of noble aims manifests his love of country;
> Refined women vow to seek revenge on behalf of their lands.
> Angry at their fate, they animatedly talk together
> Without concern for life or death; their names will go down into history.
> Their daring spirit and propitious words
> Move all who read their story.

Phan Chau Trinh, "Doc *Giai Nhan Ky Ngo*" in *Tho van Phan Chau Trinh* [Collected works of Phan Chau Trinh] (Hanoi: Nha Xuat Ban Van Hoc, 1983), 54. My discussion of Phan Chu Trinh's rendering of this work draws on Huynh Ly, "Ve quyen *Giai nhan ky ngo dien ca* cua Phan Chau Trinh" [On Phan Chau Trinh's *Rare Encounters with Beautiful Personages*], *Tap Chi Van Hoc* [Literature magazine] 1 (1969): 71, and Vinh Sinh, "'Elegant Females' Re-Encountered: From Tôkai Sanshi's *Kajin No Kigû* to Phan Chau Trinh's *Giai Nhan Ky Ngo Dien Ca*," in *Essays into Vietnamese Pasts*, ed. K. W. Taylor and John W. Whitmore (Ithaca: Cornell University Southeast Asia Program, 1995), 195–206.

27 Phan Chau Trinh, *Giai-Nhan Ky-Ngo (Anh-Hung-Ca)* [Rare encounters with beautiful personages (an epic)] (Saigon: Nha Xuat Ban Huong Duong, 1958), 6–8. An abbreviated translation, which formed the starting point of my own, along with a suggestive discussion of the political elitism of Vietnamese anticolonialism before the 1920s appears in Alexander B. Woodside, *Community and Revolution in Modern Vietnam* (Boston: Houghton Mifflin, 1976), 38–40.

28 Dang Tran Con and Phan Huy Ich, *The Song of a Soldier's Wife* [Chinh Phu Ngam] (New Haven: Yale Council on Southeast Asia Studies, 1986).

29 For an instructive discussion of this phenomenon in the Chinese context, see Duara, *Rescuing History*, 139–44.

30 "The Great Learning," in *The Chinese Classics*, vol. 1, trans. James Legge (1893; reprint, Hong Kong: Hong Kong University Press, 1960), 358–59. For a discussion of the

use of *The Great Learning* in the Vietnamese imperial examination system, see Woodside, *Vietnam and the Chinese Model*, 189.

31 My discussion of K'ang Yu-wei's republican vision of universal peace draws on Hao Chang, "Intellectual Change and the Reform Movement, 1890–98," in *The Cambridge History of China*, vol. 11, pt. 2, *Late Ch'ing, 1800–1911*, ed. John K. Fairbank and Kwang-Ching Liu (Cambridge: Cambridge University Press, 1980), 283–91; Hsiao Kung-ch'üan, *A Modern China and a New World*, 409–514; and Wm. Theodore de Bary, *East Asian Civilizations: A Dialogue in Five Stages* (Cambridge: Harvard University Press, 1988), 88–97.

32 Phan Chu Trinh's 1925 speech, "Quan Tri Chu Nghia va Dan Tri Chu Nghia" [Monarchism and democracy], is reprinted in The Nguyen (Nguyen Ba The), *Phan Chu Trinh*, 101–27.

33 The broader indigenous social and intellectual context in which I place the images of America that emerged in the Vietnamese radical political discourse of the 1920s is informed by Hue-Tam Ho Tai, *Radicalism and the Origins of the Vietnamese Revolution*, and David G. Marr, *Vietnamese Tradition on Trial, 1920–1945* (Berkeley: University of California Press, 1981).

34 The fullest discussion of the French colonial education system is Gail P. Kelly, "Franco-Vietnamese Schools, 1918–1938" (Ph.D. diss., University of Wisconsin, 1974). See also Hue-Tam Ho Tai, *Radicalism and the Origins of the Vietnamese Revolution*, 32–36, and Marr, *Vietnamese Tradition on Trial*, 35–44. The student exodus to France after 1925 is analyzed in Daniel Hémery, "Du patriotisme au marxisme: l'immigration vietnamienne en France de 1926 à 1930," *Le Mouvement Social* 90 (January–March 1975): 3–54.

35 *Cloche Fêlée*, 10 December 1923; translation in Hue-Tam Ho Tai, *Radicalism and the Origins of the Vietnamese Revolution*, 72.

36 Under the French *dépôt légal* system, all works published in Vietnam after 1921 were registered with the colonial government in Hanoi, with an additional copy of each work sent to Paris. This collection, the most comprehensive holding of Vietnamese-language (*quoc ngu*) books and pamphlets published during the colonial period, is now held by the Bibliothèque Nationale in Paris. The library's catalog of Vietnamese works lists some 338 titles published in Vietnam between 1925 and 1930 that popularized Western ideas and experiences, approximately 14 percent of the total number of volumes published in this period, including literary works, religious tracts, and government publications. As some radical works were published clandestinely and not officially registered, the actual number may be somewhat higher. See "Annexe 1: Tableau des monographies en langue vietnamienne" in *Catalogue des ouvrages du fonds indochinois 1922–1954 reproduits sur microfiches* (Paris: Bibliothèque Nationale, 1988), 27. Periodicals and newspapers edited by members of the new intelligentsia also devoted significant attention to Western ideas. Among the most important were *Cloche Fêlée*, *Youth* [*Thanh Nien*], and *Ladies' News* [*Phu Nu Tan Van*], whose editorial content in the late 1920s, despite its *Good Housekeeping*-like name, was informed by radical thought. The development of the indigenous press in this period is discussed in Huynh Van Tong, *Lich Su Bao Chi Viet-Nam tu Khoi Thuy den Nam 1930* [The history of the Vietnamese press from its origins to 1930] (Saigon: Tri Dang, 1973), and Nguyen Thanh, *Bao Chi Cach Mang*

Viet Nam, 1925–1945 [The revolutionary press in Vietnam, 1925–1945] (Hanoi: Nha Xuat Ban Khoa Hoc Xa Hoi, 1984), 13–66. The fullest analysis of Vietnamese efforts to explore European thought in the vernacular publishing boom of the 1920s is in Marr, *Vietnamese Tradition on Trial*, and Hue-Tam Ho Tai, *Radicalism and the Origins of the Vietnamese Revolution.*

37 Tinh Tien, *Van Minh Au My* [European and American civilization] (Hue: Tieng-Dan, 1928). Several other works from this period that consider aspects of American society include Vu Cong-Nghi, *Dong Tay Van Tap* [Scientific and literary works of Asia and the West] (Hanoi: Librairie Quoc-Dan, 1928); Bui Thanh-Van, *Dao Khap Hoan Cau* [A tour of the world] (Hue: Dac-Lap, 1929); and *Dong-Tay Van-Hoa Phe-Binh* [On Oriental and Occidental civilizations] (Hue: Thu-Xan, 1928).

38 On Dao Duy Anh as the likely author of *European and American Civilization*, see Le Thanh, *Cuoc Phong Van Cac Nha Van* [Interviews with writers] (Hanoi: Nha Xuat Ban Doi Moi, n.d.), 160–61. On the writings of Vietnamese proponents of national essence, see Marr, *Vietnamese Tradition on Trial*, 106–15, and Hue-Tam Ho Tai, *Radicalism and the Origins of the Vietnamese Revolution*, 48–51. As Hue-Tam Ho Tai suggests, Vietnamese neotraditional formulations of national essence drew on a much more static and elite-centered approach to Confucianism than the Chinese National Essence Movement of the same period, which sought to reinterpret Confucian tradition creatively and contained strong agrarian and democratic elements. On the Chinese movement, see Guy Allito, *The Last Confucian* (Berkeley: University of California Press, 1979), and Charlotte Furth, "Intellectual Change: From the Reform Movement to the May Fourth Movement, 1895–1920," in *The Cambridge History of China*, vol. 12, pt. 1, *Republican China, 1912–1949*, ed. John King Fairbank (Cambridge: Cambridge University Press, 1983), 350–73.

39 Tinh Tien, *Van Minh Au My*, 23, 25. The pamphlet's opposition of idealism and materialism does not appear to carry the Marxist connotations that emerged in some of the radical discourse of this period.

40 Ibid., 25–28.

41 On these French perceptions of the United States, see René Rémond, *Les Etats-Unis devant l'opinion française, 1815–1852* (Paris: Librairie Armand Colin, 1962); Charles W. Brooks, *America in France's Hopes and Fears, 1890–1920*, 2 vols. (New York: Garland, 1987); Paul A. Gagnon, "French Views of Postwar America, 1919–1932" (Ph.D. diss., Harvard University, 1960); Bernadette Galloux-Fournier, "Un regard sur l'Amérique: voyageurs français aux États-Unis, 1919–1939," *Revue d'histoire moderne et contemporaine* 37 (April–June 1990): 297–307; and Jacques Portes, *Une fascination réticente: les États-Unis dans l'opinion française, 1870–1917* (Nancy: Presses universitaires de Nancy, 1990).

42 The availability of these works is suggested by the catalog of the National Library (Thu Vien Quoc Gia) in Hanoi, which lists works by Duhamel, Siegfried, Lewis, Dreiser, and Dos Passos deposited into the collection in the 1920s. Until the 1940s, American fiction did not appear in Vietnamese translations. The United States did provide the setting for one volume of a French detective series translated into Vietnamese during the interwar period; see Tran Cong Dung, trans., *Bi-mat thanh Nuu Uoc* [The secrets of New York] (Hanoi: Vo dang thu xa, 1935).

43 Tinh Tien, *Van Minh Au My*, 25, 29.

44 The nature and impact of French censorship is revealingly discussed in Shawn Frederick McHale, "Printing, Power, and the Transformation of Vietnamese Culture, 1920–1945" (Ph.D. diss., Cornell University, 1995), 68–81, 90–110.

45 Radical biographies of American figures include *Dong Tay Vi Nhan: Lam-Khang* [Great men of Asia and Europe: Lincoln] (Saigon: n.p., 1929); Tran Huu Do, *Anh-Hung Tao Thoi The: Hoa-Thinh Don* [Great men create their own circumstances: Life of Washington] (Saigon: Réveil Saigonais, 1926); *Dong Tay Vi Nhan: Hoa-tinh-Don* [Great men of Asia and Europe: Washington] (Saigon: n.p., 1929); Lam Van Ly and Tran Huy Lieu, *Anh-Hung Yeu Nuoc: Ong Lam-Khang* [A patriotic hero: Lincoln] (Saigon: Cuong-Hoc, 1928); *Dong Tay Vi Nhan: Phat-lankhac-Linh* [Great men of Asia and Europe: Franklin] (Saigon: n.p., 1929); Vu Cong-Nghi, *Guong Kien-Nhan* [Life of Edison] (Hanoi: Nha Xuat Ban Nguyen Ngoc-Tam, 1926); and Ngo Duc Ke, *Dong Tay Vy Nhan* [Great men of the West] (Hanoi: Nha Xuat Ban Giac-Quan Thu-Xa, 1929–30). For a discussion of the place of Vietnamese, Chinese, and European figures in the radical biographical literature of the 1920s, see Marr, *Vietnamese Tradition on Trial*, 258–65.

46 *Dong Tay Vi Nhan: Lam-Khang*. As an illustration of French fears that these books could serve revolutionary purposes, this biography was among the works banned by French colonial censors in the late 1920s. See "Forbidden Books and Newspapers in Vietnam, 1927–1936," in McHale, "Printing, Power, and the Transformation of Vietnamese Culture," 106–10.

47 *Dong Tay Vi Nhan: Lam-Khang*, 35.

48 The fullest account of the Youth League is contained in Huynh Kim Khanh, *Vietnamese Communism, 1925–1945* (Ithaca: Cornell University Press, 1982), 63–89. Other radical anticolonial associations that emerged at the end of the 1920s included the Vietnam Nationalist Party (Viet Nam Quoc Dan Dang), modeled on the Chinese Kuomintang and active in northern Vietnam, and the Nguyen An Ninh Secret Society (Hoi Kin Nguyen An Ninh), inspired by French anarchism and active in southern Vietnam. Neither remained viable after 1930. On the former, see Hoang Van Dao, *Viet Nam Quoc Dan Dang: Lich Su Dau Tranh Can Dai, 1927–1954* [The Vietnamese Nationalist Party: A history of modern struggle, 1927–1954] (Saigon: Nguyen Hoa Hiep, 1965); on the latter, see Hue-Tam Ho Tai, *Radicalism and the Origins of the Vietnamese Revolution*, 187–94.

49 Accounts of the early life and revolutionary careers of Pham Van Dong, Truong Chinh, and Vo Nguyen Giap are often sketchy and sometimes contradictory. The biographical information presented here draws on a series of reports originally prepared by the Sûreté, the French colonial intelligence service, now contained in dossier 377, Fonds Service de Protection du Corps Expéditionnaire, and dossier 261, AOM-CP, and on conversations with historians at the Institute of History in Hanoi in 1989 and 1992.

50 The details of Ho Chi Minh's life are particularly difficult to ascertain. Even the exact date of his birth, officially designated in Vietnam as 19 May 1890, is not clear. Among the problems confronting biographers are Ho's use of numerous pseudonyms and skill at evading French colonial intelligence surveillance (including the staging of a mock funeral at one point in Moscow), long and poorly documented sojourns in Russia and

China in the 1920s and 1930s, and the self-conscious mythologizing of his life by the Vietnamese Communist Party. This biographical summary relies on relevant materials in dossiers 364 and 365, Fonds Service de Protection du Corps Expéditionnaire, AOM; Hémery, "Jeunesse d'un colonisé, genèse d'un exil," 83–157; Hémery, *Ho Chi Minh de l'Indochine au Vietnam*, 27–67; and Jean Lacouture, *Ho Chi Minh: A Political Biography* (New York: Vintage, 1968), 3–52.

51 The full text of Ho Chi Minh's 1927 *Duong Cach Menh* [The road to revolution] is reprinted in *Ho Chi Minh Toan Tap, Tap 2, 1930–1945* [Ho Chi Minh's collected works, vol. 2, 1930–45] (Hanoi: Nha Xuat Ban Su That, 1981), 173–254. Among the extensive analyses of this work the most important are Vu Tho, "Tu *Duong Cach Menh* den *Luan Cuong Chinh Tri cua Cong San Dong Duong*" [From the *Road to Revolution* to the *Political Theses of the Indochinese Communist Party*], *Nghien Cuu Lich Su* [Historical studies] 72 (March 1965): 14–19; Greg Lockhart, *Nation in Arms: The Origins of the People's Army of Vietnam* (Sydney: Allen and Unwin, 1989), 53–59; Marr, *Vietnamese Tradition on Trial*, 374–76; Woodside, *Community and Revolution*, 168–72; and Hue-Tam Ho Tai, *Radicalism and the Origins of the Vietnamese Revolution*, 179–81.

52 The mixture of Marxist-Leninist and indigenous political themes also emerged in the league's journal, *Youth*, edited by Ho Chi Minh. Weekly issues in the fall and winter of 1926 explicated the revolutionary history of France, Britain, Russia, China, and Java. Confucian themes were also common (see, for example, issues of 12 September 1925 and 20 February 1927), as were efforts to reprint inspirational writings of the reform generation (see, for instance, the serialization of Phan Boi Chau's *Overseas Book Inscribed in Blood* [*Hai Ngoai Huyet Thu*] beginning in the 5 September 1925 issue).

53 "Lich Su Cach Menh My" [History of the American revolution], in Ho Chi Minh, *Duong Cach Menh*, 190. Ho's *Duong Cach Menh* is not the only work in this period that popularized Marxist-Leninist ideas and drew on aspects of the American experience for parts of its arguments; see, for instance, Dao Duy Anh, *Thuc Dan Lich Su* [A history of colonialism] (Hue: n.p., 1928), and Diep Van Ky, *Su Cach Mang* [A history of revolutions] (Saigon: Bao-Ton, 1927).

54 "Lich Su Cach Menh My," 190–91.

55 Ibid., 191–92.

56 Ibid., 192; for other critical expressions of contemporary American society, see his essays on lynching and the Ku Klux Klan originally published in 1924 in *La Correspondance Internationale* and reprinted in Ho Chi Minh, *Selected Works*, vol. 1, *Articles and Speeches, 1922–1926* (Hanoi: Foreign Languages Publishing House, 1960), 99–105, 127–32.

57 "Lich Su Cach Menh My," 192.

58 Ho Chi Minh, *Duong Cach Menh*, 186. My emphasis on Ho's use of Confucian rhetoric to discuss the meaning of world revolution draws on Lockhart, *Nation in Arms*, 55.

59 Hue-Tam Ho Tai, *Radicalism and the Origins of the Vietnamese Revolution*, 246.

60 For issues of *Ladies' News* that deal with American themes, see 28 July, 11 August, 1, 29 September, 10 November 1932, 5 January, 2, 16 March, 6, 13 April, 22 June 1933, 18 January 1934, and Spring 1934 special issue. The emergence of progressive thought is discussed in Hue-Tam Ho Tai, *Radicalism and the Origins of the Vietnamese Revolution*, 243–54.

61 The formation of the ICP and its ultra-leftist leadership and ideological orientation are discussed in Huynh Kim Khanh, *Vietnamese Communism*, 99–179. On southern radical politics in the 1930s, see Daniel Hémery, *Révolutionnaires Vietnamiens et pouvoir colonial en Indochine: communistes, trotskystes, nationalistes à Saigon de 1932 à 1937* (Paris: Maspéro, 1975); Hémery explores the emphasis on European internationalist debates in the southern radical press in his "Journalisme révolutionnaire et système de la presse au Vietnam dans les années 1930," *Les Cahiers du Cursa* 8 (1978): 55–85.

62 My discussion of Ho Chi Minh's experiences in Moscow between 1934 and 1938 and quotations from the files of the Far Eastern Bureau of the Comintern rely on the pioneering work of Sophie Quinn-Judge in the Comintern files for Vietnam housed at the Russian Center for the Preservation and Study of Documents of Modern History contained in her "Ho Chi Minh: New Perspectives from the Comintern Files," *Viet Nam Forum*, no. 14 (1994): 61–81. It also draws on Do Quang Hung, "Chu Tich Ho Chi Minh Trong Thoi Ky 1934–1938, Roi Sang Them Cho Van De Dan Toc Hay Quoc Te?" [Ho Chi Minh in the period 1934–38, clearly for nationalism or internationalism?], in *Ho Chi Minh Anh Hung Giai Phong Dan Toc Danh Nhan Van Hoa* [Ho Chi Minh, national liberation and cultural hero] (Hanoi: Nha Xuat Ban Khoa Hoc Xa Hoi, 1990), 28–36, and Vera Vladimirova Vishnyakova-Akima, *Two Years in Revolutionary Russia, 1925–1927*, trans. Steven I. Levine (Cambridge: Harvard University Press, 1971), 228–29.

63 My analyses of the prison experience and its impact in this and the following paragraph draw on Khanh, *Vietnamese Communism*, 162–63; Marr, *Vietnamese Tradition on Trial*, 308–15; and the indigenous accounts of Bui Cong Trung, "Phai Song" [We must live], and Dang Kim Giang, "Truong Quan Chinh Trong Nha Tu Son La" [A military-political school inside Son La prison], in Bui Cong Trung, Truong Sinh, et al., *Nguoi Truoc Nga Nguoi Sau Tien* [The front rank falls, the rear advances] (Hanoi: Nha Xuat Ban Van Hoc, 1960), 27–32, 53–58; Le Van Hien, *Nguc Kontum* [Kontum prison] (Tourane: Tu Tuong Moi, 1938); and Hoang Quoc Viet et al., *A Heroic People: Memoirs from the Revolution* (Hanoi: Foreign Languages Publishing House, 1965), 167–72.

64 On the rise of the Popular Front and its impact in Vietnam, see Khanh, *Vietnamese Communism*, 205–25; Marr, *Vietnamese Tradition on Trial*, 392–400; and Lockhart, *Nation in Arms*, 64–72.

65 See *Soul of Youth* [*Hon Tre*], 22, 27 April, 4, 11, 23 May, 13 June 1935, and *Notre Voix*, 12 February 1939.

66 Marilyn A. Levine, *The Found Generation: Chinese Communists in Europe during the Twenties* (Seattle: University of Washington Press, 1993), 159–60, 166.

67 For a discussion of the encounter between Chinese and Vietnamese revolutionaries in southern China in the mid-1920s that draws on newly available Chinese-language memoirs, see Qiang Zhai, *China and the Vietnam Wars, 1950–1975* (Chapel Hill: University of North Carolina Press, 2000). Although both Ho Chi Minh and Mao Tse-tung were active in the Peasant Education Institute in Canton in this period, apparently the two did not meet. See William J. Duiker, "Seeds of the Dragon: The Influence of the Maoist Model in Vietnam," in *Critical Perspectives on Mao Zedong's Thought*, ed. Arif Dirlik, Paul Healy, and Nick Knight (Atlantic Highlands, N.J.: Humanities Press, 1997), 316, 338 n. 7.

68 *News* [*Tin Tuc*], 13 July, 14, 17 August 1938; *People* [*Dan Chung*], 10, 14, 17, 21 September 1938; Nguyen Duc Thuy, *Phuong Phap Khang Nhat cua Hong Quan Tau* [The method of the anti-Japanese resistance of the Chinese Red Army] (Hanoi: n.p., 1938); Nguyen Van Tay, *Lam Sao cho Tau Thang Nhat?* [What can the Chinese do to defeat the Japanese?] (My-Tho: Nha Xuat Ban Dong-Phuong Thu-Xa, 1938).

69 Nguyen Duc Thuy, *Phuong Phap Khang Nhat*, 4 (translation from Lockhart, *Nation in Arms*, 67); Nguyen Van Tay, *Lam Sao cho Tau Thang Nhat?*, 20–25.

70 For an authoritative discussion of the philosophical dimension of Mao's efforts to assert Chinese independence from Soviet tutelage in the late 1930s, see Stuart Schram, *The Thought of Mao Tse-Tung* (Cambridge: Cambridge University Press, 1989), 61–84.

71 Van Dinh (Vo Nguyen Giap), *Con Duong Chinh: Van De Dan Toc Giai Phong o Dong Duong* [The proper path: The question of national liberation in Indochina] (Hanoi: Dan Chung, 1939), 10, 13; other ICP texts that use the Chinese experience to set a course for Vietnamese policies include Sieu Hai, *Hoa Chien-Tranh voi Van De Phong-Thu Dong-Duong* [The peril of war and the problem of defending Indochina] (Vinh: Tap Sach Tien-Bo, 1938).

72 Van Dinh (Vo Nguyen Giap), *Muon Hieu Ro Tinh Hinh Quan Su o Tau* [Understanding clearly the military situation in China] (Hanoi: Dan Chung, 1939).

73 Articles in *Notre Voix* on Chinese developments appear in the following issues: 1, 8, 29 January, 5, 12 February, 5, 12, 19, 26 March, 9 April, 4 June 1939. Ho Chi Minh's eight-part "Lettre de Chine" under the pseudonym P. C. Line appeared in the following issues of *Notre Voix*: 9, 16, 30 April, 21 May, 23 June, 7, 14, 28 July 1939. Two earlier dispatches from China published in *Notre Voix* using the same pseudonym include 12 February, 5 March 1939. Ho's reports from China are collected in a Vietnamese translation in *Ho Chi Minh Toan Tap, Tap 3, 1930–1945* [Ho Chi Minh's collected works, vol. 3, 1930–45] (Hanoi: Nha Xuat Ban Su That, 1983), 60–108.

74 *Notre Voix*, 14 July 1939.

CHAPTER TWO

1 Gertrude Emerson, "Backwaters of Empire in French Indo-China," *Asia* 23, no. 9 (September 1923): 670.

2 Harris M. Cookingham (American Consul, Saigon) to Nelson T. Johnson (Assistant Secretary of State), 29 November 1927, 851G.0016, Decimal Files, Internal Affairs of France: French Indochina, 1910–39, RG 59. For existing accounts of the limited American presence in Vietnam in the interwar period, see Ronald H. Spector, "European Colonization and American Attitudes toward Southeast Asia, 1919–1941," *Proceedings of the Seventh International Association of Historians of Asia Conference*, vol. 1 (Bangkok: International Association of Historians of Asia, 1978), 269–89, and Anne L. Foster, " 'But We Didn't Know Much about You': Images of French, Vietnamese, and Americans, 1919–1939" (unpublished paper in the possession of the author).

3 American Consul, Saigon, to Department of State, 26 July 1923, RG 59. American trade with French Indochina is discussed in Gary R. Hess, *The United States' Emergence As a Southeast Asian Power, 1940–1950* (New York: Columbia University Press,

1987), 9–16; detailed statistical reporting on American trade with Indochina and the rest of Southeast Asia in the interwar period is in the U.S. Department of Commerce's annual *Foreign Commerce Yearbook.*

4 On French proposals to sell Indochina to the United States, see Pham Quynh, "Dong Phap bao gio van la Dong Phap" [French Indochina will always be French Indochina], *Nam Phong Tap Chi* [Southern wind] 37 (July 1920): 83, and *New York Times*, 5, 7 June 1920.

5 My analysis of the interwar American discourse on Vietnam draws on more than two hundred books and articles published in the 1920s and 1930s. Journal and newspaper articles were identified through the *Reader's Guide to Periodical Literature* (1919–40) and the *New York Times' Index* (1919–40). Books by journalists, missionaries, travel writers, and scholars were identified through a search of the collections held by the Harvard College libraries, the Library of Congress, and the Wason-Echols Collection at Cornell University. Virginia Thompson's *French Indo-China* (New York: Macmillan, 1937) and Thomas E. Ennis's *French Policy and Developments in Indochina* (Chicago: University of Chicago Press, 1936) were the most sustained and influential American accounts of Vietnam in the interwar period and receive particular attention in my analysis. Thompson, an independent scholar associated with the Institute of Pacific Relations, continued to write on Southeast Asia throughout World War II and the postwar period. Ennis was a professor of history at West Virginia University whose work on Vietnam became required reading for American diplomats in East and Southeast Asia. Examples of consular reporting are drawn from the following archival collections: Records of Consular Posts, Saigon, 1889–1940, and Records of Diplomatic Posts, Vietnam, 1936–40, Department of State, RG 84; Records of the Department of State Relating to the Internal Affairs of France, 1910–39, RG 59.

6 Theodore Dreiser, *Tragic America* (New York: Liveright, 1931); Edmund Wilson, *American Jitters: A Year of the Slump* (New York: Charles Scribner's Sons, 1932); Sherwood Anderson, *Puzzled America* (New York: Charles Scribner's Sons, 1935). Selections from the more than sixty thousand images that made up the Farm Security Administration project were widely disseminated in published works in the 1930s, including Archibald MacLeish, *Land of the Free* (New York: Harcourt, Brace, 1938). On the emergence of this documentary literature in the United States in the 1930s, see William Scott, *Documentary Expression and the Thirties America* (New York: Oxford University Press, 1973), and Nicholas Nathanson, *The Black Image in the New Deal: The Politics of FSA Photography* (Knoxville: University of Tennessee Press, 1992). I am indebted to Chris Appy for drawing my attention to the potential utility of these works for American reporting on Vietnam.

7 The spectacular sales of *The Good Earth*, Pearl Buck's 1931 novel about a Chinese farmer that displays many of the conventions of the reportage genre, broke a long-standing American indifference to books about China and may also have provided reassurance of potential American interest in Vietnamese society. The relationship between *The Good Earth* and interwar American writing on Vietnam will be explored later in this chapter. On the reception of *The Good Earth* in the United States, see Peter Conn, *Pearl S. Buck: A Cultural Biography* (Cambridge: Cambridge University Press, 1996), 121–35.

8 Similarly, the depression-era reportage literature discussed above was not unique to the United States but was, rather, a transnational phenomenon in the 1930s, as works by George Orwell and J. B. Priestley in England and Maryse Choisy in France suggest. See, for instance, George Orwell, *The Road to Wigan Pier* (London: Victor Gollancz, 1937); J. B. Priestley, *English Journey* (London: W. Heineman, 1934); and Maryse Choisy, *L'Amour dans les prisons, reportage* (Paris: Montaigne, 1930). Among Vietnamese writers, too, the genre of depression-era social reporting (*phong su*) was particularly important for ongoing efforts to reconceptualize the relationship between the individual and society. The most important of these writing from the 1930s are reprinted in Vuong Tri Nhan, comp. and ed., *Tam Lang, Trong Lang, Hoang Dao: Phong su chon loc* [Tam Lang, Trong Lang, Hoang Dao: Selected reportage] (Hanoi: Hoi Nha Van, 1995). For a useful introduction to these works, see Greg Lockhart and Monique Lockhart, trans., *The Light of the Capital: Three Modern Vietnamese Classics* (Kuala Lumpur: Oxford University Press, 1996), 1–49.

9 Thompson, *French Indo-China*, 42. At times U.S. observers and diplomats used the French terms "Tonkinese," "Annamite," and "Cochinchinese" to refer to Vietnamese living in northern, central, and southern Vietnam, respectively. More commonly, however, they adopted the broader French term "Annamite" to refer to the Vietnamese population as a whole. Context usually makes clear if "Annamite" is used in its broader or narrower sense. In quoted material I retain these appellations to give a better sense of the flavor of this discourse. For a useful discussion that problematizes these terms and analyzes notions of space and nation in colonial Vietnam, see Christopher E. Goscha, "Annam and Vietnam in the New Indochinese Space, 1887–1945," in *Asian Forms of the Nation*, ed. Stein Tønnesson and Hans Antlov (London: Curzon, 1996), 93–130.

10 Thompson, *French Indo-China*, 263, 161, 284; Leland L. Smith (American Consul, Saigon) to State Department, 28 August 1924, 851G.001, Saigon, 1889–1940, RG 84. See also Ennis, *French Policy and Developments*, 133–34, 139–40; Gertrude Emerson, "Backwaters of Empire," 690; W. Robert Moore, "Along the Old Mandarin Road of Indo-China," *National Geographic*, August 1931, 164; and Harold J. Coolidge Jr. and Theodore Roosevelt, *Three Kingdoms of Indo-China* (New York: Thomas Y. Crowell, 1933), 37, 149.

11 Mona Gardner, *Menacing Sun* (London: John Murray, 1939), 30; Gertrude Emerson, "Backwaters of Empire," 673; Thompson, *French Indo-China*, 43, 45, 51, 283, 284; Leland L. Smith, "An SOS in the Jungle of Indo-China," *Radio Broadcast*, May 1923, 44.

12 Thompson, *French Indo-China*, 44, 47, 252, 259, 260; Gertrude Emerson, "Backwaters of Empire," 672; Coolidge and Roosevelt, *Three Kingdoms*, 71–74.

13 Mona Gardner, *Menacing Sun*, 12–13; Ennis, *French Policy and Developments*, 56–58; Thompson, *French Indo-China*, 254.

14 Mona Gardner, *Menacing Sun*, 16, 22; Thompson, *French Indo-China*, 47. See also Gertrude Emerson, "Backwaters of Empire," 672; Marc T. Greene, "Shadows over Indo-China," *Asia* 35, no. 11 (November 1935): 676. Vietnamese women, too, were the subject of objectified comment, particularly by male observers, who either romanticized their "sinuous, supple" shapes and "seductive bosoms" or criticized their "doll-like—usually stupidly doll-like" beauty. See, for instance, Maynard Owen Williams,

"By Motor Trail across French Indo-China," *National Geographic*, October 1935, 503; Thomas Steep, "French Oppression in Indo-China," *American Mercury* 32, no. 127 (July 1934): 330; Wilbur Burton, "H. M. Bao Dai," *Asia* 35, no. 12 (December 1935): 723.

15 Thompson, *French Indo-China*, 43.

16 See, for instance, Elazar Barkan, *The Retreat of Scientific Racism: Changing Conceptions of Race in Britain and the United States between the World Wars* (Cambridge: Cambridge University Press, 1992); George W. Stocking Jr., *Race, Culture, and Evolution: Essays in the History of Anthropology* (Chicago: University of Chicago Press, 1982); Carl N. Degler, *In Search of Human Nature: The Decline and Revival of Darwinism in American Social Thought* (New York: Oxford University Press, 1991), 59–211.

17 Conn, *Pearl S. Buck*, 185.

18 Thompson, *French Indo-China*, 319, 111.

19 Grace H. Cadman, *Pen Pictures of Annam and Its People* (New York: Christian Alliance, 1920), 124; H. C. Flower Jr., "On the Trail of Lord Tiger," *Asia* 20, no. 9 (October 1920): 893; Smith, "SOS in the Jungle," 43, 48; Coolidge and Roosevelt, *Three Kingdoms*, 271. See also Douglas Burden, "The Ibex and the Elephant," *Atlantic*, July 1924, 33–35; Gertrude Emerson, "Mostly Tigers," *Asia* 23, no. 10 (October 1923): 744; Dean Sage Jr., "Annam's Elusive Elephants," *Asia* 33, no. 3 (March 1933): 168–71.

20 Thompson, *French Indo-China*, 43–44. See also Mona Gardner, *Menacing Sun*, 17–16, and Josephine Hope Westervelt, *The Green Gods* (New York: Christian Alliance, 1927), 17–18, 30–31, 66–69.

21 My discussion of the historical antecedents of climatic explanations draws on Durand Echeverria, *Mirage in the West: A History of the French Image of American Society to 1815* (Princeton: Princeton University Press, 1957), 3–38; Echeverria, "Roubaud and the Theory of American Degeneration," *French American Review* 3 (1950): 24–33; and Gilbert Chinard, "Eighteenth Century Theories of America As a Human Habitat," *Proceedings of the American Philosophical Society* 91 (1947): 27–57. Unlike French and British observers, Spanish commentators on the New World often rejected climatic arguments for the inferiority of nonwhite peoples. Their writings, however, appear to have had significantly less influence in shaping American attitudes. On the works of Spanish commentators, see Anthony Pagden, *Spanish Imperialism and the Political Imagination* (New Haven: Yale University Press, 1990), esp. 104–16; Pagden, *The Fall of Natural Man: The American Indian and the Origins of Comparative Ethnology* (Cambridge: Cambridge University Press, 1982; and Stephen Greenblatt, *Marvelous Possessions: The Wonder of the New World* (Chicago: University of Chicago Press, 1991). The eighteenth century should not be viewed as free of the discourse of race. See, for instance, the masterful analysis of racialist attitudes toward African Americans before the nineteenth century in Winthrop Jordan, *White over Black: American Attitudes toward the Negro, 1550–1812* (New York: Norton, 1968).

22 My discussion of the nineteenth-century focus on race follows Reginald Horsman, *Race and Manifest Destiny: The Origins of American Radical Anglo-Saxonism* (Cambridge: Harvard University Press, 1981); Michael H. Hunt, *Ideology and U.S. Foreign Policy* (New Haven: Yale University Press, 1987), 46–91; and Roy Harvey Peace, *Savagism and Civilization: A Study of the Indian and American Mind* (1953; reprint, Berke-

ley: University of California Press, 1988). On late nineteenth-century attitudes toward Native Americans and African Americans, see Robert N. Utley, *The Indian Frontier of the American West, 1846–1890* (Albuquerque: University of New Mexico Press, 1984); George M. Fredrickson, *The Black Image in the White Mind: The Debate on Afro-American Character and Destiny, 1817–1914* (New York: Harper and Row, 1971); and C. Vann Woodward, *The Strange Career of Jim Crow* (New York: Oxford University Press, 1974), 67–109.

23 The most important analysis of this hierarchical discourse of civilization is George W. Stocking Jr., *Victorian Anthropology* (New York: Free Press, 1987). For revealing analyses of the gendered dimension of civilizational discourse, see Kristin L. Hoganson, *Fighting for American Manhood: How Gender Politics Provoked the Spanish-American and Philippine-American Wars* (New Haven: Yale University Press, 1998), and Gail Bederman, *Manliness and Civilization: A Cultural History of Gender and Race in the United States, 1880–1917* (Chicago: University of Chicago Press, 1995).

24 On the important role of neo-Lamarckian ideas for American conceptions of cultural hierarchies, see George W. Stocking Jr., "Lamarckianism in American Social Science," in his *Race, Culture, and Evolution*, 234–69. Substantial scholarly attention has been devoted to the racialist American perceptions of non-Western peoples that emerged in the debates over U.S. imperialism at the end of the nineteenth century. Among the most important works that focus on aspects of the interconnections between notions of Anglo-Saxon superiority, Social Darwinism, and attitudes toward Native and African Americans are Stuart Anderson, *Race and Rapprochement: Anglo-Saxonism and Anglo-American Relations, 1895–1904* (Rutherford, N.J.: Fairleigh Dickinson University Press, 1981); Richard Hofstader, *Social Darwinism in American Thought* (Philadelphia: University of Pennsylvania Press, 1944), 170–200; Robert C. Bannister, *Social Darwinism: Science and Myth in Anglo-American Thought* (Philadelphia: Temple University Press, 1979); Christopher Lasch, "The Anti-Imperialists, the Philippines, and the Inequality of Man," *Journal of Southern History* 24, no. 3 (August 1958): 319–31; and James P. Shenton, "Imperialism and Racism," in *Essays in American Historiography*, ed. Donald Sheehan and Harold C. Syrett (New York: Columbia University Press, 1960), 231–50.

25 Alleyne Ireland, *The Far Eastern Tropics: Studies in the Administration of Tropical Dependencies* (New York: Houghton Mifflin, 1905); Benjamin Kidd, *The Control of the Tropics* (New York: Macmillan, 1898); Kidd, "The United States and the Control of the Tropics," *Atlantic*, December 1868, 721–27. David Healy discusses the prevalence of these interpretations, focusing on the writings of Benjamin Kidd, and their influence on American policy makers in the late nineteenth and early twentieth centuries in his *U.S. Expansionism: The Imperialist Urge in the 1890s* (Madison: University of Wisconsin Press, 1970), 127–43, and his *Drive to Hegemony: The United States in the Caribbean, 1898–1917* (Madison: University of Wisconsin Press, 1988), 58–76, as does Donald C. Bellomy in his "Social Darwinism Revisited," *Perspectives on American History*, n.s., 1 (1984): 92–94. Bernard Semmel discusses the work of Kidd in relationship to British attitudes toward imperialism in his *Imperialism and Social Reform: English Social-Imperial Thought, 1895–1914* (London: Allen and Unwin, 1960), 31–35.

26 Ireland, *Far Eastern Tropics*: 1–14, passim. See also his *Tropical Colonization: An Introduction to the Study of the Subject* (New York: Macmillan, 1899). Robert W. Rydell

explores the popularization of these assumptions about nonwhite peoples through an analysis of ethnographic exhibits organized at twelve international expositions held in the United States between 1876 and 1916, in his *All the World's a Fair* (Chicago: University of Chicago Press, 1984).

27 These characterizations of the Filipinos draw on Walter L. Williams, "U.S. Indian Policy and the Debate over Philippine Annexation," *Journal of American History* 66, no. 4 (March 1980): 810–31; Glenn A. May, *Social Engineering in the Philippines: The Aims, Execution, and Impact of American Colonial Policy, 1900–1913* (Westport, Conn.: Greenwood Press, 1980), 9–12; and Peter W. Stanley, *A Nation in the Making: The Philippines and the United States, 1899–1921* (Cambridge: Harvard University Press, 1974), 163–67. For a particularly insightful discussion of the fears of colonial administrators about the potentially degenerative impact of the tropical Philippine climate, see Warwick Anderson, "The Trespass Speaks: White Masculinity and Colonial Breakdown," *American History Review* 102, no. 5 (December 1997): 1343–70. On the ubiquity of these views for American perceptions of Latin America in this period, see Sarah E. Sherbach, *Stereotypes of Latin America: Press Images and U.S. Foreign Policy, 1920–1933* (New York: Garland, 1993).

28 On the nativism of the 1920s, see John Higham, *Strangers in the Land: Patterns of American Nativism, 1860–1925*, 2d ed. (New Brunswick, N.J.: Rutgers University Press, 1988), 264–330. The Harlem riot of 1935 and the simpleminded and comical portrayal of blacks in popular cultural forms such as *Amos 'n' Andy* and *Gone with the Wind* are among the important indicators for the continuing salience of race for interwar white Americans. See, for instance, Herbert Shapiro, *White Violence and Black Response: From Reconstruction to Montgomery* (Amherst: University of Massachusetts Press, 1988), 255–72; Melvin Patrick Ely, *The Adventures of Amos 'n' Andy: A Social History of an American Phenomenon* (New York: Free Press, 1991); and Thomas Cripps, *Slow Fade to Black: The Negro in American Film, 1900–1942* (New York: Oxford University Press, 1993).

29 According to "The Map of Civilization," in Ellsworth Huntington, *Civilization and Climate* (New Haven: Yale University Press, 1924), 417–28, areas ranked as follows (100 = highest level of civilization): England, 100; New England, 100; Germany, 96; France, 95; United States (except New England), 88; China, 57; Central America, 47; Latin America, 40; Middle East, 35; Southeast Asia, 34; Siam, 44; Philippines, 40; Burma, 40; Java, 36; Indochina (Vietnam, Cambodia, Laos), 35; Africa, 29.

The broader prevalence of scholarly writings in the interwar period linking race and climate suggests the continuing importance of these ideas in intellectual and policymaking circles as well as at the more popular level. See, for instance, Ellsworth Huntington, *The Character of Races* (New York: Charles Scribner's Sons, 1924); Franklin Thomas, *The Environmental Basis of Society* (New York: Century, 1925); Robert DeC. Ward, "The Literature of Climatology," *Annals of the Association of American Geographers*, March 1931, 34–51; and Daniel Katz and Kenneth W. Braly, "Racial Prejudice and Racial Stereotypes," *Journal of Abnormal and Social Psychology* 30, no. 2 (July–September 1935): 175–93.

30 The most important interwar American writings on Southeast Asia, from which these quotations are drawn, include Rupert Emerson, *Malaya: A Study in Direct and In-*

direct Rule (New York: Macmillan, 1937); Virginia Thompson, *Thailand: The New Siam* (New York: Macmillan, 1941); and Amry Vandenbosch, *The Dutch East Indies: Its Government, Problems, and Politics* (Grand Rapids, Mich.: Eerdmans, 1933).

31 My discussion of *Mother India* relies on Andrew J. Rotter, "Gender Relations, Foreign Relations: The United States and South Asia, 1947–1964," *Journal of American History* 81, no. 2 (September 1994): 522–23, and Harold R. Isaacs, *Scratches on Our Minds: American Views of China and India* (New York: Harper and Row, 1958), 268–90.

32 Conn, *Pearl S. Buck*, 129. For a similar analysis, see also Elizabeth J. Lipscomb, Frances E. Webb, and Peter Conn, eds., *The Several Worlds of Pearl S. Buck* (Westport, Conn.: Greenwood Press, 1994).

33 My reading of *The Good Earth* is informed by Michael H. Hunt, "Pearl Buck: Popular Expert on China, 1931–1949," *Modern China* 3, no. 1 (January 1977): 33–64. On the racialized paternalism embedded in this view of China, I am indebted to Chris Jespersen's analysis of interwar American writings on China; see T. Christopher Jespersen, *American Images of China, 1931–1949* (Stanford: Stanford University Press, 1996), esp. 73.

34 George Sánchez, *Becoming Mexican-American: Ethnicity, Culture, and Identity in Los Angeles, 1900–1945* (New York: Oxford University Press, 1993), 95–107. See also Gwendolyn Mink, *Wages of Motherhood: Inequality in the Welfare State, 1917–1942* (Ithaca: Cornell University Press, 1995).

35 See Warren I. Susman, "The Culture of the Thirties" and "Culture and Commitment," in his *Culture As Social History: The Transformation of American Society in the Twentieth Century* (New York: Pantheon, 1984), 150–210, and Frederick Lewis Allen, *Since Yesterday* (New York: Harper and Brothers, 1939), 129–35.

36 Among the dozens of French works that favor this construction of Vietnamese masculinity, several were frequently mentioned in the narratives of American observers in Vietnam, including Albert Challan de Belval, *Au Tonkin, 1884–1885: notes, souvenirs et impressions* (Paris: Plon, 1904), and Charles D. M. Rollet de l'Isle, *Au Tonkin et dans les mers de Chine: souvenirs et croquis, 1883–1885* (Paris: Plon, 1886). For an analysis of these French writings, I am indebted to Frank Proschan, "Eunuch Mandarins, Effeminate 'Boys,' and '*Soldats Mamzelles*': The Annamite As Androgyne" (paper delivered at the Association for Asian Studies Forty-ninth Annual Meeting, Chicago, Illinois, March 1996).

37 Eliacin Luro, *Le pays d'Annam* (Paris: Ernest Leroux, 1897). Other works in the French sinological tradition often cited by American observers include Gustave Dumoutier, *Essais sur les Tonkinois* (Hanoi: Imprimerie d'Extrême-Orient, 1908); Francis Garnier, *Voyages d'exploration en Indochine*, 2 vols. (Paris: Hachette, 1873); Alfred Schreiner, *Les institutions Annamites en Basse-Cochinchine avant la conquête Française*, 3 vols. (Saigon: Claude, 1900); and J. Silvestre, *L'empire d'Annam et le peuple Annam* (Paris: Félix Alcan, 1889). American observers also drew on the works of French essayists and journalists who popularized the sinological approach to Vietnam in the 1920s and 1930s, such as Albert de Pouvourville's *L'Annamite* (Paris: Éditions LaRose, 1932). Scholars have not systematically analyzed French writings on Vietnam or the connections between Orientalist writers and agents of French imperialism. Useful short introductions to the range of available French materials on Vietnam are John Cady, "Biblio-

graphical Article: The Beginnings of French Imperialism in the Pacific Orient," *Journal of Modern History* 14, no. 1 (March 1942): 71–87, and Jean Chesneaux, "French Historiography and the Evolution of Colonial Vietnam," in *Historians of South-East Asia*, ed. D. G. E. Hall (London: Oxford University Press, 1961), 235–44. More complete bibliographical and descriptive guides to French colonial writings include H. Cordier, *Bibliotheca Indosinica*, 4 vols. (Paris: Ernest Leroux, 1912–15); Paul Boudet and Rémy Bourgeois, *Bibliographie de l'Indo-Chine française, 1913–1926* (Hanoi: Imprimerie d'Extrême-Orient, 1929); and Louis Malleret, *L'Exotisme indochinois dans la littérature française depuis 1860* (Paris: Larose, 1934). For one invaluable account that begins to analyze the nature of French discourse on Vietnam, see Panivong Norindr, *Phantasmatic Indochina: French Colonial Ideology in Architecture, Film, and Literature* (Durham, N.C.: Duke University Press, 1996).

38 Luro, *Le pays d'Annam*, 76–77. For another formulation of this common French perspective used by American observers, see Schreiner, *Les institutions Annamites*, 1:54–55.

39 Thompson, *French Indo-China*, 19, 20, 27. See also Ennis, *French Policy and Developments*, 56–58, and Moore, "Along the Old Mandarin Road," 157, 180–81. Although it appeared slightly after the onset of World War II, Alan H. Brodrick's travel narrative *Little China: The Annamite Lands* (London: Oxford University Press, 1942) also focused on the centrality of Chinese cultural forms in Vietnam, arguing that the Vietnamese "have never pretended not to owe everything to China." The sinological approach to Vietnamese history and society persisted far beyond the interwar period, informing the major American interpretation of Vietnamese history published in the 1950s, Joseph Buttinger's *The Smaller Dragon: A Political History of Vietnam* (New York: Praeger, 1958). Only after 1970 did Western scholars begin to challenge this interpretative framework successfully, using Vietnamese sources to analyze indigenous perspectives on Vietnamese history. Notable examples of this pioneering work include Keith Taylor, *The Birth of Vietnam* (Berkeley: University of California Press, 1983); John K. Whitmore, *Vietnam, Ho Quy Ly, and the Ming, 1371–1421* (New Haven: Yale Center for Southeast Asian Studies, 1985); and Alexander B. Woodside, *Vietnam and the Chinese Model: A Comparative Study of Vietnamese and Chinese Government in the First Half of the Nineteenth Century* (Cambridge: Harvard University Press, 1971).

40 Alfred Meynard, "Sacrifice to Heaven and Earth," *Asia* 28, no. 10 (October 1928): 799; Achille Murat, "In 'The Purple Forbidden City' of Hue," *Asia* 27, no. 5 (May 1927): 383–87, 427–29. See also Meynard, "Time's Fresh Budding in Annam," *Asia* 31, no. 2 (February 1931): 105–7, and Meynard, "Possessed Annamese on Pilgrimage," *Asia* 31, no. 12 (December 1931): 785–87.

41 Paul Giran, *Psychologie du peuple Annamite* (Paris: Ernest Leroux, 1904). For Virginia Thompson's reliance on Giran's analysis, see Thompson, *French Indo-China*, 41–43.

42 Edward W. Said's *Orientalism* (New York: Vintage, 1979), of course, first directed scholarly attention to the significance of Orientalist constructions of non-Western societies, focusing on European and American writings on the Middle East. To date, scholars have not systematically examined European colonial studies of Southeast Asia, but for useful assessments of Said's framework in the South Asian context, see Ronald Inden, *Imagining India* (London: Basil Blackwell, 1990); Carol A. Breckinridge and Peter van

der Veer, eds., *Orientalism and the Postcolonial Predicament: Perspectives on South Asia* (Philadelphia: University of Pennsylvania Press, 1993); John D. Rogers, "Colonial Perceptions of Ethnicity and Culture in Early Nineteenth-Century Sri Lanka," in *Society and Ideology: Essays in South Asian History*, ed. Peter Robb (Delhi: Oxford University Press, 1993), 97–109; and Rogers, "Historical Images in the British Period," in *Sri Lanka: History and the Roots of Conflict*, ed. Jonathan Spencer (London: Routledge, 1990), 87–106. See also Said, *Culture and Imperialism* (New York: Knopf, 1993).

43 Ennis, *French Policy and Developments*, 9, 58.

44 Thompson, *French Indo-China*, 24, 39, 161, 248, 294, 303, 369–70; Mona Gardner, *Menacing Sun*, 16. For other examples, particularly on "Oriental" responses to French conquest, see Ennis, *French Policy and Developments*, 20–51, passim.

45 Thompson, *French Indo-China*, 19, 45, 167, 168, 303.

46 Ibid., 239.

47 See, for instance, Ann L. Stoler, "Sexual Affronts and Racial Frontiers: National Identity, 'Mixed Bloods,' and the Cultural Genealogies of Europeans in Colonial Southeast Asia," *Comparative Studies in Society and History* 34, no. 3 (July 1992): 514–51; Margaret Strobel, "Gender and Race in the Nineteenth and Twentieth Century British Empire," in *Becoming Visible: Women in European History*, ed. Renate Bridenthal and Claudia Koonz (Boston: Houghton Mifflin, 1987), 375–96; Helen Callaway, *Gender, Culture, and Empire: European Women in Colonial Nigeria* (London: Macmillan, 1987); and Frederick Cooper and Ann Laura Stoler, eds., *Tensions of Empire: Colonial Cultures in a Bourgeois World* (Berkeley: University of California Press, 1997).

48 For a sustained discussion of what Akira Iriye terms the shared "mental universe" of Americans and Europeans on these questions, see his *Across the Pacific: An Inner History of American-East Asian Relations* (New York: Harcourt Brace Jovanovich, 1967), 53–64, as well as Stuart Anderson, *Race and Rapprochement*; Bellomy, "Social Darwinism Revisited," 1–129; Mike Hawkins, *Social Darwinism in European and American Thought, 1860–1945: Nature As Model and Nature As Threat* (Cambridge: Cambridge University Press, 1997); M. G. Biddiss, *Father of Racist Ideology: The Social and Political Thought of Count Gobineau* (London: Weidenfeld and Nicholson, 1970); George M. Fredrickson, "Colonialism and Racism: The United States and South Africa in Comparative Perspective," in his *The Arrogance of Race: Historical Perspectives on Slavery, Racism and Social Inequality* (Middletown, Conn.: Wesleyan University Press, 1988), 216–35; V. G. Kiernan, *The Lords of Human Kind: European Attitudes toward the Outside World in the Imperial Age* (London: Weidenfeld and Nicholson, 1969); and Jan Breman, ed., *Imperial Monkey Business: Racial Supremacy in Social Darwinist Theory and Colonial Practice*, CASA Monographs No. 3 (Amsterdam: VU University Press, 1990).

49 Percy Standing, "French Progress in Indo-China," *Contemporary Age*, April 1931, 504–8. Although Standing's account was not published until 1931, it is based on his research and observations on Vietnam from the late 1920s. For similar views, see Helen Churchill Candee, *New Journey in Old Asia: Indo-China, Siam, Java, Bali* (New York: Frederick A. Stokes, 1927), 13–114; Moore, "Along the Old Mandarin Road," 157, 165, 175, 177, 180; and Coolidge and Roosevelt, *Three Kingdoms*, 44, 299.

50 For the admiring accounts of French journalists and travel writers, see Roland Dorgelès, *On the Mandarin Road* (New York: Century, 1926); Henry Hervy, *King Cobra: An Autobiography of Travel in French Indo-China* (New York: Cosmopolitan, 1927); and Claudius Madrolle, *Indochina: Cochinchina, Cambodia, Annam, Tonkin, Yunnan, Laos, Siam* (Paris: Librairie Hachette, 1930), the English edition of the well-known Madrolle guides to Indochina, which was available in the United States.

51 Gertrude Emerson, "Backwaters of Empire," 690. See also Henry A. Frank, *East of Siam: Ramblings in the Five Divisions of French Indo-China* (New York: Century, 1926), 219–43. In a practice that would significantly accelerate in the following decade, the reports of U.S. consuls in Saigon contained criticisms of discriminatory French protectionist practices in the 1920s. See, for instance, Leland L. Smith to Department of State, 28 August 1924, 851G.00/16, Decimal Files, RG 59.

52 Steep, "French Oppression in Indo-China," 328–30. See also Ennis, *French Policy and Developments*, 59–61; William Henry Chamberlin, "A New Deal for French Indo-China?," *Asia* 37, no. 7 (July 1937): 478; Thompson, *French Indo-China*, 86–88, 419–22, 427–42.

53 Thompson, *French Indo-China*, 109–43, 173–78; Ennis, *French Policy and Developments*, 111–34.

54 Thompson, *French Indo-China*, 205–13; Ennis, *French Policy and Developments*, 126–27; Mona Gardner, *Menacing Sun*, 17, 88. U.S. criticism that the French "couldn't make the trains run on time" was also commonplace among travelers to Vietnam in the 1920s; see, for instance, Coolidge and Roosevelt, *Three Kingdoms*, 35–36, and Flower, "On the Trail of Lord Tiger," 35–36. Americans were also critical of the French tendency to use colonial funds to build what were termed "lavish structures" to house the colonial administration in Hanoi and Saigon. See, for instance, Thompson, *French Indo-China*, 219–20; Steep, "French Oppression in Indo-China," 330; and Gertrude Emerson, "Backwaters of Empire," 690.

55 On the reporting of U.S. consuls from Saigon in the 1930s concerning French tariffs and economic policy in Vietnam, see Henry I. Waterman to Department of State, "Tariff Situation in French Indo-China," 23 May 1930, 651G.113/121; Waterman to Department of State, "Propaganda against American Automobiles," 27 January 1931, 651G.1112/11; and American Consul, Saigon, to Department of State, 7 July 1938, all in RG 59; and Waterman to Department of State, 10 June 1931, file 800-Saigon-1931, RG 84. For the commentary of other American observers on the tariff and its impact, see Thompson, *French Indo-China*, 198–205; Ennis, *French Policy and Developments*, 135–37; Wilbur Burton, "French Imperialism in China," *Current History*, January 1934, 428–31; Steep, "French Oppression in Indo-China," 330; Greene, "Shadows over Indo-China," 680, 682; and Herbert Ingram Priestly, *France Overseas: A Study of Modern Imperialism* (New York: Appleton-Century, 1938), 234.

56 Mona Gardner, *Menacing Sun*, 34–35. See also Quincy Roberts (American Consul, Saigon) to Department of State, 31 January 1936, 851G.008/22, RG 84; American Consul, Saigon, to Department of State, 25 May 1937, 851G.00, Decimal Files, RG 59; Ennis, *French Policy and Developments*, 71–72; and Thompson, *French Indo-China*, 79–87.

57 On the American criticism of the French colonial tax burden, see Henry I. Waterman to Hester (U.S. trade commissioner in Manila), December 1930, file 630-Saigon-1930, RG 84; Thompson, *French Indo-China*, 182–98; Ennis, *French Policy and Developments*, 64–65; Greene, "Shadows over Indo-China," 682; and Priestly, *France Overseas*, 230.

58 On American criticism of French educational policies in Vietnam, see Steep, "French Oppression in Indo-China," 332; Thompson, *French Indo-China*, 284–307; and Ennis, *French Policy and Developments*, 169–75.

59 "Stepchildren: Indochinese, Forgotten of France, Want Their New Deal, Too," *Literary Digest*, 3 July 1937, 14; on American views of French labor policies, see also Chamberlin, "New Deal for French Indo-China?," 476–78; Ennis, *French Policy and Developments*, 155–61; and Thompson, *French Indo-China*, 143–62.

60 On French medical policies in Vietnam, see Thompson, *French Indo-China*, 277–83, and Ennis, *French Policy and Developments*, 149–55.

61 On the character of interwar Franco-American relations, see Melvyn P. Leffler, *The Elusive Quest: America's Pursuit of European Stability and French Security, 1919–1933* (Chapel Hill: University of North Carolina Press, 1979); Henry Blumenthal, *Illusion and Reality in Franco-American Diplomacy, 1914–1945* (Baton Rouge: Louisiana State University Press, 1986); and Frank Costigliola, *Awkward Dominion: American Political, Economic, and Cultural Relations with Europe, 1919–1933* (Ithaca: Cornell University Press, 1984).

62 David G. Marr, "Vietnam: Harnessing the Whirlwind," in *Asia: The Winning of Independence*, ed. Robin Jeffrey (New York: St. Martin's Press, 1981), 165–67. For a sustained discussion of the impact of the Great Depression on the Vietnamese economy, see Pierre Brocheux, "Crise économique et société en Indochine française," *Revue française d'histoire d'outre mer* 232–33 (1976): 655–67.

63 Thompson, *French Indo-China*, 494.

64 Ennis, *French Policy and Developments*, 52. The following discussion of interwar American criticism of French policies of associative rule in Vietnam draws on ibid., 6–10, 52–72; Priestly, *France Overseas*, 226–32, 337–39; Chamberlin, "New Deal for French Indo-China?," 476–78; and Thompson, *French Indo-China*, 243, 247–48, 252–53, 399–402.

65 For two useful overviews of the historiography of Americanization and assimilation, see Russell A. Kazal, "Revisiting Assimilation: The Rise, Fall, and Reappraisal of a Concept in American Ethnic History," *American Historical Review* 100, no. 2 (April 1995): 437–71, and Gary Gerstle, "Liberty, Coercion, and the Making of Americans," *Journal of American History* 84, no. 2 (September 1997): 524–58.

66 My discussion of Robert Park relies on Kazal, "Revisiting Assimilation," 442–46. On the multiethnic celebration of the interwar period, see John Bodnar, *Remaking America: Public Memory, Commemoration, and Patriotism in the Twentieth Century* (Princeton: Princeton University Press, 1992), 70–77, and Richard Weiss, "Ethnicity and Reform: Minorities and the Ambience of the Depression Years," *Journal of American History* 66, no. 3 (December 1979): 566–85.

67 Domestic discourse on immigration and the attitudes of interwar observers in Vietnam

toward French colonialism do exhibit one intriguing difference. As Mae Ngai's recent analysis of the Immigration Act of 1924 and its implementation suggests, the increasingly common perception that Eastern and Southern European immigrants were eventually assimilable as American citizens did not extend to Asians, who were deemed "persons ineligible to citizenship" because their inferior racial characteristics were deemed to make them unassimilable. The Vietnamese case seems to suggest that outside the boundaries of the domestic national space, however, Americans saw the possibility of political and social transformation, albeit slow, toward the ideals that animated American citizenship even as they embraced broader assumptions about the hierarchical inferiority of Asians. See Mae M. Ngai, "The Architecture of Race in American Immigration Law: A Reexamination of the Immigration Act of 1924," *Journal of American History* 86, no. 1 (June 1999): 67–92.

68 Ennis, *French Policy and Developments*, 8, 58; Thompson, *French Indo-China*, 294.

69 Vandenbosch, *Dutch East Indies*, 59–60, 165.

70 Important interwar American works on the Philippines include W. Cameron Forbes, *The Philippine Islands*, 2 vols. (Boston: Houghton Mifflin, 1928); Grayson L. Kirk, *Philippine Independence* (New York: Farrar and Rinehart, 1936); and Nicholas Roosevelt, *The Philippines* (New York: J. H. Sears, 1926). On the Tydings-McDuffie Act and eventual Philippine independence, see Theodore Friend, *Between Two Empires: The Ordeal of the Philippines, 1929–1946* (New Haven: Yale University Press, 1965), 95–148.

71 Dwight F. Davis (Governor General, Philippine Islands) to Patrick J. Hurley (U.S. Secretary of War), 15 July 1931, file 18868-55, entry 5, Records of the Bureau of Insular Affairs, RG 350, National Archives, Washington, D.C. I am indebted to Anne Foster for bringing this document to my attention.

72 Ennis, *French Policy and Developments*, 7, 95; Thompson, *French Indo-China*, 494.

73 Ennis, *French Policy and Developments*, 176, 177; Greene, "Shadows over Indo-China," 683; Thompson, *French Indo-China*, 483. See also Ennis, *French Policy and Developments*, 61–62, 71–72; Thompson, *French Indo-China*, 297–99, 482–85; Mona Gardner, *Menacing Sun*, 34–35; Chamberlin, "New Deal for French Indo-China?," 478; "Stepchildren," 14–15; Quincy Roberts (American Consul, Saigon) to Department of State, 31 January 1936, 851G.008/22, RG 84; and American Consul, Saigon, to Department of State, 16 January 1937, 851G.00/01, and 25 May 1937, 851G.00, both in Decimal Files, RG 59.

74 See Lloyd C. Gardner, *Safe for Democracy: The Anglo-American Response to Revolution, 1913–1923* (New York: Oxford University Press, 1984). For a broader consideration of the American response to revolution, see Hunt, *Ideology and U.S. Foreign Policy*, 92–124.

75 Thompson, *French Indo-China*, 313, 485–93; Mona Gardner, *Menacing Sun*, 24; Ennis, *French Policy and Developments*, 191–92.

76 Foster Rhea Dulles, "French Problems in Indo-China," *Current History*, May 1927, 202; Mona Gardner, *Menacing Sun*, 55; Chamberlin, "New Deal for French Indo-China?," 478.

77 Ennis, *French Policy and Developments*, 185; Henry I. Waterman (American Consul, Saigon) to Department of State, 16 May 1930, 851G.001B/3, Decimal Files, RG 59;

Thompson, *French Indo-China*, 489–90. Waterman's reporting was criticized within the State Department, with his superiors in the Western European (WE) and Far Eastern (FE) Divisions arguing Waterman lacked "discrimination" and that "the French authorities have been stuffing him with a lot of hot air about the communistic menace." But the department did not replace Waterman or send him instructions to revise his reporting. See John F. Carter (WE) to Paul T. Culbertson (WE), Ransford S. Miller (FE), and Stanley K. Hornbeck (FE), 16 June 1931, 851G.00B/12, Decimal Files, RG 59. For other analyses that focus on the role of external forces in Vietnamese nationalism, see *New York Times*, 15 February 1930; Dulles, "French Problems in Indo-China," 198; "Soviet Light in Asia," *Literary Digest*, 21 February 1931, 14; "France's Colonial Spot of Trouble," *Literary Digest*, 1 August 1931, 15; Greene, "Shadows over Indo-China," 679; Standing, "French Progress in Indo-China," 508; and Priestly, *France Overseas*, 235–37, 243.

78 Ennis, *French Policy and Developments*, 187. On Ho Chi Minh, see Thompson, *French Indo-China*, 489–92, and Priestly, *France Overseas*, 235–36.

79 On criticism of French repression, see Greene, "Shadows over Indo-China," 679; Raymond Postgate, "Echoes of a Revolt," *New Republic*, 22 May 1935, 44–45; "France's Colonial Spot of Trouble," 15; and Thompson, *French Indo-China*, 492.

80 On assessments of French policy toward Vietnamese nationalism, see Ennis, *French Policy and Developments*, 191–93; Chamberlin, "New Deal for French Indo-China?," 478; American Consul, Saigon, to Department of State, 25 May 1937, 851G.00, and 16 January 1937, 851G.00/01, both in Decimal Files, RG 59; and Quincy Roberts (American Consul, Saigon) to Department of State, 31 January 1936, 851G.008/22, RG 84.

81 French governor general Albert Sarraut's 1919 speech on the steps of the Temple of Literature in Hanoi was among the most dramatic efforts to employ the metaphors of father and children; the text of the speech is in *Tribune Indigène*, 27 April 1919. For a discussion of the familial language used by French colonial officials in Vietnam, see Hue-Tam Ho Tai, *Radicalism and the Origins of the Vietnamese Revolution* (Cambridge: Harvard University Press, 1992), 37, 142–43. See also Agathe Larcher, "Le voie étroite des réformes coloniales et la 'collaboration franco-annamite' (1917–1928)," *Revue française d'histoire d'outre mer* 82, no. 309 (1995): 387–420. On American uses of a similar rhetoric, see Stuart Creighton Miller, *"Benevolent Assimilation": The American Conquest of the Philippines, 1899–1903* (New Haven: Yale University Press, 1982).

82 Alice L. Conklin, *A Mission to Civilize: The Republican Idea of Empire in France and West Africa, 1895–1930* (Stanford: Stanford University Press, 1997), 6–7, 187–211; Gwendolyn Wright, *The Politics of Design in French Colonial Urbanism* (Chicago: University of Chicago Press, 1991), 73–84. In a similar manner, historians of American immigration policy point to the permeability between what contemporaries sometimes viewed as antithetical approaches to Americanization; see discussions in Kazal, "Revisiting Assimilation," 442, 446, and Gerstle, "Making of Americans," 530–31.

83 On these inter-European colonial rivalries and the interconnections between the national and colonial projects, see Said, *Orientalism*, 201–25, and Said, *Culture and Imperialism*, 191–209.

CHAPTER THREE

1 T Minutes 56, 11 November 1943, Subcommittee on Territorial Problems, Division of Political Studies, box 59, Notter Files, RG 59, 4.

2 Ibid., 4–5.

3 On Japan's southward movement into Vietnam, see John E. Dreifort, "Japan's Advance into Indochina, 1940: The French Response," *Journal of Southeast Asian Studies* 13, no. 2 (September 1982): 279–95; Hata Ikuhiko, "The Army's Move into Northern Indochina," in *The Fateful Choice: Japan's Advance into Southeast Asia, 1939–41*, ed. James William Morley (New York: Columbia University Press, 1980), 155–208; Nagaoka Shinjiro, "The Drive into Southern Indochina and Thailand," in Morley, *Fateful Choice*, 209–40; and Nicholas Tarling, "The British and the First Japanese Move into Indochina," *Journal of Southeast Asian Studies* 21, no. 1 (March 1990): 35–65.

4 U.S. Army and Navy Munitions Board, *The Strategic and Critical Materials* (Washington, D.C.: Army and Navy Munitions Board, 1940), 2–3, 15–16, 18. On the significance of this document and a persuasive analysis of the broader concern within the Roosevelt administration about strategic raw materials in Southeast Asia and the role they played in the coming of war, see Jonathan Marshall, *To Have and Have Not: Southeast Asian Raw Materials and the Origins of the Pacific War* (Berkeley: University of California Press, 1995).

5 See, for instance, Michael A. Barnhart, *Japan Prepares for Total War: The Search for Economic Security, 1919–1941* (Ithaca: Cornell University Press, 1987), 198–236; Robert Dallek, *Franklin Roosevelt and American Foreign Policy, 1932–1945* (New York: Oxford University Press, 1979), 273–76; Waldo Heinrichs, *Threshold of War: Franklin D. Roosevelt and American Entry into World War II* (New York: Oxford University Press, 1988), 118–45; and Nicholas Tarling, *Britain, Southeast Asia, and the Onset of the Pacific War* (Cambridge: Cambridge University Press, 1996).

6 For penetrating discussions of the Japanese wartime occupation of Vietnam and its impact on French colonial control, see David G. Marr, *Vietnam 1945: The Quest for Power* (Berkeley: University of California Press, 1995), chap. 1, and Stein Tønnesson, *The Vietnamese Revolution of 1945: Roosevelt, Ho Chi Minh, and de Gaulle in a World at War* (London: Sage, 1991), chaps. 1 and 6.

7 For the existing scholarship on Roosevelt's plans for trusteeship in Indochina, see Lloyd C. Gardner, *Approaching Dien Bien Phu* (New York: Norton, 1988), 21–53; Gary R. Hess, "Franklin Roosevelt and Indochina," *Journal of American History* 59, no. 2 (September 1972): 353–68; Hess, *The United States' Emergence As a Southeast Asian Power, 1940–1950* (New York: Columbia University Press, 1987), 47–158; Walter LaFeber, "Roosevelt, Churchill, and Indochina, 1942–45," *American Historical Review* 80, no. 5 (December 1975): 1277–95; and Christopher Thorne, "Indochina and Anglo-American Relations, 1942–1945," *Pacific Historical Review* 45, no. 1 (February 1976): 73–96.

8 Minutes of the Pacific War Council, 21 July 1943, folder: "Naval Aide's Files, Pacific War #2," box 168, FDR-MR.

9 Elliott Roosevelt, *As He Saw It* (New York: Duell, Sloan and Pearce, 1946), 115; Roosevelt-Stalin Meeting, 28 November 1943, *FRUS: The Conferences at Cairo and Tehran, 1943* (1961), 485. See also Minutes of the Pacific War Council, 23 May, 9 December

1942, 17 March 1943, folder: "Naval Aide's Files, Pacific War #2," box 168, FDR-MR; Memorandum of Conversation by Harry Hopkins, 27 March 1943, *FRUS, 1943*, vol. 3, *The British Commonwealth, Eastern Europe, the Far East* (1963), 39; F. D. R. to the Secretary of State, 24 January 1944, *FRUS: Conferences at Cairo and Tehran*, 872; and Roosevelt-Stalin Meeting, 8 February 1945, *FRUS: The Conferences at Malta and Yalta*, 1945 (1955), 770.

10 Minutes of the Pacific War Council, 23 May 1942, folder: "Naval Aide's Files, Pacific War #2," box 168, FDR-MR. The recollections of participants in the May 1954 Princeton seminar, which gathered wartime and Cold War policy makers such as Dean Acheson, Paul Nitze, and W. Averell Harriman, also suggest that Roosevelt's critique of French rule in Vietnam was less an attack on colonialism than on France's inadequacies as a colonial power. In the printed transcript of the 15 May session of the seminar, an unidentified voice claims, "I think he [FDR] was much more amenable to the Dutch going back into Indonesian [*sic*] than he was to the French going back into Indo-China," to which Dean Acheson added, "I think he had a higher view of Queen Wilhelmina." See transcript of 15 May 1954, folder: "Reading Copy III: Princeton Seminars, May 15–16, 1954 (folder 2)," box 84, Papers of Dean Acheson, HST, reel 5, track 1, p. 8.

11 Minutes of the Pacific War Council, 17 March 1943, folder: "Naval Aide's Files, Pacific War #2," box 168, FDR-MR. See also Edward R. Stettinius Jr., *Roosevelt and the Russians: The Yalta Conference* (Garden City, N.Y.: Doubleday, 1949), 237, and Elliott Roosevelt, *As He Saw It*, 115, 165, 251.

12 Roosevelt-Stalin Meeting, 8 February 1945, *FRUS: Conferences at Malta and Yalta*, 770. The source of FDR's limited knowledge of the Vietnamese is reinforced by meetings of the Pacific War Council that included discussions of Indochina where Roosevelt often deferred to Chinese foreign minister T. V. Soong to supply even the most basic details of Vietnam's population and social organization. Beginning in 1942 Roosevelt did receive regular reports on conditions in Indochina from William J. Donovan, the director of the OSS. But these reports, which usually focused on Japanese, French, British, and Chinese policies in the region, seldom provided the historical or sociological information on the Vietnamese that OSS field officers were sending on to Washington. For FDR's reliance on Soong at the Pacific War Council, see Minutes of the Pacific War Council, 23 May 1942, 21 July 1943, folder: "Naval Aide's Files, Pacific War #2," box 168, FDR-MR. The majority of Donovan's reports to FDR on Indochina from 1942 to 1945 are in folder: "OSS Report," boxes 149–52, FDR-PS; a few additional reports from 1945 are in folder: "OSS Numbered Bulletin Jan–Apr 45," box 73, FDR-MR.

It is tempting to believe that Roosevelt's perceptions of the Vietnamese and other Southeast Asian societies might have also been influenced by experiences of Theodore Roosevelt Jr., Eleanor Roosevelt's first cousin. Theodore traveled to Vietnam in 1928–29 as a coleader of the Kelley-Roosevelt-Field Museum expedition discussed in Chapter 2. He also served as the American governor general to the Philippines in 1932–33. Theodore, however, is unlikely to have had any significant influence in shaping FDR's perceptions. By the early 1920s a feud between the Oyster Bay and Hyde Park branches of the Roosevelt family pitted Theodore against Franklin and Eleanor. Theodore campaigned vigorously against FDR's vice-presidential bid in 1920. Eleanor's very public opposition to Theodore's campaign for New York governor in 1924 permanently severed any connection with him. The similarities between FDR's and Theodore's perceptions of Vietnamese society more probably reflect prevailing negative views of non-Western societies. On the Roosevelt feud, see Blanche Wiesen Cook, *Eleanor Roosevelt*, vol. 1, *1884–1933* (New York: Viking, 1992), 278, 351–54; Kenneth S. Davis, *FDR: The Beckoning of Destiny, 1882–1928* (New York: G. P. Putnam's Sons, 1972), 621, 771–72; and Geoffrey C. Ward, *A First-Class Temperament: The Emergence of Franklin Roosevelt* (New York: Harper and Row, 1989), 532, 540, 700–701.

13 Text of "Radio Address by President Roosevelt," 15 November 1942, in the appendix to "United States Policy Regarding Dependent Territories, 1933–44 (CDA-246)," 20 February 1945, box 125, Notter Files, RG 59.

14 Ibid.

15 Roosevelt-Stalin Meeting, 28 November 1943, *FRUS: Conferences at Cairo and Tehran*, 485; FDR Press Conference (#992), 23 February 1945, in *Complete Press Conferences of Franklin D. Roosevelt*, vol. 25 (New York: Da Capo Press, 1972), 70.

16 Glenn A. May, *Social Engineering in the Philippines: The Aims, Execution, and Impact of American Colonial Policy, 1900–1913* (Westport, Conn.: Greenwood Press, 1980), xvii.

17 Vincente L. Rafael, "White Love: Surveillance and Nationalist Resistance in the U.S. Colonization of the Philippines," in *Cultures of United States Imperialism*, ed. Amy Kaplan and Donald E. Pease (Durham, N.C.: Duke University Press, 1993), 216. See also Michael Salman, "The United States and the End of Slavery in the Philippines, 1898–1914: A Study of Imperialism, Ideology, and Nationalism" (Ph.D. diss., Stanford University, 1993), 605–17.

18 The text of Roosevelt's note to the French is in Roosevelt to Leahy, 10 February 1942, *FRUS, 1942*, vol. 2, *Europe* (1962), 131; for the increasingly testy diplomatic exchanges between the French and the Americans over French negotiations with the Japanese, see ibid., 136–47, 671–87.

19 Joint Chiefs of Staff, Minutes of Meeting at the White House, 7 December 1943, *FRUS: The Conferences at Washington, 1941–42, and Casablanca, 1943* (1968), 505. For the text of Murphy's pledge as well as other official U.S. wartime statements on France and its colonies, see *FRUS, 1942*, 2:412–22; *FRUS, 1944*, vol. 3, *The British Commonwealth and Europe* (1965), 770–72; and "United States Policy Regarding Dependent Territories, 1933–44 (CDA-246)," 20 February 1945, box 125, Notter Files, RG 59.

20 On Roosevelt's refusal to allow French representation on the Pacific War Council, see Stettinius to Roosevelt, 29 October 1943, folder: "France 1943," box 29, FDR-PS.

21 On FDR's benign view of China's intentions in Indochina, see Minutes of the Pacific War Council, 9 December 1942, folder: "Naval Aide's Files, Pacific War #2," box 168, FDR-MR, and Roosevelt-Stalin Meeting, 28 November 1943, *FRUS: Conferences at Cairo and Tehran*, 485. On China's plans for the invasion of northern Vietnam, see McCloy to Acheson, 10 January 1942, and Chinese Embassy to Department of State, n.d., *FRUS, 1942: China* (1956), 750–52, 754–55. On French protests, see Memorandum of Conversation, 8 January 1942, *FRUS, 1942: China*, 749–50. For the U.S. response to China's plans, see McCloy to Acheson, 28 January 1942; Stanley Hornbeck, "French Indochina: Political and Military Strategy," 4 February 1941; and Hull to Stimson, 6 February 1942, all in *FRUS 1942: China*, 755–60. Renewed evidence of China's

invasion plans in late 1943 also produced U.S. approval and favorable assessment of Chinese intentions despite French protests. See Washington Delegation of the French Committee of National Liberation to Department of State, 20 October 1943; Stettinius to Roosevelt, 8 November 1943; and Roosevelt to Stettinius, 9 November 1943, all in *FRUS 1943: China* (1957), 882–83, 886–87.

22 "Memorandum of Conversation, by the Secretary of State," 27 March 1943, and "Memorandum of Conversation, by Mr. Harry L. Hopkins, Special Assistant to President Roosevelt," 27 March 1943, *FRUS, 1943*, 3:36–39.

23 Roosevelt to the Secretary of State, 24 January 1944, *FRUS, 1944*, 3:773.

24 The place of the Subcommittee on Territorial Problems in the complicated structure of the State Department's postwar planning organization is clearly outlined in U.S. Department of State, *Postwar Foreign Policy Preparation, 1939–1945* (Washington, D.C.: U.S. Government Printing Office, 1949), 118–19.

25 Biographical information on Kenneth P. Landon is in *Biographic Register of the Department of State: September 1, 1944* (Washington, D.C.: U.S. Government Printing Office, n.d.), 125. Landon returned from Thailand in the late 1930s to undertake a doctoral program at Cornell University. He became an analyst for the OSS just before Pearl Harbor and joined the State Department in 1942. His writings on Thailand include *Siam in Transition: A Brief Survey of Cultural Trends in the Five Year Revolution of 1932* (London: Oxford University Press, 1939) and *The Chinese in Thailand* (London: Oxford University Press, 1941). Landon's wife, Margaret, wrote *Anna and the King* (London: George C. Harrup, 1952), the basis for the Broadway musical *The King and I*. Amry Vandenbosch's writings on the Dutch East Indies were published in journals such as *Amerasia, Asia, Far Eastern Survey*, and *Pacific Affairs*. His best-known work, *The Dutch East Indies: Its Government, Problems, and Politics*, was discussed in Chapter 2. Melvin Knight's critiques of French colonialism emerged in his *Morocco As a French Economic Venture: A Study of Open Door Imperialism* (New York: Appleton-Century, 1937). Geographer Isaiah Bowman's interwar writings on Africa reflected the framework of racialized cultural hierarchies that animated U.S. perceptions of Vietnam; on Bowman, see Thomas Borstelmann, *Apartheid's Reluctant Uncle: The United States and Southern Africa in the Early Cold War* (New York: Oxford University Press, 1993), 11.

26 Vandenbosch and Knight's perceptions of French colonial rule and Vietnamese society closely followed the views of interwar American observers of Vietnam. In several cases the conclusions of writers such as Virginia Thompson and Thomas Ennis were directly incorporated into their reports. See, for instance, "Indo-China: Political and Economic Problems (T-398)," 2 November 1943, Notter Files, RG 59, 5.

27 T Minutes 56, 11 November 1943, 1–2, and T Minutes 55, 5 November 1943, Subcommittee on Territorial Problems, Division of Political Studies, box 59, Notter Files, RG 59, 2–3.

28 "Indo-China: Political and Economic Problems (T-398)," 6; T Minutes 55, 5 November 1943, 2; and Economic Relations of Indo-China (T-283), n.d., Division of Economic Studies, all in box 59, Notter Files, RG 59.

29 "Indochina: Political and Economic Problems (T-398)," 4, and T Minutes 55, 5 November 1943, 2–3, both in box 59, Notter Files, RG 59.

30 T Minutes 55, 5 November 1943, 13, and T Minutes 56, 11 November 1943, 5, box 59, Notter Files, RG 59.

31 T Minutes 56, 11 November 1943, 1, and T Minutes 55, 5 November 1943, 1, 3–4, box 59, Notter Files, RG 59.

32 T Minutes 55, 5 November 1943, 3–4, and T Minutes 5, 11 April 1942, Division of Special Research, both in box 59, Notter Files, RG 59, 5.

33 "Indo-China: Political and Economic Problems (T-398)," 2 November 1943, 4–5, box 59, Notter Files, RG 59. See also T Minutes 55, 5 November 1943, 3, ibid.

34 T Minutes 56, 11 November 1943, 5–6, box 59, Notter Files, RG 59. Prevailing skepticism of Vietnamese ability to undertake self-government immediately is also reflected in a 2 November 1943 memo from John Carter Vincent, Assistant Chief of the Division of Far Eastern Affairs, to Assistant Secretary of State Berle. Vincent argued that the Vietnamese were "capable of self-government" only after postwar administration had trained them to assume "the responsibilities of self-government." The memo was initialed by Joseph W. Ballantine, Chief of the Division of Far Eastern Affairs and a member of the subcommittee. See Memo from Vincent to Berle, 2 November 1943, *FRUS, 1943: China*, 886.

35 T Minutes 56, 11 November 1943, 1, and Indochina: Political and Economic Factors (T-398), 10, box 59, Notter Files, RG 59.

36 Indo-China: Political and Economic Factors (T-398), 2 November 1943, 10–11, box 59, Notter Files, RG 59.

37 Ibid.; T Minutes 56, 11 November 1943, 8, box 59, Notter Files, RG 59.

38 T Minutes 56, 11 November 1943, 8, box 59, Notter Files, RG 59.

39 Ibid., 3, 9.

40 Indo-China: Political and Economic Factors (T-398), 11–12, and T Minutes 56, 11 November 1943, 3, 7, 11, 12–13, box 59, Notter Files, RG 59. For a fuller discussion of this regional approach to American postwar planning in postcolonial Southeast Asia, see Hess, *United States' Emergence*, 94–104. On the origins of the Anglo-American Caribbean Commission, see Wm. Roger Louis, *Imperialism at Bay: The United States and the Decolonization of the British Empire, 1941–1945* (Oxford: Oxford University Press, 1977), 180–81.

41 T Minutes 56, 11 November 1943, 2, 3, 7, 11, box 59, Notter Files, RG 59. See also assessments of British policy in T Minutes 55, 5 November 1943, 8–9, ibid.

42 For the views of the Division of Western European Affairs in support of regional commissions, see "American Policy with Regard to Indochina," 30 June 1944, Division of Western European Affairs, Office of European Affairs, Department of State, box 9, Records of the Office of Assistant Secretary and Under Secretary of State Dean Acheson, 1941–48, and "The Advisability of International Administration for Indochina," 15 June 1944, box 2, Records of the French Desk, both in RG 59. For the viewpoint of the Committee on Colonial Problems, see minutes from 19, 22 November 1943 and 8, 23 February 1944, box 120, Notter Files, 1939–45, RG 59. On support for international trusteeship in the Division of Southwest Pacific Affairs, see Culbertson to Salisbury, 4 March 1944, and "International Trusteeship for Indochina," 2 March 1944, box 7, PSA, RG 59. The divisions within the CAC on the Far East emerge in IAC-FE Minutes, 23 February, 3 July 1944, boxes 117, 118, and in several of the committee's working

papers, including CAC Document 89, 1 March 1944; CAC 114, 13 March 1944, box 109; and CAC 239, 1 July 1944, box 112, all in Notter Files, RG 59. For a popular but nonetheless useful account of the relationship between postwar planning on Indochina and the use of regional commissions throughout the colonized world, see Joseph M. Jones, "Half of One World," *Fortune*, November 1944, 19–32.

43 "Draft Outline of an International Trusteeship Government for Indochina," CAC 114, 13 March 1944, box 109, Notter Files, RG 59.

44 CAC 89, 1 March 1944, box 109, and T Minutes 56, 11 November 1943, 6, 11, 12, box 59, Notter Files, RG 59. The nature of a Southeast Asian regional commission remained somewhat nebulous. The Committee on Colonial Problems envisioned the commission as considerably weaker than the international body that had been proposed to supervise trusteeship, suggesting the commission should be an "advisory body" concerned with "social and economic problems." But other postwar planning committees argued for a more forceful role, suggesting the commission should be granted "executive powers" over both "social and political affairs," including the right to send inspection agents to Indochina and other colonial dependencies to investigate their progress and make recommendations for the future. See CTP Minutes 38, 23 February 1944, 3, box 120, and T Minutes 55, 5 November 1943, 7, 11, box 59, Notter Files, RG 59.

45 For the views of State Department planners on Chinese intentions in Indochina, see T Minutes 55, 5 November 1943, 6, 10, 11, 12, and T Minutes 56, 11 November 1943, 3, 4, 10, box 59; "Indo-China: Military Government (T-404)," 9 November 1943, 1–2, box 65; CTP Minutes 38, 23 February 1944, 2–3, box 120, all in Notter Files, RG 59; memorandum, 28 January 1944, box 5, and "Indochina: Proposed United States Policy," 26 July 1944, box 7, both in PSA, RG 59.

46 Gauss to Secretary of State, 31 December 1942, 851G.00/81, and 23 December 1943, 851G.00/95, Decimal Files, RG 59.

47 Gauss to Secretary of State, 23 December 1943, 851G.00/95, Decimal Files, RG 59.

48 Archimedes Patti, who would head the OSS Indochina operations in 1945, aptly termed these groups and their often overlapping and poorly coordinated activities a "modern babylon." For his useful summary of the activities of intelligence-gathering operations on Vietnam between 1942 and 1944, see Patti, *Why Viet Nam? Prelude to America's Albatross* (Berkeley: University of California Press, 1980), 23–58.

49 Planning for OSS MO in Indochina began in the fall of 1943 and continued throughout the following year. Useful précis of OSS psychological warfare strategies are in "Outline of MO Objectives and Operations in Indo-China," n.d.; "Indo-China M.O. Mission," 30 October 1943; and "Indo China—M.O. Unit," 13 December 1943, all in folder 1864, box 138, entry 139, RG 226.

50 Memo from R. P. Leonard to Harley C. Stevens, 16 May 1944; "Propaganda and the War in Indo-China," n.d.; "Comments re Memorandum of Mr. Leonard," 23 May 1944; and memo from Harold C. Faxon to Betty MacDonald, 17 November 1944, all in folder 1863, box 138, entry 139, RG 226.

51 "Determining a Policy for MO Operations in Indochina," n.d., folder 1863, box 138, entry 139, RG 226.

52 "Suggestions for Leaflets to French Indo China," 7 December 1944, folder 1863, box 138, entry 139, RG 226.

53 Ibid.; emphasis in original.

54 Ibid.

55 Faxon to MacDonald, 1, 21 November 1944, folder 1863, box 138, entry 139, RG 226.

56 "The Economic Relations of Indo-China," 23 March 1943, OSS Research and Analysis Report 54073, box 616, entry 16, RG 226.

57 By "Annamite Revolutionary Alliance" Ringwalt probably referred to the Viet Nam Cach Menh Dong Minh Hoi (Vietnam Revolutionary League), a coalition of Vietnamese anticolonial groups in exile in southern China organized under the auspices of the Chinese government in August 1942. It initially excluded the ICP and the Viet Minh. In the fall and spring of 1944, however, the Chinese began to encourage the participation of the ICP. Ho Chi Minh's involvement with the Dong Minh Hoi is discussed in Chapter 4. For more on the formation of the Dong Minh Hoi and its activities at the time of Ringwalt's dispatch, see King C. Chen, *Vietnam and China, 1938–1954* (Princeton: Princeton University Press, 1969), 61–68.

58 Ringwalt to Gauss, 21 January 1944, 851G.00/98; see also Ringwalt to Gauss, 14, 23 December 1943, and 28 January 1944, 851G.00/96, 851G.00/99, all in Decimal Files, RG 59.

59 William R. Langdon (Kunming) to Kenneth P. Landon (Division of Southwest Pacific Affairs), 16 June 1944, box 10, PSA, RG 59. Direct observation of developments in Vietnam by U.S. diplomats and missionaries ended in 1942. American diplomatic posts in Indochina were closed by the Japanese on 8 December 1941. Most American consular personnel were detained by the Japanese in Indochina until July 1942. Reports of the detained consular personnel prepared in 1942 provided only limited assessments of the impact of the Japanese occupation in Indochina. See Charles S. Reed III, "General Summary of the Military, Economic, and Political Situation in French Indochina," 14 August 1942; O. Edmund Clubb, "Politico-Military Situation and Economic Conditions, Tonkin, French Indochina," 27 July 1942; Kingsley W. Hamilton, "French Indochina: Summary of Developments during the First Seven Months of War in the Pacific," 4 August 1942, 851G.00/76, all in Decimal Files, RG 59. Most American missionaries in Indochina left shortly after the outbreak of the Pacific war. The State Department and the OSS did conduct interviews between 1942 and 1944 with American missionaries who had lived in Vietnam before the war. While the interviews focused on Japanese occupation policies, many also offered critiques of French colonial rule and dismissive observations of indigenous Vietnamese society that closely followed those of other American observers. See Memorandum of Conversation with Irving R. Stebbins, 29 July 1942, 851G.00/75, and Ltr. of Irving Stebbins to Laurence Salisbury, Assistant Chief, Division of Far Eastern Affairs, U.S. Department of State, 851G.00/78, both in Decimal Files, RG 59; "Mr. Dutton—Missionary," "Interview with H. A. Jackson and Herbert Merrill Jackson," and "Mr. Travers—Missionary," ca. 1943–44, folder 344, box 43, entry 140, and "Interview with Rankin Henry Wentland," 1 December 1944, OSS Confidential Research and Analysis Report 105207, box 1156, entry 16, all in RG 226.

60 L. L. Gordon to Hall, 24 October 1944, folder 340, box 42D, entry 140, and Memo, OSS SU Detachment 202 China Theatre, 31 October 1944, folder 344, box 43, entry 140, RG 226.

61 On GBT reliance on French agents, see memo, OSS SU Detachment 202 China The-

atre, 31 October 1944, folder 344, box 43, entry 140, RG 226; memo, "G-B-T Group, French Indo-China," U.S. Naval Unit Headquarters, Fourteenth Air Force, 6 December 1944, folder 3, box 36, entry NHC-75, RG 38. The extensive records of the U.S. Naval Group, China operations in Indochina, and the Meynier mission are in folders 1–6, box 36, entry NHC-75, Papers of Vice-Admiral Milton E. Miles, USN Naval Group China, RG 38. While the planning documents propose the use of both French and Vietnamese agents (see "Plan and Operation—Meynier Group," 20 November 1943, folder 3), the surviving operational reports point to the clear reliance on French intelligence sources; see, for instance, Rapports du Lieutenant Pianelli, 26 February 1944, box 4; Memorandum to Captain Miles, 17 March 1944, box 2; Memorandums to Commander Wight, 27 February, 2 March 1944, box 2; Declarations of Major Kernevez, 3 June 1944, box 3; and Memorandums to Commander Wight, 17, 31 March, 2 April 1944, box 3, all in RG 38. The fascination of Miles's chief aid, Robert Larson, with Mme. Meynier's French-Vietnamese ancestry and purportedly royal blood as well as allegations of an affair between Mme. Meynier and Larson that emerge in these files not only provide salacious reading but recall the tropical exoticism, sensuality, and amorality that interwar U.S. observers ascribed to French and Vietnamese colonial societies; see, for example, Miles to Larson, 8 August 1943, box 4; Larson to Wight, 20 March 1944, folder 2; and Larson to Miles, 22 September 1944, folder 2, all in RG 38.

62 "Conditions of French Indo-China," 8 July 1944, OSS Research and Analysis Report 86713, box 971, entry 16, RG 226; William R. Langdon, "The Indo-China Question," 3 August 1944, 851G.00/8-344, Decimal Files, RG 59.

63 Emblac (French Military Mission in China) to Dickey [China-Burma-India Command (CBI) Headquarters], 11 December 1943; "Political Leaflets of Aerial Distribution over Indo-China," Joseph K. Dickey, CBI Headquarters, 6 January 1944; John B. Stanley (War Department) to R. T. Pell (State Department), 4 February 1944; Pell to Stanley, 12 February 1944, 851G.01/46, all in Decimal Files, RG 59.

64 "Extract from letter dated November 7, 1943 from L. Gordon to Colonel J. C. Williams," folder 3, box 36, entry NHC-75, RG 38. Divisions within the French diplomatic and military missions in southern China between supporters of de Gaulle and the Vichy regime were also a constant frustration for the U.S. Naval Group in China's intelligence operations in Indochina. See, for instance, Larson to Miles, 18 November 1943, and Kotrla to Miles, 20 November 1943, folder 3, box 36, entry NHC-75, RG 38.

65 Pechkoff to Ambassadeur de France Commissaire aux Affaires Étrangères (Alger), 25 August 1944, folder: "Indochine: Liberation de l'Indochine, 8/26/44 to 3/8/45, E166-1," vol. 29, Asie Oceanie, 1944–1955: Indochine, MAE. Pechkoff's cable of 25 August 1944 is one of several in this folder critical of American operations in southern China and suspicious of U.S. intentions toward Indochina.

66 William J. Powell, OWI Air Liaison, Kunming, "Political Conditions in Indo-China," 28 August 1944, 851G.00/9-944, Decimal Files, RG 59; "The Nationalist Movement in Indo-China," OSS SI Report, 28 August 1944, folder 273, box 35, entry 35, RG 226.

67 Langdon to Secretary of State, and Memorandum of Conversation, both 9 September 1944, 851G.00/9-944, and Langdon to Secretary of State, 20 September 1944, 851G.00/9-2044, Decimal Files, RG 59.

68 Gauss to Secretary of State, 18 August, 19 December 1942, Decimal Files, RG 59;

FRUS, 1942: China, 738, 746. See also Gauss to Secretary of State, 17, 28 March 1942, and memorandum of conversation, 29 July 1942, FRUS, 1942: China: 731, 732, 734.

69 Pechkoff to Ambassadeur de France Commissaire aux Affaires Étrangères (Alger), 25 August 1944, MAE. See also "Free French Anxiety over Future of Indo-China," 31 August 1943, 851G.00/89, Decimal Files, RG 59. For a useful account of the escalating tensions between France and China over Vietnam, one that draws upon both newly available French and Chinese sources, see Lin Hua, Chiang Kai-Shek, de Gaulle contre Hô Chi Minh: Viêt-nam 1945–46 (Paris: Éditions L'Harmattan, 1994), 45–54, 55–75.

70 Gauss to Secretary of State, 23 December 1943, 851G.00/95, Decimal Files, RG 59. See also George Atcheson Jr. (Chargé d'Affaires, Chungking) to Secretary of State, 21 July 1943, and enclosed memorandum titled "Organization of Annamite and Overseas Chinese from Indochina by Chinese Groups in China," 851G.00/88, ibid.

71 Ringwalt to Gauss, 14 December 1943, and Gauss to Secretary of State, 5 January 1944, 851G.00/96; see also Ringwalt to Gauss, 9 February 1944, 851G.00/99, all in Decimal Files, RG 59.

72 Langdon to Landon, 16 June 1944, box 10, PSA, RG 59; Langdon, "Indo-China Question," 3 August 1944, 851G.00/8-344, Decimal Files, RG 59.

73 Chen Shio Ho, "Ancient History of Indo-China and a Study of Its People and Culture," in OSS Research and Analysis Report 88367, box 986, entry 16, and "China Intentions in Indo-China," OSS SI Report—Kunming, 1 August 1944, box 1012, entry 16, both in RG 226; Powell, "Political Conditions in Indo-China," 28 August 1944, 851G.00/9-944, Decimal Files, RG 59.

74 See Michael Schaller, The U.S. Crusade in China, 1938–1945 (New York: Columbia University Press, 1979), 147–75, and Christopher Thorne, Allies of a Kind: The United States, Britain, and the War against Japan, 1941–45 (New York: Oxford University Press, 1978), 563–75.

75 Langdon, "Indo-China Question," 3 August 1944, 851G.00/8-344, Decimal Files, RG 59.

76 Gauss to Secretary of State, 26 July 1944, 851G.00/7-2644, Decimal Files, RG 59.

77 Aide-Mémoir, 25 August 1944, FRUS: The Conference at Quebec, 1944 (1972), 247–49.

78 Hull to FDR, 8 September 1944, FRUS: Conference at Quebec, 261–63.

79 Hull to Roosevelt, and Stettinius to Roosevelt, both 10 October 1944, FRUS, 1944, 3:776–79. Diplomatic reporting from Colombo in early 1945 reflected similar suspicions of European intentions at SEAC; see Stettinius to Roosevelt (enclosing Max Bishop, State Department Representative at SEAC, to Stettinius, 9 January 1945), 10 January 1945, and Bishop to Stettinius, 22 March 1945, folder: "Indochina," box 39, FDR-PS.

80 Hurley to Roosevelt, 26 November 1944, folder: "President–General Hurley, 1944–45," box 11, FDR-MR. See also Hurley to Roosevelt, 2 January 1945, ibid. General Albert Wedemeyer, commander of the American forces in the China theater, voiced similar concerns about European intentions. A 29 December 1944 memo from Wedemeyer to General George C. Marshall, later passed to Roosevelt, suggested a "close and coordinated relationship between British, French, and the Dutch exists with the primary purpose of retrieving pre-war favored position in this area" (Wedemeyer to Marshall, 29 December 1944, Wedemeyer Correspondence File, George C. Marshall Papers,

George C. Marshall Foundation, Lexington, Virginia). See also Wedemeyer to Marshall, 10 December 1944, Wedemeyer Correspondence File, Marshall Papers.

Despite these suspicions in late 1944, most U.S. observers were largely unaware that the British were also making clandestine arrangements to train and transport French forces in Indochina. See "Force 136 Future Plans French Indochina (FIC)," 16 November, 28 December 1944," WO 203/4331, Allied Land Forces in Southeast Asia and South-East Asia Command, War of 1939–45, War Office, Military Headquarters Papers Far East, PRO.

81 Hull to FDR, 8 September 1944, *FRUS: Conference at Quebec*, 261–63. Hull's recommendations closely follow the arguments of working papers on Indochina developed in July 1944 by the Division of Southwest Pacific Affairs, which had begun to back away from its unconditional support of international trusteeship; see "Indochina: Proposed United States Policy," 26 July 1944, and "Summary of Recommendations," 29 July 1944, box 7, PSA, RG 59.

82 Roosevelt to Stettinius, 1 January 1945, *FRUS, 1945*, vol. 7, *The British Commonwealth and the Far East* (1969), 293. For Roosevelt's series of responses on Indochina questions in the fall of 1944, see Roosevelt to Hull, 28 August, 16 October 1944, and Roosevelt to Stettinius, 3 November 1944, *FRUS, 1944*, 3:775, 777, 780; Roosevelt to Secretaries of Navy and War, Directors of OSS and OWI, and Admiral Leahy, 17 November 1944, box 55, FDR-PS; and Roosevelt to Stettinius, 24 November 1944, folder: "Indochina," box 39, FDR-PS.

83 Roosevelt-Stalin Meeting, 8 February 1945, *FRUS: Conferences at Malta and Yalta*, 770.

84 Memorandum of Conversation by the Adviser on Caribbean Affairs (Taussig), 15 March 1945, *FRUS, 1945*, vol. 1, *General; the United Nations* (1967), 124.

85 Prime Minister to President Roosevelt, 17 March 1945, in Warren F. Kimball, ed., *Churchill and Roosevelt: The Complete Correspondence*, vol. 2, *Alliance Declining, February 1944–April 1945* (Princeton: Princeton University Press, 1984), 572–73. On the origins of the boundary dispute, see Mountbatten to Chiefs of Staff, 9 November 1943, and Mountbatten to R. V. Soong, MB1/C280, MB; Roosevelt to Churchill, 22 June 1943 [draft not sent], and 24 June 1944, in Kimball, *Churchill and Roosevelt*, 2:275–77; and Thorne, *Allies of a Kind*, 300–301. On British-American tensions over SEAC in late 1944 and early 1945, see Memorandum by the Assistant to the President's Naval Aide (Elsey), n.d., *FRUS: The Conference of Berlin (the Potsdam Conference)* (1960), 1:915–21, and Wedemeyer to Mountbatten, 29 January 1945; deWiart to Mountbatten, 23 February 1945; and Deming to Mountbatten, 6 April 1945, MB1/C84, MB.

86 President Roosevelt to the Prime Minister, 22 March 1945, and Prime Minister to President Roosevelt, 11 April 1945, in Kimball, *Churchill and Roosevelt*, 2:582–83, 626–27.

87 The paintings of Bolívar, Hidalgo, and San Martín are now hung in the reconstruction of Truman's oval office at the Harry S. Truman Museum in Independence, Missouri. Truman is likely to have first encountered these anticolonial leaders in *Great Men and Famous Women*, a four-volume set of historical biographies his mother gave to him when he was a young boy; see Charles F. Horne, ed., *Great Men and Famous Women* (New York: Semlar Hess, 1894), 2:306–11, 3:281–85. On Truman's interest in history and heroism, see his *Memoirs*, vol. 1, *Year of Decisions* (Garden City, N.Y.: Double-

day, 1955), 119–20, and David McCullough, *Truman* (New York: Simon and Schuster, 1992), 42, 58.

88 On the decisions of May 1945, see Memorandum to Truman, 9 May 1945, 851G.oo/5-945, Decimal Files, RG 59, and Grew to Caffery, 19 May 1945, *FRUS, 1945,* vol. 6, *The British Commonwealth and the Far East* (1969), 307. Continuing tensions between Britain and the United States over SEAC emerge in Mountbatten to Wedemeyer, 6, 21 May 1945; Mountbatten to Ismay (War Cabinet Office, London), 8 May 1945; and Wedemeyer to Mountbatten, 12 May, 14 June 1945, all in MB1/C280, MB. On the military division of Vietnam at Potsdam, see Meeting of the Combined Chiefs of Staff, 18, 24 July 1945; Meeting of the Joint Chiefs of Staff, 23 July 1945; and Memorandum by the United States Chiefs of Staff, 17 July 1945, *FRUS: Conference of Berlin,* 2:83–85, 271–72, 375–78, 1313–15.

89 See, for instance, Bonnet to Ministère des Affaires Étrangères Diplomatiques, Paris [MAE], 2, 6, 21 May 1945, folder: "Indochine: Libération de l'Indochine, 3/9/45 to 9/47, E166-1," vol. 30, Indochine, Asie Oceanie, 1944–1955, and Jacques Bayyens (Conseiller d'Ambassade Charge du Consulat Général de France [San Francisco]) to MAE, 20 June 1945, folder: "Action alliée clandéstine, 10/44 to 12/45, E166-7," vol. 49, Indochine, Asie Oceanie, 1944–1955, MAE; Grew to Hurley, 2 June 1945, *FRUS, 1945,* 6:312; and FO Minute by Mr. Butler, 10 July 1945, F4240, FO371/46507, PRO.

90 Robert J. McMahon has most recently made this argument in his *The Limits of Empire: The United States and Southeast Asia since World War II* (New York: Columbia University Press, 1999), 9–13, 28, but it is more fully developed in Hess, *United States' Emergence,* 47–158. Similar interpretations emerge in two broader accounts of U.S. wartime attitudes toward decolonization; see Warren F. Kimball, " 'In Search of Monsters to Destroy': Roosevelt and Colonialism," in his *The Juggler: Franklin Roosevelt As Wartime Statesman* (Princeton: Princeton University Press, 1991), 127–57, and Louis, *Imperialism at Bay.*

91 See, for example, LaFeber, "Roosevelt, Churchill, and Indochina."

92 My discussion of time as a critical element for the exercise of power is shaped by Johannes Fabian, *Time and the Other: How Anthropology Makes Its Object* (New York: Columbia University Press, 1983); Pierre Bourdieu, *Outline of a Theory of Practice* (Cambridge: Cambridge University Press, 1977), 159–97; and Arjun Appadurai, *Modernity at Large: Cultural Dimensions of Globalization* (Minneapolis: University of Minnesota Press, 1996), 66–85, 178–99.

93 French fears that the United States sought to create an empire for itself in Vietnam are a common feature of French internal reporting on U.S. activities in Vietnam after 1945. They are discussed more fully in Chapters 4 and 5.

94 My discussion on the interrelationship of modernity and the telescoping of time draws on David Harvey, *The Condition of Postmodernity* (Cambridge: Blackwell, 1990), 201–83, and more broadly, Karl Polanyi, *The Great Transformation* (Boston: Beacon Press, 1943). Frank Ninkovich has thoughtfully explored the impact of modernity and its accompanying fears on twentieth-century American policy makers, including Franklin Roosevelt, in his *Modernity and Power: A History of the Domino Theory in the Twentieth Century* (Chicago: University of Chicago Press, 1994).

95 The conservative embrace of gradualism in the Roosevelt administration's policy to-

ward Vietnam was paralleled in U.S. wartime domestic policy toward African Americans. In the face of escalating racial violence and crises at home—in 1943 some 242 racial battles occurred in forty-seven cities across the country—the administration maintained its policy of conciliation and compromise from the 1930s. It was reluctant to challenge segregation in the South, willing to tolerate racial discrimination in managing its own relief programs, accepting of racial wage differentials, and unwilling to endorse antilynching legislation. See Harvard Sitkoff, "Racial Militancy and Interracial Violence in the Second World War," *Journal of American History* 58, no. 3 (December 1971): 661–81; Jill Quadagno, *The Color of Welfare* (New York: Oxford University Press, 1995); and Alan Brinkley, "The New Deal and the Southern Politics," in his *Liberalism and Its Discontents* (Cambridge: Harvard University Press, 1998), 66–97.

CHAPTER FOUR

1 Ho Chi Minh, "Tuyen Ngon Doc Lap" [Declaration of independence], in *Ho Chi Minh Toan Tap, Tap 3, 1930–1945* [Ho Chi Minh's collected works, vol. 3, 1930–45] (Hanoi: Nha Xuat Ban Su That, 1983), 383.

2 On the presence of American P-38 planes over Hanoi, see Michael Charlton and Anthony Moncrieff, *Many Reasons Why: The American Involvement in Vietnam* (New York: Hill and Wang, 1978), 13–14.

3 Vo Nguyen Giap's address and its discussion of the United States is reprinted in *CMCD, Tap 12, Tong Khoi Nghia Thang Tam* [vol. 12, The August Revolution] (1957), 116. The pro-American placards and banners at the independence day parade were visible in documentary footage of the event in the collection of the Vietnamese Ministry of Culture. My description also draws on a contemporary Vietnamese account of the events of 2 September 1945; see Tung Hiep, "Hom Nay la Ngay Doc Lap!" [Today is independence day!], 9 September 1945, *Trung Bac Chu Nhat* [Center and northern Sunday magazine].

4 Until recently, the place of the United States in the August Revolution received more polemical than scholarly treatments. Contemporary French colonial observers, who saw the independence day events against a broader pattern of wartime collaboration between Vietnam and the United States, have argued that "it was the Americans who made Ho Chi Minh." Official historians of the Vietnamese state, who ascribe the success of the August Revolution almost solely to Marxist-Leninist revolutionary acumen, attribute no real significance to the U.S. presence at the independence day celebrations in Hanoi. Some opponents of the war in Vietnam in the 1960s and 1970s in the U.S. Congress saw the events of 2 September as a golden age in Vietnamese-American relations, an era tragically shattered by the rise of the Cold War. For the assessments of French observers, see Général Sabattier, *Le destin de l'Indochine: souvenirs et documents* (Paris: Plon, 1952); Jean Sainteny, *Histoire d'une paix manquée* (Paris: Fayard, 1967); and Lucien Bodard, *The Quicksand War: Prelude to Vietnam* (Boston: Little, Brown, 1967), 221–22. For official Vietnamese perspectives, see *CMCD, Tap 11: Cao Trao Dau Tranh Tien Khoi Nghia* [vol. 11, The high tide of the struggle and our insurrection front] (1957), 82–83. One admiring and wistful view of this period by U.S.

opponents of the war emerges in hearings held by the Senate Committee on Foreign Relations; see, for instance, U.S. Senate, Committee on Foreign Relations, *Hearings on the Causes, Origins, and Lessons of the Vietnam War*, 92d Cong., 2d sess., 9–12 May 1972 (Washington, D.C.: U.S. Government Printing Office, 1973).

More recently, however, the important works of David Marr and Stein Tønnesson on the August Revolution have thoughtfully explored its international dimension. While these works deeply informed my understanding of this period, my own approach departs from, although I hope complements, the analyses they offer. See David G. Marr, *Vietnam 1945: The Quest for Power* (Berkeley: University of California Press, 1995), and Stein Tønnesson, *The Vietnamese Revolution of 1945: Roosevelt, Ho Chi Minh, and de Gaulle in a World at War* (London: Sage, 1991).

5 On ICP perceptions of the outbreak of World War II, see Pham Xuan Nam, "Ve Nhung Nguyen Nhan Phat Sinh Cuoc Chien Tranh The Gioi Thu Hai (Xet theo nhan dinh cua nhung nguoi cong san Viet Nam luc do)" [On the causes of the outbreak of World War II (as understood by Vietnamese communists at the time)], *Nghien Cuu Lich Su* [Historical studies] 5 (1979): 67–79, and Nguyen Khanh Toan, "Ve Nguyen Nhan Phat Sinh Cuoc Chien Tranh The Gioi Thu Hai" [On the causes of the outbreak of World War II], *Nghien Cuu Lich Su* 6 (1979): 1–16.

6 The composition of the plenum is discussed in Hoang Quang Khanh, Le Hong, and Hoang Ngoc La, *Can Cu Dia Viet Bac: Trong Cuoc Cach Mang Thang 8-1945* [The Viet Bac base area: In the August Revolution] (Hanoi: Nha Xuat Ban Viet Bac, 1976), chap. 2; Tran Huy Lieu, *Lich Su Tam Muoi Nam Chong Phap, Tap III* [History of the eighty-year anti-French resistance, vol. 3] (Hanoi: Van Su Dia, 1961), 69–71; and Huynh Kim Khanh, *Vietnamese Communism, 1925–1945* (Ithaca: Cornell University Press, 1982), 257–59.

7 Two French campaigns of repression in 1939 decimated much of the ICP's leadership who had been active in the fractious internationalist politics of the 1930s. A third campaign, in the wake of the party's Nam Ky uprising in southern Vietnam in November 1940, saw more than one hundred top southern party leaders executed and numerous others imprisoned on the penal island of Con Son, where they were detained until the close of World War II. For a discussion of these French campaigns and their significance for the development of Vietnamese communism during World War II, see Tran Van Giau, *Giai Cap Cong Nhan Viet Nam: Tu Dang Cong San Thanh Lap Den Cach Mang Thanh Cong, Tap 3, 1939–45* [The Vietnamese working class: From the formation of the Communist Party until the success of the revolution, vol. 3, 1939–45] (Hanoi: Vien Su Hoc, 1963), 24, 55; Tran Huy Lieu, *Lich Su Tam Muoi Nam*, 62–63; *CMCD, Tap 10* [vol. 10] (1957), 24; and Khanh, *Vietnamese Communism*, 250, 254–55.

8 "Chinh Sach Moi Cua Dang" [New policies of the party], in the resolutions of the Eighth Plenum of the Central Committee of the Indochinese Communist Party [Hoi Nghi Trung Uong Lan Thu VIII Dang Cong San Dong-Duong] of May 1941, as reprinted in Ban Chap Hanh Trung Uong Dang Cong San Viet-Nam (Executive Board of the Central Committee of the Communist Party of Vietnam), *Van Kien Dang, Tap III, 1930–1945* [Party documents, vol. 3, 1930–45] (Hanoi: Ban Nghien Cuu Lich Su Dang Trung Uong Xuat Ban, 1977), 203; translation in Khanh, *Vietnamese Communism*, 260.

9 "Pac-Bo Hung Vi" [Majestic Pac Bo], in Ho Chi Minh, *Ho Chi Minh Toan Tap*, 3:145.

10 My discussion of the role of mountains and water in the Vietnamese mythology of national origins follows Keith Taylor, *The Birth of Vietnam* (Berkeley: University of California Press, 1983), 1–7, 303–5. Two works by Vietnamese authors demonstrate the widespread persistence of these beliefs at both the elite and the popular levels: Tran Quoc Vuong, "Tu Tu Duy Than Thoai Den Tu Duy Lich Su" [From mythical thought to historical thought], in *Hung Vuong Dung Nuoc* [*The Hung kings found a nation*] (Hanoi: Uy Ban Khoa Hoc Xa Hoi, 1973), 402–5, and Nguyen Thi Hue, "Nguoi Dan Ha Bac Ke Chuyen Lac Long Quan–Au Co" [The people of Ha Bac tell the story of Lac Long Quan–Au Co], *Tap Chi Van Hoc* [Literature magazine] 4 (1980): 102–7.

11 The metrical structure of Ho's poem reinforces its dual sensibilities. In constructing this poem, like many he composed during the World War II period, Ho used the rigid metrical form that had governed the often patriotic Vietnamese classical poetry written by Confucian scholar-officials. Ho broke with traditional metric patterns, however, by using what was known as the double-seven (*song-that*) meter for both of the poem's couplets. In classical Vietnamese poetry, double-seven verse almost never stood alone, as its skewed rhythm and oblique rhymes went against the grain of Vietnamese speech and left the impression of an action uncompleted or unresolved. By using double-seven meter, Ho both joined himself to the traditional forms of Vietnamese patriotic verse and, more subtly, modified these structures to foreshadow a new and not yet fully realized world. My discussion of metric structure and the nature of classical Vietnamese poetry relies on Huynh Sanh Thong's analysis in the introduction to his *Heritage of Vietnamese Poetry* (New Haven: Yale University Press, 1979), xxviii–xxxvi.

12 Ban Chap Hanh Trung Uong Dang Cong San Viet-Nam, *Van Kien Dang*, 203; translation in Khanh, *Vietnamese Communism*, 261.

13 Ibid., 205; my translation.

14 Ibid., 195; my translation.

15 Mao Tse-tung, *The Chinese Revolution and the Chinese Communist Party* and *On the New Democracy*, in *Selected Works* (Peking: Foreign Languages Press, 1965), 2:305–34, 339–84.

16 This discussion draws on Stuart Schram, *The Thought of Mao Tse-tung* (Cambridge: Cambridge University Press, 1989), 68–84, and John Bryan Starr, *Continuing the Revolution: The Political Thought of Mao* (Princeton: Princeton University Press, 1979), 202–3, 263–65.

17 On Chinese influences in the construction of Vietnamese military strategy and tactics, see Greg Lockhart, *Nation in Arms: The Origins of the People's Army of Vietnam* (Sydney: Allen and Unwin, 1989), 64–73, 86, 97, 100, and Khanh, *Vietnamese Communism*, 281–84.

18 The organization and tactics of the Viet Minh are outlined in "Viet-Nam Doc Lap Dong Minh: Tuyen Ngon, Chuong Trinh, Dieu Le (25-10-41)" [Independence League of Vietnam: Declaration, program, by-laws (25 October 1941)], reprinted in Ban Chap Hanh Trung Uong Dang Cong San Viet-Nam, *Van Kien Dang*, 431–50. For existing Western scholarly analyses of the origins of the Viet Minh, see Khanh, *Vietnamese Communism*, 263–69, and William J. Duiker, *The Communist Road to Power in Vietnam* (Boulder, Colo.: Westview Press, 1981), 68–69. As both Duiker and Khanh point out, the ICP had advocated united fronts in the 1930s, including the Antiimperialist

Front (1930–31) and the Democratic Front (1937–39), but they had not been particularly successful.

19 "Viet-Nam Doc Lap Dong Minh," 435, 442; Ho Chi Minh, *Lich Su Nuoc Ta* [History of our country], in *Ho Chi Minh Toan Tap*, 3:215–24.

20 *Viet Nam Doc Lap* [Vietnam independence], 10 September, 1 December 1941, 1 January, 21 February, 11 March 1942. On the establishment of *Viet Nam Doc Lap*, see Nguyen Thanh, *Bao Chi Cach Mang Viet Nam, 1925–1945* [The revolutionary press in Vietnam, 1925–45) (Hanoi: Nha Xuat Ban Khoa Hoc Xa Hoi, 1984), 267–82. For a useful examination of Ho's efforts to use poetry as a technique of mass mobilization, see Phan Ngoc Lien, "Tim Hieu ve Cong Tac Van Dong Giao Duc Quan Chuang cua Ho Chu Tich Thoi Gian Nguoi o Pac Bo" [An investigation of president Ho's mass mobilization and education work in the period at Pac Bo], *Nghien Cuu Lich Suu* 14 (1973): 13–21, 30.

21 Ban Chap Hanh Trung Uong Dang Cong San Viet-Nam, *Van Kien Dang*, 205.

22 Ibid., 201–2; Ho Chi Minh, *Lich Su Nuoc Ta*, 3:222.

23 On party organizing efforts after the Pac Bo Plenum, see Vien Su Hoc (Board of Historical Studies), *Tai Lieu Tham Khao Cach Mang Thang Tham (Tong Khoi Nghia o Hanoi va Cac Dia Phuong), Tap 1* [Research documents on the August Revolution (in the general uprising in Hanoi and other regions, vol. 1] (Hanoi: Nha Xuat Ban Su Hoc, 1960), 9–17, 197–98, 313–30, and Nguyen Thanh, *Bao Chi Cach Mang Viet Nam*, 282–95. On French repression in 1941 and 1942, see Ban Nghien Cuu Lich Su Quan Doi Thuoc Cuc Chinh Tri (Board for the historical study of the army in the political department), *Lich Su Quan Doi Nhan Dan Viet Nam* [History of the People's Army of Vietnam] (Hanoi: Nha Xuat Ban Quan Doi Nhan Dan, 1974), 76–90; Mai Elliot, trans., *Reminiscences on the Army for National Salvation: Memoirs of General Chu Van Tan* (Ithaca: Cornell University Southeast Asia Program Data Paper Number 97, 1974), 76–114; and Lockhart, *Nation in Arms*, 84–88.

24 All forty-seven issues of *Vietnam Independence* published between August 1941 and December 1942 contained extended discussions of the war in Europe and Asia. *National Salvation*, which appeared more irregularly in this period, tended to focus on developments in the Pacific theater.

25 Ho's overtures to China and his prison experiences are discussed in Hoang Tranh, *Ho Chi Minh voi Trung Quoc* [Ho Chi Minh and China] (n.p.: Nha Xuat Ban Sao Moi, 1990), 140–66, and King C. Chen, *Vietnam and China, 1938–1954* (Princeton: Princeton University Press, 1969), 55–60.

26 Ho Chi Minh, "Cac Bao Dang Tin Hoi Hop Lon Hoan Nghenh Uy-Ki" [News report: Willkie given a warm reception] and "Doan Dai Bieu Anh Sang Tham Trung-Hoa" [A British delegation in China], in *Ho Chi Minh Toan Tap*, 3:275–76, 321; translations from "Ho Chi Minh's 'Prison Diary,'" in *Reflections from Captivity*, ed. David G. Marr (Athens: Ohio State University Press, 1978), 77, 87.

27 ICP perceptions of the changing international environment and its impact on Vietnam are discussed in a party training manual written by Truong Chinh in 1943 titled, "Chien Tranh Thai-Binh-Duong va Cach Mang Giai Phong Doan Toc Dong Duong" [The Pacific war and the Indochinese national liberation revolution]; original edition consulted at the Museum of Revolution, Hanoi. On the February 1943 meeting of the

Standing Committee, see "Nghi Quyet Cua Ban Thuong Vu Trung Uong Dang Con San Dong-Duong (hop ngay 25–28/2/1943)" [Resolutions of the Central Committee of the Indochinese Communist Party (convened 25–28 February 1943)], in Ban Chap Hanh Trung Uong Dang Cong San Viet-Nam, *Van Kien Dang*, 313–62, and Khanh, *Vietnamese Communism*, 271–72.

28 On the formation of the policy of the cultural front and its enduring significance, see "Nghi Quyet Cua Ban Thuong Vu Trung Uong Dang Con San Dong-Duong," 346; Truong Chinh, "Marxism and Vietnamese Culture," in his *Selected Writings* (Hanoi: Foreign Languages Publishing House, 1977), 255–59; Neil L. Jamieson, *Understanding Vietnam* (Berkeley: University of California Press, 1993), 182–191; and Khanh, *Vietnamese Communism*, 273–75. On the resurgence of voluntarism, see Song Hong, "La thi si" [To be a poet], *Co Giai Phong* [Banner of liberation], 18 April 1944; Pham The Ngu, *Viet Nam Van Hoc Su Gian Uoc Tan Bien, Tap 3, Van Hoc Hien Dai, 1862–1945* [A new outline history of Vietnamese literature, vol. 3, Contemporary literature, 1862–1945] (Saigon: Nha Xuat Ban Anh Phuong, 1965), 611–12.

29 Vu Dinh Hoe, along with several other prominent urban intellectuals associated with the cultural front, would serve in the cabinet of the Viet Minh's provisional government in 1945; see Philippe Devillers, *Histoire du Viêt-Nam de 1940 à 1952* (Paris: Éditions du Seuil, 1952), 177–78.

30 See *Thanh Nghi* [Impartial opinion], 1 November 1942, 1 January 1943, 25 March, 1 July, 7, 14 October, 16 December 1944, 27 January, 5 February 1945.

31 William Faulkner, "Khoi thuoc la" [Smoke], *Thanh Nghi*, 3, 10, 17, 24 June 1944; Jean-Paul Sartre, "American Novelists in French Eyes," *Atlantic Monthly*, August 1946, 114–15.

32 For the RCA discography available in Vietnam, see *Buu Thap cua Cong Ty RCA Victor* [Catalog of recordings by RCA Victor] (Saigon: Au Livre d'Or, 1940). Among the texts for learning English available in Vietnam during World War II were Nguyen Khac Kham, *Tieng Anh cho Nguoi Viet-Nam* [English for Vietnamese speakers] (Hanoi: Trung-Bac Tan-Van, 1941); Truong Anh Tu, *Nhung Tieng va Cau Huu Ich . . . : Viet-Phap-Anh* [Useful words and phrases . . . : Vietnamese-French-English] (Hanoi: Bacha, 1940); Tran Ngoc Phan, *Anh My Ngu Tu* [Self-taught English] (Hai Phong: n.p., 1945); and Nguyen Thuong Xuan and Nguyen Huu Dong, *Anh Ngu Tu Hoc* (English self-instruction] (Hanoi: Tien Hoa, 1945).

33 On reassessments within the Indochinese Communist Party of the important place of China, Britain, and the United States in Viet Minh strategy for realizing their goals in the winter and spring of 1943, see "Nghi Quyet Cua Ban Thuong Vu Trung Uong Dang Cong San Dong-Duong," 360–61; *Cuu Quoc* [Save the country], 10 February 1943; and *Viet Nam Doc Lap*, 1 May 1943.

34 *Cuu Quoc*, 10 February 1943; see also discussion in Tønnesson, *Vietnamese Revolution*, 132. On continuing French repression in 1943 and 1944 and the difficulties it posed for Viet Minh organizing, see *CMCD, Tap 1* [vol. 1] (1955), 67–73, and Lockhart, *Nation in Arms*, 87–88.

35 *Cuu Quoc*, November 1944, 3. For a discussion of Sino-Vietnamese diplomacy in this period, see Hoang Tranh, *Ho Chi Minh voi Trung Quoc*, 166–92, and Chen, *Vietnam and China*, 60–85.

36 *Cuu Quoc*, November 1944, 15, 19–20.

37 The memoirs of Hoang Quoc Viet and Hoang Van Hoan, who after Ho Chi Minh were most closely involved with the Viet Minh's Chinese initiatives, provide insight into internal party thinking on the Sino-Vietnamese relationship; see Hoang Quoc Viet, "Peuple héroïque," in *Récits de la résistance vietnamienne, 1925–1945* (Paris: François Maspéro, 1966), 190–92, and Hoang Van Hoan, *Giot Nuoc Trong Bien Ca: Hoi Ky Chach Mang* [A drop of water in the ocean: Memoirs of revolution] (Beijing: Nha Xuat Ban Tin Viet Nam, 1986), 233–52.

38 On Pham Van Dong's efforts to secure Ho's release, see Central Committee to the Indochina Section of the International Anti-Aggression Association at Hanoi to the American Ambassador, and Central Committee to Chiang Kai-shek, both 25 October 1943, in Gauss to Secretary of State, 23 December 1943, 851G.00/95, Decimal Files, RG 59.

39 On the organization of the Viet Minh delegation at Kunming and biographical information on Pham Viet Tu, see "The National Movement in Indo-China," 28 August 1944, Operational Intelligence Report, OSS, Kunming, folder 273, box 35, entry 140, RG 226.

40 Pham Viet Tu to American Ambassador in China, 18 August 1944, and "Indochina from the French Occupation in 1886 up to the Present," in Langdon to Gauss, 24 August 1944, 851G.00/8-2444, Decimal Files, RG 59. For another example of the Viet Minh delegation in Kunming to seek U.S. support, see Pham Viet Tu to Senator Arthur Capper, 29 August 1944, folder 35-273, entry 140, RG 226. The letter to Senator Capper was apparently initiated after Pham Viet Tu received a copy of the 9 July 1944 issue of the *Congressional Record* with a transcript of a speech by Capper on the Senate floor praising the courage of the Indochinese people in the face of Japanese aggression.

41 For a useful discussion of these ritual forms and assumptions embedded in them, see James L. Hevia, *Cherishing Men from Afar: Qing Guest Ritual and the Macartney Embassy of 1793* (Durham, N.C.: Duke University Press, 1995), 1–28, 116–33. For their significance in precolonial Vietnamese diplomacy, see Truong Buu Lam, "Intervention versus Tribute in Sino-Vietnamese Relations, 1788–1790," in *The Chinese World Order: Traditional China's Foreign Relations*, ed. John King Fairbank (Cambridge: Harvard University Press, 1968), 165–79, and Alexander Barton Woodside, *Vietnam and the Chinese Model: A Comparative Study of Vietnamese and Chinese Government in the First Half of the Nineteenth Century* (Cambridge: Harvard University Press, 1971), 234–46.

42 Memorandum of Conversation, 7 September 1944, in Langdon to Secretary of State, 9 September 1944, 851G.00/9-944, Decimal Files, RG 59.

43 *Viet Nam Doc Lap*, February 1945. My discussion of the Viet Minh rescue of the American pilot also draws on my interview in Hanoi in 1989 with General Dam Quang Trung, who was active in the Viet Minh militia in northern Vietnam in November 1944 and later worked worked with one of the OSS missions to Vietnam in the summer of 1945.

44 *Viet Nam Doc Lap*, February 1945. The play is discussed in the statement of Tran Minh Chau at an oral history conference in Hanoi in October 1995 organized by the Ford Foundation and the U.S.-Indochina Reconciliation Project; copy in the author's posses-

sion. For a consideration of other efforts to draw on Allied prestige, see Nguyen Trong Hau, "Van De Tim Ban Dong Minh Xa Qua Bao *Viet Nam Doc Lap*, 1941–1945" [On the issue of friendship with the allies in *Vietnamese Independence*, 1941–1945] (unpublished manuscript in author's possession).

45 Lucius, "Letter from Indochina," February 1945, box 1393, entry 16, RG 226, 8. On Ho's work with the OSS and other U.S. military personnel in China, see Charles Fenn to Robert Hall, 22 October 1944, folder 340, box 42D, entry 140, RG 226; Hoang Van Hoan, *Giot Nuoc*, 245–46; Charles Fenn, *Ho Chi Minh: A Biographical Introduction* (New York: Charles Scribner's Sons, 1973), 72–84; and Chen, *Vietnam and China*, 93. For other examples of the use of the Philippines in official discourse, see *Viet Nam Doc Lap*, 25 December 1944, and the 21 November 1944 issue of *Dong Minh* [Allies] in Royere to Pechkoff, 16 January 1945, folder: "Mouvement révolutionnaire Annamite, 8/26/44–4/49, E165-2," vol. 161, Indochine, Asie Oceanie, 1944–1955, MAE.

46 Excerpt from an irregular journal produced by the Viet Minh in Saigon titled *Rang Dong cua Dan Toc* [Dawn of a people], ca. 1944, in "Rapport: Le parti communiste en Cochinchine," 21 February 1945, AOM-CP 192.

47 See *Viet Nam Doc Lap*, 15 June, 20 July, 15 December 1944, 25 January, 13 February 1945; *Cuu Quoc*, 20 August, 30 October 1944; *Co Giai Phong*, 10 November 1944; and "Indochinese Revolutionary Party Pamphlet," 24 August 1944, box 1094, entry 16, RG 226.

48 *Cuu Quoc*, 30 January 1945; *Viet Nam Doc Lap*, 4 March 1945; translations in Tønnesson, *Vietnamese Revolution*, 209.

49 The fullest account of these events and the coming of the August Revolution is in Marr, *Vietnam 1945*, chaps. 5 and 6.

50 "Nhat Phap Dan Nhau va Hanh Dong cua Ta: Chi Thi cua Ban Tuong Vu Trung Uong Dang Cong San Dong-duong ngay 12-3-1945" [Our action in relations to the Franco-Japanese conflict: Instruction of the Standing Committee of the Central Committee of the Indochinese Communist Party, 12 March 1945], in Ban Chap Hanh Trung Uong Dang Cong San Viet-Nam, *Van Kien Dang*, 391–92.

51 Khanh, *Vietnamese Communism*, 333–38.

52 On Ho's meeting with Chennault, see Hoang Van Hoan, *Giot Nuoc*, 245–46. On OSS encounters with Ho Chi Minh following the Japanese coup, see "Position of the Annamite Communistic Group," 2 March 1945, box 434, entry 19, RG 226; Fenn, *Ho Chi Minh*, 76–79; and Archimedes Patti, *Why Viet Nam?: Prelude to America's Albatross* (Berkeley: University of California Press, 1980), 84–88. My discussion of the Deer team missions draws on "Report on Deer Mission," 17 September 1945, folder 3377, box 199, entry 154, RG 226; Vo Nguyen Giap, *Khu Giai Phong* [The liberated zone] (Hanoi: Cuu Quoc, 1946); and interviews with Allison K. Thomas in East Lansing, Michigan, and Dam Quang Trung in Hanoi in 1989.

53 No Vietnamese or American transcripts of these conversations survive. This account relies on Patti, *Why Viet Nam?*, 151–255, supplemented by my interview with Hoang Minh Giam in Hanoi in 1989.

54 This discussion relies on Gallagher's accounts of his meetings with Ho Chi Minh, including "French Indo-China (14 September '45–12 Dec 1945)"; Gallagher to McClure, 20 September 1945; and Memorandum for the Record, 29 September 1945, Papers of

Phillip E. Gallagher, U.S. Army Center for Military History, Washington, D.C., and interviews in Hanoi with Hoang Minh Giam in 1989 and Nguyen Van Tran in 1992.

55 Statement of Frank M. White, 11 May 1972, U.S. Senate, Committee on Foreign Relations, *Hearings*, 152. Ho Chi Minh's encounter with Arthur Hale is discussed in Hale to Holland, 11 December 1945, Gallagher Papers.

56 Ho Chi Minh to Truman, 16 February 1946, and Ho Chi Minh to James Byrnes, 1 November 1945, reprinted in U.S. House of Representatives, Committee on Armed Services, *United States–Vietnam Relations, 1945–1967*, vol. 1, *Vietnam and the United States, 1940–1950* (Washington, D.C.: U.S. Government Printing Office, 1971), C95–96, C90. For the complete correspondence sent to Washington by Ho Chi Minh, see also Ho Chi Minh to Truman, 29 September, 17 October, 8, 23 November 1945; Ho Chi Minh to U.S. Secretary of State, 22 October 1945; and Ho Chi Minh to James Byrnes, 26 November 1945, reprinted in ibid., 1:C69–70, C73–74, C80–81, C84–86, C87–88, C92; Ho Chi Minh to Truman, 18 January 1946, folder: "800 IC 1946," Records of the Nanking Embassy, RG 84; and Ho Chi Minh to Truman, 28 February 1946, folder 427, box 53, entry 140, RG 226.

57 Biographical material on Pham Ngoc Thach is based on conversations with scholars at the Institute of History, Hanoi, Vietnam, 1989 and 1992, and "Note sur la personnalité de Monsieur Pham Ngoc Thach," December 1947, "Communisme et relations Moscou-Hanoi-Chine," 174, Indochine, Asie Oceanie, 1944–1955, MAE.

58 Herbert J. Bluechel, "The Political Aims and Philosophy of the Viet Minh Government," 30 September 1945, folder 277, box 25, entry 100, RG 226; Pham Ngoc Thach, "Some Notable Characteristics of the Revolution in August 1945," ca. October 1945, box 1, Records of Consular Posts, Hanoi, 1950–52, RG 84. For Thach's initial approach to the OSS in Saigon in 1945, see Provisory Government of the Republic of Viet-Nam to OSS Major Peter Dewey, 2 September 1945, and Saigon to Kandy, 21 September 1945, folder: "Messages via OSS," box 10, PSA, RG 59. Conversations between Thach and American OSS officers in Saigon and the information passed by Thach to American officials are in "Who's Who of Members of Present Government," 7 November 1945, XL27712; "Viet Minh's Political, Economic, and Social Program as Outlined by Dr. Thach," 7 November 1945, XL27713; "History and Political Movements of the Viet Nam," 17 November 1945, XL27715; "Relations between Vietminh and the French . . . Report by Dr. Thach," 12 November 1945, XL27711; "Viet-Minh Evidence against the French," 13 November 1945, XL 27710; "Memorandum of the Southern Executive Committee of Vietnam," 19 November 1945, XL27716, box 360, entry 19, RG 226, and "History and Political Movements of the Viet Minh," 17 November 1945, box 365, entry 19, RG 226.

59 On the character of Sino-Vietnamese relations during the Chinese occupation of the north, see Chen, *Vietnam and China*, 115–54, and Hoang Tranh, *Ho Chi Minh voi Trung Quoc*, 196–209.

60 See, for instance, Ho Chi Minh to Stalin, 22 September 1945, list 187, file 31, box 197, year 29, fond 0136, Foreign Policy Archives of the Russian Federation (Arkhiv vneshnei politiki Rossiyskoy Federatsii), Moscow, cited in Igor Bukharkin, "Moscow and Ho Chi Minh, 1945–1969" (paper presented at Conference on New Evidence on the Cold War in Asia, University of Hong Kong, January 1996).

61 On initial Vietnamese efforts to court the British, see Pham Ngoc Thach to General Gracey, 16 September 1945, box 10, PSA, RG 59; Ho Chi Minh to Council of Ministers, 18 September 1945, FO371/46038, and "Record of an Interview with Dr. Thach on 3rd October 1945," WO203/5562, PRO. The British mission is analyzed in Peter Dennis, *Troubled Days of Peace: Mountbatten and the South East Asia Command, 1945–46* (New York: St. Martin's Press, 1987); Peter M. Dunn, *The First Vietnam War* (New York: St. Martin's Press, 1985). Dennis takes a more critical view of British policy in Vietnam than does Dunn, whose account provides an extended apologia for British actions in Vietnam. Neither author explores the nature of Viet Minh diplomacy with the British.

62 For two opposing contemporary accounts of the outbreak of fighting in southern Vietnam in late September 1945, see "History of the 20th Indian Division," n.d., Douglas David Gracey Papers 36, Liddell Hart Centre for Military Archives, King's College, University of London, London, England, an official British report of their mission in Saigon, and Hoc Tu, *Nhung Ngay Dau cua Mat Tran Nam Bo* [First days on the South Vietnamese battlefront] (Hanoi: Tranh Dao, 1945), an eyewitness account by a Viet Minh journalist of the clash between the British and the Vietnamese. On Ho Chi Minh's protest to the British government, see Ho Chi Minh to Prime Minister Attlee, 27 September 1945, WO203/5562, PRO. On Vietnam propaganda directed toward Indian troops, see "Appeal to the Indian Officers and Soldiers among the British Troops," n.d., and "Viet Minh Propaganda," ca. October 1945, Gracey Papers, 37. On Gracey's views of the Viet Minh, see Gracey to SEAC, 3 October 1945, Gracey Papers, 36. On increasing Vietnamese antagonism toward the British, see Noang Cao Nha to Gracey, 11 October 1945, Gracey Papers, 54, and Tran Van Giau to Gracey, 10 October 1945, F9532, FO371/46309, PRO. On the October meetings between the British and Pham Ngoc Thach, see Saigon Control Commission to SACSEA, 1 October 1945, and Report on Political and Economic Conditions in Saigon, ca. October 1945, WO203/5562, PRO; "Meeting between British and Vietnamese Officials," 9 October 1945, and "Appendix D: Extracts from Minutes of British-Viet Minh Meetings, Political Report, 13 September to 9 October 1945," Gracey Papers, 48, 36.

63 Hoi Viet-My Than Huu, *Dieu-Le* [By-laws] (Hanoi: Hoi Viet-My Than Huu, 1945); "History and Origins of the Annamite-American Friendship Association," 9 October 1945, folder 3426, box 202, entry 154, RG 226; "First Meeting," *Viet-My Tap Chi* [Vietnamese-American Friendship Association review], November 1945, 2–3.

64 "About Future Relations between Vietnam and the U.S.A.," *Viet-My Tap Chi* (Christmas and New Year ed., 1945–46), 18, 17.

65 *Viet-My Tap Chi* was published three times between October 1945 and February 1946. A copy of the initial issue is preserved in the Gallagher Papers, U.S. Army Center for Military History, Washington, D.C.; remaining issues are available in the library of the Institute of History in Hanoi.

66 On the U.S. commercial presence in Vietnam in 1946, see Rapport sur l'activité des étrangers, 25 September, 31 October 1946, folder: "Rapports sur l'activité des étrangers," AOM-CP 154. On American films, see *Viet-My Tap Chi* (Christmas and New Year ed., 1945–46), 17, and Hale to Holland, 11 December 1945, Gallagher Papers.

67 For American reports on declining U.S. prestige in Vietnam, see Saigon to Kandy,

27 November 1945, folder: "Kandy Cables in Nov 45," and 3 December 1945, folder: "Kandy Cables in Dec 45," box 3, entry 53, RG 226; Saigon to Singapore, 9 January 1946, folder "Singapore Cables in Jan 46," box 3, entry 53, RG 226; "Political Intentions," XL 34469, 9 January 1946, box 381, entry 19, RG 226; and Hale to Holland, 11 December 1945, Gallagher Papers.

68 On the rise of internationalist conceptions of America in this period, see "Fond Viet Minh," 3 March 1946, in Note, Conseiller diplomatique, 4 February 1948, folder: "Premeditation VN dans l'attaque du 19–12," AOM-CP supplément 17, and Bach Ho, *Lich Su Cac Cuoc Cach Menh Tren The Gioi: Cach Menh Hoa-Ky* [History of the revolutions of the world: The American revolution] (Vinh: Nha Xuat Ban Ngan Hong, 1946), esp. 33–36.

69 For discussions of Ho Chi Minh and the Viet Minh, see Patti, *Why Viet Nam?*, 83–88, 124–29, 151–256, 274–80, 337–449. Various statements of the "lost opportunity" thesis and the perceptual gap between Washington and the field include Robert Shaplen, *The Lost Revolution* (New York: Harper and Row, 1965), 27–35, 46–54; Harold Isaacs, *No Peace for Asia* (Cambridge: MIT Press, 1967), 170–75; George C. Herring, "The Truman Administration and the Restoration of French Sovereignty in Indochina," *Diplomatic History* 1, no. 2 (Spring 1977): 112, 116; and Gary R. Hess, *The United States' Emergence As a Southeast Asian Power, 1940–1950* (New York: Columbia University Press, 1987), 169–84.

70 Patti, *Why Viet Nam?*, 209–10; Patti to Kunming, 27 August 1945, folder 3373, box 199, entry 154, RG 226. For other examples of the perceptual differences between Patti's memoirs and his contemporary reporting from the field, compare Patti, *Why Viet Nam?*, 218, 221–24, with Activities Report, 28 August 1945, and Patti to Kunming, 29 August 1945, folder 3376, box 199, entry 154, RG 226.

71 James R. Withrow to Robert P. Leonard, 1 May 1945, folder 1617, box 119, entry 139, and "Position of Annamite Communistic Group," 2 March 1945, L-54540, box 434, entry 19, RG 226. See also Chow to Whampler, 18 July 1945, folder 3377, box 199, entry 154, RG 226.

72 Patti to Kunming, 29 August 1945, folder 3373, box 199, entry 154, RG 226. See also Patti to Kunming, 27, 31 August 1945, ibid.

73 "Conditions in Northern Indochina," Department of State Memorandum of Conversation with Brigadier General Philip E. Gallagher; Gallagher to McClure, 20 September 1945; and Hale to Holland, 11 December 1945, all in Gallagher Papers; "Annamite Revolutionary Movements," Robert H. Knapp, 9 October 1945, box 316, entry 19, RG 226. See, also untitled notes, Lt. Defourneaux, September 1945, folder 416, box 52, entry 140, RG 226.

74 Allison K. Thomas, "The Vietminh Party or League," in his "Report on Deer Mission," 17 September 1945, and Patti to Kunming, 2 September 1945, both in folder 3373, box 199, entry 154, RG 226; Hale to Holland, 11 December 1945, Gallagher Papers; "Interview with Ho Chi Minh," 21 January 1946, box 426, entry 19, RG 226.

75 There were some exceptions to this generally critical tone. One of the men with the Deer team mission called Giap "part of a group of intelligent young men" surrounding Ho Chi Minh; see untitled notes, Lt. Defourneaux, September 1945, folder 416, box 52, entry 140, RG 226. Allison Thomas termed Giap "sincere and able," just as he

had Ho Chi Minh; see Thomas, "Report on Deer Mission," 17 September 1945, folder 3377, box 199, entry 154, RG 226.

76 For one dissenting analysis that argued that Ho had never put nationalism "above loyalty to Moscow," see OSS Research and Analysis Report, 25 October 1945, folder: "Messages via OSS," box 10, PSA, RG 59.

77 John C. Bane to Kunming, 15 September 1945, folder 3373, box 199, entry 154, RG 226; "French Indochina," 17 October 1945, folder 416, box 52, entry 140, RG 226; OSS R&A Report, 14 October 1945, folder: "Messages via OSS," box 10, PSA, RG 59.

78 Heppner to Patti, 3 September 1945, folder 3373, box 199, entry 154, RG 226. On Swift's proposal and reactions to it, see Swift to Kunming, 10 October 1945, folder 3432, box 202, entry 154, RG 226; Swift to Kunming, 22 October 1945, folder: "Messages via OSS," box 10, PSA, RG 59; and Kunming to OSS (Washington), 22 October 1945; OSS (Washington) to Heppner, 24 October 1945; Heppner to Swift, 25 October 1945; Heppner to OSS (Washington), 25 October 1945, folder 3426, box 202, entry 154, RG 226.

79 On the instructions guiding the work of U.S. intelligence and military operatives in Vietnam, see Kunming to Chungking, 23 August 1945; Chungking to Kunming, 24, 26 August, 2, 3 September 1945; and Helliwell to Nordlinger, 7 September 1945, all in folder 3373, box 199, entry 154, RG 226.

80 "Field Mission of Capt. Phelan into French Indo-China," 17 October 1945, 851G.00/10-1745, Decimal Files, RG 59; John C. Bane to Kunming, 15 September 1945, folder 3373, box 199, entry 154, RG 226; Gallagher to McClure, 20 September 1945, Gallagher Papers. See also Robert V. Ettinger to Kunming, 17 September 1945, folder 3375, box 199, entry 154, RG 226.

81 Donovan to Truman, 31 August 1945, folder: "OSS Donovan June–Aug 1945," box 15, Rose Conway File, Papers of Harry S. Truman, HST. See also Donovan to Truman, 21 August 1945, folder: "OSS Donovan June–Aug 1945"; Donovan to Truman, 6, 25 September 1945, folder: "OSS Donovan Sep 1945"; and Donovan to Secretary of State, 22, 31 August, 5, 6 September 1945, folder: "PSA-IC," box 10, PSA, RG 59. The State Department's Division of Philippine and Southeast Asian Affairs also received copies of most of Patti's dispatches along with a number of other OSS reports from the field; see folder: "Messages via OSS," box 10, PSA, RG 59.

82 "Conditions in French Indochina," Department of State Memorandum of Conversation with Colonel Nordlinger, 5 December 1945, box 9, PSA, RG 59; Nordlinger served in Hanoi from late August to October 1945 and was responsible for evacuating American prisoners of war. See also "Situation in Northern French Indochina," Department of State Memorandum of Conversation with Major Archimedes Patti, 5 December 1945, and Vincent to Acheson, 8 February 1946, box 10, PSA, RG 59, and "Conditions in Northern Indochina," Department of State Memorandum of Conversation with Brigadier General Philip E. Gallagher, Gallagher Papers.

83 "Indochina," 26 November 1945, box 2, Records of the Department of State, Division of Western European Affairs, Office of the French Desk, 1941–1951, RG 59. For similar statements of American policy in this period, see Statement of John Carter Vincent, 20 October 1945, *Department of State Bulletin*, 21 October 1945, 13:646; "PR 36: U.S. Policy towards the Netherlands, Indies, and Indochina," December 1945, box 119A, Notter Files, RG 59. Reports from the field in the fall of 1945 conveyed similar suspi-

cions of French intentions with regard to the future status of Indochina; see, in RG 226, Patti to Kunming, 1 September 1945, folder 3376, and 8 September 1945, folder 3373, box 199, entry 154; "Interim Report of Political and Propaganda Development within Indo-China," 8, 15 October 1945, folder 2475, box 186, entry 139; Saigon to Kandy, 27 November 1945, folder: "Kandy Cables in Nov 1945," and 13 December 1945, folder: "Kandy Cables in Dec 1945," box 3, entry 53.

84 USIS-OIC Reports for September, October, November, and December 1946, Saigon, French Indochina, box 2, Records of the Saigon Embassy and Consulate, RG 84. Counterposing the establishment of the USIS reading room in 1946 with Archimedes Patti's suggestion in the summer of 1945 that the United States undertake "propaganda material illustrating the American way of living" further reveals the parallels between perceptions in Washington and the field; see Patti to Kunming, 30 August 1945, folder 3431, box 202, entry 154, RG 226.

85 Reed to Secretary of State, 11 September, 3 October 1946, box 2, Records of the Saigon Embassy and Consulate, RG 84. See also J. A. Robertson to C. R. Chartrand, 9 May 1946; "Special Survey Report: United States Information Service, Saigon," July 1946; Reed to Secretary of State, 31 May, 17 September, 16 October 1946; and Moffat to Wallner, 23 October 1946, ibid.

86 Rapport, 9 January 1946, folder: "Indochine-Amérique, 1945–11/48, E170-3," vol. 255, Indochine, Asie Oceanie, 1944–1955, MAE. See also Général LeClerc to Ministre des Affaires Étrangères, 27 September 1945, in *La guerre d'Indochine, 1945–1954*, vol. 1, *Le retour de la France en Indochine, 1945–1946*, ed. Gilbert Bodinier (Vincennes: Service Historique de l'Armée de Terre, 1987), 193; "Note: Relations du Viet Nam avec les représentatives américains au Tonkin, 2 September 1946" and Pignon to Comité Interministériel de l'Indochine, 19 November 1946, folder: "Indochine-Amérique, 1945-11/48, E170-3," vol. 255, Indochine, Asie Oceanie, 1944–1955, MAE; Rapport, 25 September 1946, folder: "Rapports sur l'activité des étrangers," AOM-CP 154, and Bulletin de Renseignements, 3 March 1946, note, 1 June 1946, Rapport, 5, 18 September 1946, folder: "Attitude américaine a l'egard du gouvernement Republicaine annamite au Tonking," AOM-CP 231. On the broader forces framing postwar French suspicion of the United States, see Richard Kuisel, *Seducing the French: The Dilemma of Americanization* (Berkeley: University of California Press, 1993).

87 "Statement of Abbot Low Moffat," 11 May 1972, in U.S. Senate, Committee on Foreign Relations, *Hearings*, 169.

88 Moffat to Secretary of State Byrnes, 12 December 1945, box 1, Records of the Saigon Embassy and Consulate, RG 84. A more complete discussion of Moffat's trip to Hanoi in December 1946 emerges in a series of letters written to his wife, reprinted in U.S. Senate, Committee on Foreign Relations, *The United States and Vietnam, 1944–1947* (Washington, D.C.: U.S. Government Printing Office, 1972), 36–44. On U.S. contacts with the Vietnamese and French in 1946, see also O'Sullivan to Reed, 13, 17 August, 7 October 1946; Caffery to Secretary of State, 12 September 1946; Reed to Secretary of State, 30 September 1946; O'Sullivan to Secretary of State, 25 October 1946, all in box 2, Records of the Saigon Embassy and Consulate, RG 84; Caffery to Secretary of State, 6 February, 7 July, 2 August 1946, 17 September, 3 December 1946; Landon to Secretary of State, 27 February 1946; Reed to Secretary of State, 27 April 1946; and

Moffat to Vincent, 9 August 1946, in *FRUS, 1946,* vol. 8, *The Far East* (1971), 25–27, 37–38, 48–51, 52–54, 58, 65–66.

89 Acting Secretary of State to Reed, 9 September 1946, and Caffery to Secretary of State, 29 November 1946, in *FRUS, 1946,* 8:57, 63; "Le parti communiste Indochinois historique," in Donovan to Secretary of State, 18 February 1946; Sûreté Memorandum on Chinese Communist Political Activity in Vietnam, in Reed to Secretary of State, 24 October 1946; and Reed to Secretary of State, 18 November 1946, box 2, Records of the Saigon Embassy and Consulate, RG 84. For one early statement of French efforts to make available material to the United States on the DRV's connections to international communism, see the French Ministry of Foreign Affairs instructions to French Ambassador to Washington Henri M. Bonnet that he "should not hide the fact that the Viet Minh contains a preponderance of communist elements"; see Ministre des Affaires Étrangères to Bonnet, 29 September 1945, folder: "Politique intérieure-dossier général 8/26/44–12/31/45, E165-1," vol. 138, Indochine, Asie Oceanie, 1944–1955, MAE.

90 Acting Secretary of State to Moffat, 5 December 1945, *FRUS, 1946,* 8:67; Moffat to Secretary of State Byrnes, 12 December 1945, box 1, Records of the Saigon Embassy and Consulate, RG 84.

CHAPTER FIVE

1 On Franco-Vietnamese negotiations in 1946 and the coming of war in Vietnam, see Stein Tønnesson, *1946: Déclenchement de la guerre d'Indochine: les vêpres tonkinoises du 19 décembre* (Paris: L'Harmattan, 1987), and Ellen J. Hammer, *The Struggle for Indochina* (Stanford: Stanford University Press, 1954), 148–91.

2 *Cuoc Khang Chien Than Thanh cua Nhan Dan Viet Nam* [The sacred resistance war of the Vietnamese people], 4 vols. (Hanoi: Nha Xuat Ban Su That, 1958–60), 2:40–41. This source is a compilation of articles from the official press, including *Su That* [Truth], *Sinh Hoat Noi Bo* [Inner life], and *Nhan Dan* [The people], for the period September 1945 to July 1954.

3 As the documents produced by the Vietnamese government on domestic affairs between September 1945 and December 1946 (captured by the French at the outbreak of the war and now housed in the French National Archives) suggest, the postcolonial state was fragile and experimental from its inception; see, for instance, dossiers contained in GF 28-68, Fonds Indochine: Gouvernement de fait, AOM. The escalating administrative chaos produced by the war also emerged in my interviews conducted in Hanoi in 1989 and 1992 with Vietnamese diplomats active in the period.

4 On Vietnamese relations with the CCP, see Hoang Tranh, *Ho Chi Minh voi Trung Quoc* [Ho Chi Minh and China] (n.p.: Nha Xuat Ban Sao Moi, 1990); Qiang Zhai, *China and the Vietnam Wars, 1950–1975* (Chapel Hill: University of North Carolina Press, 2000), chap. 1; King C. Chen, *Vietnam and China, 1938–1954* (Princeton: Princeton University Press, 1969), 187–95; and Greg Lockhart, *Nation in Arms: The Origins of the People's Army of Vietnam* (Sydney: Allen and Unwin, 1989). On Soviet influence in Vietnam, see Charles B. McLane, *Soviet Strategies in Southeast Asia* (Princeton: Princeton University Press, 1966), 261–345. On the relationship between the DRV and

the French Communist Party, see Alain Ruscio, *Les communistes français et la guerre d'Indochine, 1944–1954* (Paris: Éditions l'Harmattan, 1985), and McLane, *Soviet Strategies*, 423–43.

5 Conversations with University of Hanoi historians Pham Xanh and Do Quang Hung in 1992 yielded an alternative explanation for the lack of Soviet support for the DRV in this period. They contend that Stalin's distrust of Ho Chi Minh's revolutionary credentials significantly reduced Soviet interest in the DRV. Beginning with the rise of the ultra-leftist revolutionary line adopted at the Sixth World Congress of the Comintern in 1928, Xanh and Hung assert, Stalin criticized Ho's emphasis on national liberation rather than proletarian social revolution and remained skeptical of Ho's aims for the DRV until Mao effected a rapprochement between Stalin and Ho in 1950. As I discussed in Chapter 1, recently opened Comintern files confirm Ho's difficult relationship with the Soviet leadership in the 1930s. But because Soviet and Vietnamese party archives for the late 1940s remained closed to foreign researchers, Xanh and Hung's characterization of Stalin's motivations in this period are difficult to confirm. For one somewhat elliptical confirmation of their argument for the 1940s, see Do Quang Hung, "Chu Tich Ho Chi Minh Trong Thoi Ky 1934–1938, Roi Sang Them Cho Van De Dan Toc Hay Quoc Te?" [Ho Chi Minh in the period 1934–1938, clearly for nationalism or internationalism?], in *Ho Chi Minh Anh Hung Giai Phong Dan Toc Danh Nhan Van Hoa* [Ho Chi Minh, national liberator and cultural hero] (Hanoi: Nha Xuat Ban Khoa Hoc Xa Hoi, 1990), 28, 35–36.

6 American socialists offered little more than the French Communist Party. The DRV did establish ties with the American Socialist Party and the Socialist Workers' Party, which helped to form a Vietnamese-American friendship association in New York City under the direction of George Sheldon. The organization provided little beyond moral support expressed at several meetings, the publication of a few articles sympathetic to the DRV's position, and a demonstration held on 25 July 1947 in which two hundred people surrounded the French consulate for twelve hours chanting, "Hands Off Indochina." See Renseignements, 25 February, 25 October 1947, 4 October 1948, and Bonnet to Bidault, 28 March 1947, folder: "Vietnam American Friendship Association," AOM-CD 128.

7 "Transmission of Questions Answered by Pham Ngoc Thach," Stanton to Marshall, 14 May 1947, box 4, Confidential Records of the Saigon Consulate, RG 84.

8 "Memo to International Engineering Company," Stanton to Marshall, 24 April 1947, box 4, RG 84.

9 The DRV's intention to capitalize on its favorable wartime relations with the OSS was suggested in my interview with Hoang Minh Giam, DRV foreign minister (1946–54), in Hanoi in 1989.

10 Hammer, *Struggle for Indochina*, 204.

11 The text of Giam's appeal is in O'Sullivan to Marshall, May 9, 1947, *FRUS, 1947*, vol. 6, *The Far East* (Washington, D.C.: U.S. Government Printing Office, 1972), 95.

12 "Questionnaire Received from Dr. Thach," Stanton to Marshall, July 9, 1947, box 4, RG 84.

13 Continuing prohibitions on access to documents that would reveal the processes of Vietnamese decision making in undertaking the initiative to the Truman administra-

tion make it difficult to address authoritatively DRV motivations and aims. At the time of my research in Vietnam, the archives of the party and foreign ministry remained closed to American researchers. Existing scholarship has tended to put forward a more ideological analysis of DRV motives, suggesting the DRV's solidarity with the Soviet Union prevented it from undertaking any sustained relationship with the noncommunist world. Party doctrine, according to these analyses, viewed diplomacy as part of the political and military struggle to achieve a Leninist revolution in Vietnam. In this view, any effort to gain external support from the noncommunist world was little more than a tactical maneuver to be quickly abandoned when the government's revolutionary aims had been achieved. Such a reductionist argument, however, obscures the diverse internationalist and indigenous influences that had shaped the worldview of the DRV's leadership. For one formulation of this view, see Ton That Thien, *The Foreign Politics of the Communist Party of Vietnam: A Study of Communist Tactics* (New York: Crane Russak, 1989), 57–65.

14 The efforts of France and the other colonial powers to limit information about developments within Southeast Asia before World War II are discussed in Anne L. Foster, "Alienation and Cooperation: American, European, and Southeast Asian Perceptions of Anti-Colonial Rebellion, 1919–1937" (Ph.D. diss., Cornell University, 1995). On the orientation of the Vietnamese elites toward China and France, see Hue-Tam Ho Tai, *Radicalism and the Origins of the Vietnamese Revolution* (Cambridge: Harvard University Press, 1992), 8–9. An examination of radical Vietnamese writings from the colonial period reveals only a handful of books and articles that devoted any attention to Southeast Asia. They include Chau Van Sang, ed. and trans., *Luoc Su Cach Mang o Nam Duong Quan Dao* [Summary history of revolution in the South Seas archipelago] (Saigon: n.p., 1929), and "Le bel exemple des Philippines," *Notre Voix*, 12 February 1939. Vietnamese political elites appear to have been somewhat better informed about developments in India, with discussions of Gandhi and Indian nonviolent resistance to the British playing a larger role in anticolonial radical political discourse. See, for instance, *Lich su ong thanh Gandhi* [Life of Gandhi] (Gia Dinh: Dong-phap, 1929); *Phu Nu Tan Van* [Ladies' news], 11 August 1932, 5–8; Vo Ba Van, *Van Dong Giai Phong Dan Toc* [Activating national liberation] (Saigon: Tan Van Hoa Tong Tho, 1937); and *Thanh Nghi* [Impartial opinion], 5 February 1945.

15 On Ho's activities in Thailand, see Hoang Van Hoan, *Giot Nuoc Trong Bien Ca: Hoi Ky Cach Mang* [A drop of water in the ocean: Memoirs of revolution] (Beijing: Nha Xuat Ban Tin Viet Nam, 1986), 34–66; Tran Lam, "Adventure in the Forest," in *Days with Ho Chi Minh* (Hanoi: Foreign Languages Publishing House, 1962), 132–38; and Le Manh Tranh, "In Canton and Siam," in *Days with Ho Chi Minh*, 116–21. Substantial portions of Ho's reporting on Southeast Asia to the Comintern are preserved in Fonds service de protection du corps expéditionnaire 367 and 368, AOM; see, for instance, Nguyen Ai Quoc to "Alex," 9 June 1931, Service de protection du corps expéditionnaire 367. On Ho's role in the formation of the Malay Communist Party, see C. F. Yong, "Origins and Development of the Malayan Communist Movement, 1919–1930," *Modern Asian Studies* 25, no. 4 (1991): 646–48. Ho did direct some attention to revolutionary events in Java in the late 1920s in a few of his published works; see Ho Chi Minh, *Duong Cach Menh* [Road to revolution], in *Ho Chi Minh Toan Tap, Tap 2, 1925–1930* [Ho

Chi Minh's collected works, vol. 2, 1925–30] (Hanoi: Nha Xuat Ban Su That, 1981), 221, 226, and *Thanh Nien* [Youth], 28 November 1926.

16 Pandit Nehru to Ho Chi Minh, 26 October 1946, folder: "Le Gouvernement Viet Nam," AOM-CP 128; National Congress to Ho Chi Minh, 7 January 1947, and Note, n.d. (ca. 1948), folder: "Aide aux VM: Indes," AOM-CD 128; "Nehru: Extract of Statement at New Delhi," 8 January 1947; "Sympathy by Indians for the Viet-Namese People: Extract from Official Report of the Legislative Assembly Debates," 5 February 1947; "Report on Indian Press," 15 January 1947; Shone, Office of the Higher Commissioner to Cabinet Office, 1 February 1947; and Gandhi Statement, 8 April 1947, all in L/P&S/12/4705, IO; Sarat Bose, "Call for an Indian Volunteer Army for Vietnam, 3 January 1947," in his *I Warned My Countrymen* (Calcutta: Netaji Research Bureau, 1968).

17 On Burmese support for the DRV, see Whitteridge, Foreign Office to Gibson, Burma Desk, 15 January 1947; Governor of Burma to Secretary of State for Burma, 17, 24 January, 2 February 1947; and *New Times of Burma*, 21 January 1947, all in M/4/2802, IO; Bulletin, 22 September 1948, folder: "Aide aux VM-Birmanie," AOM-CD 128; and interview with Hoang Nguyen, Hanoi, 1992. On Indonesia, see Batavia to Paris, 21 August 1947, folder: "Aide aux VM-Indonesie," AOM-CD 128, and Renseignements, 1 October 1947, folder: "Relations avec les Étrangers," AOM-CP supplément 1. On Malaya, see report, n.d. (ca. 1947), L/P&S/12/4705, IO, and Renseignements, 7 October 1947, folder: "Relations avec les Étrangers," AOM-CP supplément 1.

18 The outlines of the DRV's broader diplomatic strategy in Southeast Asia are in Vien Quan He Quoc Te Bo Ngoai Giao (Ministry of Foreign Relations Institute of International Relations), *Chu Tich Ho Chi Minh voi Cong Tac Ngoai Giao* [Ho Chi Minh and Foreign Relations] (Hanoi: Su That, 1990), 129–31. On basing DRV diplomatic operations in Thailand, see Renseignements, 3 January 1946, and "Organization des Rebelles Indochinois au Siam," February 1949, folder: "Rebelles au Siam," AOM-CD 106; "Siam," 3 January 1946, folder: "Mouvement révolutionnaire Annamite, 8/26/44–4/49, E165-2," vol. 161, Indochine, Asie Oceanie, 1944–1955, MAE; *Cuoc Van Dong Cuu Quoc cua Viet Kieu o Thai-Lan (Gop vao Tai Lieu Lich Su Cach Mang Viet-Nam)* [The national salvation activities of the overseas Vietnamese in Thailand (a contribution to the historical research of the Vietnamese revolution)] (Hanoi: Nha Xuat Ban Su That, 1961). For a pioneering analysis of DRV diplomacy in Thailand that informs my discussion, see Christopher E. Goscha, "Thailand and the Vietnamese Resistance against the French" (M.A. thesis, Australian National University, 1991), chaps. 1–4.

19 On the activities of the DRV mission in Bangkok and its efforts to forge closer relations with Thailand, see Notes, 6 March, 15 April 1947, folder: "Etude sur le Vietminh," AOM-CP 128, and Conseiller politique to Haut Commissariat, 23 October 1948, folder: "Siam," AOM-CD 7; and Vien Quan He Quoc Te Bo Ngoai Giao, *Chu Tich Ho Chi Minh voi Cong Tac Ngoai Giao*, 130. Copies of the DRV news releases from 1947 and two more substantial Vietnamese publications, "One Year of Revolutionary Achievement" and "Vietnam: A New Stage in her History," are in box 4, Records of the Saigon Consulate, RG 84. For the connections between the DRV mission and the *Bangkok Post*, see Alexander MacDonald, *Bangkok Editor* (New York: Macmillan, 1949), 214. On the activities of DRV representatives in the rest of Southeast Asia, see Rap-

port, 2ème Bureau, 13 November 1946, folder: "Mouvement révolutionnaire Annamite, 8/26/44–4/49, E165-2," vol. 161, Indochine, Asie Oceanie, 1944–1955, MAE;
Renseignements, 1, 7 October 1947, folder: "Relations avec les Étrangers," AOM-CP
supplément 1, and "Organization des Rebelles Indochinois au Siam," February 1949,
folder: "Rebelles au Siam," AOM-CD 106; Report on Indian Press, 15 January 1947,
L/P&S/12/4705, IO; and *Voice of Burma*, 21 January 1947, enclosure to Packer, Burma
to Secretary of State, 25 January 1947, box 4, Records of the Saigon Consulate, RG 84.

20 My discussion of the lines of authority in Vietnamese foreign policy making is based
on my interviews with Hoang Nguyen and a member of the Vietnamese Foreign Ministry's Institute of International Relations in Hanoi in 1992 and Vien Quan He Quoc
Te Bo Ngoai Giao, *Chu Tich Ho Chi Minh voi Cong Tac Ngoai Giao*, 120–31. Biographical information on Nguyen Duc Quy, Le Hy, and Tran Van Luan is based on
"Organization des Rebelles Indochinois au Siam," February 1949, folder: "Rebelles au
Siam," AOM-CD 106, and Renseignements, 22 March 1947, folder: "Conference panasiatique de New Delhi," AOM-CP supplément 10; and Goscha, "Thailand and the
Vietnamese Resistance," 85, 127.

21 The selection of Tran Van Giau points to the presence of some ambiguity in the
DRV's diplomatic strategy, suggesting, as Huynh Kim Khanh argues in his study of Vietnamese communism, that the role of class and nationalism continued to be a "thorny
issue" for the DRV leadership. Unlike the more moderate individuals who were associated with the DRV's diplomacy, Giau is often characterized by Western scholars of
Vietnamese communism such as Khanh and Philippe Devillers as an uncompromising
internationalist. When Ho Chi Minh dissolved the ICP in November 1945 to minimize
the official communist presence in the DRV, Giau and other like-minded leaders of
the ICP reorganized in the form of the Marxist Study Group, which stressed internationalist notions of radical social revolution over the DRV's more moderate policy of
all-class nationalism. Moreover, as chairman of the Viet Minh executive committee in
Nam Bo, Giau oversaw radical efforts to consolidate control in Saigon and the Mekong
Delta in 1945 and 1946, including the assassinations of prominent Vietnamese Trotskyists and anticommunists. Before his appointment to the DRV mission in Bangkok,
however, Giau was forced to undergo *kiem thao* (self-criticism) and was removed from
leadership positions in Nam Bo. See Huynh Kim Khanh, *Vietnamese Communism,
1925–1945* (Ithaca: Cornell University Press, 1982), 255, and Philippe Devillers, *Histoire
du Viêt-Nam de 1940 à 1952* (Paris: Éditions du Seuil, 1952), 144–76, 197, 247.

22 On the difficulties facing the DRV mission in Bangkok after the November 1947 coup,
see Notes, 2, 20 December 1947; Renseignement, 2 November 1948; de la Grandville
(Bangkok) to Haut Commissariat, 18 November 1948; Bulletin, 6 May 1949; and Annexe I to Bulletin, 29 September 1949, folder: "Siam," AOM-CD 7; and Note, 29 July
1948, folder: "Rebelles Viet-Minh," AOM-CD 108; and *Bangkok Post*, 22 September
1948. My discussion of the establishment and operations of the DRV mission in Burma
draws on my 1992 interview with Hoang Nguyen in Hanoi and his "Hoi Ky: Toi Tham
Gia Doan Can Bo Doi Ngoai Dau Tien Di Dong Nam A" [Memoirs: I took part in
the first delegation of foreign affairs cadres going to Southeast Asia], *Nghien Cuu Dong
Nam A* [Southeast Asian studies] 1, no. 2 (1991): 51–56, as well as Notes sur la Delegation Viet Minh de Rangoon, November 1953, folder: "Mouvement révolutionnaire

Annamite, 1/1/53 to 12/31/53, E165-2," vol. 165, Indochine, Asie Oceanie, 1944–1955, MAE; and Renseignement, 12 October 1948, folder: "Aide aux VM-Birmanie," AOM-CD 128.

23 A useful history of the conference and its organization is in *Asian Relations: Being a Report of the Proceedings and Documentation of the First Asian Relations Conference, New Delhi, March–April 1947* (New Delhi: Asian Relations Organization, 1948). See also "Rapport sur la Conference de New Delhi," n.d., folder: "Asian Relations Organization," dossier 220, carton 62, Fonds Haut Commissariat de France en Indochine, AOM, and Renseignements, Bureau Federal de Documentation, Haut Commissariat, Saigon, 13 February 1947, folder: "Conference panasiatique de New Delhi," AOM-CP supplément 10; "Brief: Inter-Asian Relations Conference," February 1947, F926, FO371/63539, PRO; and Tilman Remme, "Britain, the 1947 Asian Relations Conference, and Regional Co-operation in South-East Asia," in *Post-War Britain, 1945–64,* ed. Anthony Gorst, Lewis Johnmann, and W. Scott Lucas (London: Pinter, 1989), 109–34.

24 "Inaugural Address by Pandit Nehru" and "Address of Mahatma Gandhi," in *Asian Relations,* 22–24, 242–44; see also "Address of Shri Ram," in *Asian Relations,* 17–18. Inter-Asian cultural ties were also emphasized in a large art exhibition organized in conjunction with the conference that devoted particular attention to Indic influences in Southeast Asia; see "Appendix E: Exhibitions," in *Asian Relations:* 290, 302–5, and Renseignements, n.d., folder: "Conference panasiatique de New Delhi," AOM-CP supplément 10.

25 Nehru invited Ho Chi Minh to send a delegation to the conference as early as October 1946; see Nehru to Ho, 3, 26 October 1946, folder: "Le Gouvernement Viet Nam," AOM-CP 128, and 15 December 1946, dossier 661, carton 227, Haut-Commissariat de France en Indochine, AOM. The French also organized an alternative delegation of representatives from Vietnam, Cambodia, and Laos that apparently caused some confusion at the conference. The French-sponsored delegate from Cambodia, British observers reported, was "a charming girl who looked the part of a revolutionary" and was "loudly applauded in some quarters in the belief that she was a member of the Resistance Movement and not an 'Imperialist lackey.'" See "The Inter-Asian Relations Conference: Report by Sir Abe Bailey, Research Professor of British Commonwealth Relations, Dr. P. N. S. Mansergh, Chatham House Observer," 16 April 1947, F7102, FO371/63541, PRO, 11.

26 *Asian Relations,* 71–76, 79–90.

27 "Activité de la Delegation VN à la Conference de New-Delhi," 2ème Bureau, n.d., folder: "Conference panasiatique de New Delhi," AOM-CP supplément 10; *Asian Relations,* 76–77, 89; and Vien Quan He Quoc Te Bo Ngoai Giao, *Chu Tich Ho Chi Minh voi Cong Tac Ngoai Giao,* 130.

28 *Asian Relations,* 77. On the Indonesian delegation, see also Mackereth (Batavia) to Foreign Office, 21 March 1947, F3972, and Mackereth to Foreign Office, 31 March 1947, F4438, FO371/63540, PRO.

29 Notes, 15 April, 20 May 1947, folder: "Conference panasiatique de New Delhi," AOM-CP supplément 10; *Asian Relations,* 77–79, 246.

30 "The Inter-Asian Relations Conference," 16 April 1947, F7102, FO371/63541, PRO, 11.

31 *Asian Relations,* 255–57.

32 "Constitution of the South East Asia League," 8 September 1947, F1216, FO371/69686, PRO. See also Drumright to Whitteridge, 30 September 1947, and Whitteridge to Drumright, 1 October 1947, F13408, FO371/63557, PRO.

33 Ho Chi Minh to the President of the Republic of Indonesia, 17 November 1945, and "Proposed Text of Common Declaration by Viet Nam and Indonesia," in Hanna Papanek, "Note on Soedjatmoko's Recollection of a Historical Moment: Sjahrir's Reaction to Ho Chi Minh's 1945 Call for a Free People's Federation," *Indonesia*, no. 44 (April 1990): 142–43. For a discussion of Ho's calls for regional solidarity during World War II, see Chapter 4.

34 On DRV motivations for participating in the league, see Vien Quan He Quoc Te Bo Ngoai Giao, *Chu Tich Ho Chi Minh voi Cong Tac Ngoai Giao*, 130; Renseignements, Bureau Federal de Documentation, Haut Commissariat, 17 December 1947, folder: "Relations avec les Étrangers: Siam," AOM-CP supplément 1; "The South-East Asia League," minute prepared by John Coast, 12 January 1948, F1216, FO371/69686, PRO; and John Coast, *Some Aspects of Siamese Politics* (New York: Institute of Pacific Relations, 1953), 52, 73, 290.

35 Rapport, 2ème Bureau, 13 November 1946, folder: "Mouvement révolutionnaire Annamite, 8/26/44–4/49, E165-2," vol. 161, Indochine, Asie Oceanie, 1944–1955, MAE; Note, 12 August 1947, folder: "Etude sur le Vietminh," AOM-CP 128; Renseignements, 11 April 1947, folder: "Relations avec les Étrangers: Siam," AOM-CP supplément 1; and Notes, 4, 27 March, 15 June 1949, folder: "Trafic d'armes Siam," AOM-CD 30.

36 On the support given to the DRV arms network from supporters of the Pridi government, see Renseignements, 5, 6 May, 29 July, 29 December 1947, folder: "Trafic d'armes Siam," AOM-CD 30, and Note, 2ème Bureau, Saigon, 5 June 1947, folder: "Siam," AOM-CD 7. On Khuang Aphaiwang and the Bangkok arms network, see Renseignements, 28 February, 29 April 1947, and 1 August 1948, folder: "Trafic d'armes Siam," AOM-CD 30, and Renseignement, 1 August 1948, folder: "Macao," AOM-CD 34. On the nature of Thai politics in this period and its international dimensions, see Daniel Fineman, *A Special Relationship: The United States and Military Government in Thailand, 1947–1958* (Honolulu: University of Hawaii Press, 1997), 11–63, and Thak Chaloemtiarana, *Thailand: The Politics of Despotic Paternalism* (Bangkok: Social Science Association of Thailand, Thammasat University, 1979).

37 On the difficulties facing the operation of the DRV arms network in Thailand after April 1948, see Conseiller politique to Haut Commissariat, 23 October 1948; Note, 18 November 1948; and Annexe I to Bulletin, Saigon, 29 September 1949, folder: "Siam," AOM-CD 7. On Burma and the arms trade, see Note, 18 March 1949, folder: "Aide aux VM-Birmanie," AOM-CD 128. On the arms trade with the Philippines, see Renseignements, 8 August, 8 October 1947, 19 August 1948, 30 June, 5, 17 August, 7, 24 October, 1949, folder: "Trafic d'armes Manille," AOM-CD 34, and Notes, 7 July, 5 August 1949, folder: "Trafic d'armes Siam," AOM-CD 30. On the arms trade with the Kuomintang in southern China, see Notes, 7 February 1947, 4 October, 6 December 1948, folder: "Chine," AOM-CD 34; Renseignement, 12 May 1947, folder: "Trafic d'armes Siam," AOM-CD 30; Notes, 9, 17 June 1947, folder: "Annamites," AOM-CP supplément 24; and Notes, 19 January 1949, 4 March 1950, folder: "Nguyen Van Thao," Service de protection du corps expéditionnaire 385, AOM. On the sources for the clan-

destine arms trade, see Minute by R. C. Blackham, 8 June 1949, F8477; British Embassy, Stockholm, to Foreign Office, 13 June 1949, F8948/G; British Embassy, Brussels, to Foreign Office, 17 June 1949, F8884/G; and British Embassy, Rome, to Foreign Office, 19 October 1949, F16243/G, FO371/76051, PRO; and Note, 15 October 1949, folder: "Panama," AOM-CD 34.

38 On the tonnage and value of arms entering Vietnam by land and sea from Thailand, see Note, 12 August 1947, folder: "Etude sur le Vietminh," AOM-CP 128, and Note, 29 April 1947, folder: "Trafic d'armes Siam," AOM-CD 30; "Trafic d'Armées et Activités du Siam," 15 February 1947, 10H101; "Fiche hebdomadaire," 28 November 1950, 10H609; and "Synthèses d'Exploitation du Rallié [x]: IV-Voies de liaisons V. M. Siam-Nam Bo," 12 October 1951, 10H5585, Fonds Indochine, Service Historique de l'Armée de Terre, Vincennes, Paris, France; and Jacques Mordal, *Marine Indochine* (Paris: Amiot-Dumont, 1953), 200–205. On the quantities and value of the arms trade with the Philippines, see Notes, 17 September 1948 and 6 May 1949, folder: "Trafic d'armes Manille," AOM-CD 34. On the value of the arms trade with China, see Note, 15 August 1947, folder: "Chine," AOM-CD 34, and Renseignement, 15 January 1949, FF1433, FO371/75972, PRO. For one contemporary Vietnamese assessment of the arms traffic and its significance for the war against the French, see Carnet de notes de Vo Ba Nhac, Ex-chef des Services d'Intendance et des Finances du Commandement supérieur du Nam Bo, n.d., 10H636, Fonds Indochine, Service Historique de l'Armée de Terre; I am grateful to Chris Goscha for drawing this document to my attention.

39 Hoang Tranh, *Ho Chi Minh voi Trung Quoc*, 209–14; Nguyen Duy Thanh, *My Four Years with the Viet-Minh* (Bombay: Democratic Research Service, 1950), 18; Renseignements, 5 April 1947, folder: "Relations avec les Étrangers: Siam," AOM-CP supplément 1; Chen, *Vietnam and China*, 175–76.

40 Hoang Tranh, *Ho Chi Minh voi Trung Quoc*, 214–17; Note, 9 June 1947, folder: "Annamites," AOM-CP supplément 24, and Renseignement, 4 October 1948, folder: "Chine," AOM-CD 34; Virginia Thompson and Richard Adloff, *The Left Wing in Southeast Asia* (New York: William Sloane Associates, 1950), 42; interview with Hoang Nguyen, Hanoi, 1992.

41 On the April directive, see William J. Duiker, *The Communist Road to Power in Vietnam* (Boulder, Colo.: Westview Press, 1981), 131; on local arms workshops, see Lockhart, *Nation in Arms*, 207–8.

42 Andrew Vickerman, *The Fate of the Peasantry: Premature 'Transition to Socialism' in the Democratic Republic of Vietnam*, Yale University Southeast Asian Studies Monograph Series No. 28 (New Haven: Yale Center for International and Asian Studies, 1986), 49–72; for an analysis of the impact of DRV military and socioeconomic reforms on one northern village, see Hy V. Luong, *Revolution in the Village: Tradition and Transformation in North Vietnam, 1925–1988* (Honolulu: University of Hawaii Press, 1992), 147–58.

43 On the origins of containment and U.S. policy in Europe and Asia more broadly, see Melvyn P. Leffler, *A Preponderance of Power: National Security, the Truman Administration, and the Cold War* (Stanford: Stanford University Press, 1992). On the significance of France in U.S. policy toward Western Europe, see John W. Young, *France, the Cold War, and the Western Alliance, 1944–49: French Foreign Policy and Post-War*

Europe (Leicester: Leicester University Press, 1990), and Irwin M. Wall, *The United States and the Making of Postwar France, 1945–1954* (Cambridge: Cambridge University Press, 1991).

44 On confusion in the Truman administration's policy toward China, see Ernest R. May, *The Truman Administration and China, 1945–1949* (Philadelphia: Lippincott, 1975); Dorothy Borg and Waldo Heinrichs, eds., *Uncertain Years: Chinese-American Relations, 1947–1950* (New York: Columbia University Press, 1980); and Nancy Bernkopf Tucker, *Patterns in the Dust: Chinese-American Relations and the Recognition Controversy, 1949–50* (New York: Columbia University Press, 1983).

45 Secretary of State Marshall to Embassy in France, 3 February 1947, FRUS, 1947, vol. 6, *The Far East* (1972), 67–68.

46 O'Sullivan to Marshall, March 28, 1947, FRUS, 1947, 6:83.

47 Stanton to Marshall, 24 April 1947, box 4, RG 84.

48 O'Sullivan to Marshall, ibid.

49 Marshall to O'Sullivan, 2 May 1947, box 4, RG 84.

50 Stanton to Marshall, 7 May 1947, FRUS, 1947, 6:92.

51 Marshall to O'Sullivan, 9 May 1947, box 4, RG 84.

52 Note, 30 March 1946, "Activités américaines en Indochine," Haut-Commissariat de France en Indochine, AOM-CP 231.

53 Stanton to Marshall, 7 May 1947, FRUS, 1947, 6:92.

54 Marshall to Reed, 3 May 1947, FRUS, 1947, 6:90.

55 On divisions in the American embassy in China, see Ernest R. May, *Truman Administration*, 12–14.

56 Stuart to Marshall, 15 May 1947, FRUS, 1947, 6:90. For a useful account of Stuart's views, see Yu-ming Shaw, *An American Missionary in China: John Leighton Stuart and Chinese-American Relations* (Cambridge: Harvard University Press, 1992).

57 American Embassy, China, to Marshall, 16 March 1947, box 4, RG 84.

58 Reed to Marshall, 29 April 1947, box 4, RG 84; Reed to Marshall, 3 May 1947, FRUS, 1947, 6:99.

59 O'Sullivan to Marshall, 3 May 1947, FRUS, 1947, 6:90.

60 Reed to Marshall, 7 May 1947, FRUS, 1947, 6:94.

61 Marshall to Reed, 17 July 1947, FRUS, 1947, 6:117.

62 Reed to Marshall, 11, 24 July 1947, FRUS, 1947, 6:114–15, 124–25.

63 O'Sullivan to Marshall, 21 July 1947, FRUS, 1947, 6:121–22.

64 Caffery to Marshall, July 31, 1947, FRUS, 1947, 6:128.

65 "Memorandum of Conversation between Bullitt and Ogburn," 29 May 1947, box 4, RG 84.

66 O'Sullivan to Marshall, 21 July 1947, and Reed to Marshall, 24 July 1947, FRUS, 1947, 6:122, 125.

67 French efforts to shape the Truman administration's perceptions of the links between Ho Chi Minh and international communism, which had begun in 1946 as discussed in the preceding chapter, intensified in this period and focused primarily on the rising influence of Chinese communism. See, for instance, Ministre des Affaires Étrangères to Bonnet (Washington), 10 July 1948, folder: "Communisme et relations Moscou-Hanoi-Chine, 8/26/49 to 5/30/53, E165-3," vol. 174, and Rapport, 8 July 1947, and Traduction,

3 January 1949, folder: "Mouvement révolutionnaire Annamite, 1/5/49 to 12/31/49, E165-2," vol. 162, Indochine, Asie Oceanie, 1944–1955, MAE, and Notes, 12, 22 October 1949, folder: "P. Communiste en INDO," AOM-CD 105.

68 O'Sullivan to Marshall, 19 July 1947, *FRUS, 1947,* 6:120.

69 Biographical information on Jefferson Caffery, William C. Bullitt, James O'Sullivan, and Charles S. Reed was obtained from the *Biographic Register of the Department of State* (Washington, D.C.: U.S. Government Printing Office, 1940–47); material on Bullitt was supplemented by Will Brownell and Richard N. Billings, *So Close to Greatness: A Biography of William C. Bullitt* (New York: Macmillan, 1987).

70 Hugh DeSantis, *The Diplomacy of Silence: The American Foreign Service, the Soviet Union, and the Cold War, 1933–1947* (Chicago: University of Chicago Press, 1983), 33. For an extended analysis of Bullitt's anticommunism, see Beatrice Farnsworth, *William C. Bullitt and the Soviet Union* (Bloomington: Indiana University Press, 1967).

71 Marginal notation by Woodruff Wallner, Department of Western European Affairs, on Landon to Butterworth, 18 November 1947, 856D.00/11-1847, Records of the Office of Western European Affairs, 1941–54, RG 59.

72 My conclusions reverse what has become the common wisdom in the long-standing debate about the "lost chance" for Sino-American relations in the late 1940s that now tends to see the Americans willing to work with Mao's China in 1949 and 1950 but the Chinese as almost implacably opposed. For a recent airing of this controversy drawing on new Chinese sources, see "Symposium: Rethinking the Lost Chance in China," *Diplomatic History* 21, no. 1 (Winter 1997): 71–115.

73 For Gaddis's discussion of the wedge strategy, see his *The Long Peace: Inquiries into the History of the Cold War* (New York: Oxford University Press, 1987), 149–64.

74 On the nature of the State Department's Division of Philippine and Southeast Asian Affairs in this period, see "Oral History Interview with John F. Cady," 31 July 1974, HST, 15–18, 33–34.

75 The contrast with reports from Belgrade and Moscow on Tito and the Yugoslav communists in 1948 is sharp, reinforcing the sense that racial hierarchies were an important factor inhibiting the use of the wedge strategy in Vietnam. While U.S. diplomats were concerned about Tito's Marxist-Leninist ideology, Tito's or the Yugoslavian capacity for independent self-government was never at issue. See, for instance, Ambassador to the Soviet Union (Smith) to Secretary Marshall, 1–2 July 1948; Chargé in Yugoslavia (Reams) to Marshall, 7 July, 15 September 1948; and Ambassador to Yugoslavia (Cannon) to Marshall, 28 October, 24 November 1948, *FRUS, 1948,* vol. 4, *Eastern Europe and the Soviet Union* (1974), 1082–84, 1088–92, 1106–1110, 1113–16. See also Beatrice Heuser, *Western "Containment" Policies in the Cold War: The Yugoslav Case, 1948–1953* (London: Routledge, 1989).

76 George M. Abbott, "Remarks on Agenda for Bangkok Regional Conference As Pertaining to Indochina," 18 June 1948, file: "Southeast Asia File (1)," box 10, Papers of John F. Melby, HST. For other discussions of Ho Chi Minh and the DRV at the Southeast Asia Regional Conference, see "Discussion of Recommendations Submitted by Summary Committee for Solution of Indochina Problem," n.d.; "Proposed Solution of Indochina Problem," n.d.; and Proceedings of Southeast Asia Conference, 21 June 1948, file: "Southeast Asia File (1)"; "Regional Repercussions of Continued Hostility in

Indochina," n.d., and "Communist Activities in Southeast Asia," file: "Southeast Asia File (2)," box 10, Melby Papers, HST.

77 Department of State Policy Statement on Indochina, 27 September 1945, *FRUS, 1948*, vol. 6, *The Far East and Australasia* (1974), 43, 45. See also "Southeast Asia: Communist Penetration," n.d., box 5, and Butterworth to Hickerson, 25 May 1948, and "Draft Policy Statement on Indochina," 12 July 1948, box 9, PSA, RG 59; Secretary of State to American Consul in Hanoi, 20 May 1949, *FRUS, 1949*, vol. 7, *The Far East and Australasia* (1975), pt. 1, pp. 196–97.

78 Department of State Policy Statement on Indochina, 27 September 1945, *FRUS, 1948*, 6:45, 49.

79 See Robert J. McMahon, *Colonialism and Cold War: The United States and the Struggle for Indonesian Independence, 1945–49* (Ithaca: Cornell University Press, 1981); Gary R. Hess, *The United States' Emergence As a Southeast Asian Power, 1940–1950* (New York: Columbia University Press, 1987), 275–332; Evelyn Colbert, "The Road Not Taken: Decolonization and Independence in Indonesia and Indochina," *Foreign Affairs* 51, no. 2 (April 1973): 608–28.

80 On Roosevelt's favorable views of Dutch colonialism, see McMahon, *Colonialism and Cold War*, 64–65.

81 The assumptions embedded in the overarching U.S. postcolonial vision produced divisions in perceptions of other areas of Asia as well. Andrew J. Rotter thoughtfully explores the differences separating American views of India and Pakistan in this period, an analysis that, given their shared colonial histories under the British, rests on gendered use of language by U.S. policy makers and its larger significance, in his "Gender Relations, Foreign Relations: The United States and South Asia, 1947–1964," *Journal of American History* 81, no. 2 (September 1994): 518–42.

82 Thomas Borstelmann, *Apartheid's Reluctant Uncle: The United States and Southern Africa in the Early Cold War* (New York: Oxford University Press, 1993), 8.

83 Kennan to Acheson, "United Nations," 14 November 1949, in *The State Department Policy Planning Staff Papers*, vol. 3 (New York: Garland, 1983), 189, cited in Borstelmann, *Apartheid's Reluctant Uncle*, 246. On the pervasiveness of these sentiments, see Anders Stephanson, *Kennan and the Art of Foreign Policy* (Cambridge: Harvard University Press, 1989), 148, 172, 101–2; Douglas Brinkley, *Dean Acheson: The Cold War Years, 1953–71* (New Haven: Yale University Press, 1992), 303; and Alan Brinkley, "Icons of the American Establishment," in his *Liberalism and its Discontents* (Cambridge: Harvard University Press, 1998), 164–209.

84 See William Berman, *The Politics of Civil Rights in the Truman Administration* (Columbus: Ohio State University Press, 1970). For a penetrating discussion of the parallels African Americans drew between their own situation and the colonial order as well the interconnections between the Truman administration's domestic race policy and its diplomacy in Africa, see Penny M. Von Eschen, *Race against Empire: Black Americans and Anticolonialism, 1937–1957* (Ithaca: Cornell University Press, 1997).

85 For a comparative discussion of the economies of Western Europe in this period, see Alan S. Milward, *The Reconstruction of Western Europe, 1945–51* (Berkeley: University of California Press, 1984), chap. 1.

86 The work of Michael Hogan and Charles Maier is particularly helpful for locating

the place of post-1945 U.S. order-building in a context broader than the exigencies of the Cold War. See Hogan, *The Marshall Plan: America, Britain, and the Reconstruction of Western Europe, 1947–1952* (Cambridge: Cambridge University Press, 1987), and Charles S. Maier, "The Two Postwar Eras and the Conditions for Stability in Twentieth-Century Western Europe," *American Historical Review* 86, no. 2 (April 1981): 327–52.

87 On Thach's efforts in February 1948 and the U.S. response, see Lacy to Penfield, 12 February 1948, and Landon to Penfield, 17 February 1948, box 7, PSA, RG 59, and Note, 2 August 1948, folder: "Relations avec le Viet-Minh et le chinois," AOM-CP supplément 1.

88 "Bulletin de renseignement: activities politiques américaines en Indochine dues par les V.M.," 12 November 1948, and "Traduction: La question de notre comportement à l'égard de l'impérialisme Américain," 14 January 1948, dossier 415, carton 91, Fonds Etats Associés, MAE. I am indebted to Chris Goscha for making his copies of these documents available to me. For Ho Chi Minh's more public appeals, see *Newsweek*, 25 April 1949, 44, and *Nation*, 10 September 1949, 244.

89 "Traduction du rapport de Dang Xuan Khu (alias Truong Trinh [*sic*]) à la Vième Conférences des 'Can Bo' en janvier 1949," folder: "Mouvement révolutionnaire Annamite, 1/5/49 to 12/31/49, E165-2," vol. 162, Indochine, Asie Oceanie, 1944–1955, MAE. For internal party memorandums and press accounts increasingly critical of the United States, see Ban Chap Hanh Trung Uong Dang Cong San Viet Nam (Executive Board of the Central Committee of the Communist Party of Vietnam), *Vien Kien Dang ve Khang Chien Chong Thuc Dan Phap, Tap 1, 1945–50* [Party documents on the resistance war against the French colonialists, vol. 1, 1945–50] (Hanoi: Nha Xuat Ban Su That, 1986), 95–97, 168; "Attitude de la République Democratique du Vietnam vis-à-vis de la politique des USA . . . ," 21 May 1949, and Note, 6 October 1948, folder: "Mouvement révolutionnaire Annamite, 1/5/49 to 12/31/49, E165-2," vol. 162, Indochine, Asie Oceanie, 1944–1955, and Note, 20 May 1949, folder: "Activités Nationalistes," dossier 344, carton 108, Fonds Haut Commissariat de France en Indochine, AOM.

CONCLUSION

1 Reed to Secretary of State Marshall, 14 June 1947, *FRUS, 1947*, vol. 6, *The Far East* (1972), 103–5; Edwin C. Rendall (Hanoi) to Secretary of State Marshall, 7 June 1948, 851G.01/6-748, RG 59.

2 Marshall to Embassy in France, 3 July, 30 August 1948, and Marshall to Abbott (Saigon), 27 August 1948, *FRUS, 1948*, vol. 6, *The Far East and Australasia* (1974), 30, 38, 40; Acheson to Embassy in France, 25 February, 1 December 1949, and Bruce to Secretary of State, 29 June 1949, *FRUS, 1949*, vol. 7, *The Far East and Australasia* (1975), pt. 1, pp. 8, 66, 101–2. See also Caffery to Secretary of State, 9 July 1948, and Abbott to Marshall, 28 August 1948, *FRUS, 1948*, 6:33, 39; Acheson to Consulate General at Saigon, 10, 20 May 1949; Memorandum by the Department of State to the French Foreign Office in Butterworth to Bruce, 6 June 1919; and Webb to Embassy in India, 18 June 1949, *FRUS, 1949*, vol. 7, pt. 1, pp. 24, 28–29, 39–45, 60.

3 Gullion to Secretary of State, 23 June 1950, *FRUS, 1950*, vol. 6, *East Asia and the Pacific* (1976), 827.

4 Bernard B. Fall, *The Viet Minh Regime: Government and Administration in the Democratic Republic of Vietnam* (New York: Institute of Pacific Relations, 1956), 34. The calculus of Vietnamese decision making in 1950 has largely gone unexamined except in undocumented, ideologically driven accounts that view the DRV's recognition by the Soviets and the Chinese both as a strategic move and as confirmation of the regime's political and intellectual domination by external forces. Moreover, they suggest that the formal embrace of the Vietnamese government by the international communist world only made explicit what the DRV's leaders had privately hoped for since 1945. See, for instance, Ton That Thien, *The Foreign Politics of the Communist Party of Vietnam: A Study in Communist Tactics* (New York: Crane Russak, 1989).

5 This interpretation of the Vietnamese and Chinese negotiations over diplomatic recognition was suggested to me in an interview in Hanoi in 1992 with an anonymous Vietnamese diplomat active in the period. Continuing restrictions on access to Vietnamese diplomatic papers make this admittedly speculative interpretation impossible to confirm with certainty. Several pieces of corroborating evidence, however, point to its plausibility as well as continuing Vietnamese interest in maintaining a wider diplomatic presence. DRV Foreign Minister Hoang Minh Giam's message of 15 January seeking diplomatic recognition from the PRC and the Chinese response several days later point to some measure of advance discussion between the Vietnamese and the Chinese. The day before Giam's message, however, Ho Chi Minh issued another appeal, calling for diplomatic recognition of the DRV by all the world's powers, which suggests that the Vietnamese continued to frame their diplomatic petitions in more universalistic terms. For Ho's message, see "Loi Tuyen Bo Cua Chinh Phu Nuoc Viet-Nam Dan Chu Cong Hoa Cung" Chinh Phu Cac Nuoc Tren The Gioi [Proclamation of the Democratic Republic of Vietnam to all the nations of the world], in *Ho Chi Minh Toan Tap, Tap 5, 1948–1950* [Ho Chi Minh's collected works, vol. 5, 1948–50] (Hanoi: Nha Xuat Ban Su That, 1985), 334–35. The discussion in the following paragraph of the impact of Soviet and Chinese recognition in Southeast Asia also supports the continuing salience of the diplomacy of revolutionary nationalism for the DRV. Finally, the limited success of Mao's work to repair relations between Stalin and Ho suggests that the DRV retained its suspicions of Soviet ideological direction and maintained its efforts to chart a more independent internationalist course. In what may be an apocryphal account of the first meeting between the two leaders since the 1930s in Moscow in February 1950, Stalin told Ho when he entered the room, "You may sit in either of these two chairs. This one is the nationalist chair. The other is the internationalist chair." Ho reportedly replied, "I'll stand." This story was told to me in an interview with an anonymous Vietnamese diplomat in Hanoi in 1992 who had been active in Sino-Vietnamese diplomacy in 1950. The chilly tone of relations between Stalin and Ho in Moscow also emerges in Nikita Khrushchev, *Khrushchev Remembers: The Glasnost Tapes*, ed. and trans. Jerrold Schecter (Boston: Little, Brown, 1990), 154–56.

6 Secretary of State Acheson to Embassy in Thailand, 17 January 1950; Stanton to Secretary of State, 19 January 1950; and memorandum of conversations, 10 March 1950, *FRUS, 1950*, 6:617, 752. On the concerted U.S. efforts to seek recognition of the Bao

Dai government by India and the newly independent states of Southeast Asia, see Embassy in the Philippines to Secretary of State, 17 February 1950; Gullion to Acheson, 8 June 1950; Acheson to Djakarta, 2 June 1950; Secretary of State to Embassy in Manila, 26 July 1952, folder: "360: Other SEA Countries Recog of Bao Dai," box 14, Records of the Saigon Embassy and Consulate Confidential Files, 1950–52, RG 84; Acheson to Embassy in the Philippines, 7 January 1950; Henderson (India) to Acheson, 7 January 1950; Cochran (Indonesia) to Acheson, 11 January 1950; Stanton (Thailand) to Acheson, 12 January 1950; Acheson to Embassy in Paris, 13 January 1945; Acheson to Consulate General at Saigon, 20 January 1950; Acheson to Embassy in France, 29 March 1950; and Henderson (India) to Acheson, *FRUS, 1950*, 6:691–94, 699–700, 768–771, 778–79. On the negative attitudes of India and the Southeast Asian states toward Bao Dai, see "Burmese Reaction to Recognition of Viet Minh by the Soviet Union," 6 February 1950; "Analysis of Thai Attitudes toward Recognition," 7 April 1950; and Stanton to Acheson, 1 March 1950, folder: "360: Other SEA Countries Recog of Bao Dai," box 14, Records of the Saigon Embassy and Consulate Confidential Files, 1950–52, RG 84; U.K. High Commissioner in India to Commonwealth Relations Office, 9 February, 2 November 1950, FF1063/14, FO371/83635, and Spearight (Rangoon) to Foreign Office, 11 November 1950, FF1063/15, FO 371/83635, PRO.

7 On the debates in the Indonesian parliament, see Kermode to Foreign Office, 4, 13 June 1950, FF10362/2, FO 371/83622, PRO; Gauguie (Djakarta) to Paris, 3 October 1951, folder: "Aide aux VM-Indonesie," AOM-CD 128; and Cochran (Djarkarta) to Secretary of State, 4, 6 June 1950, folder: "360: Other SEA Countries Recog of Bao Dai," box 14, Records of the Saigon Embassy and Consulate Confidential Files, 1950–52, RG 84. On relations between Burma and the DRV, see Freese-Pennefather (Rangoon) to Foreign Office, 7 September 1951, FF10379/1, FO371/83623; British Embassy (Rangoon) to J. D. Murray, 12 September 1951, FF10379/2, FO371/92421; and Freese-Pennefather (Rangoon) to Foreign Office, 25 September 1950, FF10379/2, FO371/83623, PRO; and Plion-Bernier (Rangoon) to Ministre des Affaires Étrangères, 6 September 1951, folder: "Mouvement révolutionnaire Annamite, 1/1/50 to 10/30/50, E165-2," vol. 164, Indochine, Asie Oceanie, 1944–1955, MAE. On the continuing clandestine traffic in arms in Thailand and the Philippines, see Renseignement, n.d., and Note, 12 January 1951, folder: "Trafic d'armes Siam," AOM-CD 30, and Note, 17 February 1950, and Renseignements, 23 June 1950, folder: "Trafic d'armes Manille," AOM-CD 34; Foreign Office to Saigon, 4 October 1950, FF1197/1, and Whittington (Bangkok) to J. D. Murray, Foreign Office, 1 November 1950, FF1197/2, FO371/83654, PRO.

8 Qiang Zhai, *China and the Vietnam Wars, 1950–75* (Chapel Hill: University of North Carolina Press, 2000), chap. 2. On the problems Chinese aid presented to the Vietnamese state, see Greg Lockhart, *Nation in Arms: The Origins of the People's Army of Vietnam* (Sydney: Allen and Unwin, 1989), 222–52. In addition to Zhai's important work, useful analyses of Chinese diplomacy toward Vietnam in this period also based on newly available Chinese sources are in Chen Jian, "China and the First Indo-China War, 1950–1954," *China Quarterly*, no. 133 (March 1993): 85–110, and Shu Guang Zhang, *Mao's Military Romanticism: China and the Korean War, 1950–1953* (Lawrence: University of Kansas Press, 1995), 41–44, 69–70.

9 On Sino-Vietnamese disagreements at Dien Bien Phu, see Georges Boudarel, "Com-

ment Giap a falli perdre la bataille de Dien Bien Phu," *Nouvel Observateur*, 8 April 1983, 97, and Lockhart, *Nation in Arms*, 252–63.

10 On Chinese pressure at the Geneva Conference, see François Joyaux, *La Chine et le règlement du premier conflit d'Indochine genève 1954* (Paris: Publications de la Sorbonne, 1979), 276–86, 301–52; "The Truth about Vietnam-China Relations over the Last 30 Years," 4 October 1979, Ministry of Foreign Relations, Socialist Republic of Vietnam, in *BBC Summary of World Broadcasts (Far East)*, 6 October 1979, FE/6238/A3/7-12; Kuo-khang Shao, "Zhou Enlai's Diplomacy and the Neutralization of Indo-China, 1954–55," *China Quarterly*, no. 107 (September 1986): 483–504; Keith W. Taylor, "China and Vietnam: Looking for a New Version of an Old Relationship," in *The Vietnam War: Vietnamese and American Perspectives*, ed. Jayne S. Werner and Luu Doan Huynh (Armonk, N.Y.: M. E. Sharpe, 1993), 272–78; and Qiang Zhai, "China and the Geneva Conference of 1954," *China Quarterly*, no. 129 (March 1992): 103–22. Transcripts of conversations between Chinese and Vietnamese leaders that have recently been made available reinforce the significance of the Geneva episode for Vietnamese thinking about China; see "Mao Zedong and Pham Van Dong, 17 November 1968," in *Seventy-seven Conversations between Chinese and Foreign Leaders on the Wars in Indochina, 1964–1977*, ed. Odd Arne Westad et al., Cold War International History Project Working Paper No. 22 (Washington, D.C.: Woodrow Wilson International Center for Scholars, 1998), 140–55.

11 On the land reform campaigns and their impact on Sino-Vietnamese relations, see Edwin Moise, "Land Reform and Land Reform Errors in North Vietnam," *Pacific Affairs* 49, no. 1 (Spring 1976): 70–92, and Bui Tin, *Following Ho Chi Minh: Memoirs of a North Vietnamese Colonel* (Honolulu: University of Hawaii Press, 1995), 23–34.

12 In the absence of archival documentation from the Vietnamese side, the memoirs of Bui Tinh remain essential for understanding the views of the Vietnamese leadership on the Sino-Soviet split; see Bui Tin, *Following Ho Chi Minh*, 44–46, 52, 54–56. Also important for their discussion of the impact of these events on the regime's domestic policy is Hirohide Kurihara, "Changes in the Literary Policy of the Vietnamese Workers' Party, 1956–1958," in *Indochina in the 1940s and 1950s*, ed. Takashi Shiraishi and Motoo Furuta (Ithaca: Cornell University Southeast Asia Program, 1992), 165–96, and Georges Boudarel, *Cent fleurs ecloses dans la nuit du Vietnam: communisme et dissidence, 1954–1956* (Paris: J. Bertoin, 1991). For useful analyses of strains in the Sino-Vietnamese relationship in the 1960s based on newly available Chinese sources, see Zhai, *China and the Vietnam Wars*, chaps. 4–7, and Chen Jian, "China's Involvement in the Vietnam War, 1964–69," *China Quarterly*, no. 142 (June 1995): 380–87. On the tensions in Soviet-Vietnamese relations as early as the late 1950s, see Mari Olsen, *Solidarity and National Revolution: The Soviet Union and the Vietnamese Communists, 1954–1960* (Oslo: Norwegian Institute for Defence Studies, 1997); on the Soviet relationship in the 1960s, see Ilya V. Gaiduk, *The Soviet Union and the Vietnam War* (Chicago: Ivan R. Dee, 1996).

13 "East and South Asia," 6 June 1950, box 26, Records of the Policy Planning Staff, 1947–53, Lot 54D190/7, RG 59.

14 For an insightful analysis of Vietnamese communist military strategy in the war against the French and the primacy of indigenous factors in explaining its increasing success

after 1949, see Greg Lockhart, *Nation in Arms: The Origins of the People's Army of Vietnam* (Sydney: Allen and Unwin, 1989), chaps. 5 and 6.

15 Harold R. Isaacs, *Scratches on Our Minds: American Views of China and India* (New York: Harper and Row, 1958), 227, 229, 238. For a discussion of the transformation of U.S. perceptions of Chinese military capabilities during the Korean War, see ibid., 225–38.

16 Central Intelligence Agency, "National Intelligence Estimate, Indochina: Current Situation and Probable Developments," 29 December 1950, and "Analysis Prepared for the Joint Chiefs of Staff by the Joint Strategic Survey Committee," 17 November 1950, *FRUS, 1950,* 6:951, 961. For the sustained discussion among U.S. policy makers in the fall of 1950 on the role of China and the failure of French military tactics and strategy as the explanation for Vietnamese communist military victories, see Rusk to Secretary of State, 11 September 1950; Heath to Secretary of State, 15 October, 1 November 1950; Memorandum of the Joint Chiefs of Staff, 28 November 1950, *FRUS, 1950,* 6:878, 894, 914–17, 946. American policy makers offered the same explanatory variables during the spring of 1954 to account for the likely Vietnamese military victory over the French at Dien Bien Phu, a development that effectively brought an end to French rule in Vietnam. See, for instance, Memorandum of Conversation, 4 April 1954; Dillon to Department of State, 5 April 1954; Memorandum of Discussion, National Security Council, 6 April 1954, *FRUS, 1952–1954,* Vol. 13, *Indochina* (1982), pt. 2, pp. 1233, 1237, 1251–66. Robert Buzzanco has recently argued that the U.S. military consistently drew attention to the difficulties facing American military intervention in Vietnam. But as I read the evidence he puts forward for the early 1950s, the military's desire to protect its limited forces for use in Europe, rather than a reconceptualization of the Vietnamese themselves, seems to have shaped their approach to Vietnam. See Buzzanco, *Masters of War: Military Dissent and Politics in the Vietnam Era* (Cambridge: Cambridge University Press, 1996), chap. 2.

17 Acheson to Legation at Saigon, 1 September, 30 October, 28 November 1950; Heath (Saigon) to Secretary of State, 27 November 1950; and "National Intelligence Estimate, Indochina: Current Situation and Probable Developments," 29 December 1950, *FRUS, 1950,* 6:868–69, 894, 915, 939, 960.

18 Strum (Hanoi) to Department of State, 10 June 1952, *FRUS, 1952–1954,* vol. 13, pt. 1, pp. 177–78.

19 American views on the clash between French and U.S. perspectives on nation building and on military and other issues emerge in Indochina Subject Files, 1950–54, Records of the Office of Far Eastern Operations, and Office of the Director; memos sent by Dr. W. W. Winklestein (Regional Director, 1952–53), Hanoi Office; and Subject Files of J. P. Guttinger (Assistant Agricultural Reform Specialist, 1951–57), Agricultural and Natural Resources Division, Records of the Mission to Vietnam, 1950–59, Records of U.S. Foreign Assistance Agencies, 1948–61, Record Group 469, National Records Center, Suitland, Maryland; "Southeast Asia Files," Papers of John F. Melby and "Vietnam Files," Papers of James P. Hendrick, HST; and Records of the French Desk, 1941–55, and Records of the Office of Western European Affairs, 1941–54, RG 59.

French views emerge in "Aide Américaine," dossier 45, Fonds Conseiller Politique; "US Rapports," dossiers 49 and 57, Fonds Conseiller Diplomatique; "Aide Américaine," dossiers 201–598, and "Comité Franco-Amérique," dossiers 189–566, Fonds Haut-Commissariat de France en Indochine, AOM, and "Aid Américaine," Série Asie-Oceanie, 1944–1955, Indochine, MAE.

20 Collins to Dulles, 29 March 1955, Confidential U.S. State Department Central Files, Indochina Internal Affairs, 1955–59, RG 59. For one useful analysis of U.S. attitudes toward the French in this period, see George C. Herring, "Franco-American Conflict in Indochina, 1950–1954," in *Dien Bien Phu and the Crisis of Franco-American Relations, 1954–1955*, ed. Lawrence S. Kaplan, Denise Artaud, and Mark R. Rubin (Wilmington, Del.: Scholarly Resources Books, 1990), 29–48.

21 Collins to Dulles, 22 March, 10 April 1955, 757G.oo/3-2255 and 757G.oo/4-1055, RG 59. See also Kidder to Dulles, 8, 10 February 1955, 757G.oo/2-855 and 757G.oo/2-955, RG 59.

22 The relationship between the United States and South Vietnam remains one of the least-studied aspects of the war. For a valuable discussion of the issues that require scholarly attention, see George C. Herring, " 'Peoples Quite Apart': Americans, the South Vietnamese, and the War in Vietnam," *Diplomatic History* 14, no. 1 (Winter 1990): 1–23. Two recent works on the Diem period do begin to redress this imbalance; see Anne Blair, *Lodge in Vietnam: A Patriot Abroad* (New Haven: Yale University Press, 1995), and Joseph G. Morgan, *The Vietnam Lobby: The American Friends of Vietnam, 1955–1975* (Chapel Hill: University of North Carolina Press, 1997).

23 The best-known proponent of modernization theory is Walt Rostow, from whose work these commonalities are drawn; see Rostow, *The Stages of Economic Growth: A Non-Communist Manifesto* (Cambridge: Cambridge University Press, 1960). For a thoughtful discussion of modernization theory and its relationship to the Kennedy policy toward Latin America, see Michael E. Latham, "Ideology, Social Science, and Destiny: Modernization and the Kennedy-Era Alliance for Progress," *Diplomatic History* 22, no. 3 (Spring 1998): 199–229.

24 David Halberstam, *The Best and the Brightest* (New York: Random House, 1972), 512, 564.

25 Lyndon Baines Johnson, speech of 7 April 1965, reprinted in U.S. Senate, Committee on Foreign Relations, *Background Information Relating to Southeast Asia and Vietnam*, 90th Cong., 2d sess. (Washington, D.C.: U.S. Government Printing Office, 1965), 197–202.

26 My reading of the Johns Hopkins speech and the notion of internal colonization relies on a wonderful essay by Lloyd Gardner; see his "From the Colorado to the Mekong," in *Vietnam: The Early Decisions*, ed. Lloyd C. Gardner and Ted Gittinger (Austin: University of Texas Press, 1997), 37–57, and his *Pay Any Price: Lyndon Johnson and the Wars for Vietnam* (Chicago: Ivan R. Dee, 1995).

27 Doris Kearns Goodwin, *Lyndon Johnson and the American Dream* (New York: Harper and Row, 1976), 267, and Stanley Karnow, *Vietnam: A History* (New York: Viking Press, 1983), 416, cited in Lloyd Gardner, "From the Colorado," 53.

28 On the perceptions of the U.S. business community before the lifting of the trade embargo, see *New York Times*, 31 March, 8 May 1992, 8 February, 3 October 1993, 2, 3 February 1994. On post-embargo disillusionment, see *New York Times*, 13 November 1994,

and "Romance Meets Reality," *Far Eastern Economic Review*, 22 September 1994, 72–73.

29 Warren Christopher, "U.S.–Vietnam Relations: A New Chapter," *U.S. Department of State Dispatch* 6 (14 August 1995): 627–29.

30 "Nike Shoe Plan in Vietnam Is Called Unsafe for Workers," *New York Times*, 8 November 1997.

31 "Who Went Under in the World's Sea of Cash" and "How the U.S. Wooed Asia to Let Cash Flow In," *New York Times*, 15, 16 February 1999.

32 One manifestation of the contemporary concern for reconceptualizing the boundaries of the national space that emphasizes a single civic rather than a plural ethnic national identity is the work of the self-titled liberal nationalists. See, for instance, David A. Hollinger, *Postethnic America: Beyond Multiculturalism* (New York: Basic Books, 1995), and Michael Lind, *The Next American Nation: The New Nationalism and the Fourth American Revolution* (New York: Free Press, 1995).

33 On the coming of the *doi moi* reforms and their significance, see Börje Ljunggren, ed., *The Challenge of Reform in Indochina* (Cambridge: Harvard Institute for International Development, 1993), and William S. Turley and Mark Selden, eds. *Reinventing Vietnamese Socialism* (Boulder, Colo.: Westview Press, 1993).

34 "About Future Relations between Vietnam and the U.S.A.," *Viet-My Tap Chi* [Vietnamese-American Friendship Association review] (Christmas and New Year ed., 1945–46), 18. On the coming of Pepsi to Ho Chi Minh City in 1994, see *New York Times*, 5, 7, 10 February 1994, and "Making Up for Lost Time: U.S. Firms Rush in Where Once They Could Not Tread," *Far Eastern Economic Review*, 17 February 1994, 16–17.

35 Nguyen Huy Thiep, "The General Retires" ["Tuong ve huu"], in his *Nhung Ngon Gio Hua Tat* [The breezes of Hua Tat] (Hanoi: Nha Xuat Ban Van Hoa, 1989), 23.

36 Bao Ninh, *Sorrows of War* [*Noi buon chien tranh*] (Hanoi, 1991; reprint, Westminster: Hong Linh, 1992), 67. For a more sustained examination of the implications of these works, focusing on contemporary film, see my "Contests of Memory: Remembering and Forgetting War in Contemporary Vietnamese Cinema," in *Remembering New Pasts: Commemoration in Contemporary Vietnam*, ed. Hue-Tam Ho Tai (Berkeley: University of California Press, forthcoming).

37 Hue-Tam Ho Tai draws attention to the unrealized agendas of Vietnamese radicalism in her *Radicalism and the Origins of the Vietnamese Revolution* (Cambridge: Harvard University Press, 1992), 262–63. For a recent sweeping historical consideration of the fragility of Vietnamese identities and their continual reconstructions, see Keith Taylor, "Surface Orientations in Vietnam: Beyond Histories of the Nation and Region," *Journal of Asian Studies* 59, no. 4 (November 1998): 949–78.

38 Tran Huy Quang's "The Prophecy" ["Linh Nghiem"] was published in *Literature and Arts Journal* [*Bao Van Nghe*] in 1992; translation by Sherée Carey in *Viet Nam Forum*, no. 14 (1994): 55–60.

BIBLIOGRAPHY

PRIMARY SOURCES

Socialist Republic of Vietnam

ARCHIVES

Thu Vien Quoc Gia (National library), Hanoi
    The national library holds the only collection of *quoc ngu*, or Vietnamese-language,
        material printed in the resistance zones held by Ho Chi Minh's Democratic
        Republic of Vietnam in the period 1946–54. A number of these works were
        consulted for this study.
Trung Tam Luu Tru Quoc Gia-1 (National archives center no. 1), Hanoi
    Fonds du Résidence Supérieure au Tonkin, 1920–1945

INTERVIEWS

Unless otherwise noted, all personal interviews were conducted in Hanoi.
Bui Dinh Thanh, 1989, 1992
Dam Quang Trung, 1989
Do Quang Hung, 1992
Hoang Dao Thuy, 1992
Hoang Minh Giam, 1989
Hoang Nguyen, 1992
Hoang Phong, 1992
Luu Doan Huynh, 1989, 1992, 1997
Luu Van Loi, 1992
Nguyen Van Tran, 1992
Pham Van Dong (private correspondence), 1992
Pham Xanh, 1992

Ta Dinh De, 1992
Tran Van Giao (private correspondence), 1989, 1992
Vo Nguyen Giap (private correspondence), 1992
Vu Ky, 1992

NEWSPAPERS AND JOURNALS

L'Avenir du Tonkin, Hanoi, 1887
La Cloche Fêlée, Saigon, 1926–28
Co Giai Phong [Banner of liberation], 1943–45
Cuu Quoc [Save the country], 1942–45
La Lutte, Saigon, 1933–38
Le Militant, Saigon, 1936–37
Nam Phong [Southern wind], Saigon, 1917–34
Ngay Nay [This day], Hanoi, 1937–40
Nghien Cuu Dong Nam A, Hanoi, 1991
Nghien Cuu Lich Su [Historical studies], Hanoi, 1960–93
Nhan Dan [The people], Hanoi, 1954, 1989–93
Notre Voix, Hanoi, 1939
Phu Nu Tan Van [Ladies' news], Saigon, 1929–34
Tap Chi Bon-so-vich [Bolshevik review], 1934–36
Tap Chi Cong San [Communist review], 1933–34
Tap Chi Van Hoc [Literature magazine], Hanoi, 1980
Thanh Nghi [Impartial opinion], Hanoi, 1941–45
Thanh Nien [Youth], Canton, 1925–30
Tin Tuc [News], Hanoi, 1938
Le Travail, Hanoi, 1936–37
Tribune Indigène, Saigon, 1919
Trung Bac Chu Nhat [Center and northern Sunday magazine], Hanoi, 1945
Viet-My Tap Chi [Vietnamese-American Friendship Association review], Hanoi, 1945
Viet Nam Doc Lap [Vietnam independence], 1941–45

PUBLISHED DOCUMENTS, MEMOIRS, AND
REVOLUTIONARY WRITINGS

Bac Ho: Hoi Ky [Memoirs of Uncle Ho]. Hanoi: Nha Xuat Ban Van Hoc, 1960.
Ban Chap Hanh Trung Uong Dang Cong San Viet-Nam (Executive Board of the
    Central Committee of the Communist Party of Vietnam). *Van Kien Dang, Tap III,
    1930–1945* [Party documents, vol. 3, 1930–45]. Hanoi: Ban Nghien Cuu Lich Su
    Dang Trung Uong Xuat Ban, 1977.
———. *Van Kien Dang ve Khang Chien Chong Thuc Dan Phap, Tap 1, 1945–1950*
    [Party documents on the resistance war against the French colonialists, vol. 1,
    1945–50]. Hanoi: Nha Xuat Ban Su That, 1986.
Ban Nghien Cuu Lich Su Dang (Board for the historical study of the party). *Cuoc*

Khang Chien Chong Thuc Dan Phap va Can Thiep My o Ha Noi [The resistance war against the French colonialists and the American interventionists in Hanoi]. Hanoi: n.p., 1980.

Ban Nghien Cuu Lich Su Quan Doi Thuoc Cuc Chinh Tri (Board for the historical study of the army in the political department). *Lich Su Quan Doi Nhan Dan Viet Nam* [History of the People's Army of Vietnam]. Hanoi: Nha Xuat Ban Quan Doi Nhan Dan, 1974.

Bui Cong Trung, Truong Sinh, et al. *Nguoi Truoc Nga Nguoi Sau Tien* [The front rank falls, the rear advances]. Hanoi: Nha Xuat Ban Van Hoc, 1960.

Bui Lam et al. *Souvenirs sur Ho Chi Minh.* Hanoi: Éditions en langues étrangères, 1965.

Bui Tin. *Following Ho Chi Minh: Memoirs of a North Vietnamese Colonel.* Honolulu: University of Hawaii Press, 1995.

Chien Tranh Thai-Binh-Duong va Cach Mang Giai Phong Dan Toc Dong Duong [The Pacific war and the Indochinese national liberation revolution]. N.p.: Ban Tuyen Truyen Huan Luyen Trung Uong Dang Cong San Dong Duong Xuat Ban, 1942.

Chu Tich Ho Chi Minh o Phap [Ho Chi Minh in France]. Hanoi: Nha Xuat Ban Thong Tin Ly Luan, 1988.

Cuoc Khang Chien Than Thanh cua Nhan Dan Viet Nam [The sacred resistance war of the Vietnamese people]. 4 vols. Hanoi: Nha Xuat Ban Su That, 1958–60.

Dang Cong San Viet Nam Ban Chap Hanh Trung Uong (Vietnam Communist Party Central Committee). *Van Kien Dang, 1945–1954* [Party documents, 1945–54]. 3 vols. Hanoi: Ban Nghien Cuu Lich Su Dang Trung Uong Xuat Ban, 1979.

Dang Cong San Viet Nam Ban Chap Hanh Trung Uong, 1930–1945 [Party documents, 1930–45]. Hanoi: Ban Nghien Cuu Lich Su Dang Trung Uong Xuat Ban, 1977.

Dang Thai Mai. *Van Tho Cach Mang Viet-Nam Dau The Ky XX* [Vietnamese revolutionary poetry and prose in the early twentieth century]. Hanoi: Nha Xuat Ban Van Hoc, 1964.

Dang Van Cap. *Dau Nguon: Hoi Ky va Bac Ho* [The source: Memories of Uncle Ho]. Hanoi: Nha Xuat Ban Van Hoc, 1975.

Days with Ho Chi Minh. Hanoi: Foreign Languages Publishing House, 1962.

Elliot, Mai, trans. *Reminiscences on the Army for National Salvation: Memoirs of General Chu Van Tan.* Ithaca: Cornell University Southeast Asia Program Data Paper Number 97, 1974.

Hoang Quoc Viet et al. *A Heroic People: Memoirs from the Revolution.* Hanoi: Foreign Languages Publishing House, 1965.

———. *Récits de la résistance vietnamienne, 1925–1945.* Paris: François Maspéro, 1966.

Hoang Van Hoan. *Giot Nuoc Trong Bein Ca: Hoi Ky Cach Mang* [A drop of water in the ocean: Memoirs of revolution]. Beijing: Nha Xuat Ban Tin Viet Nam, 1986.

Ho Chi Minh. *Ho Chi Minh Toan Tap* [Ho Chi Minh's collected works]. 10 vols. Hanoi: Nha Xuat Ban Su That, 1980–90.

———. *Selected Works.* Vol. 1, *Articles and Speeches, 1922–1926.* Hanoi: Foreign Languages Publishing House, 1960.

Mai Van Bo. *Ha Noi–Paris: Hoi Ky Ngoai Giao* [Hanoi-Paris: Memoirs of foreign relations]. Ho Chi Minh City: Nha Xuat Ban Van Nghe, 1993.

Ministry of Foreign Affairs, Socialist Republic of Vietnam. *The Truth about Vietnam-China Relations over the Last Thirty Years*. Hanoi: Vietnamese Ministry of Foreign Affairs, 1979.

Nghi Quyet Cua Ban Thuong Vu Trung Uong Dang Cong San Dong Duong: 25-28-2-1943 [Resolutions of the Central Committee of the Indochinese Communist Party: 25–28 February 1943]. N.p., n.d.

Nguyen Khanh Toan et al. *Avec l'oncle Ho*. Hanoi: Éditions en langues étrangères, 1972.

Phan Boi Chau. *Phan Boi Chau Toan Tap, Tap 1–2* [Phan Boi Chau's collected works, vols. 1–2]. Hue: Nha Xuat Ban Thuan Hoa, 1990.

Phan Chau Trinh. *Giai-Nhan Ky-Ngo (Anh-Hung-Ca)* [Rare encounters with beautiful personages (an epic)]. Saigon: Nha Xuat Ban Huong Duong, 1958.

———. *That Dieu Thu* [Seven point letter]. Hue: Anh Minh Xuat Ban, 1958.

———. *Tho Van Phan Chau Trinh* [Collected works of Phan Chau Trinh]. Hanoi: Nha Xuat Ban Van Hoc, 1983.

Quan Su Cua Dang, 1930–1945 [Military documents of the party, 1930–45]. Hanoi: Nha Xuat Ban Quan Doi Nhan Dan, 1968.

Souverains et notabilités d'Indochine. Hanoi: Éditions du Gouvernement Général de l'Indochine (IDEO), 1943.

The Nguyen (Nguyen Ba The). *Phan Chu Trinh*. Saigon: Nha Xuat Ban Tan Viet, 1956.

Tran Huy Lieu et al., eds. *Tai Lieu Tham Khao Lich Su Cach Mang Can Dai Viet Nam* [Research materials on the history of the contemporary Vietnamese revolution]. 12 vols. Hanoi: Nha Xuat Ban Van Su Dia, 1955–58.

Tran Trung Kim. *Mot Con Gio Bui* [A puff of dust]. Saigon: Vinh Son, 1969.

Truong Chinh. *Selected Writings*. Hanoi: Foreign Languages Publishing House, 1977.

Van Kien Lich Su Dang [Party history documents]. 6 vols. Hanoi: n.p., n.d.

Vien Quan He Quoc Te Bo Ngoai Giao (Ministry of Foreign Relations Institute of International Relations). *Chu Tich Ho Chi Minh voi Cong Tach Ngoai Giao* [Ho Chi Minh and foreign relations]. Hanoi: Su That, 1990.

Vien Su Hoc (Board of Historical Studies). *Tai Lieu Tham Khao Cach Mang Thang Tam (Tong Khoi Nghia o Hanoi va Cac Dia Phuong)* [Research documents on the August Revolution (in the general uprising in Hanoi and other regions)]. 2 vols. Hanoi: Nha Xuat Ban Su Hoc, 1960.

Vo Nguyen Giap. *Khu Giai Phong* [The liberated zone]. Hanoi: Cuu Quoc, 1946.

Vu Dinh Lien et al., eds. *Hop Tuyen Tho Van Viet-Nam, 1858–1930* [A collection of Vietnamese poetry and prose, 1858–1930]. Hanoi: Nha Xuat Ban Van Hoa, 1963.

France

ARCHIVES

Archives du Ministère des Affaires Étrangères Diplomatiques, Paris
Série Asie-Oceanie 1944–1955: Indochine
Série Asie-Oceanie 1944–1955: Sous-Série Dossiers Généraux
Série E, Asie-Oceanie, Sous-Série Indochine Française, 1930–1940
Série Guerre 1939–1945, Sous-Série E-Vichy-Asie-Indochine

Archives Nationales, Paris
    Archives de la Présidence du Conseil des ministres: Dossiers Indochine
    Fonds Présidence du Conseil: Dossiers Indochine
Bibliothèque Nationale, Paris
    Fonds du dépôt légal indochinois des livres en *quoc ngu*, 1922–1954
Dépôt des Archives d'Outre Mer, Archives Nationales, Aix-en-Provence
    Fonds Conseiller Diplomatique
    Fonds Conseiller Economique à Saigon
    Fonds Conseiller Politique
    Fonds Conseiller Politique supplément
    Fonds Gouvernement Général Indochine: Cabinet Militaire
    Fonds Haut-Commissariat de France en Indochine
    Fonds Indochine: Gouvernement de fait
    Fonds Service de Protection du Corps Expéditionnaire
    Indochine Nouveau Fonds
Service Historique de l'Armée de Terre, Vincennes, Paris
    Fonds Etat-Major Général de la Défense Nationale
    Fonds Indochine, Sous-Série 10H, 1945–1956

COLLECTIONS OF PERSONAL PAPERS
AND ORAL INTERVIEWS

George Bidault, Archives Nationales, Paris
Émile Bollaert, Archives Privée, Dépôt des Archives d'Outre Mer, Archives Nationales, Aix-en-Provence
Henri Bonnet, Papiers d'Agents, Archives Privée, Archives du Ministère des Affaires Étrangères Diplomatiques, Paris
Henri Hoppenot, Papiers d'Agents, Archives Privée, Archives du Ministère des Affaires Étrangères Diplomatiques, Paris
Ho Ta Khanh (personal interview), Paris, 1991
Henri Laurenti, Archives Nationales, Paris
René Mayer, Archives Nationales, Paris
Pierre Mendès France, Documents Pierre Mendès France, Series CED, Fuites, Indochine, Institute Pierre Mendès France
Marius Moutet, Archives Privée, Dépôt des Archives d'Outre Mer, Archives Nationales, Aix-en-Provence
Pham Ngoc Tuan (personal interview), Paris, 1991
Léon Pignon, Archives Privée, Dépôt des Archives d'Outre Mer, Archives Nationales, Aix-en-Provence
Jean Sainteny, Foundation Nationale des Sciences Politiques, Paris
Tran Van An (personal interview), Paris, 1991

PUBLISHED DOCUMENTS

Documents diplomatiques Français, 1954 (21 juillet–31 décembre). Paris: Imprimerie Nationale, 1987.

Documents diplomatiques Français, 1954: Annexes (21 juillet–31 décembre). Paris: Imprimerie Nationale, 1987.

Documents diplomatiques Français, 1955: Tome 1 (1 janvier–30 juin). Paris: Imprimerie Nationale, 1987.

Documents diplomatiques Français, 1955: Annexes, Tome 1 (1 janvier–30 juin). Paris: Imprimerie Nationale, 1987.

Documents diplomatiques Français, 1955: Tome 2 (1 juillet–31 décembre). Paris: Imprimerie Nationale, 1988.

La guerre d'Indochine, textes et documents: le retour de la France en Indochine, 1945–1946. Vincennes: Service Historique de l'Armée de Terre, 1987.

La guerre d'Indochine, textes et documents: Indochine 1947, règlement politique ou solution militaire? Vincennes: Service Historique de l'Armée de Terre, 1989.

Ruscio, Alain, ed. *Ho Chi Minh: Textes, 1914–1969*. Paris: L'Harmattan, 1990.

Great Britain

ARCHIVES

India Office Library and Records, Orbit House, London
   Burma Office Records (M), 1932–48
      M/4 Burma Office—Annual Department Files, Frontier and Frontier Areas, 1946–48
   India Office Departmental Records
   Political and Secret (P&S) Department Records, 1756–1950
      P&S/18, Political and Secret Memorandum
      P&S/12, Political (External) Files and Collections, 1931–50
Public Records Office, Kew
   CAB 78. Cabinet Office, Coordination of Policy in Southeast Asia, 1945
   CAB 79. Cabinet Office, War Cabinet, Chiefs of Staff Committee, Minutes of Meetings, 1939–45
   CAB 99. Cabinet Office, War Cabinet, Commonwealth and International Conferences, 1938–45
   CAB 120. Cabinet Office, Minister of Defense, Secretariat Files, 1938–47
   CAB 122. Cabinet Office, British Joint Staff Mission, Washington Office Files, 1940–58
   CO 537. Colonial Office, Colonies General Supplementary Correspondence: Straits Settlement, Internal Relations, 1946–51
   FO 371. Foreign Office, Political Correspondence: Indochina, 1941–56
   FO 628. Foreign Office, Embassy and Consular Archives: Thailand (Siam), 1945–51
   FO 810. Foreign Office, Embassy and Consular Archives: Netherlands, Djakarta (Batavia), 1946–48
   FO 924. Foreign Office, Cultural Relations Files, 1948

FO 959. Foreign Office, Embassy and Consular Archives: France, Indochina, 1945–59

WO 106. War Office, Directorate of Military Operations and Intelligence

WO 172. War Office, War Diaries: South-East Asia Command

WO 193. War Office, Director of Military Operations Collation Files

WO 203. War Office, Military Headquarters Papers Far East, War of 1939–45, Allied Land Forces in Southeast Asia and South-East Asia Command

COLLECTIONS OF PERSONAL PAPERS

Arthur Reginald Chater, Liddell Hart Centre for Military Archives, King's College, University of London, London

Tom Driberg, Christ Church College, Oxford University, Oxford

Douglas David Gracey, Liddell Hart Centre for Military Archives, King's College, University of London, London

Earl Mountbatten of Burma, Hartley Library, University of Southampton, Highfield

William Ronald Campbell Penney, Liddell Hart Centre for Military Archives, King's College, University of London, London

Henry Royds Pownall, Liddell Hart Centre for Military Archives, King's College, University of London, London

United States

ARCHIVES

National Archives, Washington, D.C.

Record Group 38. Records of the Office of the Chief of Naval Operations
Naval Intelligence Unit—China Files
Office of Naval Intelligence Files

Record Group 59. Records of the Department of State
Decimal Files
French Indochina, Vietnam, Thailand, Philippines, 1940–55
Internal Affairs of France: French Indochina, 1910–39
Lot Files
Papers of Charles Bohlen, 1942–52
Papers of Philip C. Jessup, 1946–53
Records of Harley A. Notter, 1939–45
Records of the Bureau of Far Eastern Affairs, 1953, 1955
Records of the Bureau of Far Eastern Affairs (Economic Aid), 1948–59
Records of the Bureau of Far Eastern Affairs (Files Relating to Southeast Asia and the Geneva Conference), 1954
Records of the French Desk, 1941–55
Records of the Griffin Mission to Southeast Asia, 1950
Records of the Office of Assistant Secretary and Under-Secretary of State Dean Acheson, 1941–48, 1950

Records of the Office of China Affairs, 1944–50
Records of the Office of China Affairs (Econ Files), 1948–56
Records of the Office of European Affairs, 1935–47 (Matthews-Hickerson Files)
Records of the Office of Southeast Asian Affairs, 1950–56
Records of the Office of Southeast Asian Affairs (Cambodia and Vietnam), 1953–58
Records of the Philippine and Southeast Asia Division, 1944–52
Records of the Policy Planning Staff, 1947–53
Records of the Southeast Asia Policy Committee (June 1950–April 1953)
Records of the Vietnam Desk Officer, 1954–55
Records of the Office of Western European Affairs, 1941–54
Research Reports of the Foreign Policy Studies Branch, Division of History Policy Research, 1944–50
Record Group 165. Records of the War Department
American-British Conversations File
Records of the Operations and Plans Division
Record Group 226. Records of the Office of Strategic Services
China Theater Correspondence
Far East Division Correspondence
Indochina Files of Morale Operations (MO), Secret Intelligence (SI), Special Operations (SO), Strategic Services Unit (SSU) and X-2
Records of the Research and Analysis Branch
Record Group 350. Records of the Bureau of Insular Affairs
Record Group 353. Records of the State-War-Navy Coordinating Committee and the State-Army-Navy-Air Force Coordinating Committee, 1944–49
National Records Center, Suitland, Maryland
Record Group 84. Records of Foreign Service Posts
Records of Consular Posts, Hanoi, 1939–50
Records of Consular Posts, Nanking, 1946
Records of Consular Posts, Saigon, 1889–1940, 1946–55
Records of Diplomatic Posts, Thailand, 1942–54
Records of Diplomatic Posts, Vietnam, 1936–55
Record Group 319. Records of the Office of the Assistant Chief of Staff
G-2 "ID" Files: Indochina
G-2 Project Decimal Files: Indochina
Record Group 332. Records of the China-Burma-India Theatres
French Indochina Files
Wedemeyer Files
Record Group 469. Records of Foreign Assistance Agencies
Records of the Mission to Vietnam, 1950–59
Records of the Office of Far East Operations
Indochina Subject Files, 1950–54
Vietnam Subject Files, 1955–59

Dean Acheson, Harry S. Truman Library, Independence, Missouri
Stanley Andrews, Harry S. Truman Library, Independence, Missouri
Adolph Berle, Franklin D. Roosevelt Library, Hyde Park, New York
J. Lawton Collins, Dwight D. Eisenhower Library, Abilene, Kansas
Mathew J. Connelly, Harry S. Truman Library, Independence, Missouri
Lauchlin Currie, Franklin D. Roosevelt Library, Hyde Park, New York
Dwight D. Eisenhower, Dwight D. Eisenhower Library, Abilene, Kansas
    Diaries, 1948–53
    Papers As President, 1953–61 (Ann Whitman File)
    Pre-Presidential Papers, 1916–52
    Records As President, While House Central Files, 1953–61
    White House Office, National Security Council Staff: Papers, 1948–61
    White House Office, Office of the Special Assistant for National Security Affairs
        (Robert Culter, Dillon Anderson, and Gordon Gray): Records, 1952–61
George M. Elsey, Harry S. Truman Library, Independence, Missouri
Philip E. Gallagher, U.S. Army Center for Military History, Washington, D.C.
Alfred M. Gruenther, Dwight D. Eisenhower Library, Abilene, Kansas
James P. Hendrick, Harry S. Truman Library, Independence, Missouri
Christian A. Herter, Dwight D. Eisenhower Library, Abilene, Kansas
Harry L. Hopkins, Franklin D. Roosevelt Library, Hyde Park, New York
Charles M. Hulten, Harry S. Truman Library, Independence, Missouri
C. D. Jackson, Dwight D. Eisenhower Library, Abilene, Kansas
Kevin McCann, Dwight D. Eisenhower Library, Abilene, Kansas
George C. Marshall, George C. Marshall Foundation, Lexington, Virginia
John F. Melby, Harry S. Truman Library, Independence, Missouri
Milton E. Miles, National Archives, Washington, D.C.
Henry J. Morgenthau Jr., Franklin D. Roosevelt Library, Hyde Park, New York
Franklin D. Roosevelt, Franklin D. Roosevelt Library, Hyde Park, New York
    Papers As President, Alphabetical File, 1933–45
    Papers As President, Map Room File, 1941–45
    Papers As President, Official File, 1933–45
    Papers As President, President's Personal File, 1933–45
    Papers As President, President's Secretary's File, 1933–45
Harold Stein, Harry S. Truman Library, Independence, Missouri
Edward Stettinius, Alderman Library, University of Virginia, Charlottesville, Virginia
John D. Sumner, Harry S. Truman Library, Independence, Missouri
Charles W. Taussig, Franklin D. Roosevelt Library, Hyde Park, New York
Harry S. Truman, Harry S. Truman Library, Independence, Missouri
    Papers As President, Map Room File, 1945
    Papers As President, National Security Council Files, 1947–53
    Papers As President, President's Secretary's Files, 1945–53
    Papers As President, Psychological Strategy Board Files, 1945–53
    Papers As President, While House Central Files, 1945–53

ORAL HISTORIES AND PERSONAL INTERVIEWS

Theodore C. Achilles, Harry S. Truman Library, Independence, Missouri
Dillon Anderson, Dwight D. Eisenhower Library, Abilene, Kansas
Leland Barrows, Harry S. Truman Library, Independence, Missouri
Charles Bohlen, Dwight D. Eisenhower Library, Abilene, Kansas
Robert Bowie, Dwight D. Eisenhower Library, Abilene, Kansas
John F. Cady, Harry S. Truman Library, Independence, Missouri
Clark M. Clifford, Harry S. Truman Library, Independence, Missouri
Thomas J. Corcoran, Foreign Affairs Oral History Program, Georgetown University,
    Washington, D.C.
Olcott H. Deming, Foreign Affairs Oral History Program, Georgetown University,
    Washington, D.C.
Clarence Dillon, Dwight D. Eisenhower Library, Abilene, Kansas
Alan Fisher, Foreign Affairs Oral History Program, Georgetown University, Washington,
    D.C.
Dennis Fitzgerald, Dwight D. Eisenhower Library, Abilene, Kansas
Andrew Goodpaster, Dwight D. Eisenhower Library, Abilene, Kansas
Arthur Hummel, Foreign Affairs Oral History Program, Georgetown University,
    Washington, D.C.
William Lacy, Dwight D. Eisenhower Library, Abilene, Kansas
Lyman Lemnitzer, Dwight D. Eisenhower Library, Abilene, Kansas
Charlotte Loris, Foreign Affairs Oral History Program, Georgetown University,
    Washington, D.C.
Jack Lydman, Foreign Affairs Oral History Program, Georgetown University,
    Washington, D.C.
Richard McCarthy, Foreign Affairs Oral History Program, Georgetown University,
    Washington, D.C.
Edwin W. Martin, Foreign Affairs Oral History Program, Georgetown University,
    Washington, D.C.
Robert Murphy, Dwight D. Eisenhower Library, Abilene, Kansas
Arthur Nevis, Dwight D. Eisenhower Library, Abilene, Kansas
Thomas R. O'Brien, Foreign Affairs Oral History Program, Georgetown University,
    Washington, D.C.
Bromley Smith, Dwight D. Eisenhower Library, Abilene, Kansas
R. Burr Smith, Harry S. Truman Library, Independence, Missouri
Philip D. Sprouse, Harry S. Truman Library, Independence, Missouri
Elmer B. Staats, Harry S. Truman Library, Independence, Missouri
Emory C. Swank, Foreign Affairs Oral History Program, Georgetown University,
    Washington, D.C.
Allison K. Thomas (personal interview), East Lansing, Michigan, 1989
Earl Wilson, Foreign Affairs Oral History Program, Georgetown University, Washington,
    D.C.

NEWSPAPERS AND JOURNALS

American Mercury, 1934
Asia, 1920–37
Atlantic, 1924–50
Bangkok Post, 1946–55
Christian Science Monitor, 1930–50
Congressional Record, 1944
Contemporary Review, 1931–39
Current History, 1927–34
Department of State Bulletin, 1945–50
Far Eastern Economic Review, 1994–99
Foreign Affairs, 1938–94
Fortune, 1944
Ladies' Home Journal, 1928
Literary Digest, 1922–37
Living Age, 1922–39
Nation, 1945–55
National Geographic, 1931–50
New Republic, 1935–55
New York Times, 1919–55, 1990–99
Radio Broadcast, 1923
Time, 1945–55
Washington Post, 1946–55

PUBLISHED DOCUMENTS

All published in Washington, D.C., by the U.S. Government Printing Office, unless otherwise indicated.
Biographic Register of the Department of State, 1940–55.
Christopher, Warren. "U.S.–Vietnam Relations: A New Chapter." U.S. *Department of State Dispatch* 6 (14 August 1995): 627–29.
Complete Press Conferences of Franklin D. Roosevelt. Vol. 25. New York: Da Capo Press, 1972.
Foreign Commerce Yearbook 1933. 1933.
Foreign Commerce Yearbook 1935. 1935.
Foreign Commerce Yearbook 1938. 1939.
Foreign Commerce Yearbook 1939. 1942.
Foreign Relations of the United States, 1939. Vol. 3, *The Far East*. 1955.
Foreign Relations of the United States, 1940. Vol. 1, *General*. 1959
Foreign Relations of the United States, 1940. Vol. 2, *General and Europe*. 1957.
Foreign Relations of the United States, 1940. Vol. 4, *The Far East*. 1955.
Foreign Relations of the United States, 1941. Vol. 2, *Europe*. 1959.
Foreign Relations of the United States, 1941. Vols. 4 and 5, *The Far East*. 1956.
Foreign Relations of the United States, 1942. Vol. 1, *General, the British Commonwealth; the Far East*. 1960.

Foreign Relations of the United States, 1942. Vol. 2, *Europe.* 1962.

Foreign Relations of the United States, 1942: China. 1956.

Foreign Relations of the United States, 1943. Vol. 3, *The British Commonwealth; Eastern Europe; The Far East.* 1963.

Foreign Relations of the United States, 1943: China. 1957.

Foreign Relations of the United States, 1944. Vol. 3, *The British Commonwealth and Europe.* 1965.

Foreign Relations of the United States, 1944. Vol. 5, *The Near East; South Asia and Africa; the Far East.* 1965.

Foreign Relations of the United States, 1944. Vol. 6, *China.* 1967.

Foreign Relations of the United States, 1945. Vol. 1, *General; the United Nations.* 1967.

Foreign Relations of the United States, 1945. Vol. 4, *Europe.* 1968.

Foreign Relations of the United States, 1945. Vol. 6, *The British Commonwealth and the Far East.* 1969.

Foreign Relations of the United States, 1945. Vol. 7, *The British Commonwealth and the Far East.* 1969.

Foreign Relations of the United States, 1946. Vol. 8, *The Far East.* 1971.

Foreign Relations of the United States, 1947. Vol. 6, *The Far East.* 1972.

Foreign Relations of the United States, 1947. Vol. 7, *The Far East: China.* 1972.

Foreign Relations of the United States, 1948. Vol. 1, *General; the United Nations.* 1976.

Foreign Relations of the United States, 1948. Vol. 3, *Western Europe.* 1974.

Foreign Relations of the United States, 1948. Vol. 4, *Eastern Europe and the Soviet Union.* 1974.

Foreign Relations of the United States, 1948. Vol. 6, *The Far East and Australasia.* 1974.

Foreign Relations of the United States, 1948. Vol. 8, *The Far East: China.* 1973.

Foreign Relations of the United States, 1949. Vol. 1, *National Security Affairs; Foreign Economic Policy.* 1976.

Foreign Relations of the United States, 1949. Vol. 2, *The United Nations; the Western Hemisphere.* 1975.

Foreign Relations of the United States, 1949. Vol. 4, *Western Europe.* 1975.

Foreign Relations of the United States, 1949. Vol. 7, pts. 1 and 2, *The Far East and Australasia.* 1975.

Foreign Relations of the United States, 1949. Vol. 8, *The Far East: China.* 1978.

Foreign Relations of the United States, 1949. Vol. 9, *The Far East: China.* 1974.

Foreign Relations of the United States, 1950. Vol. 1, *National Security Affairs; Foreign Economic Policy.* 1977.

Foreign Relations of the United States, 1950. Vol. 2, *The United Nations; the Western Hemisphere.* 1976.

Foreign Relations of the United States, 1950. Vol. 3, *Western Europe.* 1977.

Foreign Relations of the United States, 1950. Vol. 6, *East Asia and the Pacific.* 1976.

Foreign Relations of the United States, 1950. Vol. 7, *Korea.* 1976.

Foreign Relations of the United States, 1951. Vol. 1, *National Security Affairs; Foreign Economic Policy.* 1979.

Foreign Relations of the United States, 1951. Vol. 2, *The United Nations; the Western Hemisphere.* 1979.

Foreign Relations of the United States, 1951. Vol. 3, *European Security and the German Questions.* 1981.

Foreign Relations of the United States, 1951. Vol. 6, pts. 1 and 2, *Asia and the Pacific.* 1977.

Foreign Relations of the United States, 1951. Vol. 7, pts. 1 and 2, *Korea and China.* 1983.

Foreign Relations of the United States, 1952–1954. Vol. 1, pts. 1 and 2, *General; Economic and Political Matters.* 1983.

Foreign Relations of the United States, 1952–1954. Vol. 2, pts. 1 and 2, *National Security Affairs.* 1984.

Foreign Relations of the United States, 1952–1954. Vol. 3, *The United Nations.* 1979.

Foreign Relations of the United States, 1952–1954. Vol. 5, pts. 1 and 2, *Western European Security.* 1983.

Foreign Relations of the United States, 1952–1954. Vol. 6, pts. 1 and 2, *Western Europe and Canada.* 1986.

Foreign Relations of the United States, 1952–1954. Vol. 12, pts. 1 and 2, *East Asia and the Pacific.* 1984, 1987.

Foreign Relations of the United States, 1952–1954. Vol. 13, pts. 1 and 2, *Indochina.* 1982.

Foreign Relations of the United States, 1952–1954. Vol. 14, pts. 1 and 2, *China and Japan.* 1985.

Foreign Relations of the United States, 1952–1954. Vol. 15, pts. 1 and 2, *Korea.* 1984.

Foreign Relations of the United States, 1952–1954. Vol. 16, *The Geneva Conference.* 1981.

Foreign Relations of the United States, 1955–1957. Vol. 1, *Vietnam.* 1985.

Foreign Relations of the United States, 1955–1957. Vols. 2 and 3, *China.* 1986.

Foreign Relations of the United States, 1955–1957. Vol. 9, *Foreign Economic Policy; Foreign Information Program.* 1987.

Foreign Relations of the United States, 1955–1957. Vol. 10, *Foreign Aid and Economic Defense.* 1989.

Foreign Relations of the United States, 1955–1957. Vol. 11, *The United Nations and General International Matters.* 1988.

Foreign Relations of the United States, 1955–1957. Vol. 19, *National Security Policy.* 1990.

Foreign Relations of the United States, 1955–1957. Vol. 21, *East Asian Security; Cambodia; Laos.* 1989.

Foreign Relations of the United States, 1955–1957. Vol. 22, *Southeast Asia.* 1986.

Foreign Relations of the United States, 1958–1960. Vol. 1, *Vietnam.* 1986.

Foreign Relations of the United States: Japan, 1931–1941. Vols. 1 and 2. 1943.

Foreign Relations of the United States: The Conference at Quebec, 1944. 1972.

Foreign Relations of the United States: The Conferences at Cairo and Tehran, 1943. 1961.

Foreign Relations of the United States: The Conferences at Malta and Yalta, 1945. 1955.

Foreign Relations of the United States: The Conferences at Washington, 1941–42, and Casablanca, 1943. 1968.

Foreign Relations of the United States: The Conference of Berlin (the Potsdam Conference). Vols. 1 and 2. 1960.

Kimball, Warren F., ed. *Churchill and Roosevelt: The Complete Correspondence.* 3 vols. (Princeton: Princeton University Press, 1984).

Porter, Gareth, ed. *Vietnam: The Definitive Documentation of Human Decisions.* Vol. 1,

The First Indochina War and the Geneva Agreements, 1941–1955. Stanfordville, N.Y.: Earl M. Coleman Enterprises, 1979.

U.S. Army and Navy Munitions Board. *The Strategic and Critical Materials.* Washington, D.C.: Army and Navy Munitions Board, 1940.

U.S. House of Representatives. Committee on Armed Services. *United States–Vietnam Relations, 1945–1967 (U.S. Department of Defense Study).* 12 vols. 1971.

U.S. Senate. Committee on Foreign Relations. *Background Information Relating to Southeast Asia and Vietnam.* 90th Cong., 2d sess.

———. *Hearings on the Causes, Origins, and Lessons of the Vietnam War.* 92d Cong., 2d sess., 9–12 May 1972. 1973.

———. *The United States and Vietnam, 1944–1947.* 1972.

SECONDARY SOURCES

Adas, Michael. *Machines as the Measure of Men: Science, Technology, and Ideologies of Western Dominance.* Ithaca: Cornell University Press, 1989.

Ageron, Charles-Robert. *Modern Algeria: A History from 1830 to the Present.* Translated and edited by Michael Brett. London: Hurst, 1991.

Allen, Frederick Lewis. *Since Yesterday.* New York: Harper and Brothers, 1939.

Anderson, Benedict. *Imagined Communities: Reflections on the Origins and Spread of Nationalism.* Rev. ed. London: Verso, 1991.

Anderson, David L. *Trapped by Success: The Eisenhower Administration and Vietnam, 1953–61.* New York: Columbia University Press, 1991.

Anderson, Sherwood. *Puzzled America.* New York: Charles Scribner's Sons, 1935.

Anderson, Stuart. *Race and Rapprochement: Anglo-Saxonism and Anglo-American Relations, 1895–1904.* Rutherford, N.J.: Fairleigh Dickinson University Press, 1981.

Anderson, Warwick. "The Trespass Speaks: White Masculinity and Colonial Breakdown." *American Historical Review* 102, no. 5 (December 1997): 1343–70.

Appadurai, Arjun. *Modernity at Large: Cultural Dimensions of Globalization.* Minneapolis: University of Minnesota Press, 1996.

Apter, David E., and Tony Saich. *Revolutionary Discourse in Mao's Republic.* Cambridge: Harvard University Press, 1994.

Arkush, R. David, and Leo O. Lee, eds. *Land without Ghosts: Chinese Impressions of America from the Mid-Nineteenth Century to the Present.* Berkeley: University of California Press, 1989.

Asian Relations: Being a Report of the Proceedings and Documentation of the First Asian Relations Conference, New Delhi, March–April 1947. New Delhi: Asian Relations Organization, 1948.

Austin, J. L. *How to Do Things with Words.* Cambridge: Harvard University Press, 1962.

Ayoob, Mohammed. *India and Southeast Asia: Indian Perceptions and Policies.* London: Routledge, 1990.

Bannister, Robert C. *Social Darwinism: Science and Myth in Anglo-American Thought.* Philadelphia: Temple University Press, 1979.

Bao Dai. *Le dragon d'Annam.* Paris: Plon, 1980.

Bao Ninh. *Sorrow of War* [*Noi buon chien tranh*]. Hanoi, 1991. Reprint, Westminster: Hong Linh, 1992.

Barkan, Elazar. *The Retreat of Scientific Racism: Changing Conceptions of Race in Britain and the United States between the World Wars.* Cambridge: Cambridge University Press, 1992.

Barnett, Susan Wilson. "Protestant Expansion and Chinese Views of the West." *Modern Asian Studies* 6, no. 2 (1972): 129–49.

Barnhart, Michael A. *Japan Prepares for Total War: The Search for Economic Security, 1919–1941.* Ithaca: Cornell University Press, 1987.

Bederman, Gail. *Manliness and Civilization: A Cultural History of Gender and Race in the United States, 1880–1917.* Chicago: University of Chicago Press, 1995.

Bellomy, Donald C. "Social Darwinism Revisited." *Perspectives on American History*, n.s., 1 (1984): 1–129.

Berman, William. *The Politics of Civil Rights in the Truman Administration.* Columbus: Ohio State University Press, 1970.

Biddiss, M. G. *Father of Racist Ideology: The Social and Political Thought of Count Gobineau.* London: Weidenfeld and Nicholson, 1970.

Blair, Anne. *Lodge in Vietnam: A Patriot Abroad.* New Haven: Yale University Press, 1995.

Blum, Robert M. *Drawing the Line: The Origins of the American Containment Policy in East Asia.* New York: Norton, 1982.

Blumenthal, Henry. *Illusion and Reality in Franco-American Diplomacy, 1914–1945.* Baton Rouge: Louisiana State University Press, 1986.

Bodard, Lucien. *The Quicksand War: Prelude to Vietnam.* Boston: Little, Brown, 1967.

Bodnar, John. *Remaking America: Public Memory, Commemoration, and Patriotism in the Twentieth Century.* Princeton: Princeton University Press, 1992.

Boime, Albert. *Hollow Icons: The Politics of Sculpture in Nineteenth-Century France.* Kent, Ohio: Kent State University Press, 1987.

Boon, James. "Cosmopolitan Moments: Echoey Confessions of an Ethnographer-Tourist." In *Crossing Cultures: Essays in the Displacement of Western Civilization*, edited by Daniel Segal, 226–54. Tucson: University of Arizona Press, 1992.

Borden, William S. *The Pacific Alliance: United States Foreign Economic Policy and Japanese Trade Recovery, 1947–1955.* Madison: University of Wisconsin Press, 1984.

Borg, Dorothy, and Heinrichs, Waldo, eds. *Uncertain Years: Chinese-American Relations, 1947–1950.* New York: Columbia University Press, 1980.

Borstelmann, Thomas. *Apartheid's Reluctant Uncle: The United States and Southern Africa in the Early Cold War.* New York: Oxford University Press, 1993.

Bose, Sarat. *I Warned My Countrymen.* Calcutta: Netaji Research Bureau, 1968.

Boudarel, Georges. *Cent fleurs ecloses dans la nuit du Vietnam: communisme et dissidence, 1954–1956.* Paris: J. Bertoin, 1991.

———. "Comment Giap a falli perdre la bataille Dien Bien Phu." *Nouvel Observateur*, 8 April 1983, 97.

Boudet, Paul, and Rémy Bourgeois. *Bibliographie de l'Indo-Chine française, 1913–1926.* Hanoi: Imprimerie d'Extrême-Orient, 1929.

Bourdieu, Pierre. *Language and Symbolic Power.* Cambridge: Harvard University Press, 1991.
———. *Outline of a Theory of Practice.* Cambridge: Cambridge University Press, 1977.
Bradley, Mark. "Contests of Memory: Remembering and Forgetting War in Contemporary Vietnamese Cinema." In *Remembering New Pasts: Commemoration in Contemporary Vietnam,* edited by Hue-Tam Ho Tai. Berkeley: University of California Press, forthcoming.
———. "Imagining America: The United States in Radical Vietnamese Anticolonial Discourse." *Journal of American-East Asian Relations* 4, no. 4 (Winter 1995): 299–329.
———. *Vietnamese Archives and Scholarship on the Cold War.* Cold War International History Project Working Paper No. 7. Washington, D.C.: Woodrow Wilson International Center for Scholars, 1993.
Brands, H. W. *The Specter of Neutralism: The United States and the Emergence of the Third World.* New York: Columbia University Press, 1989.
Breman, Jan, ed. *Imperial Monkey Business: Racial Supremacy in Social Darwinist Theory and Colonial Practice.* CASA Monographs No. 3. Amsterdam: VU University Press, 1990.
Brinkley, Alan. *Liberalism and Its Discontents.* Cambridge: Harvard University Press, 1998.
Brinkley, Douglas. *Dean Acheson: The Cold War Years, 1953–71.* New Haven: Yale University Press, 1992.
Brocheux, Pierre. "Crise économique et société en Indochine française." *Revue française d'histoire d'outre mer* 232–33 (1976): 655–67.
Brodrick, Alan H. *Little China: The Annamite Lands.* London: Oxford University Press, 1942.
Brooks, Charles W. *America in France's Hopes and Fears, 1890–1920.* 2 vols. New York: Garland, 1987.
Brownell, Will, and Richard N. Billings. *So Close to Greatness: A Biography of William C. Bullitt.* New York: Macmillan, 1987.
Buhite, Russell D. *Patrick J. Hurley and American Foreign Policy.* Ithaca: Cornell University Press, 1973.
Butcher, John. *The British in Malaya, 1880–1941: The Social History of a European Community in Colonial Southeast Asia.* Kuala Lumpur: Oxford University Press, 1979.
Buttinger, Joseph. *The Smaller Dragon: A Political History of Vietnam.* New York: Praeger, 1958.
Buzzanco, Robert. *Masters of War: Military Dissent and Politics in the Vietnam Era.* Cambridge: Cambridge University Press, 1996.
Cadman, Grace H. *Pen Pictures of Annam and Its People.* New York: Christian Alliance, 1920.
Cady, John. "Bibliographical Article: The Beginnings of French Imperialism in the Pacific Orient." *Journal of Modern History* 14, no. 1 (March 1942): 71–87.
Callaway, Helen. *Gender, Culture, and Empire: European Women in Colonial Nigeria.* London: Macmillan, 1987.

Candee, Helen Churchill. *New Journey in Old Asia: Indo-China, Siam, Java, Bali.* New York: Frederick A. Stokes, 1927.

Carrère d'Encausse, Hélène, and Stuart R. Schram. *Marxism and Asia.* London: Allen Lane, 1969.

Chaloemtiarana, Thak. *Thailand: The Politics of Despotic Paternalism.* Bangkok: Social Science Association of Thailand, Thammasat University, 1979.

Chamberlin, William Henry. "A New Deal for French Indo-China?" *Asia* 37, no. 7 (July 1937): 478.

Chan, Wing-Tsit. *A Sourcebook in Chinese Philosophy.* Princeton: Princeton University Press, 1963.

Chang, Hao. "Intellectual Change and the Reform Movement, 1890–98." In *The Cambridge History of China*, vol. 11, pt. 2, *Late Ch'ing, 1800–1911*, edited by John K. Fairbank and Kwang-Ching Liu, 274–338. Cambridge: Cambridge University Press, 1980.

———. *Liang Ch'i-ch'ao and Intellectual Transition in China, 1890–1907.* Cambridge: Harvard University Press, 1971.

Charlton, Michael, and Anthony Moncrieff. *Many Reason Why: The American Involvement in Vietnam.* New York: Hill and Wang, 1978.

Chen, King C. *Vietnam and China, 1938–1954.* Princeton: Princeton University Press, 1969.

Chesneaux, Jean. "French Historiography and the Evolution of Colonial Vietnam." In *Historians of South-East Asia*, edited by D. G. E. Hall, 235–44. London: Oxford University Press, 1961.

Chinard, Gilbert. "Eighteenth Century Theories of America as a Human Habitat." *Proceedings of the American Philosophical Society* 91 (1947): 27–57.

Choisy, Maryse. *L'Amour dans les prisons, reportage.* Paris: Montaigne, 1930.

Clifford, James, and George Marcus, ed. *Writing Culture: The Poetics and Politics of Ethnography.* Berkeley: University of California Press, 1986.

Coast, John. *Some Aspects of Siamese Politics.* New York: Institute of Pacific Relations, 1953.

Cohn, Bernard. *An Anthropologist among the Historians and Other Essays.* Delhi: Oxford University Press, 1987.

Colbert, Evelyn. "The Road Not Taken: Decolonization and Independence in Indonesia and Indochina." *Foreign Affairs* 51, no. 2 (April 1973): 608–28.

———. *Southeast Asia in International Politics, 1941–1956.* Ithaca: Cornell University Press, 1977.

Conklin, Alice L. *A Mission to Civilize: The Republican Idea of Empire in France and West Africa, 1895–1930.* Stanford: Stanford University Press, 1997.

Conn, Peter. *Pearl S. Buck: A Cultural Biography.* Cambridge: Cambridge University Press, 1996.

Cook, Blanche Wiesen. *Eleanor Roosevelt.* Vol. 1, 1884–1933. New York: Viking, 1992.

Coolidge, Harold J., Jr., and Theodore Roosevelt. *Three Kingdoms of Indo-China.* New York: Thomas Y. Crowell, 1933.

Cooper, Frederick, and Anne Laura Stoler, eds. *Tensions of Empire: Colonial Cultures in a Bourgeois World.* Berkeley: University of California Press, 1997.

Cordier, H. *Bibliotheca Indosinica*. 4 vols. Paris: Ernest Leroux, 1912–15.

Costigliola, Frank. *Awkward Dominion: American Political, Economic, and Cultural Relations with Europe, 1919–1933*. Ithaca: Cornell University Press, 1984.

———. *France and the United States: The Cold Alliance since World War II*. New York: Twayne, 1992.

Cripps, Thomas. *Slow Fade to Black: The Negro in American Film, 1900–1942*. New York: Oxford University Press, 1993.

Cumings, Bruce. *The Origins of the Korean War: Liberation and the Emergence of Separate Regimes, 1945–47*. Princeton: Princeton University Press, 1981.

———. *The Origins of the Korean War*. Vol. 2, *The Roaring of the Catarac, 1947–1950*. Princeton: Princeton University Press, 1990.

Cuoc Van Dong Cuu Quoc cua Viet Kieu o Thai-Lan (Gop vao Tai Lieu Lich Su Cach Mang Viet-Nam) [The national salvation activities of the overseas Vietnamese in Thailand (a contribution to the historical research of the Vietnamese revolution)]. Hanoi: Nha Xuat Ban Su That, 1961.

Dalleck, Robert. *Franklin Roosevelt and American Foreign Policy, 1932–1945*. New York: Oxford University Press, 1979.

Dang Tran Con and Phan Huy Ich. *The Song of a Soldier's Wife*. New Haven: Yale Council on Southeast Asian Studies, 1986.

David, Steven R. "Why the Third World Still Matters." *International Security* 17, no. 3 (Winter 1992/93): 127–59.

Davis, Kenneth S. *FDR: The Beckoning of Destiny, 1882–1928, a History*. New York: G. P. Putnam's Sons, 1972.

de Bary, Wm. Theodore. *East Asian Civilizations: A Dialogue in Five Stages*. Cambridge: Harvard University Press, 1988.

de Belval, Albert Challan. *Au Tonkin, 1884–1885: notes, souvenirs et impressions*. Paris: Plon, 1904.

de Certeau, Michael. *The Practice of Everyday Life*. Berkeley: University of California Press, 1979.

Degler, Carl N. *In Search of Human Nature: The Decline and Revival of Darwinism in American Social Thought*. New York: Oxford University Press, 1991.

Dennis, Peter. *Troubled Days of Peace: Mountbatten and South East Asia Command, 1945–46*. New York: St. Martin's Press, 1987.

de Pouvourville, Albert. *L'Annamite*. Paris: Éditions LaRose, 1932.

DeSantis, Hugh. *The Diplomacy of Silence: The American Foreign Service, the Soviet Union, and the Cold War, 1933–1947*. Chicago: University of Chicago Press, 1983.

Despuech, Jacques. *Le trafic de piastres*. Paris: Deux Rives, 1953.

Devillers, Philippe. *Histoire du Viêt-Nam de 1940 à 1952*. Paris: Éditions du Seuil, 1952.

Dikötter, Frank. *The Discourse of Race in Modern China*. Stanford: Stanford University Press, 1992.

Do Quang Hung. "Chu Tich Ho Chi Minh Trong Thoi Ky 1934–1938, Roi Sang Them Cho Van De Dan Toc Hay Quoc Te?" ["Ho Chi Minh in the period 1934–1938, clearly for nationalism or internationalism?"], in *Ho Chi Minh Anh Hung Giai Phong Dan Toc Danh Nhan Van Hoa* [Ho Chi Minh, national liberator and cultural hero], 28–36. Hanoi: Nha Xuat Ban Khoa Hoc Xa Hoi, 1990.

Dorgelès, Roland. *On the Mandarin Road.* New York: Century, 1926.

Dower, John W. *War without Mercy: Race and Power in the Pacific War.* New York: Pantheon, 1986.

Drachman, Edward R. *United States Policy toward Vietnam, 1940–1945.* Rutherford, N.J.: Fairleigh Dickinson University Press, 1970.

Drake, Fred W. *China Charts the World: Hsü Chi-yü and His Geography of 1848.* Cambridge: Harvard University Press, 1975.

———. "A Nineteenth-Century View of the United States of America from Hsü Chi-yü's *Ying-huan chih-lüeh.*" *Papers on China* 19 (December 1965): 48–49.

Dreifort, John E. "Japan's Advance into Indochina, 1940: The French Response." *Journal of Southeast Asian Studies* 13, no. 2 (September 1982): 279–95.

Dreiser, Theodore. *Tragic America.* New York: Liveright, 1931.

Duara, Prasenjit. *Rescuing History from the Nation: Questioning Narratives of Modern China.* Chicago: University of Chicago Press, 1995.

Duiker, William J. *The Communist Road to Power in Vietnam.* Boulder, Colo.: Westview Press, 1981.

———. "Seeds of the Dragon: The Influence of the Maoist Model in Vietnam." In *Critical Perspectives on Mao Zedong's Thought,* edited by Arif Dirlik, Paul Healy, and Nick Knight, 313–41. Atlantic Highlands, N.J.: Humanities Press, 1997.

Dumoutier, Gustave. *Essais sur les Tonkinois.* Hanoi: Imprimerie d'Extrême-Orient, 1908.

Dunn, Peter M. *The First Vietnam War.* New York: St. Martin's Press, 1985.

Echeverria, Durand. *Mirage in the West: A History of the French Image of American Society to 1815.* Princeton: Princeton University Press, 1957.

———. "Roubaud and the Theory of American Degeneration." *French American Review* 3 (1950): 24–33.

Ely, Patrick. *The Adventures of Amos 'n' Andy: A Social History of an American Phenomenon.* New York: Free Press, 1991.

Emerson, Gertrude. "Backwaters of Empire in French Indo-China." *Asia* 23, no. 9 (September 1923): 670–74.

Emerson, Rupert. *Malaya: A Study in Direct and Indirect Rule.* New York: Macmillan, 1937.

Ennis, Thomas E. *French Policy and Developments in Indochina.* Chicago: University of Chicago Press, 1936.

Esherick, Joseph W., and Jeffrey N. Wasserstrom. "Acting Out Democracy: Political Theater in Modern China." *Journal of Asian Studies* 49, no. 4 (November 1980): 835–65.

Fabian, Johannes. *Time and the Other: How Anthropology Makes Its Object.* New York: Columbia University Press, 1983.

Fairbank, John King, ed. *The Chinese World Order: Traditional China's Foreign Relations.* Cambridge: Harvard University Press, 1968.

Fall, Bernard B. "Truong Chinh: Portrait of a Party Thinker." In *Primer for Revolt,* vii–xxii. New York: Praeger, 1963.

———. *The Viet-Minh Regime: Government and Administration in the Democratic Republic of Vietnam.* New York: Institute of Pacific Relations, 1956.

Farnsworth, Beatrice. *William C. Bullitt and the Soviet Union.* Bloomington: Indiana University Press, 1967.

Faulkner, William. *Doctor Martino and Other Stories.* New York: Harrison Smith and Robert Hass, 1934.

Fenn, Charles. *Ho Chi Minh: A Biographical Introduction.* New York: Charles Scribner's Sons, 1973.

Fifer, J. Valerie. *United States Perceptions of Latin America, 1850–1930: A "New West" South of Capricorn?* Manchester: Manchester University Press, 1991.

Fifield, Russell H. *Americans in Southeast Asia: The Roots of Commitment.* New York: Crowell, 1973.

————. *The Diplomacy of Southeast Asia, 1945–1958.* New York: Harper and Brothers, 1958.

Fineman, Daniel. *A Special Relationship: The United States and Military Government in Thailand, 1947–1958.* Honolulu: University of Hawaii Press, 1997.

Forbes, W. Cameron. *The Philippine Islands.* 2 vols. Boston: Houghton Mifflin, 1928.

Foster, Anne L. "Alienation and Cooperation: American, European, and Southeast Asian Perceptions of Anti-Colonial Rebellion, 1919–1937." Ph.D. diss., Cornell University, 1995.

————. " 'But We Didn't Know Much about You:' Images of French, Vietnamese, and Americans, 1919–1939." Unpublished paper in the possession of the author.

Foucault, Michel. *The Archaeology of Knowledge and the Discourse on Language.* New York: Pantheon, 1972.

————. *The Order of Things: An Archaeology of the Human Sciences.* New York: Vintage, 1994.

Frank, Henry A. *East of Siam: Ramblings in the Five Divisions of French Indo-China.* New York: Century, 1926.

Fredrickson, George M. *The Black Image in the White Mind: The Debate on Afro-American Character and Destiny, 1817–1914.* New York: Harper and Row, 1971.

————. "Colonialism and Racism: The United States and South Africa in Comparative Perspective." In *The Arrogance of Race: Historical Perspectives on Slavery, Racism, and Social Inequality.* Middletown, Conn.: Wesleyan University Press, 1988.

Friend, Theodore. *Between Two Empires: The Ordeal of the Philippines, 1929–1946.* New Haven: Yale University Press, 1965.

Furth, Charlotte. "Intellectual Change: From the Reform Movement to the May Fourth Movement, 1895–1920." In *The Cambridge History of China*, vol. 12, pt. 1, *Republican China, 1912–1949*, edited by John K. Fairbank, 332–405. Cambridge: Cambridge University Press, 1983.

Gaddis, John Lewis. *The Long Peace: Inquiries into the History of the Cold War.* New York: Oxford University Press, 1987.

————. *Strategies of Containment: A Critical Appraisal of Postwar American National Security Policy.* New York: Oxford University Press, 1982.

————. *We Now Know: Rethinking Cold War History.* New York: Oxford University Press, 1997.

Gagnon, Paul A. "French Views of Postwar America, 1919–1932." Ph.D. diss., Harvard University, 1960.

Gaiduk, Ilya V. *The Soviet Union and the Vietnam War*. Chicago: Ivan R. Dee, 1996.

Gallicchio, Marc S. *The Cold War Begins in Asia: American East Asian Policy and the Fall of the Japanese Empire*. New York: Columbia University Press, 1988.

Galloux-Fournier, Bernadette. "Un regard sur l'Amérique: voyageurs français aux Etats-Unis, 1919–1939." *Revue d'histoire moderne et contemporaine* 37 (April–June 1990): 297–307.

Gardner, Lloyd C. *Approaching Vietnam: From World War II through Dienbienphu, 1941–1954*. New York: Norton, 1988.

———. "From the Colorado to the Mekong." In *Vietnam: The Early Decisions*, edited by Lloyd C. Gardner and Ted Gittinger, 37–57. Austin: University of Texas Press, 1997.

———. *Pay Any Price: Lyndon Johnson and the Wars for Vietnam*. Chicago: Ivan R. Dee, 1995.

———. *Safe for Democracy: The Anglo-American Response to Revolution, 1913–1923*. New York: Oxford University Press, 1984.

Gardner, Mona. *Menacing Sun*. London: John Murray, 1939.

Garnier, Francis. *Voyages d'exploration en Indochine*. 2 vols. Paris: Hachette, 1873.

Garver, John W. *Chinese-Soviet Relations, 1937–1945: The Diplomacy of Chinese Nationalism*. New York: Oxford University Press, 1988.

Gasster, Michael. *Chinese Intellectuals and the Revolution of 1911*. Seattle: University of Washington Press, 1969.

Geertz, Clifford. *The Interpretation of Cultures*. New York: Basic Books, 1973.

Gerstle, Gary. "Liberty, Coercion, and the Making of Americans." *Journal of American History* 84, no. 2 (September 1997): 524–58.

Gidden, Anthony. *Central Problems in Social Theory*. Berkeley: University of California Press, 1979.

———. *The Consequences of Modernity*. Stanford: Stanford University Press, 1990.

Giran, Paul. *Psychologie du peuple Annamite*. Paris: Ernest Leroux, 1904.

Goodwin, Doris Kearns. *Lyndon Johnson and the American Dream*. New York: Harper and Row, 1976.

Goscha, Christopher E. "Annam and Vietnam in the New Indochinese Space, 1887–1945." In *Asian Forms of the Nation*, edited by Stein Tønnesson and Hans Antlov, 93–130. London: Curzon, 1996.

———. "Thailand and the Vietnamese Resistance against the French." M.A. thesis, Australian National University, 1991.

"The Great Learning." In *The Chinese Classics*, vol. 1, translated by James Legge, 355–81. 1893. Reprint, Hong Kong: Hong Kong University Press, 1960.

Greenblatt, Stephen. *Marvelous Possessions: The Wonder of the New World*. Chicago: University of Chicago Press, 1991.

Greene, Marc T. "Shadows over Indo-China." *Asia* 35, no. 11 (November 1935): 676–83.

Halberstam, David. *The Best and the Brightest*. New York: Random House, 1972.

Hammer, Ellen J. *The Struggle for Indochina*. Stanford: Stanford University Press, 1954.

Hampshire, Stuart. "Nationalism." In *Isaiah Berlin: A Celebration*, edited by Edna Margalit and Avishai Margalit, 127–34. London: Hogarth Press, 1991.

Harvey, David. *The Condition of Postmodernity*. Cambridge: Blackwell, 1990.

Hawkins, Mike. *Social Darwinism in European and American Thought, 1860–1945: Nature As Model and Nature As Threat.* Cambridge: Cambridge University Press, 1997.

Healy, David. *Drive to Hegemony: The United States in the Caribbean, 1898–1917.* Madison: University of Wisconsin Press, 1988.

———. *U.S. Expansionism: The Imperialist Urge in the 1890s.* Madison: University of Wisconsin Press, 1970.

Hébrard, Ernest. "L'Urbanisme en Indochine." In *L'Urbanisme aux colonies et dans les pays tropicaux,* edited by Jean Royer, 282–86. La Charité-sur-Loire: Delayance, 1932.

Heinrichs, Waldo. *Threshold of War: Franklin D. Roosevelt and American Entry into World War II.* New York: Oxford University Press, 1988.

Hémery, Daniel. "Du patriotisme au marxisme: l'immigration vietnamienne en France de 1926 à 1930." *Le Mouvement Social* 90 (January–March 1975): 3–54.

———. *Ho Chi Minh de l'Indochine au Vietnam.* Paris: Gallimard, 1990.

———. "Jeunesse d'un colonisé, genèse d'un exil: Ho Chi Minh jusqu'en 1911." *Approches-Asie* 4, no. 11 (1992): 83–157.

———. "Journalisme révolutionnaire et système de la presse au Vietnam dans les années 1930." *Les Cahiers du Cursa* 8 (1978): 55–85.

———. *Révolutionnaires Vietnamiens et pouvoir colonial en Endochine: communistes, trotskystes, nationalistes à Saigon de 1932 à 1937.* Paris: Maspéro, 1975.

Herring, George C. " 'Peoples Quite Apart': Americans, the South Vietnamese, and the War in Vietnam." *Diplomatic History* 14, no. 1 (Winter 1990): 1–23.

———. "The Truman Administration and the Restoration of French Sovereignty in Indochina." *Diplomatic History* 1, no. 2 (Spring 1977): 97–117.

Hervy, Henry. *King Cobra: An Autobiography of Travel in French Indo-China.* New York: Cosmopolitan, 1927.

Hess, Gary R. "Franklin Roosevelt and Indochina." *Journal of American History* 59, no. 2 (September 1972): 353–68.

———. *The United States' Emergence As a Southeast Asian Power, 1940–1950.* New York: Columbia University Press, 1987.

Heuser, Beatrice. *Western "Containment" Policies in the Cold War: The Yugoslav Case, 1948–53.* London: Routledge, 1989.

Hevia, James L. *Cherishing Men from Afar: Qing Guest Ritual and the Macartney Embassy of 1793.* Durham, N.C.: Duke University Press, 1995.

Higham, John. *Strangers in the Land: Patterns of American Nativism, 1860–1925.* 2d ed. New Brunswick, N.J.: Rutgers University Press, 1988.

Hoang Quang Khanh, Le Hong, and Hoang Ngoc La. *Can Cu Dia Viet Bac: Trong Cuoc Cach Mang Thang 8-1945* [The Viet Bac base area: In the August Revolution]. Hanoi: Nha Xuat Ban Viet Bac, 1976.

Hoang Trang. *Ho Chi Minh voi Trung Quoc* [Ho Chi Minh and China]. N.p.: Nha Xuat Ban Sao Moi, 1990.

Hoang Van Dao. *Viet Nam Quoc Dan Dang: Lich Su Dau Tranh Can Dai, 1927–1954* [The Vietnamese Nationalist Party: A history of modern struggle, 1927–1954]. Saigon: Nguyen Hoa Hiep, 1965.

Hofstader, Richard. *Social Darwinism in American Thought.* Philadelphia: University of Pennsylvania Press, 1944.

Hogan, Michael J. *The Marshall Plan: America, Britain, and the Reconstruction of Western Europe, 1947–1952.* Cambridge: Cambridge University Press, 1987.

Hoganson, Kristin L. *Fighting for American Manhood: How Gender Politics Provoked the Spanish-American and Philippine-American Wars.* New Haven: Yale University Press, 1998.

Hollinger, David A. *Postethnic America: Beyond Multiculturalism.* New York: Basic Books, 1995.

Holt, Thomas C. "Marking: Race, Race-making, and the Writing of History." *American Historical Review* 100, no. 1 (February 1995): 1–20.

Horne, Charles F., ed. *Great Men and Famous Women.* 4 vols. New York: Semlar Hess, 1894.

Horsman, Reginald. *Race and Manifest Destiny: The Origins of American Radical Anglo-Saxonism.* Cambridge: Harvard University Press, 1981.

Hsiao Kung-ch'üan. *A Modern China and a New World: K'ang Yu-wei, Reformer and Utopian, 1858–1927.* Seattle: University of Washington Press, 1975.

Hua, Lin. *Chiang Kai-sek, de Gaulle contre Hô Chi Minh: Viêt-nam 1945–46.* Paris: Éditions L'Harmattan, 1994.

Hue-Tam Ho Tai. *Radicalism and the Origins of the Vietnamese Revolution.* Cambridge: Harvard University Press, 1992.

Hung Vuong Dung Nuoc [The Hung kings found a nation]. Hanoi: Uy Ban Khoa Hoc Xa Hoi, 1973.

Hunt, Michael H. *The Genesis of Chinese Communist Foreign Policy.* New York: Columbia University Press, 1996.

———. *Ideology and U.S. Foreign Policy.* New Haven: Yale University Press, 1897.

———. *The Making of a Special Relationship: The United States and China to 1914.* New York: Columbia University Press, 1983.

———. "Pearl S. Buck: Popular Expert on China, 1931–1949." *Modern China* 3, no. 1 (January 1977): 33–64.

Huntington, Ellsworth. *The Character of Races.* New York: Charles Scribner's Sons, 1924.

———. *Civilization and Climate.* New Haven: Yale University Press, 1924.

Huynh Kim Khanh. *Vietnamese Communism, 1925–1945.* Ithaca: Cornell University Press, 1982.

Huynh Ly. "Ve quyen *Giai nhan ky ngo dien ca* cua Phan Chau Trinh" [On Phan Chau Trinh's *Rare Encounters with Beautiful Personages*]. *Tap Chi Van Hoc* [Literature magazine] 1 (1969): 71.

Huynh Sanh Thong, ed. and trans. *Heritage of Vietnamese Poetry.* New Haven: Yale University Press, 1979.

Huynh Van Tong. *Lich Su Bao Chi Viet-Nam tu Khoi Thuy den Nam 1930* [The history of the Vietnamese press from its origins to 1930]. Saigon: Tri Dang, 1973.

Hy V. Luong. *Revolution in the Village: Tradition and Transformation in North Vietnam, 1925–1988.* Honolulu: University of Hawaii Press, 1992.

Inden, Richard. *Imagining India*. London: Basil Blackwell, 1990.

"Interpreting the Declaration of Independence by Translation: A Round Table." *Journal of American History* 85, no. 4 (March 1999): 1279–1460.

Ireland, Alleyne. *The Far Eastern Tropics: Studies in the Administration of Tropical Dependencies*. New York: Houghton Mifflin, 1905.

———. *Tropical Colonization: An Introduction to the Study of the Subject*. New York: Macmillan, 1899.

Iriye, Akira. *Across the Pacific: An Inner History of American–East Asian Relations*. New York: Harcourt Brace Jovanovich, 1967.

———. *Pacific Estrangement: Japanese and American Expansion, 1897–1911*. Cambridge: Harvard University Press, 1972.

Irving, R. E. M. *The First Indochina War: French and American Policy, 1945–54*. London: Croom Helm, 1975.

Isaacs, Harold. *No Peace for Asia*. Cambridge: MIT Press, 1967.

———. *Scratches on Our Minds: American Views of China and India*. New York: Harper and Row, 1958.

Isoart, Paul. *Le phénomène national Viêtnamien de l'indépendance unitaire a l'indépendance fractionnée*. Paris: Librairie Générale Droit et de Jurisprudence, 1961.

Jamieson, Neil. *Understanding Vietnam*. Berkeley: University of California Press, 1993.

Jervis, Robert. *Perceptions and Misperceptions in International Politics*. Princeton: Princeton University Press, 1976.

Jesperson, T. Christopher. *American Images of China, 1931–1949*. Stanford: Stanford University Press, 1996.

Jian, Chen. "China and the First Indo-China War, 1950–1954." *China Quarterly*, no. 133 (March 1993): 85–110.

———. "China's Involvement in the Vietnam War, 1964–69." *China Quarterly*, no. 142 (June 1995): 380–87.

———. *China's Road to the Korean War: The Making of the Sino-American Confrontation*. New York: Columbia University Press, 1994.

Johnston, Alastair Iain. *Cultural Realism: Strategic Culture and Grand Strategy in Chinese History*. Princeton: Princeton University Press, 1995.

Jordan, Winthrop. *White over Black: American Attitudes toward the Negro, 1550–1812*. New York: Norton, 1968.

Jorgensen-Dahl, Arnfinn. *Regional Organization and Order in South-East Asia*. New York: St. Martin's Press, 1982.

Joyaux, François. *La Chine et le règlement du premier conflit d'Indochine genève 1954*. Paris: Publications de la Sorbonne, 1979.

Kaplan, Lawrence S., Denise Artaud, and Mark R. Rubin, eds. *Dien Bien Phu and the Crisis of Franco-American Relations, 1954–1955*. Wilmington: Scholarly Resources Books, 1990.

Karl, Rebecca E. "Creating Asia: China in the World at the Beginning of the Twentieth Century." *American Historical Review* 103, no. 4 (October 1988): 1096–1118.

Karnow, Stanley. *Vietnam: A History*. New York: Viking, 1983.

Katz, Barry M. *Foreign Intelligence: Research and Analysis in the Office of Strategic Service, 1942–1945*. Cambridge: Harvard University Press, 1989.

Katzenstein, Peter J., ed. *The Culture of National Security: Norms and Identity in World Politics.* New York: Columbia University Press, 1996.

Kazal, Russell A. "Revisiting Assimilation: The Rise, Fall, and Reappraisal of a Concept in American Ethnic History." *American Historical Review* 100, no. 2 (April 1995): 437–71.

Kelly, Gail P. "Franco-Vietnamese Schools, 1918–1938." Ph.D. diss., University of Wisconsin, 1974.

Khrushchev, Nikita. *Khrushchev Remembers: The Glasnost Tapes.* Translated and edited by Jerrold Schecter. Boston: Little, Brown, 1990.

Kidd, Benjamin. *The Control of the Tropics.* New York: Macmillan, 1898.

Kiernan, V. G. *The Lords of Human Kind: European Attitudes toward the Outside World in the Imperial Age.* London: Weidenfeld and Nicholson, 1969.

Kimball, Warren F. *The Juggler: Franklin Roosevelt As Wartime Statesman.* Princeton: Princeton University Press, 1991.

Kirk, Grayson L. *Philippine Independence.* New York: Farrar and Rinehart, 1936.

Knight, Melvin M. *Morocco As a French Economic Venture: A Study of Open Door Imperialism.* New York: Appleton-Century, 1937.

Kuisel, Richard F. *Seducing the French: The Dilemma of Americanization.* Berkeley: University of California Press, 1993.

Kurihara, Hirohide. "Changes in the Literary Policy of the Vietnamese Workers' Party, 1956–1958." In *Indochina in the 1940s and 1950s,* edited by Takashi Shiraishi and Motoo Furuta, 165–96. Ithaca: Cornell University Southeast Asia Program, 1992.

Lacouture, Jean. *Ho Chi Minh: A Political Biography.* New York: Vintage, 1968.

LaFeber, Walter. "Roosevelt, Churchill, and Indochina, 1942–45." *American Historical Review* 80, no. 5 (December 1975): 1277–95.

Landon, Kenneth P. *The Chinese in Thailand.* London: Oxford University Press, 1941.

———. *Siam in Transition: A Brief Survey of Cultural Trends in the Five Year Revolution of 1932.* London: Oxford University Press, 1939.

Landon, Margaret. *Anna and the King.* London: George C. Harrup, 1952.

Lasch, Christopher. "The Anti-Imperialists, the Philippines, and the Inequality of Man." *Journal of Southern History* 24, no. 3 (August 1958): 319–31.

Latham, Michael E. "Ideology, Social Science, and Destiny: Modernization and the Kennedy-Era Alliance for Progress." *Diplomatic History* 22, no. 3 (Spring 1998): 199–229.

Latham, Robert. *The Liberal Moment: Modernity, Security, and the Making of Postwar International Order.* New York: Columbia University Press, 1977.

Leahy, William D. *I Was There: The Personal Study of the Chief of Staff to Presidents Roosevelt and Truman Based on His Notes and Diaries Made at the Time.* New York: Whittlesey House, 1950.

Leffler, Melvyn P. *The Elusive Quest: America's Pursuit of European Stability and French Security, 1919–1933.* Chapel Hill: University of North Carolina Press, 1979.

———. "Inside Enemy Archives: The Cold War Reopened." *Foreign Affairs* 75, no. 4 (July/August 1996): 120–34.

———. *A Preponderance of Power: National Security, the Truman Administration, and the Cold War.* Stanford: Stanford University Press, 1992.

Le Thanh. *Cuoc Phong Van Cac Nha Van* [Interviews with writers]. Hanoi: Nha Xuat Ban Doi Moi, n.d.

Levenson, Joseph R. *Liang Ch'i-Ch'ao and the Mind of Modern China*. Berkeley: University of California Press, 1970.

Levine, Marilyn A. *The Found Generation: Chinese Communists in Europe during the Twenties*. Seattle: University of Washington Press, 1993.

Lind, Michael. *The Next American Nation: The New Nationalism and the Fourth American Revolution*. New York: Free Press, 1995.

Lipscomb, Elizabeth J., Frances E. Webb, and Peter Conn, eds. *The Several Worlds of Pearl S. Buck*. Westport, Conn.: Greenwood Press, 1994.

Liu, Lydia H. *Translingual Practice: Literature, National Culture, and Translated Modernity: China, 1900–1937*. Stanford: Stanford University Press, 1995.

Ljunggren, Börje, ed. *The Challenge of Reform in Indochina*. Cambridge: Harvard Institute for International Development, 1993.

Lo, Jung-Pang, ed. *K'ang Yu-wei: A Biography and a Symposium*. Tucson: University of Arizona Press, 1967.

Lockhart, Greg. *Nation in Arms: The Origins of the People's Army of Vietnam*. Sydney: Allen and Unwin, 1989.

Lockhart, Greg, and Monique Lockhart, trans. *The Light of the Capital: Three Modern Vietnamese Classics*. Kuala Lumpur: Oxford University Press, 1996.

Louis, Wm. Roger. *Imperialism at Bay: The United States and the Decolonization of the British Empire, 1941–1945*. Oxford: Oxford University Press, 1977.

Luro, Eliacin. *Le pays d'Annam*. Paris: Ernest Leroux, 1897.

McAlister, John T., Jr. *Viet Nam: The Origins of the Revolution*. New York: Knopf, 1969.

McCullough, David. *Truman*. New York: Simon and Schuster, 1992.

MacDonald, Alexander. *Bangkok Editor*. New York: Macmillan, 1949.

McHale, Shawn Frederick. "Printing, Power, and the Transformation of Vietnamese Culture, 1920–1945." Ph.D. diss., Cornell University, 1995.

McLane, Charles B. *Soviet Strategies in Southeast Asia*. Princeton: Princeton University Press, 1966.

MacLeish, Archibald. *Land of the Free*. New York: Harcourt, Brace, 1938.

McMahon, Robert J. *Colonialism and Cold War: The United States and the Struggle for Indonesian Independence, 1945–49*. Ithaca: Cornell University Press, 1981.

———. *The Limits of Empire: The United States and Southeast Asia since World War II*. New York: Columbia University Press, 1999.

Madrolle, Claudius. *Indochina: Cochinchina, Cambodia, Annam, Tonkin, Yunnan, Laos, Siam*. Paris: Librairie Hachette, 1930.

Maier, Charles S. "The Two Postwar Eras and the Conditions for Stability in Twentieth-Century Western Europe." *American Historical Review* 86, no. 2 (April 1981): 327–52.

Malleret, Louis. *L'Exotisme indochinois dans la littérature français depuis 1860*. Paris: Larose, 1934.

Mao Tse-Tung. *Basic Tactics*. Translated by Stuart R. Schram. New York: Praeger, 1966.

———. *On Guerilla Warfare*. Translated by Samuel B. Griffith. New York: Praeger, 1961.

————. *Selected Works.* Vol. 2. Peking: Foreign Languages Press, 1965.

Marr, David G. "Vietnam: Harnessing the Whirlwind." In *Asia: The Winning of Independence,* edited by Robin Jeffrey, 163–207. New York: St. Martin's Press, 1981.

————. *Vietnam 1945: The Quest for Power.* Berkeley: University of California Press, 1995.

————. *Vietnamese Anticolonialism, 1885–1925.* Berkeley: University of California Press, 1971.

————. *Vietnamese Tradition on Trial, 1920–1945.* Berkeley: University of California Press, 1981.

————, ed. *Reflections from Captivity.* Athens: Ohio State University Press, 1978.

Marshall, Jonathan. *To Have and Have Not: Southeast Asian Raw Materials and the Origins of the Pacific War.* Berkeley: University of California Press, 1995.

Masson, Andre. *Hanoi pendant la périod héroïque, 1873–1888.* Paris: Librairie Orientaliste Paul Geuthner, 1929.

Mastny, Vojtech. *The Cold War and Soviet Insecurity: The Stalin Years.* New York: Oxford University Press, 1996.

May, Ernest R. *The Truman Administration and China, 1945–1949.* Philadelphia: Lippincott, 1975.

May, Glenn A. *Social Engineering in the Philippines: The Aims, Execution, and Impact of American Colonial Policy, 1900–1913.* Westport, Conn.: Greenwood Press, 1980.

Miller, Robert Hopkins. *The United States and Vietnam, 1787–1941.* Washington, D.C.: National Defense University Press, 1990.

Miller, Stuart Creighton. *"Benevolent Assimilation": The American Conquest of the Philippines, 1899–1903.* New Haven: Yale University Press, 1982.

Milward, Alan S. *The Reconstruction of Western Europe, 1945–51.* Berkeley: University of California Press, 1984.

Mink, Gwendolyn. *Wages of Motherhood: Inequality in the Welfare State, 1917–1942.* Ithaca: Cornell University Press, 1995.

Moise, Edwin. "Land Reform and Land Reform Errors in North Vietnam." *Pacific Affairs* 49, no. 1 (Spring 1976): 70–92.

Moore, W. Robert. "Along the Old Mandarin Road of Indo-China." *National Geographic,* August 1931, 157–99.

Mordal, Jacques. *Marine Indochine.* Paris: Amiot-Dumont, 1953.

Morgan, Joseph G. *The Vietnam Lobby: The American Friends of Vietnam, 1955–1975.* Chapel Hill: University of North Carolina Press, 1997.

Morley, James William, ed. *The Fateful Choice: Japan's Advance into Southeast Asia, 1939–1941.* New York: Columbia University Press, 1980.

Mosse, George. *Nationalism and Sexuality.* Madison: University of Wisconsin Press, 1985.

Mus, Paul. *Le Viêt-Nam chez lui.* Paris: Éditions l'Harmattan, 1946.

————. *Viêt-Nam sociologie d'une guerre.* Paris: Éditions du Seuil, 1952.

Nathanson, Nicholas. *The Black Image in the New Deal: The Politics of FSA Photography.* Knoxville: University of Tennessee Press, 1992.

Ngai, Mae N. "The Architecture of Race in American Immigration Law:

A Reexamination of the Immigration Act of 1924." *Journal of American History* 86, no. 1 (June 1999): 67–92.

Nguyen Duy Thanh. *My Four Years with the Viet-Minh*. Bombay: Democratic Research Service, 1950.

Nguyen Huy Thiep. *Nhung Ngon Gio Hua Tat* [The breezes of Hua Tat]. Hanoi: Nha Xuat Ban Van Hoa, 1989.

Nguyen Khach Vien and Huu Ngoc, eds. *Vietnamese Literature*. Hanoi: Foreign Languages Publishing House, n.d.

Nguyen Thanh. *Bao Chi Cach Mang Viet Nam, 1925–1945* [The revolutionary press in Vietnam, 1925–1945]. Hanoi: Nha Xuat Ban Khoa Hoc Xa Hoi, 1984.

Nguyen Trong Hau. "Van De Tim Ban Dong Minh Xa Qua Bao *Viet Nam Doc Lap*, 1941–1945" [On the issue of friendship with the allies in *Vietnamese Independence*, 1941–1945]. Unpublished manuscript in author's possession.

Nguyen Van Uan, *Hanoi Nua Dau The Ky XX, Tap 1* [Hanoi in the first half of the twentieth century, vol. 1]. Hanoi: Nha Xuat Ban Hanoi, 1994.

Ninkovich, Frank. *Modernity and Power: A History of the Domino Theory in the Twentieth Century*. Chicago: University of Chicago Press, 1994.

Norindr, Panivong. *Phantasmatic Indochina: French Colonial Ideology in Architecture, Film, and Literature*. Durham, N.C.: Duke University Press, 1996.

Novick, Peter. *That Noble Dream: The "Objectivity Question" and the American Historical Profession*. Cambridge: Cambridge University Press, 1988.

Olsen, Mari. *Solidarity and National Revolution: The Soviet Union and the Vietnamese Communists, 1954–1960*. Oslo: Norwegian Institute for Defence Studies, 1997.

O'Neill, Robert J. *General Giap: Politician and Strategist*. Melbourne: Cassell Australia, 1969.

Orwell, George. *The Road to Wigan Pier*. London: Victor Gollancz, 1937.

Pagden, Anthony. *The Fall of Natural Man: The American Indian and the Origins of Comparative Ethnology*. Cambridge: Cambridge University Press, 1982.

———. *Spanish Imperialism and the Political Imagination*. New Haven: Yale University Press, 1990.

Papanek, Hanna. "Note on Soedjatmoko's Recollection of a Historical Moment: Sjahrir's Reaction to Ho Chi Minh's 1945 Call for a Free People's Federation." *Indonesia*, no. 44 (April 1990): 141–44.

Patti, Archimedes. *Why Viet Nam? Prelude to America's Albatross*. Berkeley: University of California Press, 1980.

Peace, Roy Harvey. *Savagism and Civilization: A Study of the Indian and American Mind*. 1953. Reprint, Berkeley: University of California Press, 1988.

Pham The Ngu. *Viet Nam Van Hoc Su Gian Uoc Tan Bien, Tap 3, Van Hoc Hien Dai, 1862–1945* [A new outline history of Vietnamese literature, vol. 3, Contemporary literature, 1862–1945]. Saigon: Nha Xuat Ban Anh Phuong, 1965.

Pike, Douglas. *History of Vietnamese Communism, 1925–1976*. Stanford: Hoover Institution Press, 1978.

Pike, Frederick B. *The United States and Latin America: Myths and Stereotypes of Civilization and Nature*. Austin: University of Texas Press, 1992.

Polanyi, Karl. *The Great Transformation*. Boston: Beacon Press, 1943.

Porter, Gareth. *Vietnam: The Politics of Bureaucratic Socialism.* Ithaca: Cornell University Press, 1993.

Portes, Jacques. *Une fascination réticente: Les Etats-Unis dans l'opinion française, 1870–1917.* Nancy: Presses universitaires de Nancy, 1990.

Prakash, Gyan, ed. *After Colonialism: Imperial Histories and Post Colonial Displacements.* Princeton: Princeton: University Press, 1995.

———. "Writing Post-Orientalist Histories of the Third World: Perspectives from Indian Historiography." *Comparative Studies in Society and History* 32, no. 2 (April 1990): 383–408.

Priestley, J. B. *English Journey.* London: W. Heinemann, 1934.

Priestly, Herbert Ingram. *France Overseas: A Study of Modern Imperialism.* New York: Appleton-Century, 1938.

Prochaska, David. "Between *Algérie Française* and *Algérie Algérienne.*" In *Crossing Cultures: Essays in the Displacement of Western Civilization,* edited by Daniel Segal, 182–225. Tucson: University of Arizona Press, 1992.

Proschan, Frank. "Eunuch Mandarins, Effeminate 'Boys,' and '*Soldats Mamzelles*': The Annamite As Androgyne." Paper delivered at the Association for Asian Studies Forty-ninth Annual Meeting, Chicago, Illinois, March 1996.

Quang, Gérard Le. *Giap ou la guerre du peuple.* Paris: Éditions Denoël, 1973.

Quinn-Judge, Sophie. "Ho Chi Minh: New Perspectives from the Comintern Files." *Viet Nam Forum,* no. 14 (1994): 61–81.

Rabinow, Paul. *French Modernism: Norms and Forms of the Social Environment.* Chicago: University of Chicago Press, 1989.

Rafael, Vincente L. "White Love: Surveillance and Nationalist Resistance in the U.S. Colonization of the Philippines." In *Cultures of United States Imperialism,* edited by Amy Kaplan and Donald E. Pease, 185–218. Durham, N.C.: Duke University Press, 1993.

Remme, Tilman. "Britain, the 1947 Asian Relations Conference, and Regional Co-operation in South-East Asia." In *Post-War Britain, 1945–64,* edited by Anthony Gorst, Lewis Johnmann, and W. Scott Lucas, 109–34. London: Pinter, 1989.

Robequain, Charles. *The Economic Development of French Indo-China.* London: Oxford University Press, 1944.

Robinson, Ronald. "Non-European Foundations of European Imperialism: Sketch for a Theory of Collaboration." In *Studies in the Theory of Imperialism,* edited by Roger Own and Bob Sutcliffe, 117–40. London: Longman Group, 1972.

Rodgers, Daniel T. "Exceptionalism." In *Imagined Histories: American Historians Interpret the Past,* edited by Anthony Molho and Gordon S. Wood, 21–40. Princeton: Princeton University Press, 1998.

Rogers, John D. "Colonial Perceptions of Ethnicity and Culture in Early Nineteenth-Century Sri Lanka." In *Society and Ideology: Essays in South Asian History,* edited by Peter Robb, 97–109. Delhi: Oxford University Press, 1993.

———. "Historical Images in the British Period." In *Sri Lanka: History and the Roots of Conflict,* edited by Jonathan Spencer, 87–106. London: Routledge, 1990.

Rollet de l'Isle, Charles D. M. *Au Tonkin et dans les mers de Chine: souvenirs et croquis, 1883–1885.* Paris: Plon, 1886.

Roosevelt, Elliott. *As He Saw It.* New York: Duell, Sloan and Pearce, 1946.

Roosevelt, Nicholas. *The Philippines.* New York: J. H. Sears, 1926.

Roosevelt, Theodore. *Colonial Policies of the United States.* Garden City, N.Y.: Doubleday, Doran, 1937.

Rostow, W. W. *The Stages of Economic Growth: A Non-Communist Manifesto.* Cambridge: Cambridge University Press, 1960.

Rotter, Andrew J. "Gender Relations, Foreign Relations: The United States and South Asia, 1947–1964." *Journal of American History* 81, no. 2 (September 1994): 518–42.

———. *The Path to Vietnam: Origins of the American Commitment to Southeast Asia.* Ithaca: Cornell University Press, 1987.

Ruscio, Alain. *Les communistes français et la guerre d'Indochine, 1944–1954.* Paris: Éditions l'Harmattan, 1985.

Rydell, Robert W. *All the World's a Fair.* Chicago: University of Chicago Press, 1984.

Sabattier, Général. *Le destin de l'Indochine: souvenirs et documents.* Paris: Plon, 1952.

Said, Edward W. *Culture and Imperialism.* New York: Knopf, 1993.

———. *Orientalism.* New York: Vintage, 1979.

Sainteny, Jean. *Histoire d'une paix manquée.* Paris: Fayard, 1967.

Salman, Michael. "The United States and the End of Slavery in the Philippines, 1898–1914: A Study of Imperialism, Ideology, and Nationalism." Ph.D. diss., Stanford University, 1993.

Sánchez, George. *Becoming Mexican-American: Ethnicity, Culture, and Identity in Los Angeles, 1900–1945.* New York: Oxford University Press, 1993.

Schaller, Michael. *The Origins of the Cold War in Asia: The American Occupation of Japan.* New York: Oxford University Press, 1985.

———. *The U.S. Crusade in China, 1938–1945.* New York: Columbia University Press, 1979.

Schram, Stuart. *The Thought of Mao Tse-Tung.* Cambridge: Cambridge University Press, 1989.

Schreiner, Alfred. *Les institutions Annamites en Basse-Cochinchine avant la conquête Française.* 3 vols. Saigon: Claude, 1900.

Schwartz, Benjamin. *In Search of Wealth and Power: Yen Fu and the West.* Cambridge: Harvard University Press, 1964.

Scott, William. *Documentary Expression and the Thirties America.* New York: Oxford University Press, 1973.

Semmel, Bernard. *Imperialism and Social Reform: English Social-Imperial Thought, 1895–1914.* London: Allen and Unwin, 1960.

Seton-Watson, Hugh. *From Lenin to Khrushchev: The History of World Communism.* New York: Praeger, 1960.

Shao, Kuo-khang. "Zhou Enlai's Diplomacy and the Neutralization of Indo-China, 1954–55." *China Quarterly*, no. 107 (September 1986): 483–504.

Shapiro, Herbert. *White Violence and Black Response: From Reconstruction to Montgomery.* Amherst: University of Massachusetts Press, 1988.

Shaplen, Robert. *The Lost Revolution.* New York: Harper and Row, 1965.

Shaw, Yu-ming. *An American Missionary in China: John Leighton Stuart and Chinese-American Relations.* Cambridge: Harvard University Press, 1992.

Shenton, James P. "Imperialism and Racism." In *Essays in American Historiography*, edited by Donald Sheehan and Harold C. Syrett, 231–50. New York: Columbia University Press, 1960.

Shewmaker, Kenneth E. *American and Chinese Communists, 1927–1945: A Persuading Encounter*. Ithaca: Cornell University Press, 1971.

Silvestre, J. *L'empire d'Annam et le peuple Annam*. Paris: Félix Alcan, 1889.

Smith, Tony. *America's Mission: The United States and the Worldwide Struggle for Democracy in the Twentieth Century*. Princeton: Princeton University Press, 1994.

Spector, Ronald H. *Advice and Support: The Early Years of the U.S. Army in Vietnam, 1941–1960*. New York: Free Press, 1985.

———. "European Colonization and American Attitudes toward Southeast Asia, 1919–1941." *Proceedings of the Seventh International Association of Historians of Asia Conference*, vol. 1. Bangkok: International Association of Historians of Asia, 1978.

Spence, Jonathan D. *The Gate of Heavenly Peace: The Chinese and Their Revolution, 1895–1980*. New York: Penguin, 1981.

Stanley, Peter W. *A Nation in the Making: The Philippines and the United States, 1899–1921*. Cambridge: Harvard University Press, 1974.

Starr, John Bryan. *Continuing the Revolution: The Political Thought of Mao*. Princeton: Princeton University Press, 1979.

Steep, Thomas. "French Oppression in Indo-China." *American Mercury* 32, no. 127 (July 1934): 330.

Stephanson, Anders. *Kennan and the Art of Foreign Policy*. Cambridge: Cambridge University Press, 1989.

Stettinius, Edward R., Jr. *Roosevelt and the Russians: The Yalta Conference*. Garden City, N.Y.: Doubleday, 1949.

Stocking, George W., Jr. *Race, Culture, and Evolution: Essays in the History of Anthropology*. Chicago: University of Chicago Press, 1982.

———. *Victorian Anthropology*. New York: Free Press, 1987.

Stoler, Ann L. "Making Empire Respectable: The Politics of Race and Sexual Morality in Twentieth-Century Colonial Cultures." *American Ethnologist* 16, no. 4 (November 1989): 634–60.

———. "Sexual Affronts and Racial Frontiers: National Identity, 'Mixed Bloods,' and the Cultural Genealogies of Europeans in Colonial Southeast Asia." *Comparative Studies in Society and History* 34, no. 3 (July 1992): 514–51.

Strobel, Margaret. "Gender and Race in the Nineteenth and Twentieth Century British Empire." In *Becoming Visible: Women in European History*, edited by Renate Bridenthal and Claudia Koonz, 375–96. Boston: Houghton Mifflin, 1987.

Susman, Warren. *Culture As Social History: The Transformation of American Society in the Twentieth Century*. New York: Pantheon, 1984.

Swisher, Earl. *China's Management of the American Barbarians: A Study of Sino-American Relations, 1841–1861, with Documents*. New Haven: Far Eastern Publications, 1953.

"Symposium: Rethinking the Lost Chance in China." *Diplomatic History* 21, no. 1 (Winter 1997): 71–115.

"Symposium: Soviet Archives: Recent Revelations and Cold War Historiography." *Diplomatic History* 21, no. 2 (Spring 1997): 215–305.

Tanaka, Stefan. *Japan's Orient: Rendering Pasts into History.* Berkeley: University of California Press, 1993.

Tang, Xiaobing. *Global Space and the Nationalist Discourse of Modernity: The Historical Thinking of Liang Qichao.* Stanford: Stanford University Press, 1996.

Tarling, Nicholas. *Britain, Southeast Asia, and the Onset of the Pacific War.* Cambridge: Cambridge University Press, 1996.

———. "The British and the First Japanese Move into Indo-China." *Journal of Southeast Asian Studies* 21, no. 1 (March 1990): 35–65.

Taussig, Michael. *Mimesis and Alterity: A Particular History of the Senses.* New York: Routledge, 1993.

Taylor, Charles. *The Sources of the Self: The Making of Modern Identity.* Cambridge: Harvard University Press, 1989.

Taylor, Keith. *The Birth of Vietnam.* Berkeley: University of California Press, 1983.

———. "China and Vietnam: Looking for a New Version of an Old Relationship." In *The Vietnam War: Vietnamese and American Perspectives,* edited by Jayne S. Werner and Luu Doan Huynh, 271–85. Armonk, N.Y.: M. E. Sharpe, 1993.

———. "Surface Orientations in Vietnam: Beyond Histories of the Nation and Region." *Journal of Asian Studies* 59, no. 4 (November 1998): 949–78.

Taylor, Robert. *The State in Burma.* Honolulu: University of Hawaii Press, 1987.

Thomas, Franklin. *The Environmental Basis of Society.* New York: Century, 1925.

Thompson, Virginia. *French Indo-China.* New York: Macmillan, 1937.

———. *Thailand: The New Siam.* New York: Macmillan, 1941.

Thompson, Virginia, and Richard Adloff. *The Left Wing in Southeast Asia.* New York: William Sloane Associates, 1950.

Thorne, Christopher. *Allies of a Kind: The United States, Britain, and the War against Japan, 1941–1945.* New York: Oxford University Press, 1978.

———. "Indochina and Anglo-American Relations, 1942–1945." *Pacific Historical Review* 45, no. 1 (February 1976): 73–96.

Timperley, H. J. *Japanese Terror in China.* New York: Modern Age Books, 1938.

———. *What War Means: The Japanese Terror in China, a Documentary Record.* London: Victor Gollancz, 1938.

Tinh Tien. *Van Minh Au My* [European and American civilization]. Hue: Tieng-Dan, 1928.

Tønnesson, Stein. *1946: Déclenchement de la guerre d'Indochine: les vêpres tonkinoises du 19 décembre.* Paris: L'Harmattan, 1987.

———. *The Vietnamese Revolution of 1945: Roosevelt, Ho Chi Minh, and de Gaulle in a World at War.* London: Sage, 1991.

Ton That Thien. *The Foreign Politics of the Communist Party of Vietnam: A Study in Communist Tactics.* New York: Crane Russak, 1989.

———. *India and South East Asia, 1947–1960.* Geneva: Librairie Droz, 1963.

Trachtenberg, Marvin. *The Statue of Liberty.* New York: Penguin, 1976.

Tran Huy Quang. "The Prophecy" ["Linh Nghiem"]. Trans. Sherée Carey. *Viet Nam Forum,* no. 14 (1994): 55–60.

Tran Van Giau. *Giai Cap Cong Nhan Viet Nam: Tu Dang Cong San Thanh Lap Den Cach Mang Thanh Cong, Tap 3, 1936–45* [The Vietnamese working class: From the formation of the Communist Party until the success of the revolution, vol. 3, 1936–45]. Hanoi: Vien Su Hoc, 1963.

———. *Su Phat Trien Cua Tu Tuong o Viet Nam tu The Ky XIX den Chach Mang Thang Tam, Tap II* [The development of ideas in Vietnam from the nineteenth century to the August Revolution, vol. 2]. Hanoi: Nha Xuat Ban Khoa Hoc, 1975.

Trinh Van Tao. *Vietnam du confucianisme au communisme*. Paris: L'Harmattan, 1990.

Truman, Harry S. *Memoirs*. Vol. 1, *Year of Decisions*. Garden City, N.Y.: Doubleday, 1955.

Truong Buu Lam. "Intervention versus Tribute in Sino-Vietnamese Relations, 1788–1790." In *The Chinese World Order: Traditional China's Foreign Relations*, edited by John King Fairbank, 165–79. Cambridge: Harvard University Press, 1968.

Tsing-yuan, Tsao. "The Birth of the Goddess of Democracy." In *Popular Protest and Political Culture in Modern China*, edited by Jeffrey N. Wasserstrom and Elizabeth Perry, 140–47. Boulder, Colo.: Westview Press, 1994.

Tucker, Nancy Bernkopf. *Patterns in the Dust: Chinese-American Relations and the Recognition Controversy, 1949–50*. New York: Columbia University Press, 1983.

Turley, William S., and Mark Selden, eds. *Reinventing Vietnamese Socialism*. Boulder, Colo.: Westview Press, 1993.

U.S. Department of State. *Postwar Foreign Policy Preparation, 1939–1945*. Washington, D.C.: Government Printing Office, 1949.

———. Division of Research for Far East. Office of Intelligence Research. *Political Alignments of Vietnamese Nationalists*. OIR Report No. 3708. October 1949.

Utley, Robert N. *The Indian Frontier of the American West, 1846–1890*. Albuquerque: University of New Mexico Press, 1984.

Vandenbosch, Amry. *The Dutch East Indies: Its Government, Problems, and Politics*. Grand Rapids, Mich.: Eerdmans, 1933.

Van Evera, Stephen. "Why Europe Matters, Why the Third World Doesn't: America's Grand Strategy after the Cold War." *Journal of Strategic Studies* 13, no. 2 (June 1990): 1–51.

Vickerman, Andrew. *The Fate of the Peasantry: Premature 'Transition to Socialism' in the Democratic Republic of Vietnam*. Yale University Southeast Asian Studies Monograph Series No. 28. New Haven: Yale Center for International and Asian Studies, 1986.

Vinh Sinh. " 'Elegant Females' Re-Encountered: From Tôkai Sanshi's *Kajin No Kigû* to Phan Chau Trinh's *Giai Nhan Ky Ngo Dien Ca*." In *Essays into Vietnamese Pasts*, edited by K. W. Taylor and John W. Whitmore, 195–206. Ithaca: Cornell University Southeast Asia Program, 1995.

Von Eschen, Penny M. *Race against Empire: Black Americans and Anticolonialism, 1937–1957*. Ithaca: Cornell University Press, 1997.

Vuong Tri Nhan, ed. *Phan Boi Chau and the Dong-Du Movement*. New Haven: Yale Southeast Asia Studies, 1988.

———, comp. and ed. *Tam Lang, Trong Lang, Hoang Dao: Phong su chon loc* [Tam Lang, Trong Lang, Hoang Dao: Selected reportage]. Hanoi: Hoi Nha Van, 1995.

Wall, Irwin M. *The United States and the Making of Postwar France, 1945–1954.* Cambridge: Cambridge University Press, 1991.

Ward, Geoffrey. *A First-Class Temperament: The Emergence of Franklin Roosevelt.* New York: Harper and Row, 1989.

Ward, Robert DeC. "The Literature of Climatology." *Annals of the Association of American Geographers,* March 1931, 34–51.

Watt, D. Cameron. "Britain, America, and Indo-China, 1942–1945." In *Succeeding John Bull: America in Britain's Place, 1900–1975,* 194–219. Cambridge: Cambridge University Press, 1984.

Weiss, Richard. "Ethnicity and Reform: Minorities and the Ambience of the Depression Years." *Journal of American History* 66, no. 3 (December 1979): 566–85.

Westad, Odd Arne. *Cold War and Revolution: Soviet-American Rivalry and the Origins of the Chinese Civil War, 1944–1946.* New York: Columbia University Press, 1993.

Westad, Odd Arne, et al., eds. *Seventy-seven Conversations between Chinese and Foreign Leaders on the Wars in Indochina, 1964–1977.* Cold War International History Working Paper No. 22. Washington, D.C.: Woodrow Wilson International Center for Scholars, 1998.

Westervelt, Josephine Hope. *The Green Gods.* New York: Christian Alliance, 1927.

Whitmore, John K. *Vietnam, Ho Quy Ly, and the Ming, 1371–1421.* New Haven: Yale Center for Southeast Asian Studies, 1985.

Williams, Raymond. *Keywords: A Vocabulary of Culture and Society.* New York: Oxford University Press, 1976.

Williams, Walter L. "U.S. Indian Policy and the Debate over Philippine Annexation." *Journal of American History* 66, no. 4 (March 1980): 810–31.

Wilson, Edmund. *American Jitters: A Year of the Slump.* New York: Charles Scribner's Sons, 1932.

Wolfe, Patrick. "Imperialism and History: A Century of Theory, from Marx to Postcolonialism." *American Historical Review* 102, no. 2 (April 1997): 388–420.

Woodside, Alexander B. *Community and Revolution in Modern Vietnam.* Boston: Houghton Mifflin, 1976.

————. *Vietnam and the Chinese Model: A Comparative Study of Vietnamese and Chinese Government in the First Half of the Nineteenth Century.* Cambridge: Harvard University Press, 1971.

Woodward, C. Vann. *The Strange Career of Jim Crow.* New York: Oxford University Press, 1974.

Woodworth, Stanley D. *William Faulkner en France, 1931–1952.* Paris: M. J. Minard, 1959.

Wright, Gwendolyn. *The Politics of Design in French Colonial Urbanism.* Chicago: University of Chicago Press, 1991.

Yong, C. F. "Origins and Development of the Malayan Communist Movement, 1919–1930." *Modern Asian Studies* 25, no. 4 (1991): 625–48.

Young, John W. *France, the Cold War, and the Western Alliance, 1944–49: French Foreign Policy and Post-War Europe.* Leicester: Leicester University Press, 1990.

Zhai, Qiang. "China and the Geneva Conference of 1954." *China Quarterly,* no. 129 (March 1992): 103–22.

———. *China and the Vietnam Wars, 1950–1975.* Chapel Hill: University of North Carolina Press, 2000.

———. "Transplanting the Chinese Model: Chinese Military Advisers and the First Vietnam War, 1950–1954." *Journal of Military History* 57, no. 4 (October 1993): 689–715.

Zhang, Shu Guang. *Mao's Military Romanticism: China and the Korean War, 1950–53.* Lawrence: University of Kansas Press, 1995.

Zubok, Vladislaw, and Constantine Pleshakov. *Inside the Kremlin's Cold War: From Stalin to Khrushchev.* Cambridge: Harvard University Press, 1996.

INDEX

Kai-shek regime; Democratic Republic of Vietnam: relations of with Chinese communists; Democratic Republic of Vietnam: relations of with People's Republic of China; Ho Chi Minh: relations of with Chiang Kai-shek regime; Ho Chi Minh: relations of with Chinese communists; Indochinese Communist Party: impact of Maoist thought on; Indochinese Communist Party: relations of with Chiang Kai-shek regime; Mao Tse-tung; Vietnamese Reform Movement: Sinic influences on

Chou En-lai, 41, 183

Christian and Missionary Alliance, 45, 50

Christopher, Warren, 188, 189

Churchill, Winston, 81, 103

Clinton administration, 188

Cold War: in Vietnam, 6–7, 177–78, 179, 183; historiography, 6–9, 173–75, 187, 195 (n. 7), 196 (n. 9); end of, 187, 188

Collins, J. Lawton, 186

Comintern, 37, 109

Con Son (Poulo Condore), 16, 39

Coolidge, Harold J., Jr., 48–49

Dao Duy Anh, 27, 116, 204 (n. 53); *European and American Civilization [Van Minh Au My]*, 27–29

Davis, Dwight F., 66

Decolonization, 7–8, 105–6

Deer team. *See* Office of Strategic Services: "Deer" team

De Gaulle, Charles, 102

Democratic Party (Dan Chu Dang), 154

Democratic Republic of Vietnam (DRV): perceptions of U.S. by, 107–8, 128, 175, 176, 189; diplomacy with U.S. of, 126–33, 146, 149–51, 170, 171, 189; diplomacy in southern Vietnam of, 127–28, 129–30; relations of with Chinese communists, 129, 147, 148, 176, 180, 181; relations of with Soviet Union, 129, 147, 148–49, 176, 177, 180, 181, 183; relations of with Chiang Kai-shek regime, 129, 147,

157, 160–61, 166; diplomacy in South and Southeast Asia of, 129, 151–60, 157, 158, 181–82; influence of Vietnamese radicalism on, 130, 132, 151, 162, 180; internationalism of, 133, 176; and French war, 147, 148, 242 (n. 3); and French Communist Party, 149; clandestine arms network of, 158–60; domestic reforms of, 161; relations of with People's Republic of China, 177, 180, 181, 182, 183, 254 (n. 5); land reform of, 183; and American socialists, 243 (n. 6). *See also* Ho Chi Minh; Vietnam News Service

Democratic Republic of Vietnam Representational Office (Van Phong Dai Dien Viet Nam Dan Chu Cong Hoa), 153, 154, 155, 157–58

Dewey, Peter, 128

Dien Bien Phu, 183, 185

Donovan, William J., 141, 142

Dreiser, Theodore, 46

Dulles, Foster Rhea, 69

Dulles, John Foster, 186

Dutch East Indies. *See* Indonesia

Eden, Anthony, 80, 81

Edison, Thomas, 5, 12, 16

Eisenhower administration, 185–86

Emerson, Gertrude, 45, 48, 59

Ennis, Thomas, 46, 57, 68, 69, 207 (n. 5)

Evans, Walker, 46

Faulkner, William: "Smoke," 117

Flower, H. C., Jr., 50–51

Ford, Henry, 5, 133

France: offers to sell Vietnam to U.S., 45–46; and Franco-American relations, 63, 86, 87; on U.S. intentions in Vietnam, 95, 104, 143–44; on Chinese intentions in Vietnam, 97–98; efforts of to influence U.S. Vietnam policy, 98, 99, 145, 169, 242 (n. 89), 251 (n. 67); repression of ICP by, 109, 114, 118, 231 (n. 7); and Bao Dai regime, 177, 178

French Communist Party, 149

Gaddis, John Lewis, 171
Gallagher, Philip E., 126, 127, 131, 136, 137, 139, 141, 142
Gandhi, Mahatma, 152, 155
Gardner, Mona, 48, 49, 57–58, 59–60, 66
Gauss, Clarence E., 89, 90, 97, 100
GBT Group, 90, 94, 132
Geneva Conference (1954), 178, 183
Giran, Paul, 56
Globalization, 188, 189
Gordon, Laurence, 90, 94, 95, 132
Gracey, Douglas, 130
Great Britain: policy toward Vietnam of, 80, 81, 85, 86, 87, 100, 103, 130; on Asian Relations Conference, 157
Greene, Marc, 68
Groupe des Patriotes Annamites, 10–11
Gullion, Edmund, 180

Hale, Arthur, 127, 137, 138
Halifax, Lord, 81, 102
Henry, Patrick, 12
Heppner, Richard, 140
Hoa Hao, 186
Hoang Minh Giam, 150, 163
Hoang Nguyen, 155
Ho Chi Minh (Nguyen Ai Quoc): independence day speech of, 4, 106, 107, 126; "Revendications du Peuple Annamite," 10–11; biographical information on, 32–33, 37, 203 (n. 50); *The Road to Revolution* [*Duong Cach Menh*], 33–36, 133; on American revolution, 34–36; relations with Soviet Union of, 38–39, 129, 176, 181, 243 (n. 5), 254 (n. 5); relations with Chinese communists of, 41; "Lettre de Chine," 43–44; and Viet Minh, 96, 114; and ICP Eighth Plenum, 109–11; "Majestic Pac Bo," 110–11, 232 (n. 11); *History of Our County* [*Lich Su Nuoc Ta*], 113, 114; *Prison Diary* (*Nhat Ky Trong Tu*], 115; relations with Chiang Kai-shek regime of, 115, 118–19, 120; on pan-Asian solidarity, 119, 158; rela-

tions with U.S. of, 123, 125–33, 144, 146, 150, 171, 176; negotiations with France of, 133; experiences in Southeast Asia of, 151, 153; Vietnamese reassessments of, 192. *See also* Democratic Republic of Vietnam; Indochinese Communist Party; Vietnamese radicalism; Vietnamese Revolutionary Youth League; Viet Minh
Hopkins, Harry, 81
Holland, 175
Hull, Cordell, 80, 81, 101, 102
Hurley, Patrick, 101

Impartial Opinion [*Thanh Nghi*], 116–17
Independence League of Vietnam (Viet Nam Doc Lap Dong Minh). *See* Viet Minh
India, 152, 156, 157, 181
Indochinese Communist Party (ICP): early history of, 37–38, 67; prison experiences of members of, 39–40; impact of Popular Front on, 40–44; impact of Maoist thought on, 41–43, 108, 110, 111–12, 205 (n. 67); attitude toward U.S. of, 43–44, 108, 113–14, 116–17, 121, 122–23; Eighth Plenum of, 109–13, 125; influences of Vietnamese radicalism on, 110, 112–13; formation of Viet Minh by, 112–13; World War II diplomacy of, 113–14, 115, 117–18, 121, 123–25; relations of with Chiang Kai-shek regime, 114–15, 118–20; cultural front of, 116–17, 130; contact of with Americans, 120–21, 125–26. *See also* France: repression of ICP by; Ho Chi Minh; Pham Van Dong; Sino-Japanese war; Truong Chinh; Viet Minh; Vietnamese Revolutionary Youth League; Vo Nguyen Giap; World War II: impact of on ICP policy
Indonesia: under Dutch colonialism, 45, 65, 74, 77, 82, 174; relations of with DRV, 152, 156, 157, 182; at Asian Relations Conference, 155, 156; U.S. recognition of, 173–75

DRV, 137, 139; internal tensions and rivalries in, 139–41; impact of reports by in Washington, 141–42; in Thailand, 153. *See also* Patti, Archimedes

Orientalism: in shaping U.S. images of Vietnam, 6, 55–59, 186, 188; as shared Euro-American discourse, 47, 56–59, 67, 71–72, 78–79, 95–96, 104–6, 169

O'Sullivan, James, 163, 164, 165, 166, 167, 168, 169

Pacific War Council, 76, 77, 78, 79, 80

Paris Peace Conference (1919), 10

Park, Robert, 65

Patti, Archimedes, 125, 126, 127, 134, 135, 136, 137, 141, 142

Pechkoff, Zinovi, 97, 98

Pham Ngoc Thach: and DRV diplomacy in southern Vietnam, 127, 128, 130; and DRV diplomacy with U.S., 146, 149, 150, 154, 163, 164, 165, 175

Pham Quynh, 27

Pham Van Dong: and Vietnamese Revolutionary Youth League, 32, 36; prison experience of, 37, 38, 39, 40; activities of during Popular Front period, 41, 42, 44; and ICP activities during World War II, 109, 114, 120, 122, 123, 124; at Geneva Conference, 183

Pham Viet Tu, 120–21, 122

Phan Boi Chau, 14–15, 31, 113; anticolonial organizing of, 15, 19–20; "Telling the Story of Five Continents" ["Ke Chuyen Nam Chau"], 17–19, and images of U.S., 17–20. *See also* Vietnamese Reform Movement

Phan Chu Trinh, 15–16, 31, 33; *Rare Encounters with Beautiful Personages* [*Giai Nhan Ky Ngo*], 20–25, 190, 200 (n. 26); and images of U.S., 22–25; on republican government, 25. *See also* Vietnamese Reform Movement

Phibun Songkhram, 159

Philippines: in ICP thought, 41, 123; commercial relations with U.S. of, 45; as

American colonial model: 53–54, 66–67, 75, 83, 88, 89; in DRV appeals to U.S. 127, 150–51; in DRV clandestine arms network, 159; attitudes of toward Bao Dai regime, 181, 182. *See also* Roosevelt, Franklin D.: and Philippines as colonial model

Powell, William, 96, 99

Pridi Phanomyong, 153, 158

Racialized cultural hierarchies (in American thought), 6, 46–58 passim, 65, 68, 71, 75, 77, 91, 105, 167–88 passim, 211 (n. 29)

Reed, Charles S., 165, 166, 167, 168, 169, 179

Reformation Society (Duy Tan Hoi), 15, 19

Renovation (*doi moi*). *See* Vietnam: market economic reforms

Revolutionary nationalism (Vietnamese), 5, 109, 125, 133, 147, 151, 162, 180, 189, 190

Ringwalt, Arthur R., 93, 98

Romulo, Carlos P., 182

Roosevelt, Franklin D.: and trusteeship for Vietnam, 74, 75, 76–81, 85, 102, 134; critiques of French colonialism by, 76–77, 79–80, 81, 88; attitudes toward Vietnamese of, 77, 220 (n. 12); and Philippines as colonial model, 77–79, 88; on Chinese intentions in Vietnam, 80; on British policy toward Vietnam, 80, 81, 101; on Dutch colonialism, 174, 220 (n. 10); policies toward African-Americans of, 229 (n. 95)

Roosevelt, Theodore, Jr., 51

Roosevelt administration. *See* Office of Strategic Services; Roosevelt, Franklin D.; United States; U.S. Department of State; World War II: impact of on U.S. policy toward Vietnam

Said, Edward, 56, 57

Sainteny, Jean, 134, 137

ism; Philippines: as American colonial
model; Racialized cultural hierarchies;
Roosevelt, Franklin D.; Social Darwin-
ism; U.S. Department of State; World
War II: impact of on U.S. policy toward
Vietnam

U.S. Department of State: post–World
War II planning for Vietnam, 74, 81–89;
U.S. models and postcolonial Vietnam,
75, 88, 89, 100, 135, 142, 147, 162, 163,
168, 170, 172, 173, 179, 180, 185, 186;
critiques of French colonialism, 82–83,
95, 142, 144, 162, 163, 179, 180, 184, 185;
attitudes toward Vietnamese, 83–85,
138, 139, 162, 167, 168, 170, 172, 173, 179,
180, 183, 184, 185, 186; on trusteeship,
85–89, 100, 108–9, 144, 163, 224 (n.
44); perceptions of Ho Chi Minh, 89,
90, 138, 139, 142, 164, 166–67, 168, 170,
172–73, 178, 179; on Chinese intentions
in Vietnam, 89, 91, 97, 98, 99, 100, 101;
wartime reporting on Vietnam from
China, 89–100; deference to French
views on Vietnam, 90–91, 93–95, 97–
99, 164, 169–70; attitudes toward Viet
Minh, 93, 96–97 121–22; fears of Soviet
influence in Vietnam, 137, 139, 144,
147, 164, 166–70, 170, 172–73; attitudes
toward DRV, 146, 162–75, 184; attitudes
toward Chiang Kai-shek regime, 147,
162, 165–66, 171; Cold War diplomacy,
147, 162, 174, 175; "Asian Titoism" of,
171, 251 (n. 75); recognition of Indonesia, 173–75; and domestic attitudes
and images of Vietnam, 175; support of
Bao Dai regime, 175, 177, 178–80, 181,
184–85; tensions with France, 180, 184–
85; perceptions of People's Republic of
China, 184. See also Office of Strategic Services; Orientalism; Philippines:
as American colonial model; Racialized cultural hierarchies; Roosevelt,
Franklin D.; Truman, Harry S.; World
War II: impact of on U.S. policy toward
Vietnam

U.S. Information Service (USIS): in Viet-
nam: 143–44
U.S. Naval Group in China: operations in
Vietnam, 90, 94, 225 (n. 61), 226 (n. 64)
U Nu, 154

Vandenbosch, Amry, 66, 82, 83, 84, 222
(n. 25)
Viet Minh, 96, 97, 112–13, 118, 120–21, 126,
127, 128, 135. See also Democratic Republic of Vietnam; Ho Chi Minh: and
Viet Minh; Indochinese Communist
Party; World War II: impact of on ICP
policy
Vietnam: independence day of, 3–4, 106,
107–8; national essence (quoc tuy)
debates in, 27, 202 (n. 38); impact of
worldwide depression on, 63–64; August
Revolution of 1945 in, 109, 115–16, 124–
26, 134, 140, 142, 146, 161, 230 (n. 4);
mythological origins of, 110; traditional
diplomacy with China of, 121; Japanese
coup in, 124; American films in, 132–
33; outbreak of war with French in, 144,
146, 147; sect crisis in, 185–86; market
economic reforms of, 187, 189; legacies of postcolonial visions in, 189–92;
reportage of, 208 (n. 8)
Vietnamese-American Friendship Association (Hoi Viet-My Than Huu), 130–33,
140, 141; Vietnamese-American Friendship Association Review [Viet-My Tap
Chi], 131–32, 189
Vietnamese communism. See Democratic
Republic of Vietnam; Ho Chi Minh;
Indochinese Communist Party; Viet
Minh; Vietnamese radicalism
Vietnamese radicalism: participants in,
25–7; French influences on, 26, 29, 30,
36; images of U.S. in, 27–29, 31–32,
33–36, 108, 202 (n. 42); revolutionary
heroism in, 30–32, 36; and Marxism-
Leninism, 33–36, 44, 108; and 1930s,
37; publishing, 201 (n. 36); and knowledge of South and Southeast Asia, 244

(n. 14). *See also* Dao Duy Anh; Ho Chi Minh; Vietnamese Revolutionary Youth League; Voluntarism

Vietnamese Reform Movement: Sinic influences on, 11, 13–14, 22–25, 34, 36, 44, 199 (nn. 18, 23, 24); participants in, 11–12; *The Civilization of New Learning [Van Minh Tan Hoc Sach]*, 13, 14, 16–17; Japanese influences on, 13, 14, 17, 18, 20; *Asia [A-te-a]*, 14; projects, 14. *See also* League for the Restoration of Vietnam; Phan Boi Chau; Phan Chu Trinh; Reformation Society; Social Darwinism; Voluntarism

Vietnamese Revolutionary Youth League (Viet Nam Thanh Nien Kach Menh Hoi), 32, 33, 36, 37, 109, 204 (n. 52)

Vietnam Independence [Viet Nam Doc Lap], 113, 122, 123, 124, 233 (n. 24)

Vietnam News Service, 153, 154, 158

Vietnam Revolutionary League (Viet Nam Cach Menh Dong Minh Hoi), 119, 225 (n. 57)

Voluntarism (Vietnamese), 5, 23–25, 30–32, 36, 109, 112, 113

Vo Nguyen Giap: as young radical, 32, 36; and ICP, 38, 39, 40, 41, 44, 109, 110; *The Proper Path: The Question of National Liberation in Indochina [Con Duong Chinh: Van De Dan Toc Giai Phong o Dong Duong]*, 42–43; *Understanding Clearly the Military Situation in China [Muon Hieu Ro Tinh Hinh Quan Su o Tau]*, 43; and U.S., 108, 126, 144; and DRV, 132, 134, 138, 150, 153, 154, 161; and People's Republic of China, 182, 183

Washington, George, 4, 12, 21, 22–23, 24, 117, 190

Waterman, Henry I., 69

Wedemeyer, Albert, 103, 227 (n. 80)

White, Frank M., 127, 138

Willkie, Wendell L., 115

Wilson, Edmund, 46

Wilson, Woodrow, 10, 11, 117

Withrow, James R., 135–36

World Bank, 189

World Trade Organization, 189

World War II: impact of on U.S. policy toward Vietnam, 47, 72, 74, 75, 105, 147; impact of on ICP policy, 109, 124–25

Yuen Tse Kien, 166